"This is a daring book. Amy Peeler tackles a co[...]
God and its implications for women. For som[...]
is objectionable. For others, Peeler's high view of Scripture will suggest that
she herself is captive to patriarchy. However, readers who take the time to
engage her argument will find that neither critique has merit. Peeler patiently
shows why these questions are worth asking and how the Bible offers a robust response that both affirms women and glorifies God, without making
God male. Peeler's grasp of the secondary literature is impressive. Her arguments are sophisticated and theologically astute. She is attentive to nuance
in Scripture, and her faithful reading yields an illuminating vision of a good
God who invites women to be full participants in God's work in the world.
I'm so grateful for her work. I expect it will be an essential resource for years
to come."

— **Carmen Joy Imes**
Biola University

"The story of God is the story of Jesus Christ, and the story of Christ is also the
story of Mary of Nazareth. No story of the Christian God can be told without
the story of Mary. Incarnation through a woman reveals who God is. Pause
with that thought as you consider most Protestant theologies, most Protestant
sermons, most Protestant approaches to Christian formation, and most Protestant Sunday school curricula. All the way down, Mary has disappeared from
the only story we know in the Bible. Protestant theology needs to be schooled
in *theotokos* theology. Amy Peeler's *Women and the Gender of God* has done this
for us, dismantling the patriarchy by exclaiming precisely what Mary prophesied, 'From now all generations will call me blessed!'"

— **Scot McKnight**
Northern Seminary

"Peeler's book is a tremendous contribution to the discussion. Bridging so
many disciplinary gaps, she provides a holistic picture of how women can
relate to God and how all of us can think better about gender. I am hopeful that her generous reflections will have a significant effect on our theology
and practice."

—**Madison Pierce**
Western Theological Seminary

"Peeler refutes a view that shouldn't even need discussing because it is so absurd—that God is male. Readers might pick up this book because of the harmful effects of 'masculine Christianity' on the Christian faith. But what made this book a page-turner for me is the profound exposition of the story of Jesus, the perfect image of God, man from woman, a testimony to the beauty of God's dual human creation—both men and women finding honor and dignity in Word made flesh. Peeler navigates a volatile topic with patience, meticulous research, wisdom, and grace."

—**Nijay K. Gupta**
Northern Seminary

Women and the Gender of God

Amy Peeler

WILLIAM B. EERDMANS PUBLISHING COMPANY
GRAND RAPIDS, MICHIGAN

Wm. B. Eerdmans Publishing Co.
4035 Park East Court SE, Grand Rapids, Michigan 49546
www.eerdmans.com

28 27 26 25 24   4 5 6 7

ISBN 978-0-8028-7909-7

Library of Congress Cataloging-in-Publication Data

A catalog record for this book is available from the Library of Congress.

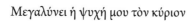

Μεγαλύνει ἡ ψυχή μου τὸν κύριον

Contents

Acknowledgments

Although the idea for this project began while I was working on my dissertation, the work began in earnest in 2018 when I was granted a sabbatical at the Logos Institute at the University of St. Andrews. I am incredibly grateful to the John Templeton Foundation and Wheaton College for their financial support. This work was supported by the Templeton Religion Trust [TRT0095/58801] and the University of St. Andrews (School of Divinity). Alan (and Margaret) Torrance's warm invitation, advocacy, insight, and friendship made that period of time one of the best of our lives. Thank you to the many friends and colleagues in St. Andrews, including those at St. Mary's, All Saints, St. Andrews Nursery School, Canongate, and FFSA who made my work and our lives so rich.

I am also grateful to the many colleagues who have read or responded to drafts of this book. Carey Newman gave invaluable advice in the early stages of the project. Michael Rae, Michelle Panchuk, Timothy and Faith Pawl, and all those involved in Logos, especially the 2018 conference, were formative in the chapters on Mary. Aubrey Buster, Julie Newberry, Brittany Wilson, Christa McKirland, Hannah Craven, Marc Cortez, Emily McGowin, Beth Felker Jones, George Kalantzis, Amanda Drury, David Lauber, Madeline Hazel Urban, Nate Thom, Kristen Page, Keith Johnson, fellow members of the Augustine Fellowship through the Center for Pastor Theologians, attendees at the 2021 meeting of the Chicago Theological Initiative, and, chiefly, Matthew Milliner carefully read and commented on particular chapters. The two anonymous readers greatly improved the argument with their insightful suggestions. Several research assistants have faithfully aided me in this project: Matthew Monkemeier, Ben Mandley, Joshua Mauer, Andy Iversen, Bethany

Grainger, Virginia Johnston, Bryan Condra, Addison Ream, and with particular insights as we compared our work, Megan Stidham. Trevor Thompson has been a supportive and insightful editor, giving shape to the present volume and necessary encouragement in the final stages. Jenny Hoffman, Justin Howell, Kristine Nelson, Sarah Gombis, and the rest of the editorial and marketing team brought my ideas to life with clarity and beauty. Questions and insights from all my students, particularly those I get to mentor and those in the Mary course and First Year Seminar and the Gender in the New Testament class, have clarified my understanding of the problems and potentials of this work. It is a gift to live out my calling as an educator at Wheaton.

It is also a gift to live out my calling as a priest in such a vibrant faith community, St. Mark's Episcopal Church in Geneva, IL. All of the congregation, but especially my Cornerstone Group, has been gracious in receiving my excitement about these topics. I am honored to work alongside Marcus and Stacie Johnson and Mark Tusken as we seek to be gospel people. Insights from my spiritual director, Angela Wisdom, have often brought breakthroughs for me, both in content and in my own worries about the project.

Family and friends have also offered such kind support. Thank you particularly to Cody and Allie Beverage, Sarah and Herb Merrill, Les and Benita Peeler, Claude and Linda Peeler, Monica Marquez, Sheila Barthell, Christine and Andrew Marquez-Hudson, Sharron Geer, Randy and Bobbie Sanders, Jim and Myrna Sanders, Jessica and Mark Fields, Savannah and Robby Doland, Dawn Orr, James and Alli Arcadi, Laura Sweat Holmes, Janette Ok, Carla Works, Kara Lyons-Pardue, Brookes Ebetsch and her late husband Drew Sandler, and Blake and Courtney Fields Connelly for being so thoughtful to ask how the work is going.

I've been especially grateful for exchanges with Cherry and Lorenzo Marquez, my aunt and uncle who showed me from an early age the beauties of Catholicism and a commitment to the flourishing of all people.

Much like Mary, I, too, have had an Elizabeth to whom I can turn. Elizabeth Hubbard, our regular walks together restore my soul. Your belief in and prayer for me and this project has, more than once, given me the strength to persevere. Along with these walks, coaches and friends at FTX CrossFit keep me healthy, happy, and sane.

I am so grateful for my mother, Pam Beverage, and her constant pride in me. Her quiet acts of service to me and my family have made our complicated lives not only feasible but also good. Wouldn't Dad just bust his buttons to see me publish another book?

My children have equipped and empowered me to write about motherhood. During the time this project has been germinating, all of them have been born and developed into intricately beautiful human beings. Kate, your strength and maturity awe me. Maxson, I'm sorry I didn't include a section about Mary fighting zombies, but I'm confident that you could write that, and it would be a best seller. Kindred, your tender heart makes mine melt.

I dedicate this book to my greatest treasure on earth, my first and final editor, bibliography complier, greatest cheerleader, and best friend, my husband, Lance. I love you beyond words.

Feast of the Annunciation

Introduction

God values women. Through study of the biblical texts, experience in healthy communities, and vibrant personal faith, many know in the core of their beings that this is true. Evidence to the contrary, however, if given honest attention, raises questions and concerns and, at times, threatens even to overwhelm the affirmation. With each fresh recovery of a misogynistic statement from Christian history, with each new revelation of misconduct in the contemporary church, Christians may wonder why a faith that affirms the divinely created goodness of all humans has so often failed women. Not always, of course. I am convinced that there is nowhere else to go where humans—women fully included—may find truly abundant life, nowhere other than *this* God as revealed in *these* texts.

Nevertheless, the failures against women proceed unabated, sometimes malicious and predatory, sometimes subconscious and unintended, practiced by both men and women, on each other and on themselves. Consequently, for many, this claim that God values women sounds audacious given Christianity's checkered history and, infuriatingly, its tabloid-worthy present. The words and actions of a shocking number of followers of the Christian God have not displayed a robust esteem for women, to say the least. Way more often than one would expect or hope for, Christians have not lived up to the faith's central anthropological claim—the *imago Dei*—with respect to women.

Considering Christianity's too frequent misogynistic expressions, it would be easy to lay the blame for the mistreatment of women at the feet of anthropology, particularly the anthropology of the historical context in which the faith developed. Christianity was birthed and cultivated in patriarchal soil, and therefore, it simply got women wrong. Its thinkers often assumed, like many of their contemporaries, that women, generally weaker in body, were also weaker in mind, that women lacked capacity for intellect and virtue. This anthropological analysis of Christianity is not incorrect—egregious statements about women in this vein are easy to find—but this analysis does not capture, I will argue, the full cause of the problem.[1] The deeper, often hidden, and therefore more insidious cause of Christianity's failure to value women is that Christianity often gets God wrong. Although many Christian theologians would assert the contrary, the assumptions and actions of interpreters from the past to the present disclose an underlying belief that God is male.

I recognize that this is a provocative charge. Certainly, the affirmation that "God, qua God, is beyond gender" is a "persistent orthodox refrain."[2] Many orthodox theologians, nonetheless, support masculine language and conceptions of God with analogical reasoning that is limited to males alone. God initiates like men initiate. God begets like men beget. God the Son was male like men are male. When it is added, in some Christian circles, that *only* males can represent God—not because of God's free choice but because of a certain male-like quality in God—the underlying but unstated belief rises to the surface of reality. The arguments and actions that manifest a belief in the maleness of God render protestations to the contrary—no matter how persistent—null and void.

Theology has consequences. It is easier to devalue and then mistreat those humans who are believed to be less like God. If Christians really want to live out their own claims and value women fully and consistently, they must disabuse themselves of the false idea that men, over and above women, favor this male God.[3]

Given the language of the scriptural text and the statements in the theological tradition, the assumption of God's maleness is certainly understandable. The unrelenting masculine language for God in Israel's Scriptures, the

1. Elizabeth A. Clark has compiled an influential collection of quotations and analysis (*Women in the Early Church*, Message of the Fathers of the Church 13 [Collegeville, MN: Liturgical, 1983]).

2. Sarah Coakley, *God, Sexuality, and the Self: An Essay 'On the Trinity'* (Cambridge: Cambridge University Press, 2013), 248.

3. I intentionally use the word "favor" in two respects: asserting both that God does not "look like" men and also that God does not "privilege" men.

New Testament, and Christian theology has, unsurprisingly, led many to the conclusion that God is male, or at least the conclusion of *the text's* assertion of God's maleness. A growing body of literature at the intersection of biblical and masculinity studies catalogs this overwhelming masculine presentation of God with critical frankness. These scholars show that from Christian art to contemporary exegesis, all inspired by the text itself, the affirmation of God's maleness has always existed alongside its denial.[4]

The situation thus stands: on the one hand, conservative theologians retain a tight grip on the male-like masculinity of God. In their view, this grip is released at the very cost of the faith. To lose this concept, or the language that attests to it, is to fail to acknowledge God as God.[5] In another discourse

4. For an introduction to the complexities of artistic representation of God, see "Seeing God: Trinitarian Thought through Iconography," in Coakley, *God, Sexuality, and the Self*, 190–248. For bold readings of God's maleness in the biblical text, see Howard Eilberg-Schwartz, *God's Phallus: And Other Problems for Men and Monotheism* (Boston: Beacon, 1994); Stephen D. Moore, *God's Gym: Divine Male Bodies of the Bible* (New York: Routledge, 1996); Carolyn J. Sharp, "Character, Conflict, and Covenant in Israel's Origin Tradition," in *The Hebrew Bible: Feminist and Intersectional Perspectives*, ed. Gale A. Yee (Minneapolis: Fortress), 41–73, esp. 46; David J. A. Clines, "The Most High Male: Divine Masculinity in the Bible," in *Hebrew Masculinities Anew*, ed. Ovidiu Creanga, Hebrew Bible Monographs 79 (Sheffield: Sheffield Phoenix, 2019), 61–82; Colleen M. Conway, "'Behold the Man!' Masculine Christology and the Fourth Gospel," in *New Testament Masculinities*, ed. Stephen D. Moore and Janice Capel Anderson, Semeia Studies 45 (Leiden: Brill, 2004), 163–80. David J. A. Clines concludes, "The fact is, though, that the Yahweh of the Hebrew Bible is a thoroughly male god" ("Alleged Female Language about the Deity in the Hebrew Bible," *Journal of Biblical Literature* 140 [2021]: 249).

God's sex and gender is closely related to the growing field of studies on God's embodiment. See Brittany E. Wilson, *The Embodied God: Seeing the Divine in Luke-Acts and the Early Church* (Oxford: Oxford University Press, 2021). The argument that more Jewish and Christian interpreters than modern theology might assume affirmed some sort of embodiment for God appears both plausible and beneficial. If this is the case, that divine body of God the Father, according to the text of the New Testament as I read it, would not be a male body.

5. Stanley J. Grenz puts it this way: "Theologians often connect these seemingly masculine activities with God as the transcendent one and view God's transcendence as lying behind the consistent use of masculine pronouns that refer to God" ("Is God Sexual?," in *This Is My Name Forever: The Trinity and Gender Language for God*, ed. Alvin F. Kimel Jr. [Downers Grove, IL: InterVarsity Press, 2001], 194). In other words, certain theologians fear that if God is not masculine, then God cannot be transcendent. If God is not transcendent, then God is not God. The result is a loss of God. That fear, I will argue, is unfounded because it begins with a false equation between transcendence and masculinity.

community, post-Christian critics dare interpreters to deny the seemingly obvious male God of the biblical text. This book rises to meet the challenges from each and aims to prove them both wrong. The triune God of the biblical text is not simply male. Therefore, privileging the masculine over the feminine is the way the world *has* often run but should not and need not continue forever.

For Christian theology, the way to end masculine privilege is to attend to the doctrinal center of the faith, the incarnation.[6] As the chief revelation of God, what is disclosed about God in the coming of Jesus Christ defines all knowledge of God. The claim that God sent forth the Son to be born of a woman (Gal 4:4) as narrated by Matthew and Luke provides the bulk of the exegetical material for this project. The persons at work in this event, Father, Son, Holy Spirit, and Mary of Nazareth, reveal that the heart of the Christian narrative rejects the damaging assumptions of God's maleness. What better location to tackle this assumption than the narratives in which God is revealed as Father, where God incarnate is born as a son. Instead of ferreting out small exceptions in the biblical text to the overwhelmingly male language for God, I devote attention to the most dominant and influential names for God at the heart of the Christian confession, Father and Son. My claim is this: the God revealed there harbors no preference for males because God the Father is not male and God the Son is male like no other.[7] Moreover, these are also the same narratives that provide the ideal textual location from which to assert this God's honoring of a woman. Because the centrality of this event reveals the identity and character of God, God's actions toward Mary—though unrepeatable in the specificity of her particular vocation to bear the Son of God—provide the standard for God's actions with all women.

Mary has frequently been addressed as *Mother of God*, the English translation of the conciliar title for Mary, "Theotokos." Accepted by the Council of Ephesus in 431, this title aimed to quell the christological confusions raised by Nestorius as well as accept the popular piety that had arisen around

6. Many are the theologians who have penned poetic utterances and persuasive arguments about the centrality of the incarnation. I share this conviction but believe more needed to be said. Having contemplated, researched, written on, and lived out gender issues as an embodied female in Christian spaces for the entirety of my adult life, I am equally convicted that the treasures of the incarnation—on this pressing question—remain to be (re)discovered.

7. I will more fully explain and argue for this highly condensed sentence throughout the book.

Mary.[8] Attention to her was never solely about her. She, like John the Baptist (John 3:30), pointed to God's revelation in the Son. Affirming her role, her title as "God bearer," was the way of proclaiming the story of God. Cyril's third letter to Nestorius states, "For the very reason that the holy Virgin gave fleshly birth to God substantially united with flesh we declare her to be 'Mother of God', not because the Word's nature somehow derived its origin from flesh (he was, after all, *'in the beginning,' 'the Word was God,' 'the Word was with God'* and is personally the creator of the worlds, co-eternal with the Father and artificer of the universe) but because, as we previously affirmed, he substantially united humanity with himself, and underwent fleshly birth from her womb."[9] Addressing Mary as "Theotokos" is to show appropriate respect for Mary, but fundamentally—and this is my interest in this project—it is to speak rightly of God. That God chose to reveal Godself to humanity, to redeem humanity, by taking on flesh, *by being born of a woman* sets the appropriate ways to conceive of God. Hence, though she, like John, directs attention to God, she is also different from John the Baptist. Both point to Christ, but the story of Jesus can exist without mention of the forerunner. The story is less rich, for sure, but it is possible. Conversely, one cannot proclaim even the most basic Christian confession—Jesus is Lord—without assuming her. Without birth through a woman, Jesus of Nazareth did not live. The title "Mother of God" is the indispensable prolegomena to the gospel. If she is forgotten, the whole theological project goes askew. Protestants, particularly those in nonliturgical traditions, have a great deal to learn from our brothers and sisters who never lost their connection to the ancient and healthy Marian piety. Whereas everyone, high church and low, benefits from a reconsideration of the biblical texts to ensure that even retention of her is not held along with an inappropriately masculine view of God.

My argument unfolds in three movements—a consideration of sex, gender, and then roles, each with attention both to Mary and to God.[10] First, I engage

---

8. Stephen J. Shoemaker, *Mary in Early Christian Faith and Devotion* (New Haven: Yale University Press, 2016), 205–28.

9. Cyril of Alexandria, *Selected Letters*, ed. and trans. Lionel R. Wickham (Oxford: Clarendon, 1983), 27–29.

10. Judith Butler's work has—beneficially in my opinion—unsettled a neat bifurcation between sex and gender. See discussion in Benjamin H. Dunning, "The New Testament and Early Christian Literature," in *The Oxford Handbook of New Testament, Gender, and Sexuality*, ed.

seriously with the claims of God's maleness, present in the Scriptures of Israel but made all the more pressing when, in the opening pages of the New
Testament, God fathers a child. The evangelists tell this story at great risk of
associating their God with common myths but do so in such a way that they
explicitly deny them. Continuing the theme of embodiment, in the second
chapter, I consider the ramifications of Mary's pregnancy and birthing of Jesus
the Messiah. Existing within the purity laws of Judaism, her body is deemed
worthy of the most holy presence of God.

The second section broadens beyond bodies to consider the characteristics
of those bodies in action—in other words, the gender of God and Mary. The
trope of the oppressive masculine God and the oppressed feminine woman
does not hold up under exegetical scrutiny. She, honored by God, exercises
the strength of agency; and while God is certainly God, sovereign and the one
who takes initiative, to claim that these divine actions are *masculine* is as false
as it is dangerous.

Finally, I engage with the controversial topic of gender roles, beginning
with an analysis of Jesus's own maleness. Accepting his particular embodiment
and enactment of that embodiment as described by the texts of the New Testament, I argue that the doctrine of the virginal conception makes that maleness
different from all others.[11] Hence, the roles of men and women who confess
this particular Messiah need not be dictated by a less than full affirmation of
his incarnate body. Mary provides the test case. She flourishes in the roles of
mother as well as proclaimer, presenting the robust possibility of God's yes to
other women who are called to do the same.

This God who honors women and does not favor men is revealed with daz-
zling clarity in the pregnancy that is the epicenter of the Christian faith.[12] The in-

Benjamin H. Dunning (Oxford: Oxford University Press, 2019), 5–7. Recognizing that nuance,
I have chosen to emphasize the sexual questions involved in pregnancy first before turning to
the character of God and Mary, perceived as masculine and feminine respectively.

11. "Virginal birth" introduces complexities in the tradition dealing with Mary's virginity
in the act of having Jesus. I seek to focus on Jesus's conception and embodiment; therefore,
"virginal conception" is the better term.

12. Although I will show ways in which our interpretations and applications stand at odds,
my affirmation of the centrality of Mary's story finds a kindred spirit in Pope John Paul II: "At
the beginning of the New Covenant, which is to be eternal and irrevocable, there is a woman:
the Virgin of Nazareth" ("Mulieris Dignitatem: Apostolic Letter of the Supreme Pontiff John

carnation contains within it countless fraught problems of sex, gender, and roles, but, I argue, it holds the answers to those problems as well. I join those who seek to unsettle the accepted and disastrous norms of a male God by recovering the implications of the well-known good news, "unto us a child is born."[13]

That God was born of a woman—the mode of the incarnation—determines how all Christians view the triune God as well as all people made in the divine image. Consequently, if the Christian God does not value women, the entire system crumbles, and we Christians are, of all people, most to be pitied. Blessedly, it is the very same, the incarnation itself—the fact that God chose to have a mother—that proves true the audacious claim: God does indeed value women.

Paul II on the Dignity and Vocation of Women on the Occasion of the Marian Year" [sec. 9], The Holy See, https://www.vatican.va/content/john-paul-ii/en/apost_letters/1988/documents /hf_jp-ii_apl_19880815_mulieris-dignitatem.html).

13. Grace Jantzen, in her proposal for a feminist philosophy of religion, often appeals to this good news to argue for a "new religious imaginary" that privileges natality rather than mortality and therefore leads to flourishing. The things that she desires, including positing women as subjects, affirming embodiment, honoring uniqueness, recognizing limitations, cultivating community, and caring for the world are possible, I argue, within a healthy Christianity. Hence, I do not share some of her central assumptions or aims, but her insightful work clarified my own hunger for women's flourishing and how it can be satisfied by turning one's attention to birth. I differ from her, however, by attending not only to the birth of all humans but, specifically, to the birth of the Son of God (*Becoming Divine: Toward a Feminist Philosophy of Religion*, Manchester Studies in Religion, Culture and Gender [Manchester: Manchester University Press, 1998]).

one

The Father Who Is Not Male

The Trinity appears still hierarchical, still male—maleness, indeed, seems enshrined in God's eternity.

—Janet Martin Soskice, *The Kindness of God*

God the Father is not male. While the basic grammar of this sentence appears contradictory, it strikes a majority of Christian theologians as obvious. The one being to whom Christian theology has attributed the source of all life has revealed the divine self as being (Exod 3), as Spirit (John 4:24), as imaged in both male and female (Gen 1:26). Hence, this denial may seem an odd place to begin. Few thoughtful Christians today believe that God the Father is a bearded gentleman who lives in the sky. It is a myth quickly released through development into the most basic theological maturity. It would be more efficient to assume this dictum and move on to more complicated matters.

Efficient, maybe, but not wise. I begin with an extended treatment of the nonmale nature of God the Father for two reasons. First, while it may not be the typical reaction of readers from more conservative theological spaces, many interpreters have read the biblical texts and arrived at precisely that conclusion, that God is depicted as a male.[1] Their boldness in naming what they

1. Feminist philosopher Luce Irigaray stated plainly, "God has been created out of man's gen-

see on the page invites, or maybe better said, *demands* an honest reconsideration of the texts. If they are correct, and God is male, my desire to affirm the full value of women made in God's image is damned from the start. Second, I begin here because the denial of God the Father's maleness lays the foundation for the next stages of my theological argument. If I am to claim that God is not more masculine than feminine, I must first be certain that God the Father is not male. If I am to argue that Jesus's maleness does not exclude women, I must be clear that his maleness does not image God his Father's.

In order to respond to those who believe, evidenced by their explicit statements or their implicit actions, that the biblical God is male, I begin with this claim. I contend that the New Testament accounts of the incarnation dispel any notion that God the Father is male.

Challenge

It is easy to picture God the Father as male because this idea is part and parcel of the language of traditional Christianity. This is true throughout the Scriptures of Israel, but maleness as communicated through fatherhood becomes even more prominent when one attends to the transition between Israel's Scriptures and the New Testament.

In Israel's Scriptures, paternal language appears but does so infrequently.[2]

---

der" (*Sex and Genealogies*, trans. Gillian Gill [New York: Columbia University Press, 1993], 62). I mentioned the biblical scholars who have read the text in this way in the introduction. Stephen Moore's concluding description of God is chilling: "the hypermasculine hulk that is the biblical God lumbers across the examining room, an imperious frown furrowing his perfectly handsome features, and a pair of handcuffs dangling ominously from his weight-lifting belt, which is cinched around his bloodstained butcher's apron, from the pocket of which a blindfold protrudes. 'You do not believe because you have seen me,' he intones. 'Blessed are those who have not seen and therefore believe'" (*God's Gym: Divine Male Bodies of the Bible* [New York: Routledge, 1996], 139–40).

2. Diane Chen notes that the term "father" is applied to God only nineteen times in the Scriptures of Israel, but the ideas of begetting, discipline, and inheritance expand the concept a bit further (*God as Father in Luke-Acts*, Studies in Biblical Literature 92 [New York: Lang, 2005], 79). Abera M. Mengestu concludes that this group of ideas "creates a narrative that identifies and sets an orienting framework for how Israel understands itself in relation to God, in relation to each other, and in relation to the surrounding nations" (*God as Father in Paul: Kinship Language*

As God is planning to redeem the Israelite people from slavery, God reveals to Moses the threat to kill Pharaoh's son if Pharaoh does not release Israel, who is God's firstborn son (Exod 4:22–23). God, through the covenant, caused the people of Israel to exist as the chosen nation, and so authors say God "fathered" (read "caused") the people to exist as a nation (Deut 32:4–6; Jer 3:19; 31:9; Isa 1:2; 63:16; 64:8). When procreation is the focus, the Hebrew text explicitly depersonalizes God so as to avoid a sexualized association: God is the "Rock" (צוּר [*tsur*]) who begot you (Deut 32:18). The Greek translations do not replicate this geological metaphor but says that God is the *God* who begot and fed the nation (32:18).[3]

Much more often than the creation of the people, when God is invoked as "Father" of Israel, the texts emphasize God's care for the nation. Deuteronomy describes God as the Father of Israel, nursing them (Deut 1:31) and disciplining them (14:1). Hosea recalls how God the Father called Israel out of Egypt, taught the nation how to walk, and embraced the people (Hos 11:1, 3). The Psalms speak of the compassion of the Lord in a fatherly way (Pss 27:10; 68:5; 103:13). As fathers do, God also provides an inheritance to the people of Israel (Jer 3:19; 31:9; Isa 61:7–10; 63:16; Zech 9:12). God's redemption of the nation in the past acts as a promise that God will call back the sons and daughters in the future (Isa 43:6–7).

The king is the only individual singled out within that nation, who stands in an intimate relationship with God, as a son with a father (2 Sam 7:14;

---

and Identity Formation in Early Christianity [Eugene, OR: Pickwick, 2013], 100). Nevertheless, Marianne Meye Thompson notes, "it is unwise to exaggerate the number of passages that present God as Father. The relative infrequency of the term 'Father' for God does contrast sharply with the regular use of the term in the New Testament" (*The Promise of the Father: Jesus and God in the New Testament* [Louisville: Westminster John Knox, 2000], 39).

3. John William Wevers, ed., *Septuaginta Vetus Testamentum Graecum: Auctoritate Academiae Scientiarum Gottingensis editum*, vol. 3/2: *Deuteronomium* (Göttingen: Vandenhoeck & Ruprecht, 1977), 350.

Janet Martin Soskice observes, "Paternal and maternal imagery in quick succession effectively rules out literalism, as does the astonishing invocation of a parturient rock" (*The Kindness of God: Metaphor, Gender, and Religious Language* [Oxford: Oxford University Press, 2008], 2). So also, "The God of Israel is defined then over and against father gods, gods who beget the world; and paradoxically, it is this abolition of the biological father God that makes non-idolatrous, metaphorical 'father language' about God possible." See Janet Martin Soskice, "Can a Feminist Call God Father?," in *Speaking the Christian God: The Holy Trinity and the Challenge of Feminism*, ed. Alvin F. Kimel Jr. (Grand Rapids: Eerdmans, 1992), 89.

1 Chr 17:13; 22:10; 28:6; Pss 2:7; 68:5; 89:26; 109:3 LXX).[4] Though a debate
about Israel's conception of a divine king continues, scholars recognize a hesitancy in Israel's texts to deify their kings to the same degree as their neighbors.[5]
This was sonship by election, not by divine begetting and birth, and so the king
was not worshiped as God but led the people in worship of God.[6] His intimate
relationship with God, described in familial terms, allowed him to function as
his Father's representative on earth.

In response to divine care for the king and the nation, the people who are
God's children should live in particular ways. They should be pure because of
their identity as God's children (Deut 8:5). The prophets appeal to this relationship to summon God to action (Isa 63:16; 64:8), to remember their former
relationship with God (Deut 32:6; Hos 11:1–4), or to call the people back to
God (Jer 3:4, 19, 22; 31:9, 20; Mal 1:6, 2:10; 3:17).[7]

References to God as the Father of creation continue in Jewish literature and
are especially prominent in the writings of Josephus and Philo. God's particular
fatherhood over the nation of Israel, expressed in God's election and continued provision, also appears.[8] Hence, divine paternity continues to play a role
in the thought life of Jewish authors. God has taken Israel, and preeminently
their king, to be his son, and so God stands in relationship to them as a Father.
The Scriptures of Israel gender God as male only insofar as they use paternal
titles for God rather than maternal ones, though at times, authors described
God with maternal images (Hos 11:3–4; 13:8; Deut 32:11–12, 18; Isa 42:14; 49:15;

4. See also examples in the Apocrypha (Wis 2:16; 14:3; Tob 13:4; Sir 23:1, 4; 51:10; 3 Macc 5:7;
6:4, 8), Pseudepigrapha (Jub. 1.24, 28; 19.29; T. Levi 18.6; T. Jud. 24.2), and Dead Sea Scrolls
(1 QH IX, 35–36).

5. See Adela Yarbro Collins and John J. Collins, *King and Messiah as Son of God: Divine, Human, and Angelic Messianic Figures in Biblical and Related Literature* (Grand Rapids: Eerdmans,
2008), ch. 1, esp. 19. He concludes, "The fact that the dominant attitude in biblical tradition
insists on a sharp distinction between divinity and humanity and is sharply critical of kingship
makes the preservation of the royal psalms all the more remarkable. It requires that we take
them seriously as a witness to preexilic religion, before it was chastened by the harsh historical
experiences that led to the demise of the monarchy" (24).

6. Yarbro Collins and Collins, *King and Messiah*, 23.

7. For a robust treatment of the theme, see Christopher J. H. Wright, *Knowing God the Father
through the Old Testament* (Downers Grove, IL: InterVarsity Press, 2007).

8. See Thompson, *Promise of the Father*, 48–53; Chen, *God as Father*, 113–35; Mengestu, *God
as Father in Paul*, 128–58.

66:13; Ps 123:2–3), but the texts resist any portrayal of a sexualized male deity. God as the Father of Israel or Israel's King remains figurative, contained within the ideas of founding or care, never procreation.[9] Paul Mankowski sums up the paternal theme well, "YHWH becomes a father not by approaching a woman but by electing a son, an election that in virtue of itself creates the son."[10]

The New Testament does not play it so safe. The first pages of the canonized form of the text make just that claim: God caused the birth of a baby. The metaphorical use of "Father" and "Son" language from the traditions of Israel become actualized at Mary's pregnancy. At this event, God causes the literal conception and birth of a child. Jesus, the son of Mary, exists as human because of the action of the Holy God. God is his Father. Much more explicitly than is true in the texts of Israel, God plays the role of the male, and consequently, "Father" language becomes more sexualized, more gendered, and more exclusive. In light of the beginning of the canonical New Testament, it seems impossible to call God Father without asserting at the same time that God is male.

This concern captures author Andrew Lincoln's difficulty with the way the story of the evangelists runs. He has written one of the most extensive and richly exegetical, historical, and theological critiques of the doctrine of the virginal conception to date, *Born of a Virgin*. His argument affirms that if the male is absent (in the evangelists' accounts of Jesus's birth), then God is the male. In his view, an acceptance of the virginal conception, particularly in light of modern biology, "requires that God acted in a biological fashion to provide the genetic material that a man normally provides and comes much closer to ancient pagan notions of the divine impregnating a woman than the patristic writers would ever countenance." If God is providing not just the energizing (nonphysical force), as Lincoln asserts many ancient theories of conception might have led early Christians to believe, but also the Y chromosome, then "this is in danger of reinforcing the notion of a male God the Father who provides the complement to human motherhood in the origins of Jesus."[11]

9. Howard Eilberg-Schwartz highlights the dissonance in the texts of Judaism between God as Father and God not acting as a male acts ("The Father, the Phallus, and the Seminal World: Dilemmas of Patrilineality in Ancient Judaism," in *Gender, Kinship, Power: A Comparative and Interdisciplinary History*, ed. Mary Jo Maynes et al. [New York: Routledge, 1996], 27–42).

10. Paul Mankowski, "The Gender of Israel's God," in Kimel, *This Is My Name Forever*, 58.

11. Andrew T. Lincoln, *Born of a Virgin? Reconceiving Jesus in the Bible, Tradition, and Theology* (Grand Rapids: Eerdmans, 2013), 262, 264.

He articulates the intensity of the problem in the modern era but by di-
minishing a similar insinuation of God's maleness in the first-century world.
Certainly, humans know more about conception than they did two thousand
years ago, but it is *not* the case that the modern understanding is *radically
more difficult for theology* than the ancient one. The biological models may be
different, but in both instances, God supplies what the male would normally
supply, be it the energizing force or the Y chromosome. Hence with either
conceptional understanding, the theological gender implications of the evangelists' concept of the fatherhood of God demand an explanation.

Solutions

Several wide roads open before interpreters. It is quite easy to acquiesce to the
normal meanings of the language, tacitly allowing the assumption that God is
a male similar to any father. In some faith communities, as I will demonstrate
in the fourth chapter, such assumptions are usually not stated and are therefore more insidious. It is also quite easy to cease speaking about God at all. In
some cases, silence is intentional, born of frustration. If calling God "Father"
is messy, and the paternal language is so replete, then the answer might be to
stop calling out to God at all.

The consensus of the Christian tradition, however, affirms that because
humans are finite, sinful, and exist on this side of eternity, no one can speak
comprehensively of God's being, but text and tradition encourage the act of
speaking to and about God. The ancient theologian Pseudo-Dionysius affirmed
that "we must not then dare to speak, or indeed to form any conception, of
the hidden super-essential Godhead, *except those things* that are revealed to
us from the Holy Scriptures."[12] Moments for silence as well as moments for
proclamation and voiced address both have an appropriate time and place.
Those who remain within the fold can and, in fact, must speak of God. The
question is how to do so rightly.

Linn Marie Tonstad seeks to follow this path by embracing a certain kind
of chastened apophaticism. Noting that theological discourse has frequently

---

12. *On the Divine Names* 1.1–2; see Pseudo-Dionysius the Areopagite, *The Divine Names and
Mystical Theology* (Milwaukee: Marquette University Press, 1980), 22–23.

neglected the Holy Spirit, she suggests that theologians should follow suit with the other two persons as well, articulating conceptions of their personhood as "less-vigorous" and more "underdetermined."[13] She does not deny their "personhood," for the "New Testament texts ensure that, as characters or actors, the narrated relationship between the persons cannot but generate thickly personal impressions." Nevertheless, "the primary meaning of trinitarian personhood is incommunicability; 'person' is a placeholder (like most trinitarian language) indicating something we must say but do not understand." She finds light imagery most appropriate for several reasons, including its concept of hiddenness: "the more light there is, the closer we get to loss of sight . . . darkness and the cloud."[14] Her epistemic humility results not in a lazy silence, for she goes on to speak of what she sees as true of God based on God's revelation to us. Her work reminds theologians that language for the divine must always recognize its temptation toward hubris, toward imagining that it can describe God fully this side of the eschaton.

R. Kendall Soulen offers another example. He argues for a threefold approach to speaking the name of the Trinity, including the *pneumatological* pattern that allows naming God with an "open-ended variety," and the *christological* pattern, "Father, Son, and Holy Spirit," that follows Jesus's paternal address of God. He affords privilege to the *theological* pattern, the "giving, receiving, and glorification of the divine Name, the unspoken Tetragrammaton." His goal is for the "recovery of the abiding significance of the unspoken Tetragrammaton for Christian faith."[15] Soulen is careful to note that he sets up the patterns in a Trinitarian way, in that each of the patterns, pneumatological, christological, and theological, are "distinct, interrelated, and equally important," but he also argues that the *theological* pattern serves as the *fons divinitatis*, the "fountain of divinity, as the first person of the Trinity stands in relationship to the second and third persons." The theological way of speaking is, in fact, an act of "pointing, in gesturing away from itself to the transcendent,

---

13. Linn Marie Tonstad, *God and Difference: The Trinity, Sexuality, and the Transformation of Finitude* (New York: Routledge, 2016), 227. Were I to engage with her work holistically, I would have critiques to offer, but her frank assessment of theological appeals to paternal language provided an important step in the development of my own thinking.

14. Tonstad, *God and Difference*, 228.

15. R. Kendall Soulen, *The Divine Name(s) and the Holy Trinity*, vol. 1 of *Distinguishing the Voices* (Louisville: Westminster John Knox, 2011), 23.

unfathomable mystery of its bearer," which indicates "the divine name *obliquely* . . . thus pointing away from every speaker but the one who alone is competent to declare this name." According to Soulen, at the fount of divine speaking is, for humanity, a lack of speech. Even though this pattern stands as the font, it flows forth into the others: "The most appropriate way of naming the persons of the Trinity consists precisely in the three patterns together."[16]

These authors are building upon the long and venerable tradition in the church and the academy that knows the limits of human language. Pseudo-Dionysius notes, "Only we must have a care lest, in expounding these different forms and figures we unwittingly confound the incorporeal meaning of the Divine Names with the terms of the sensible symbols" (*On the Divine Names* 9.5). As mentioned, many interpreters are calling into question the assurance of God's incorporeality, but his primary point still stands.[17] The language of the Bible is language that accommodates the human experience. Revelation from God can be trusted to be true of God but does not indicate that humans who use the revealed language have mastered God. For if God could be mastered, such an entity would no longer be God.

As the balance of speech and silence has proven fruitful, linguistic balance has also offered a promising way forward in the arena of gendered language. "Father" does not exhaust the scriptural witness to the one to whom the tra-

<hr />

16. Soulen, *Divine Name(s)*, 123, 254, 255.

17. In addition to Brittany E. Wilson, *The Embodied God: Seeing the Divine in Luke-Acts and the Early Church* (Oxford: Oxford University Press, 2021), see Christoph Markschies, *God's Body: Jewish, Christian, and Pagan Images of God* (Waco, TX: Baylor University Press, 2019); Benjamin D. Sommer, *The Bodies of God and the World of Ancient Israel* (New York: Cambridge University Press, 2009); Esther J. Hamori *"When Gods Were Men": The Embodied God in Biblical and Near Eastern Literature* (Berlin: de Gruyter, 2008); Esther J. Hamori, "Divine Embodiment in the Hebrew Bible and Some Implications for Jewish and Christian Incarnational Theologies," in *Bodies, Embodiment, and Theology of the Hebrew Bible*, ed. S. Tamar Kamionkowski and Wonil Kim (New York: T&T Clark, 2010); Mark S. Smith, *Where the Gods Are: Spatial Dimensions of Anthropomorphism in the Biblical World* (New Haven: Yale University Press, 2016); Kamionkowski and Kim, *Bodies, Embodiment, and Theology*; Anne K. Knafl, *Forming God: Divine Anthropomorphism in the Pentateuch* (Winona Lake, IN: Eisenbrauns, 2014); Tyson L. Putthoff, *Gods and Humans in the Ancient Near East* (Cambridge: Cambridge University Press, 2020); Andreas Wagner, *Göttliche Körper—Göttliche Gefühle: Was leisten anthropomorphe und anthropopathische Götterkonzepte im Alten Orient und Alten Testament?* (Göttingen: Vandenhoeck & Ruprecht, 2014); Andreas Wagner, *God's Body: The Anthropomorphic God in the Old Testament* (New York: T&T Clark, 2019).

dition refers as the first person of the Trinity. Affirming what the text and tradition gives does not mean overstepping its bounds, bounds erected by other names for God. The text gives other ways of articulating divine identity and relations, so many theologians and denominations urge as much variety as that which is found in the canonical text.[18] The triune identity "Father, Son, and Holy Spirit" is voiced alongside the unified divine actions of "Creator, Sustainer, Redeemer." God is described as "Father," or "Mother," or "Rock."[19] To think of God as beyond gender in the sense that God encompasses aspects of both genders, that God is Parent or Mother and not only Father, helps to work against the "phallacy" that God is male.

These suggestions are certainly helpful, but they do not completely eliminate the challenges raised by male language for God. One of those challenges is the imbalanced quantity in the text and tradition. Christians affirm that the primary lens for knowing that God is through the one who came as a human, and a significant, even overwhelming portion of the divine language of the Jesus tradition is paternal. This is replicated in the tradition. For those groups of Christians who desire to remain tethered to the text and tradition, whose language for God is dominantly masculine, this suggestion of the "Parent God" gives no sure way to proceed with practice. Even if this nongendered ("Parent") or dual-gendered ("Mother or Father God") language resonates with an orthodox principle of belief, some Christians might be hesitant to practice something very different from the traditional language.

Moreover, and more problematically, such balancing practices do not explain the *meaning* of the paternal language. Adding the feminine terms does not address the assumptions and implications of the male terms. In other words, nonmale additions do not make the male-coded terms any less male.[20]

---

18. "The Trinity: God's Love Overflowing," Presbyterian Mission, https://www.presby terianmission.org/resource/trinity-gods-love-overflowing/; Juliana M. Claassens, *Mourner, Mother, Midwife: Reclaiming God's Delivering Presence in the Old Testament* (Louisville: Westminster John Knox, 2012); Johanna W. H. van Wijk-Bos, *Reimagining God: The Case for Scriptural Diversity* (Louisville: Westminster John Knox, 1995).

19. See, for example, the arguments of Paul R. Smith, *Is It Okay to Call God "Mother"? Considering the Feminine Face of God* (Peabody, MA: Hendrickson, 1993), or Virginia Ramey Mollenkott, *The Divine Feminine: The Biblical Imagery of God as Female* (Eugene, OR: Wipf & Stock, 1984).

20. Kathryn Green-McCreight, after articulating problems with approaches that add feminine language for God, asks, "Doesn't this just confirm the stereotypes one is trying to overturn?

Another solution, then, is to use male language for God but with intense education that the terms mean something different when applied to God. God is Father, but God is *not like* other fathers. Every time one utters "Father" or "he" for God, then, it is necessary to think against the grain of the natural associations of the word. I might be saying "Father," but I must keep in mind that the first person of the Trinity is not bound within any cultural matrix of fatherhood, nor is this father an embodied male.

Such reeducation may exacerbate the precise problem it seeks to eliminate. In her analysis of Jürgen Moltmann's arguments for the uniqueness of paternal language for God, Tonstad captures the conundrum perfectly: "Remember to forget the patriarchal father, as it were! The result is precisely the opposite of what Moltmann says he intends."[21] The fallen patriarchal father looms in the background of thoughts evoked by the language if only, but persistently and strongly, by negation. Even (and maybe especially) negating human maleness when speaking the Christian God as Father keeps maleness ever present. Tonstad describes this as "stipulative language." The language says one thing but is used to mean something rather different. Her work calls attention to the way language works, namely, "the effects it engenders beyond intention or control."[22] The crossed-out patriarchal father remains a dominant force. By continually denying what the language asserts, that which is denied remains ever present. The reeducation approach asserts that God is not a normal human father, *even though* in the language of the text God sounds like one. Tonstad concludes, "these *even thoughs* are hopelessly inadequate."[23]

. . . What [is] needed . . . is not a few more pictures or an extra metaphor here and there, but better catechesis" (*Feminist Reconstructions of Christian Doctrine: Narrative Analysis and Appraisal* [New York: Oxford University Press, 2000], 126).

21. Linn Marie Tonstad, "The Logic of Origin and the Paradoxes of Language: A Theological Experiment," *Modern Theology* 30 (2014): 61.

22. Tonstad, "Logic of Origin," 61.

23. Tonstad, "Logic of Origin," 10. Alan Torrance argues for the same reality of language: "To use the word 'father' of god while simultaneously using it of male, gendered parents, for example may serve to ratify and mould the subliminal associations of the term in such a way that these associations are transferred to other contexts of the word usage" ("Call No Man Father! The Trinity, Patriarchy and Godtalk," in *The Gospel and Gender: A Trinitarian Engagement with Being Male and Female in Christ*, ed. Douglas A. Campbell, Studies in Theology and Sexuality 7 [New York: T&T Clark, 2003], 182).

One of Tonstad's recommendations in the work of speaking of God is to keep one's focus appropriately anthropological. Our knowledge of God must begin with emphasizing God's coming *for us*. I affirm this commitment with vigor, in this way. It is the incarnation that defines the terms "Father" and "Son" for Christian thought.[24] Instead of heresy, or absolute silence, or balanced but unexplained language, or the necessity of continual negation, I suggest those who call God "Father" do so because God *is* like other fathers. God invited a woman to bear a son.

Danger looms large here. Such a sentence may suggest that God is a sexual male being who impregnated a human mother. For that reason, attention to the birth narratives in the gospels are so vital. They open themselves up to the charge, but they escape it. They are willing to take the risk because the mode of the incarnation not only honors Jesus as the Son of God but also discloses a truth about the God of Israel: God is a Father, but God is not male. That denial of God the Father's maleness comes via the most sexualized of all events: pregnancy.

Story Is Not Sexualized

The New Testament says comparatively very little about Jesus's beginning. Paul says he was born of a woman (Gal 4:4), and Matthew and Luke with brevity attest that God caused Mary's pregnancy. No New Testament author recounts the precise moment of conception; they state that it will be and then has become true.

Even the brief way the evangelists recount Jesus's beginning, however, denies the maleness of God his Father, and I will demonstrate this with three arguments. First, the way in which they recount the event makes clear that this God is not like the other gods who have intercourse with women. Instead, God

---

24. This deserves much more explanation, which appears in chapter 4, but let me assuage any fears by asserting that I affirm the eternal begottenness of the Son, and hence the eternal relational reality that God is Father. I would also affirm, however, that believers know to use this *precise* language about God's eternal relation because of the incarnation. It is this birth of the God-man that provides the lens for speaking fittingly about God as Father in eternity.

acts in ways similar to other accounts of divine birth in the ancient world, by causing Mary's pregnancy without intercourse, and these similarities provide the second denial of God's maleness. In those instances, the gods explicitly do *not* act like males. Nevertheless, even if God acts in more respectable ways, God still is left standing in the place of the male, providing what the male normally provides. Finally, then, with appeal to both Jewish and Christian theology, I argue that in the incarnation, the numbers simply do not add up. God is not portrayed as a male because the triad of female, male, and child is not followed in the event of the incarnation. All three arguments coalesce to support the assertion: God is Father because God causes a pregnancy, but in no way does the text ever depict God as a male.

Divine Rape

Some readers have suggested that the birth narratives portray an invasion of Mary's body. Interpreters—some inside the Christian fold, and some decidedly out of it—have called upon the faithful to give a reason for the hope that lies within, literally the hope that lay within Mary. Infamously, the feminist theologian Mary Daly called her Christian namesake the "Total Rape Victim."[25] Conquered in both body and mind, "Like all rape victims in male myth she submits joyously to this unspeakable degradation."[26] Daly easily plays the strawman—straw woman better said—but more recent and less extreme voices also recognize the danger of the text.

The possibility of a supernatural rape remains a reading of Luke's annunciation narrative. Michael Pope argues that interpreters could see a sexualized Mary, marked as such because of being referred to as a betrothed virgin, then depicted as a victim of sexual violence. In Luke's account, Gabriel enters into her space, and she identifies herself as a slave of a male master.[27] If these echoes are given full weight, Luke presents her as a victim of "the distinctive violence faced by women in antiquity."[28] Courtney Hall Lee calls attention

25. Mary Daly, *Gyn/Ecology: The Metaethics of Radical Feminism* (Boston: Beacon, 1990), 84.

26. Mary Daly, *Pure Lust: Elemental Feminist Philosophy* (Minneapolis: Women's Press, 1998), 74.

27. Michael Pope, "Gabriel's Entrance and Biblical Violence in Luke's Annunciation Narrative," *Journal of Biblical Literature* 137 (2018): 701–10.

28. Pope, "Gabriel's Entrance," 710.

to the difficulty of the annunciation scene, especially for those women who have experienced cultural violence against their bodies: "for women who have experienced sexual violence and lack of sexual agency, the idea of faithfully accepting a womb invasion is still undesirable. . . . For ordinary women the womb invasions they have experienced were non-consensual, violent, and coercive. A womanist Mariology must not romanticize or venerate victimization."[29]

Readers of Matthew and Luke are excused for making comparisons with the conception of demigods and heroes in the ancient world. The similarities are close at hand, for frequent is the trope in which a god joins with a woman so that a child is produced: Hermes with the dancing girl,[30] Poseidon with Tyro,[31] Apollo with Perictione,[32] Jupiter with Olympias,[33] Zeus with any number of women.[34] Some stories include force,[35] and most deception. Historians debate whether "rape" is a fitting description,[36] for the women in the stories often enter into the encounter willingly (though often through deception), often receive good out of the births, and even experience pleasure. "Consent" may not be totally free in these instances,[37] but it is often present. The lack of explicit

---

29. Courtney Hall Lee, *Black Madonna: A Womanist Look at Mary of Nazareth* (Eugene, OR: Cascade, 2017), 112.

30. Homer, *Iliad* 16.180–186.

31. Homer, *Odyssey* 11.235–260.

32. Both Plutarch, in *Moralia* 717–718 (*Table-Talk* 8, question 1.2), and Diogenes Laertius, in *Lives of Eminent Philosophers* 3.2, present that Plato was conceived by Apollo.

33. Plutarch, *Life of Alexander* 2.4.

34. Zeus himself recounts a long list in *Iliad* 14.315–321. With Alcmene, Zeus looked like her husband, and with Lena, Zeus appeared as a swan. Io, Antiope, and Moschus Europa were all seduced by Zeus (*Odyssey* 11.260–265). Many from the nobility claimed descent from the gods in the Roman Empire. See Michael Peppard, *The Son of God in the Roman World: Divine Sonship in Its Social and Political Context* (Oxford: Oxford University Press, 2011), 48.

35. Mars raped Rhea Silvia/Ilia in Dio Cassius (*Roman Antiquities* 1.5.1) and Livy, *History of Rome* 1.3.10–1.4.4. See discussion in Celene Lillie, *The Rape of Eve: The Transformation of Roman Ideology in Three Early Christian Retellings of Genesis* (Minneapolis: Fortress, 2017), 23–33.

36. Mary R. Lefkowitz argues that the women in the tales are *seduced* by gods outside the home (which respects the virtue of hospitality), and they often offer consent; the results bring good for them, and, hence, the term "rape" does not fit (*Women in Greek Myth*, 2nd ed. [Baltimore: Johns Hopkins University Press, 2007], 54–69). Lillie counters that these narratives "should be read as rape narratives" (*Rape of Eve*, 22n1).

37. "It is significant that, despite the gods' undeniably greater power, they ask for the woman's consent and honor her right of refusal, even though that refusal may bring about her death,

violence against an unwilling victim in the ancient accounts actually increases the risk of Luke's guilt by association. A socially aware modern reader wonders whether Mary was brainwashed not unlike the women in the myths, for it is unlikely that a mortal woman would have the freedom to resist a god.

In full recognition of the threat this text evokes, the charge of divine sexual violence—or better said, divine sexual coercion—is not appropriate to Gabriel's statement and the event it foretells.

The two evangelists who include the birth narrative assiduously avoid any hint of sexual encounter. They assert that the child is from the Holy Spirit (Matt 1:18, 20), who came over Mary in a way that evokes imagery of light (Luke 1:35). God supplies what a male supplies in a normal pregnancy—no matter what theory of conception one assumes. God does so, however, *without intercourse*, no apparition taking the form of a human or animal, no euphemisms,[38] only the ephemeral Spirit and shadow. Such scripts for divine intercourse were available, but the evangelists did not follow them.[39]

In what follows, I walk through the annunciation narrative, noting where the threat of divine rape arises but how Luke circumvents it. I begin with the weighty language of Mary's self-identification. Once Gabriel has told her about the birth of her son, she accepts by referring to herself as the slave (δούλη [doulē]) of the Lord (Luke 1:38).

---

as it did for Cassandra and for Caenis, or transformation into a tree or fountain" (Lefkowitz, *Women in Greek Myth*, 67). Consent under the threat of death may not really be consent, but I wish not to set up the mythological world unfairly as a foil for Luke's narrative.

38. Michael Pope argues to the contrary, highlighting that Luke's naming of Mary as a betrothed virgin makes Gabriel's entrance language carry sexual connotations, reiterated by her naming of herself as a slave ("Gabriel's Entrance," 702–8). I disagree for three reasons. First, such entrance language is so common it cannot bear the weight he gives to it, even if there is one instance in the Septuagint where angelic entrance language implies sex (Gen 6:1–4). Second, it cannot bear this weight because Luke's pointing toward Mary's virginal status could just as easily emphasize the innocence she maintains throughout the encounter. Finally, as I will argue in chapter 3, Mary's slave language *in reference to God* is a term of empowerment and not oppression, including sexual violence.

39. David Litwa observes concerning Luke 1:35, "Such delicate and indeterminate theological language allowed Luke to present his narrative of Jesus's divine birth as both plausible and reliable history, and thus to distance himself from stories of sexual divine conception that he deemed mythical (with the sense of *untrue*) and unworthy of Yahweh" (*Iesus Deus: The Early Christian Depiction of Jesus as a Mediterranean God* [Minneapolis: Fortress, 2014], 43).

In Luke's context in the Greco-Roman world, the role of a female slave carried heavy sexual overtones.[40] Especially in a context in which the point of the conversation concerns pregnancy, her self-description puts into sharp relief the highly uncomfortable suggestion of divine transgression of her body. It can be the case that God calls Mary to a life of service as God does with many other followers.[41] It can also be true that her unique call to bear this Messiah stands as an incredibly honorable invitation. Nevertheless, both could stand as statements of veracity, and even so, the annunciation could remain a forcible imposition on her body.[42]

Her servitude, even to the point of bearing a child, to Luke's κύριος (*kyrios*) makes a profound difference.[43] This master is God. Mary is not submitting to any human; hers is an agreement to a situation proposed between Creator and created. Theologians as vastly different *on their concept of gender* as Orthodox priest Alexander Schmemann and Reformed feminist Serene Jones agree on the difference between Mary's acceptance of slavery to the divine and any slavery to a human. Schmemann comments: "She, however, accepts, she obeys, she humbles herself before—not her 'dependence' on something or somebody—but the living Truth itself, a Presence, a Beauty, a Life, a Call so overwhelmingly evident that it makes the notion of 'dependence' an empty one, or rather identical and coextensive with that of 'freedom.'"[44] So too Serene Jones, who also asserts the power that comes to Mary in relating to this God

---

40. Although some of the emperors passed laws for the benefit of slaves, "there is no evidence for any imperial interference with slaveholders' total physical domination of their slaves (even torture and killing were justified for sufficient cause) or with the owners' sexual use of their own slaves." See S. Scott Bartchy, "Slaves and Slavery in the Roman World," in *The World of the New Testament: Cultural, Social, and Historical Contexts*, ed. Joel B. Green and Lee Martin McDonald (Grand Rapids: Baker, 2013), 177.

41. F. Scott Spencer shows the pattern of agency in response to God's call with figures throughout the testaments (*Salty Wives, Spirited Mothers, and Savvy Widows: Capable Women of Purpose and Persistence in Luke's Gospel* [Grand Rapids: Eerdmans, 2012], 55–56).

42. Jennifer A. Glancy argues that slaves are seen simply as bodies to be owned and controlled according to the will of the owner (*Slavery in Early Christianity* [Minneapolis: Fortress, 2002]).

43. Courtney Hall Lee acknowledges the threat of a woman described as a slave giving up her body, her womb. Yet she concludes, "when Mary's fiat is considered a moment of saying yes *to her son* the meaning changes" (*Black Madonna*, 112.)

44. Alexander Schmemann, *Celebration of Faith*, vol. 3 of *The Virgin Mary* (Yonkers, NY: St. Vladimir's Seminary Press, 2001), 54.

in such a way: "Mary's belief in a transcendent God, far from entrenching her in her own sense of depravity and incapacitation, frees her to remember the past, envision the future, and act in the present."[45]

The difference is not just between divine and human, for divine beings in the ancient world, as the parallels attest, were no guarantee of benevolence. The *character* of the divine, in Luke's narrative, takes shape based on Israel's traditions. Luke utilizes common terms in the medical and philosophical texts of his day to describe the agent responsible for the conception of the child: *spirit* and *power*, πνεῦμα (*pneuma*) and δύναμις (*dynamis*);[46] yet the way that he describes those common terms associates this animating power with the God of Israel.[47] The Spirit responsible is holy, and the power at work is the power of the Most High. Within the thought world of Luke, the Spirit who is holy is a trusted source who works for good in line with the Most High, who is none other than the God of Israel. This Creator has the best in mind for humanity through the people with whom God has made covenant, and this includes Mary. Interpretation of this passage, and her statement in particular, hinges on what one thinks of the character of God. The narrative setting may set off alarm bells, but only when read in a vacuum. Luke has presented a God who does not perform malicious acts against those who give their lives, and bodies, as service. This child will not be the result of a lustful god taking advantage

---

45. Serene Jones, *Trauma and Grace: Theology in a Ruptured World*, 2nd ed. (Louisville: Westminster John Knox, 2019), 117. Feminist journalist Sally Cunneen states the paradox similarly as she describes Mary's agreement as "the creative submission of a fully liberated human being to the will of God" (*In Search of Mary: The Woman and the Symbol* [New York: Ballantine Books, 1996], 285).

46. See also the discussion of *pneuma* in ancient ideas of conception in Alicia Myers's *Blessed among Women? Mothers and Motherhood in the New Testament* (Oxford: Oxford University Press, 2017), 47, where she states, "The importance of the *pneuma*, or 'spirit,' in this process should not be overlooked."

47. In another article, Michael Pope helpfully presents the evidence of the association of the terms σπέρμα, πνεῦμα, and δύναμις (*sperma, pneuma,* and *dynamis*), which leads him to this conclusion: "Jesus's conception, both the mechanics and the resulting embryo, is not articulated according to spermatic biblical begetting stories or medical explanation. Rather, it is ἅγιον, 'other,' otherness being the most basic factor sequestering off from all the rest something as sacred or hallowed. What realizes conception in Mary's uterus is ever so much like semen, but other" ("Luke's Seminal Annunciation: An Embryological Reading of Mary's Conception," *Journal of Biblical Literature* 138 [2019]: 807). He stops short of reflecting upon the character of the one causing the child whom Luke describes as holy.

of a man's betrothed. This conception is a virtuous one because it is, indeed, orchestrated by the God who is holy. The character of God rightly leads the Christian tradition to reject with vehemence the suggestion of divine rape.

In addition to the character of the agent, the actions of the agent are nonviolating. Interpreters have noted that "the Spirit fulfills the role of the father in Jesus's birth. Mary has indeed been impregnated by the Holy Spirit,"[48] but the way in which that happens demands close attention. The annunciation comes in spatially "above" language. The Holy Spirit comes upon (ἐπέρχομαι [*epercho-mai*]) Mary but not *into* Mary. The power of the Most High will *over*shadow (ἐπισκιάζω [*episkiazō*]) her. Like the cloud that rested upon the tabernacle when it was filled with the glory of the Lord (Exod 40:29 LXX), so too will the power of the Most High overshadow her with the result that she will conceive.[49] As the spirit of God hovered over the waters of creation at the beginning of time, at the dawn of the eschatological age, Mary's body will be the source for the creative act of God. Her body will be cultivated, but her body will not be penetrated. God impregnates Mary with an overshadowing presence. On this point, Luke departs from many of the tales of his time. Most often the gods impregnate women through intercourse, even if they conceal themselves in the form of a human or an animal. Women are penetrated. This is not the case in Luke.[50] He avoids any kind of insinuation of intercourse.[51]

Tina Beattie, with appeals to the work of Luce Irigaray, sees a schema-shattering reality in this kind of impregnating. About the annunciation, Irigaray asserts that it portrays "the advent of a divine one who does not burst in violently, like the god of Greek desire."[52] Beattie elucidates, "Irigaray suggests that the Christian story of the annunciation offers the possibility of displac-

48. Heikki Räisänen, "Begotten by the Holy Spirit," in *Sacred Marriages: The Divine-Human Sexual Metaphor from Sumer to Early Christianity*, ed. Martti Nissinen and Risto Uro (Winona Lake, IN: Eisenbrauns, 2008), 330.

49. Darrell L. Bock, *Luke*, IVP New Testament Commentary Series 3 (Downers Grove, IL: InterVarsity Press, 1994), 121–22.

50. "There is *no possibility* of male semen within Mary's womb. Instead, in language that reminds readers of other divine births of Greco-Roman fame, she will be 'overshadowed' by a 'power of the Most High' (1:35)" (Myers, *Blessed among Women?*, 64).

51. Michael Pope concludes similarly, "my conclusion falls within a traditional interpretive scope that cannot find textual grounds for sex between God and Mary" ("Luke's Seminal Annunciation," 807).

52. Luce Irigaray, *Marine Lover of Friedrich Nietzsche*, trans. Gillian C. Gill (New York: Columbia University Press, 181).

ing the symbolic phallus by appealing to the angel as a life-giving symbol of mediation. . . . In this interpretation, Mary's virginal conception might signify an event outside the domain of the phallus, in a way that is not circumscribed with the values and laws of patriarchy."[53]

The message Gabriel brings does herald the birth of a child, but the conception of this child will be a nonsexual act by a holy being. There can be no rape or sexual coercion if there is no sex. Luke took the risk of association with well-known stories by choosing to include this conversation, but in the way in which he presented it, he avoided the danger. This God would not and, in fact, does not force pregnancy upon this young woman.

The lack of force becomes even more clear when readers attend to Mary's words.[54] The form of Gabriel's statement, "you will conceive" leaves an opening for response. Gabriel does speak with indicative verbs—statements of fact—but these appear in the future tense. This is what will happen; it has not happened already. Gabriel does not tell Mary of events that have already occurred within her without her knowledge or assent. Note also that Gabriel's words include no alternative, no punishment or threat if she does not embrace this word. Without such a statement, if she rejects, she would miss out on the blessing of mothering the Messiah, but there is no threat of repercussion if she chooses not to accept.

The evangelist's revelation of God's fatherhood denies that God is a coercive male. Therefore, Mary provides what a woman normally does to bring about a new human life, and God provides what a male normally does. *Because God does not act as a male acts, this account gives no justification to view God as a male.* Instead of reinforcing the notion of a male God, the virginal conception explicitly denies it.

Divine Breath

Earlier I argued against Andrew Lincoln by asserting that all views of conception, ancient and modern, are equally challenging for the Christian story of the incarnation because God supplies what the male normally supplies. This is true *if one views the accounts as similar to some kind of divine-human sexual*

53. Tina Beattie, *God's Mother, Eve's Advocate: A Marian Narrative of Women's Salvation* (London: Continuum, 2002), 125.

54. Mary's actions in this event provide the focus for chapter 3.

encounter. Because the gospel writers reject this motif, they resonate with an approach similar to other ancient authors, those who are open to the idea of some kind of divine conception albeit nonsexual.

Such a trope also existed in the ancient world. In his essay, "Miraculous Conceptions and Births in Mediterranean Antiquity," Charles H. Talbert catalogs several examples of this kind of conception.[55] Io becomes pregnant by Zeus, but only by the "onbreathing of his love" (Aeschylus, *Suppliant Women* 17–19). Io's child Epaphus is so named because he was born only by the touch of Zeus's hand (*Prometheus Bound* 848–852). In *Life of Numa*, Plutarch notes that the Egyptians believe that a human woman can conceive by the spirit of a god.[56] Plutarch's comments on Plato are the most extensive in this regard and often cited.[57] In this instance, Florus and Tyndarus are discussing Plato's birthday. They float a story in which Plato was the child of Apollo. If this is fitting for him, they take comfort in knowing that it cannot have been through intercourse, but as God creates the world, so too might have the divine begot Plato through a potency other than semen.[58] Second Enoch records a similarly inexplicable pregnancy when Sopanim conceives the child Melchizedek when she was old and had not slept with her husband Nir.[59] Philo makes a similar but more expansive move when he describes God as the Father of all creation:[60]

> God as the father of the world with a mother *but not as a male!* . . . we shall speak with justice, if we say that the Creator of the universe is also the father of his creation; and that the mother was the knowledge of the Creator with whom God uniting, *not as a man unites*, became the father of creation. And

---

55. Charles H. Talbert, "Miraculous Conceptions and Births in Mediterranean Antiquity," in *The Historical Jesus in Context*, ed. Amy-Jill Levine, Dale C. Allison Jr., and John Dominic Crossan, Princeton Readings in Religions 31 (Princeton: Princeton University Press, 2006), 79–86.

56. Plutarch, *Life of Numa* 4.3.

57. J. R. Daniel Kirk, *A Man Attested by God: The Human Jesus of the Synoptic Gospels* (Grand Rapids: Eerdmans, 2016), 371; James D. G. Dunn, *Christology in the Making: A New Testament Inquiry into the Origins of the Doctrine of the Incarnation*, 2nd ed. (Grand Rapids: Eerdmans, 1996), 14; Litwa, *Iesus Deus*, 45–67.

58. Plutarch, *Moralia* 717–718 (*Table-Talk* 8, question 1.2).

59. 2 Enoch 71 (*Old Testament Pseudepigrapha*, ed. James H. Charlesworth [New York: Doubleday, 1983], 1:206–8).

60. This idea does appear in Israel's Scriptures, for example, in Isa 45:9–13.

this knowledge having received the seed of God, when the day of her travail arrived, brought forth her only and well-beloved son, perceptible by the external senses, namely this world.[61]

Although Philo is speaking about creation and not one person, note his comfort in describing God as Creator-Father—even giving a seed—joined with an explicit statement, which he proclaims twice, that God is not acting as a male. God is not creating or fathering as a human man would. These examples show that creating life and even fathering a child could be performed by a god in the ancient world without that God being thought of as a male.[62] The gospels reside firmly in this perspective.[63]

Divine Presence

Later Jewish and early Christian reflections on conception offer another perspective that also denies the conclusion that God is male because God is Father of Jesus Christ. Jews articulated a belief that in the process of conception, God was the one who caused and sustained the birth of a new life.[64] The story the evangelists tell of the incarnation affirms this same theological commitment. God is the one who causes this new life. Whether a birth is normal or miraculously virginal, God is always present. From this perspective, for an ancient readership already committed to divine providence in birth, God remains in-

---

61. Philo, *On Drunkenness* 30 (trans. Colson and Whitaker; emphasis mine).

62. "When Plutarch speaks of a *pneuma* interacting with a woman, he is not assuming that a god in a male body has sex with a female" (Litwa, *Iesus Deus*, 49).

63. In conclusion, Litwa states the congruence between Luke and Plutarch: "both Luke and Plutarch effectively speak of divine *pneuma* and power as the efficient cause of pregnancy without hinting at perceived theologically crass features such as metamorphosis into a male body, penetration by a divine penis, and the ejaculation of divine seed into the womb" (Litwa, *Iesus Deus*, 58).

64. "[Rabbinic] traditions consistently emphasize God's roles in procreation, articulating rabbinic distinctiveness vis-à-vis Greco-Roman 'medical' writers in that seed(s), without God, do not make an embryo." See Gwynn Kessler, *Conceiving Israel: The Fetus in Rabbinic Narratives* (Philadelphia: University of Pennsylvania Press, 2009), 90. She urges that modern readers seriously consider "the extent to which rabbinic theories of procreation implicate God in this process" (90).

volved as is always true.[65] Stated clearly in the Babylonian Talmud Niddah 31a, "There are three partners in [making a] man, the Holy One, Blessed be He, his father, and his mother."[66] From this perspective, in the instance of Mary's pregnancy, God does not replace the man, God removes the man.[67] God is provident over the process as is always the case, present as God, not as a male.

Finally, the incarnation by virginal conception does not "cast God as a male" because, simply stated, in robust Christian theology, the numbers do not add up. Whereas in a normal pregnancy, mother and father unify to conceive a child, in the incarnation of the Son of God, mother gives birth to a child, but not by partnering with God the Father alone but because of the work of God the Father and God the Holy Spirit. Readers do not have access to the mental schema of the evangelists with regard to the ontology of the *pneuma hagion*, but distinct actions reveal that four persons are involved in this situation, not just three. In Matthew, the pregnancy is from the Holy Spirit (Matt 1:18, 20), and also the Lord called the child "my son" (2:15). In Luke, Jesus is the "Son of the Most High" (Luke 1:32), but it is the Holy Spirit who comes over Mary and the power of the Most High that overshadows Mary (1:35). Any comparison between the dyad of sexuality—male and female—by which God the Father plays the role of the male dissolves because of the presence of the Holy Spirit, a Spirit whose linguistic representation is feminine in Hebrew (רוח [*ruakh*])

65. Drawing upon Kessler's work, Myers concurs: "OT writings . . . emphasize God's role as the one who 'knits' and forms the fetus within the woman. . . . Where these texts differ from the larger Greco-Roman writings is in the identification of the source of this animation—God alone rather than the male human" (*Blessed among Women?*, 61). See also Lincoln's explanation of this theme of three involved in conception (*Born of a Virgin?*, 83–87).

66. See also Eccl 11:5 LXX: "When one does not know what the way of the spirit is, like bones in the belly of the pregnant woman, so you will not know the works of God, whatever he will do" (*A New English Translation of the Septuagint*, ed. Albert Pietersma and Benjamin G. Wright [New York: Oxford University Press, 2007]). Myers comments, "While unfathomable, Ecclesiastes asserts that it is God 'who makes all things,' thus firmly establishing God's life-giving role in giving the spirit and causing fetal growth" (*Blessed among Women?*, 61–62).

67. Howard Eilberg-Swartz observes the same potential with the account of Jesus's conception: "The story of the virgin birth of Jesus makes explicit what had always been a latent tension in monotheism: God fathers a son and the human father becomes irrelevant" (*God's Phallus and Other Problems for Men and Monotheism* [Boston: Beacon, 1994], 4). This need not be read as a devaluation of men. See discussion of the inclusion of female and male in the incarnation in chapter 5.

and neuter in Greek (πνεῦμα [*pneuma*]). Stated differently, any idea of the singular maleness of God is destroyed by the triunity of God.[68] In the virginal conception, God causes the birth of a son, even provides what a male normally supplies but in a nonsexualized, divine, and even triune way. As revealed by the narratives of the incarnation, God the Father is not male.

Conclusion

Speaking of God as "Father" does well to speak with a limp, as Jacob encountered God but could henceforth never walk with prideful self-dependence. With this posture, a most difficult path stretches out before interpreters, one that demands speaking of God as Father without the false affirmation that God is male. The account of the incarnation provides the best guardrail on this path. God is not sexualized even in the account of a pregnancy. The God of Israel and that God's Holy Spirit respond to Mary's yes with the same provision and protection that ensures the healthy conception and delivery of all children, but without the presence of a man.

The lack of sexuality in God the Father as revealed in the incarnation reveals that what is true of God the first person there is true of God always. While Christian confession has recognized that humans can never fully comprehend God, it has also widely held that the God revealed *pro nobis* cannot be at odds with God *in se*.[69] Just as God the Father is not male in the incarnation, so too the first person of the Trinity is not male in eternity. Few would disagree. Careful consideration of the evangelists' birth narratives in their contexts confirms that widely held consensus.

This consensus, however, does not prevent many from weighting conceptions of this nonmale God toward one end of the gendered spectrum, namely,

---

68. Spencer calls attention to the presence of the Spirit and the unsettling of gendered expectations: "Ascribing Jesus's conception to the divine Holy Spirit—the feminine *ruach* in Hebrew and the neuter *pneuma* in Greek—subverts notions of Mary's passive body being somehow penetrated and impregnated by God the Father's 'seed'" (*Salty Wives*, 72).

69. Thomas F. Torrance states, "[Humans] need a bridge across the infinite distance between God and ourselves which is grounded both in God and in man [*sic*]. That is precisely what we are given through the incarnation of God's word and Son in Jesus Christ, the one Mediator between God and man" ("The Christian Apprehension," in Kimel, *Speaking the Christian God*, 133.)

that of masculinity. Many people (and even those just casually familiar with the Christian tradition) will answer in the negative when asked whether God the Father is an embodied male. If asked, however, whether God is more like men or women, preference for the male, or even stumbling over the question, often reveals the presence of an underlying assumption. In the next section, then, I make the case that the incarnation affirms paternal language for God while at the same time denying not only God's maleness but also any preferential option for the male's godlikeness. The mode of God's self-revelation in Jesus Christ prohibits any notion that God the Father is more like men than women, that God the Father is more fittingly masculine than feminine.

Before moving to gender, however, I have more to consider concerning bodies. Next, I attend not to the body of God the Father but instead that from which the body of God the Son was formed, namely, the body of Mary.

two

Holiness and the Female Body

Then bring to birth,
push out into air, a Man-child
needing, like any other,
milk and love—
but who was God.

—Denise Levertov, "Annunciation"

Levertov's is one beautiful example of countless who seek to express in the art of poetry the mysterious paradox of God the babe, of Mary's maternity. To enter into such holy mysteries, for faith to seek not mastery but understanding, demands caution and clarity. Potential problems abound. For the purposes of this chapter, which investigates Jewish purity laws regarding women's bodies in order to place Mary's pregnancy in its historical as well as theological context, I am most concerned with two challenges. First, a carnal focus, especially upon issues unique to women's bodies, raises numerous concerns, including the fact that such treatments can serve to diminish the beautiful complexity of females to their status as menstruants or mothers alone.[1] The historical record of the Jewish people avoids this error. In it, women's bodily purity is

---

1. I address this concern in chapter 5 as well.

not the most important issue, either by frequency or weight. Women appear as players in the narrative by virtue of their covenant keeping, wisdom, strength, leadership, property ownership, relationships, and even failures, with all the variety and color of fulsome human characters.[2] Israel's Scriptures simply do not define women solely by their bodily rhythms. With this richness in mind, the last chapter of the book will broaden out to consider the various roles that Mary herself plays.

Because of the nature of the Christian confession, however, pausing to consider Mary's *body*, and the purity laws that attended to the unique experiences of the female body, is a necessity. Jewish theologians, too, affirm the goodness of the created human body, and many throughout the ages have looked forward to its resurrection, but the incarnation—that God was born of a woman—places an added demand upon Christian theologians to consider the human body. The singular focus of this chapter is not meant to reduce women to their biology but to give due attention to the rather shocking way in which God came. As the evangelists tell the story, God has decided that women's bodies are deemed worthy to receive the ultimate expression of holiness, the very body of God.

This leads to a second problematic challenge and necessary clarification. Frequently, this kind of affirmation—that Christianity offered women something uniquely affirming—builds upon a negative construct of Judaism. This sentiment is typically articulated along the lines of statements that the Jewish faith deemed women especially sinful because they were frequently impure and therefore that barred them from access to God. Such blanket characterizations not only ignore the complicated nuances of Jewish law and practice throughout different communities over time, but particularly damning for the Christian who aims to be orthodox, such portrayals posit two Gods: the God of Judaism who set up these misogynistic laws and the God of Jesus who destroyed them.

The incarnation does indeed make a radical affirmation concerning the female body's proximity to holiness but not by destroying Judaism or its purity

2. Amy-Jill Levine, "Jewish Women in the New Testament," *Shalvi/Hyman Encyclopedia of Jewish Women*, https://jwa.org/encyclopedia/article/jewish-women-in-the-new-testament. See also Lynn Cohick, *Women in the World of the Earliest Christians: Illuminating Ancient Ways of Life* (Grand Rapids: Baker, 2009).

laws. God's embrace of the flesh makes this affirmation by arriving within the
structures of Judaism. To stand in awe of this grace demands first an appropriate understanding of the gender dynamics of the Jewish law. Then, and only
then, can attention to the depth of simple affirmations of Mary's motherhood
in the New Testament reveal God's placement of the holy with the body of a
woman. This chapter considers women in the Jewish law, particularly their
access to the divine presence and the purity laws. Then I investigate Matthew
and Luke's treatment of Mary's story with the same double interest, her participation in the purity laws and her access to God.

Judaism

The trope of the misogynistic Jewish villain makes many false and yet woefully
popular statements:

"The God of the Old Testament is only for men."
"Women are more sinful because of their impurity."
"Their impurity is more pronounced, and any imbalance between the genders
    arises out of a desire to oppress women."[3]

The texts of Israel's Scriptures, however, simply will not prop up this straw
man.[4]

This is not the place for a comprehensive treatment of women in the Scriptures of Israel. Instead, I focus on the particular question of access to God's

3. Amy-Jill Levine, "Second Temple Judaism, Jesus, and Women Yeast of Eden," *Biblical
Interpretation* 2 (1994): 8–33, Paula Fredriksen, "Did Jesus Oppose the Purity Laws?," *Bible
Review* 11 (1995): 18–25, 42–45, and Katharina von Kellenbach, *Anti-Judaism in Feminist Religious
Writings* (Atlanta: Scholars Press, 1994), aptly catalog this trope in many Christian writings.

4. This is not to deny that these texts reflect the patriarchy of the societies in which they
were written. Many faithful Jewish and Christian feminists wrestle with the multiple difficult
texts in Israel's Scriptures that do not align with modern convictions of gender equality. The
particular statements I list above, however, are either completely unfounded or at least open to
various interpretations. Many interpreters have not denied the ugliness of patriarchy portrayed
in the text but have concluded that the text itself is not unredeemable. The God portrayed
therein values women, but often (and frustratingly) within the structures of patriarchal societies.

presence.[5] It is false to claim that the gates to God's presence open to women only with the arrival of Jesus. Quite the contrary. In the very beginning of the grand narrative, male and female in the image of God are granted stewardship over creation (Gen 1:26–27). When they hide themselves from God's presence after their disobedience, the text assumes it had been the habit of both to walk with the Lord God prior to this fateful event (3:8). At the beginning of the covenant with Abraham, not only does God bless Sarah along with Abraham (18:9–15; 21:1–2), but the angel of God ministers to Hagar twice, seeing her (16:7–15) and hearing her (21:17–21). She, in turn, names God (16:13).[6] At the beginning of the covenant with the people of Israel, all of the people (כל העם [*kal ha'am*]) hear and receive the covenant (Exod 19:8; 24:4, 7) and are anointed with blood (24:8).[7] When Joshua reads the covenant again, all Israel—women being explicitly included—is there to hear and respond (Josh 8:34–35). Women are involved in some cultic activity at the tent of meeting (1 Sam 2:22), interpretation ranging from prayer to fasting to offering sacrifices or serving as an honor guard.[8] When the place of worship is established, full families are instructed to bring sacrifices and eat in the presence of God (Deut 12:6–7; see Hannah's enactment of this in 1 Sam 1–2). In language

---

5. Other issues in Judaism, such as the covenantal mark of circumcision, attend to men in ways that they do not attend to women. For a treatment of this particular issue, see Shaye J. D. Cohen, *Why Aren't Jewish Women Circumcised? Gender and Covenant in Judaism* (Berkeley: University of California Press, 2005). My aim here is to say not that Judaism is completely balanced between the genders but only that it is not completely negative with regard to its treatment of women in comparison with Christianity.

6. Phyllis Trible's treatment of Hagar remains a powerful reading of this text (*Texts of Terror: Literary-Feminist Readings of Biblical Narratives* [Philadelphia: Fortress, 1984], 9–36).

7. Exodus 19:15 does instruct the "people" (עם [*am*]) not to "go near a woman," leading interpreters like Judith Plaskow to note, "At this critical moment of Jewish history, women are invisible. Whether they too stood there trembling in fear and expectation, what they heard when the men heard these words of Moses, we do not know" (*Standing Again at Sinai: Judaism from a Feminist Perspective* [San Francisco: HarperSanFrancisco, 1991], 25). On the other hand, Jewish midrash explicitly includes women here: "the house of Jacob—these are the women—the house of Israel—these are the men" (Mekhilta Bahodesh 2.207 [ed. Horovitz-Rabin] and parallels). See Cohen, *Why Aren't Jewish Women Circumcised?*, 134.

8. Susan Grossman, "Women and the Jerusalem Temple," in *Daughters of the King: Women and the Synagogue; A Survey of History, Halakhah, and Contemporary Realities*, ed. Susan Grossman and Rivka Haut (Philadelphia: Jewish Publication Society, 1993), 18.

reminiscent of Joel's prophecy cited by Peter at Pentecost, the rejoicing at the Festival of Weeks is for "you and your sons and your daughters, your male and female slaves, the Levites resident in your towns, as well as the strangers, the orphans, and the widows who are among you—at the place that the Lord your God will choose as a dwelling for his name" (Deut 16:11). The Lord commands everyone to hear the law during the Festival of Booths (3:9–13). When David brings the ark to Jerusalem and the sacrifices are consumed, all Israel is present, men and women (2 Sam 6:12–19). Based on previous examples, the comprehensiveness and importance of the inauguration of the temple makes it likely that women are present again when Solomon's temple is inaugurated and the cloud of God's presence arrives (1 Kgs 8). Time would fail me to tell of Miriam, Huldah, Deborah, Ruth, Jael, and the countless unnamed women of Israel who experienced and facilitated the presence of God. The texts attest to the rich participatory religious experience of women throughout Israel's past.

It is the purity laws, however, that so frequently give rise to the idea that Judaism was derogatory toward women.[9] At times, authors inappropriately allow impurity to bleed into the concept of sin. There is a false idea that women were more impure than men and therefore to be regarded as more sinful.[10] Such equations appear less frequently in more recent scholarship, as the work of scholars like Mary Douglas, Jacob Milgrom, and Jonathan Klawans has clarified the similarities and, vitally, the distinctions between moral sin and ritual impurity.[11] Normal processes like menstruation and good events like birth

9. "Many scholars, however, while emphasizing Jesus's articulation of Jewish ethics, or his Jewish scriptural sensibility, or the apocalyptic convictions he shared with so many contemporaries, draw the line at the biblical laws of purity" (Paula Fredriksen, "Did Jesus Oppose the Purity Laws?," 20).

10. Jonathan Klawans names as a common error the idea that "women were considered to be impure all of the time" and the "blind identification of impurity and sin" wherein one finds claims that "sinners were considered impure and that, by extension, those who associated with sinners were violating norms of purity" (*Impurity and Sin in Ancient Judaism* [Oxford: Oxford University Press, 2000], 137).

11. Mary Douglas, *Purity and Danger: An Analysis of Concepts of Pollution and Taboo* (London: Routledge, 2005), 1966; Jacob Milgrom, *Leviticus 1–16: A New Translation with Introduction and Commentary*, Anchor Bible 3 (New York: Doubleday, 1998); Milgrom, *Leviticus 17–22: A New Translation with Introduction and Commentary*, Anchor Bible 3A (New York: Doubleday, 2000); Milgrom, *Leviticus 23–27: A New Translation with Introduction and Commentary*, Anchor Bible 3B (New York: Doubleday, 2001); Milgrom, *Leviticus: A Book of Ritual and Ethics* (Minneapolis:

render women impure, but that does not mean they are sinful in a moral way. They and those who are in close contact with them need cleansing before they can come near the sanctuary, but they do not bring an abomination upon the land. The purity laws do not indicate in any way that Judaism renders women as more innately sinful than men.

In fact, the laws concerning bodily purity are rather well balanced between the genders. No difference exists for men or women in the obedience required for the food laws (Lev 11) or for the skin diseases (14–15), save a recognition of the commonality of male pattern baldness (14:40). If a male or female has an unusual discharge, each is unclean and can render others unclean. Normal expulsion of bodily fluids in menstruation or seminal emission renders the person unclean, one day for the seminal emission and seven days for menstruation, in congruence with the average length of the discharge. Pregnancy receives its own treatment, and in that way is unbalanced, but since this bodily reality affects women alone, if instructions for it were not included, the absence would likely be rendered as dismissive.

That dominant equality being recognized, it is still true that the most striking lack of balance appears in the event of pregnancy, in that a woman is rendered impure for *double* the amount of time if she has a daughter rather than a son (Lev 12:5). For ages, interpreters have suggested reasons for the difference since the text does not.[12] The extended time for a daughter might be an indication that women have a greater potency for impurity given the frequency of pregnancy or menstruation or as the representatives of Eve,[13] or it could be evidence of a desire to give more support to a daughter by providing unbroken time with her mother in a society where she might face more threats on her life. Because the text does not say, interpreters must situate this difference in time not only within the rest of Leviticus but also within Judaism as a whole.[14]

Fortress, 2004); Klawans, *Impurity and Sin in Ancient Judaism*, 2000; Klawans, *Purity, Sacrifice, and the Temple: Symbolism and Supersessionism in the Study of Ancient Judaism* (New York: Oxford University Press, 2009).

12. See Linda S. Schearing, "Double Time . . . Double Trouble? Gender, Sin, and Leviticus 12," in *Leviticus: Composition and Reception*, ed. Rolf Rendtorff, Robert A. Kugler, and Sarah Smith Bartel (Leiden: Brill, 2003), for a history of interpretation of this passage.

13. Dorothea Erbele-Küster, *Body, Gender and Purity in Leviticus 12 and 15* (London: Bloomsbury T&T Clark, 2017), 53–54.

14. See the treatment of these laws in Elizabeth W. Goldstein, *Impurity and Gender in the*

First-century Judaism had become more gender lopsided. Herod's Temple included a feature for which there is no evidence either in the tabernacle or the First Temple, namely, the Court of the Women. Here both men and women mixed and participated in religious events, but beyond this area, women could not proceed. Josephus discusses the admonitions that parturients and menstruating women are not allowed to come into the temple, yet he does not repeat the instructions that prevent impure men from approaching.[15] Whereas the law regarded impure women and men similarly, in that neither could approach the sacred space, and restricted both lay women and non-Levite men from the priesthood, in this manifestation of sacred space, ritually pure lay women were restricted from more proximate access to the temple than ritually pure lay men.[16]

Moreover, throughout time, menstruating women received more and often negative attention. Following a tradition evident in Ezekiel in which the menstruant became a pervasive metaphor for a sinner (Ezek 36:17), some rabbis urged that menstruating women (which would include parturient as well) be restricted from Torah reading and, at times, even the synagogue itself.[17]

Hebrew Bible (Lanham, MD: Lexington Books, 2017), 15–44. Klawans reaches a more positive conclusion: "But when we take into account all that we have said about ritual impurity—that it is natural, unavoidable, and not sinful—and we add to that the observation that capacity to defile can reflect positive value, then it becomes clear that we cannot simply assume that the prolonged defilement after the birth of a daughter is to be understood as articulating a negative attitude toward women or girls" (*Impurity and Sin in Ancient Judaism*, 38–41, here 39). Conversely, Sarah Whitear concludes that this law aligns with the wider pattern of women's "cultic inferiority" throughout P ("Solving the Gender Problem in Leviticus 12: From Philo to Feminism," *Annali di Storia dell'Esegesi* 37 [2020]: 299–319). Erbele-Küster argues that the Masoretic Text "stresses the female body's innate activity [menstruation] and sets it in a positive [even purificatory] light" (*Body, Gender and Purity*, 47–49, 54). My intention is not to solve the meaning of this text but only to indicate that the interpretations do not uniformly decide that the Jewish approach to women was a negative one.

15. Josephus, *Jewish War* 5.5.6. Discussed in Cohick, *Women in the World of the Earliest Christians*, 220–21.

16. Grossman, "Women and the Jerusalem Temple," 15–37.

17. Goldstein, *Impurity and Gender*; Charlotte Elisheve Fonrobert, *Menstrual Purity: Rabbinic and Christian Reconstructions of Biblical Gender* (Stanford: Stanford University Press, 2009). See also Shaye J. D. Cohen, "Menstruants and the Sacred in Judaism and Christianity," in *Women's History and Ancient History*, ed. Sarah B. Pomeroy (Chapel Hill: University of North Carolina Press, 1991), 273–99.

So too did some Christians.[18] Dionysius, bishop of Alexandria and a student of Origen, thought it ridiculous that pious menstruating women would come to receive Eucharist. He praised the woman with the issue of blood who touched only the hem of Jesus's robe because she was showing respect for the Lord. He was aghast at the thought that bleeding women would disrespect the same Lord by coming to the gathering to receive Eucharist when in that condition.[19] Theodore of Tarsus, bishop of Canterbury, was of the same opinion.[20] This prohibition continues in some expressions of the Orthodox church.[21]

Bodily differences are connected to another frustration with Judaism (and Christianity as well), namely, the paucity of female religious leadership. In the Hebrew Bible, only Levites may serve in the temple. God has chosen some and not others, and this exclusion is not exclusively along gendered but more prominently along tribal lines. The prohibition against priesthood applies to all

18. Not all. See this response to the question from Gregory (although scholars debate whether this is really from the pen of Gregory): "But this woman, while she endures her usual menstruation, should not be prohibited from entering a church, because the natural overflowing cannot be used as a charge against her, and it is not just to deprive her of entry into a church because of what she suffers unwillingly. . . . And a woman ought not to be prohibited from receiving the mystery of Holy Communion during those same days. And if, from great reverence, she does not presume to receive it, she should be applauded, but if she receives it, she should not be judged. . . . For menstruation is not a sin at all for women, because of course it happens naturally. . . . And for that reason, let women make up their own minds and if they do not presume to approach the sacrament of the Lord's body and blood during their menstruation, let them be praised for their righteous consideration, but when they are carried away by the love they feel for the same mystery, due to the manner of their religious life, they are not to be reprimanded, as we said before. . . . why should what a woman with a pure mind suffers from natural causes be brought against her as impurity?" See *The Letters of Gregory the Great*, trans. John R. C. Martyn (Toronto: Pontifical Institute of Medieval Studies, 2004), 2:539–40.

19. Dionysius, *Epistle to the Bishop Basilides* 2 (*Nicene and Post-Nicene Fathers*, Series 2, 14:179). See discussion in Fonrobert, *Menstrual Purity*, 196.

20. Joan Morris, *The Lady Was a Bishop: The Hidden History of Women with Clerical Ordination and the Jurisdiction of Bishops* (New York: Macmillan, 1973), 110. She mentions other examples in the West up through 1684.

21. Andreas Kalkun, "How to Ask Embarrassing Questions about Women's Religion: Menstruating Mother of God," in *Orthodox Christianity and Gender: Dynamics of Tradition, Culture and Live Practice*, ed. Helena Kupari and Elina Vuola (New York: Routledge, 2020), 97–114. The author catalogs testimonies from women in the Seto settlement area of Estonia who find Mary as an aid for their "women's problems."

men who are not Levites just as it applies to all women who are not Levites. At the same time, no explanation is given for why ritually pure men from the tribe of Levi may serve as priests and not ritually pure women from the same tribe.[22] If the worry is that the woman might suddenly menstruate in the temple, this reason is never stated. The impurity of a bodily discharge is also a problem for men, who were allowed to eliminate the impurity with both time and washing. Instead of a sexed difference in purity, the division along gender lines seems more likely a division of biological labor (literally). In a small agrarian society, not many need to serve as priests, but the women are needed to have and nurse future generations or care for the women who are doing so.[23]

Early Christians who prohibit women's leadership will develop their own justifications, but strikingly—possibly because the Hebrew Bible does the same—they do not persistently supply gender impurity as a reason for the restrictions. This might be implied through the scattered instructions that women should not approach Eucharist because of their impurity,[24] but this is never fronted as the primary argument. In addition to christological, apostolic, and anthropological reasons,[25] some early Christian documents also show a preference for women to care for children, including the Pastoral Epistles, where overseers and presbyters are assumed to be men, and women are instructed to care for their families (1 Tim 5:14).

These restrictions in Judaism and Christianity—to attendance, to participation, to leadership—are open to various interpretations. What some women view as restrictive expressions of repulsion, others view as respectful care. As recorded in the *Didascalia apostolorum*, a group of women in the early church wished to stay away from Eucharist while they were menstruating but were urged by its author not to do so.[26] Rather than ignoring the seasons of the

22. Klawans says it this way: "The real question is why ritually *pure* women were excluded from sacred roles in the ancient Israelite cult, but that question is not likely to be answered by an analysis of biblical ritual legislation" (*Impurity and Sin in Ancient Judaism*, 39).

23. Goldstein, *Impurity and Gender*, 44; Elyse Goldstein, *The Women's Torah Commentary: New Insights from Women Rabbis on the 54 Weekly Torah Portions* (Woodstock, VT: Jewish Lights, 2000), 489.

24. As Morris argues in *Lady Was a Bishop*, 111–12.

25. Elizabeth A. Clark, *Women in the Early Church*, Message of the Fathers of the Church 13 (Collegeville, MN: Liturgical, 1990), 16–21.

26. *Didascalia apostolorum* 6.21. See R. Hugh Connolly, ed. and trans., *Didascalia Apostol-*

body and urging a stoic fortitude through the times of the monthly cycle, restriction from synagogue or church can also be viewed as a gentle freedom for rest and self-care. Some women, in the ancient world and today, may see the limitations of women from religious leadership as respect for the difference between male and female bodies and the high calling for women to have and nurse babies. These women might say that they *get to stay home* rather than that they have to stay home.

Hence, Judaism cannot be erected as a misogynistic foil to Christianity. The Jewish God and the Jewish cultic law largely treat men and women the same, and when this is not the case, some women have interpreted this as for their good. Christianity also asserts a God who encounters both men and women, and its development gives evidences of similar kinds of gender imbalances as does Judaism. If Judaism is redeemable by feminists, so too is Christianity. If Judaism stands condemned, Christianity can't ignore the same misogynistic skeletons in its own closet. Moreover, not all interpreters see the "skeletons" as evidence of misogyny but instead view them as boundaries born out of respect for the distinct experiences of the female body. Judaism harbors no misogynistic villain that heroic Christianity can vanquish. With appreciation of the textual nuance and varied interpretations of that nuance, I now turn to the story of Mary.

Incarnation

If the Jesus movement does not radically redeem women from the oppressiveness of Judaism, both because it is not consistently radical and Judaism is not lopsidedly oppressive, then what of my claim about the radical affirmation of women's bodies in the incarnation? I stand by the claim but now have laid the groundwork to show that God's enfleshed arrival through conception and birth does not speak against the religious traditions that prepare for it but with deep resonance stands within them. It is a resonance that will allow several different faithful interpretations, even as it forecloses any possible misogynistic misinterpretation of the ritual tradition.

orum: The Syriac Version; Translated and Accompanied by the Verona Latin Fragments, Ancient Texts and Translations (Eugene, OR: Wipf & Stock, 2010).

With the villain of Judaism and the hero of Christianity both unmasked, I turn now to the texts of the New Testament, chiefly the writings of Matthew and Luke, that show the surprising continuity of the God of Israel's actions with Mary who mothers Jesus. Both of the birth narratives simply yet powerfully affirm her role in bearing and caring for Jesus the Son of God and in so doing do make a radical statement about divine holiness encountering women's bodies.

Conception

The Son of God's coming *by being born* reveals an unparalleled divine proximity to Mary, an embodied female. Both Luke and Matthew assert that it is Mary who conceives and bears the child.

Matthew does so in an artful way with his genealogy, with the unique way he introduces Jesus as well as its overarching structure. Matthew breaks the rhythm of his genealogy when he asserts not that Joseph begot Jesus, as have all the other fathers in the extensive list—forty-one of them!—but that Jesus the Messiah *was begotten* from Mary (Matt 1:16). Matthew names Joseph as Mary's husband, not—strikingly—Jesus's father. The fathers had been the subject of the active form of the verb γεννάω (*gennaō*), "to bear," but with this family not only is Joseph the husband and not the father, but also the son, Jesus, stands as the subject, and the verb appears in the passive form, he "was born" (ἐγέννησεν [*egennēsen*]). As with the women in the genealogy before her, a prepositional phrase is added indicating Mary's role: Jesus was born "from her" (ἐξ ἧς [*ex hēs*]). With changes to the descriptions of the father and the son, the spotlight has come to shine on Joseph, Jesus, and Mary in a unique way. Moreover, as the evangelist continues, he states twice that Mary was found pregnant independent of Joseph (1:18, 20). The anomaly in the genealogy is an early pointer toward Joseph's nonpaternity.[27]

In addition to the unique introduction, the entire structure points toward Mary's unparalleled role in Jesus's conception. The beginning of Matthew's

---

27. About the genealogy, Andrew T. Lincoln concludes, "Matthew's account relates that, while Mary was the mother of Jesus, Joseph was not actually his biological father. The evangelist has already alluded to this in the somewhat strange way he concluded the genealogy" (*Born of a Virgin? Reconceiving Jesus in the Bible, Tradition, and Theology* [Grand Rapids: Eerdmans, 2013], 70).

Gospel is a symbolically structured ancestry of Jesus. Matthew makes his organization explicit: three groups of fourteen generations trace Jesus's descent from Abraham through David (Matt 1:17). One noticeable wrinkle is that Matthew's system of accounting (supposed tax collector that he is [Matt 9:9 // Mark 2:13 // Luke 5:27]) does not stay consistent.[28] The first two groupings do equal fourteen, but the third, if the first name Jeconiah is not counted again (Matt 1:11–12) just as David is not counted again at the beginning of the second group (1:6),[29] leaves Matthew with only thirteen names, counting Jesus.

Since Mary's is the only other name in this group and since the story Matthew is about to tell asserts that Jesus is born of Mary and not Joseph, the best solution, in my opinion, is that she is the necessary piece to complete the symmetry of the fourteen generations.[30] Donald A. Hagner states, "It is impossible that both Joseph and Mary are to be counted as separate generations."[31] I disagree. Joseph possesses a Davidic lineage that he can use for Jesus's benefit,[32] but Mary provides something more. Without her, Jesus would

28. See discussion of Papias's testimony and the questions of authorship in Donald A. Hagner, *Matthew 1–13*, Word Biblical Commentary 33a (Dallas: Word, 1993), xliii–xlvi, lxxv–lxxvii.

29. John Nolland suggests that Matthew does have Jechoniah in both groups, but "the genealogist probably does not consider this to be double counting because in counting Jechoniah in the second fourteen, he really had in mind Jehoiakim" (*The Gospel of Matthew: A Commentary on the Greek Text*, New International Greek Testament Commentary [Grand Rapids: Eerdmans, 2005], 86). Donald A. Hagner also supports the Jeconiah/Jehoiakim confusion (*Matthew 1–13*, Word Biblical Commentary 33a [Dallas: Word, 1993], 6). Another option includes distinguishing Jesus from Christ to arrive at fourteen. I understand that including Mary in the genealogical record goes against the norm, as evidenced by Matthew's inclusion of the other women in the genealogy, but her unparalleled status in this story seems to be Matthew's point.

30. For support, see Frederick Dale Bruner, *The Christbook: Matthew 1–12*, vol. 1 of *Matthew: A Commentary*, rev. and exp. ed. (Grand Rapids: Eerdmans, 2007), 20; Nolland, *Gospel of Matthew*, 223–24; F. V. Filson, *The Gospel according to St. Matthew* (London: Harper & Row, 1960), 53; A. W. Argyle, *The Gospel according to Matthew* (Cambridge: Cambridge University Press, 1963), 25.

31. Hagner instead suggests a scribal error with the name Jeconiah (*Matthew 1–13*, 5).

32. If it is true that Joseph has no biological role, then one must explain why both Luke and Matthew emphasize that Joseph comes from the house of David (Luke 2:4, 11; Matt 1:20). First, for both evangelists, although in different ways, Joseph's standing in the line of David gets the couple to Bethlehem, where Jesus is born in the city of David. Second, Joseph also has value as a person in his own right, and so his existence matters because he fathers Jesus, not biologically

have no generations at all.[33] She fills the gap. Mary, independent of Joseph, has conceived Jesus. She plays a vital and exclusive role (at least as regards humans) in his coming to be.[34]

Various theories about women's contribution to conception existed at this time. One view followed Aristotle: To be male was to be "able to concoct, to cause to take shape, to discharge semen possessing the 'principle' of the 'form,'" by which he means "the proximate motive principle, whether it is able to act thus in itself or in something else."[35] Conversely, the definition of female is to be a being that "receives the semen, but is unable to cause semen to take shape or to discharge it."[36] The male possessed "the principle of movement and gen-

---

but functionally. As such, for some readers, Joseph's gracious actions connect the son of his betrothed to his own family, the line of David and, as Luke has it (Luke 3:38), the line of God.

This multiple attestation of divine descent is similar to that of Augustus, who was styled as divinely conceived by Apollo and, because he was adopted by Julius, could through him trace his ancestry to Mars. Michael Peppard states, "The more sources of legitimacy that Luke could articulate for Jesus, the better. Such an approach is similar to how the divine sonship of the Roman emperors in the Julio-Claudian era was legitimated, as explained in chapter 2. Augustus was son of the divine Apollo by begetting and son of the divine Julius by adoption; he traced ancestry to the divine Mars and styled himself as a new Romulus. In the Julio-Claudian dynasty—and again later in the second-century imperial successions—the adoptive relations turned out to be the most important. But like the supporters of Roman divine sons, Luke might have thought, why not claim all the different sources of legitimation, to reach the widest possible audience?" (*The Son of God in the Roman World: Divine Sonship in Its Social and Political Context* [New York: Oxford University Press, 2011], 135). Similarly, Michael Kochenash argues, "Since Luke has already described Jesus' divine conception (1.35), the genealogy in chapter 3 issues Jesus a second connection to God, through his ancestor Adam, son of God" ("'Adam, Son of God' [Luke 3.38]: Another Jesus-Augustus Parallel in Luke's Gospel," *New Testament Studies* 64 [2018]: 319). That does not demand, however, that Joseph is Jesus's biological father. In fact, in line with similar Roman narratives, it suggests the opposite. Both through direct (virginal conception) and (Joseph's) adoptive fatherhoods, Jesus descends from God.

33. Gianna Pomata argues that in the Roman system, women could not pass on their family line because they had neither the power nor the blood necessary to create kinship recognized by law ("Blood Ties and Semen Ties: Consanguinity and Agnation in Roman Law," in *Gender, Kinship, and Power: A Comparative and Interdisciplinary History* [New York: Routledge, 1995], 43–64). The evangelists place Mary as the reversal of this patrilineal system.

34. If Mary fills the gap in the genealogy, so too does God. The paternal absence is filled by the divine, a provocative and problematic reality I discussed in chapter 1.

35. *Generation of Animals* 765b10–15.

36. *Generation of Animals* 765b15–16.

eration," whereas the female possessed "that of matter."[37] A mother is like the earth utilized by the plant (the seed of life implanted by the father) to grow.[38]

An alternative view followed the Hippocratics. They believed that both men and women contributed seed. In fact, men and women possessed both strong/masculine and weak/feminine seed that they might provide in conception.[39] Centuries later in Rome, the medical writer Galen also believed that both men and women contributed seed, but the male semen was "thick viscous, and full of vital *pneuma* [πνεῦμα]," whereas female semen was "scantier, colder and wetter."[40] Hence, "male semen represents the principle of motion and . . . the female contributes something toward the generation of the animal."[41]

In whatever theory was at play, be it one seed (from men alone) or two seed (from both men and women), men always remained the ultimate actors who caused life.[42] So too, these theories acknowledged that women contributed the *material* of the child. Interpreters cannot be confident of the mechanics of Luke's and Matthew's thoughts on the precise nature of Mary's contributions, but the overwhelmingly dominant position in the church has been that Jesus took his flesh solely from Mary.[43] When Irenaeus argues for his real humanity,

37. Full quotation: "That is why wherever possible and so far as possible the male is separate from the female, since it is something better and more divine in that it is the principle of movement for generated things, while the female serves as their matter" (*Generation of Animals* 732a7–10).

38. *Generation of Animals* 740a25–30.

39. From Hippocrates of Cos: "Sometimes what is ejaculated by a woman is stronger, and sometimes it is weaker, and the same for a man. Furthermore, in a man there are both female semen and male semen, and the same in a woman" (*Genitals* 6.478).

40. *On the Usefulness of the Parts of the Body* 14.9 2.315; 14.6 2.301.

41. *On the Usefulness of the Parts of the Body* 14.7 2.304. Alicia Myers summarizes, "it is the male semen that provides the governing motion of life, which the female semen then supports" (*Blessed among Women? Mothers and Motherhood in the New Testament* [Oxford: Oxford University Press, 2017], 51). See also Lesley Dean-Jones, *Women's Bodies in Classical Greek Science* (Oxford: Clarendon, 1994), 148–209.

42. Myers, *Blessed among Women?*, 50–51.

43. A minority opinion suggested that she could have been the place where the human embryo created by the Holy Spirit dwelt and entered the world. Monophysites argued for this, as did some Anabaptists, and the recent theologian Stephen H. Webb makes a case for this position (*Jesus Christ, Eternal God: Heavenly Flesh and the Metaphysics of Matter* [New York: Oxford University Press, 2012], 105–6). I find the tradition's interpretation of the biblical narrative most convincing.

he states that the Son would not have been human if he "took nothing from the Virgin."[44] Tertullian gives evidence of this discussion when he pinpoints the difference between saying "of her" and "in her." He concludes after extensive and adamant argument that "he was born of a virgin's flesh."[45] Origen affirms this as well in his assertion that Mary provided Jesus the flesh from David.[46] At the Council of Ephesus, Cyril emphasized that the title "Mother of God" indicated that "he united to himself hypostatically the human and underwent a birth

---

44. Irenaeus, *Against Heresies* 3.22.1 (*Ante-Nicene Fathers* 1:454). See also 3.22.2 (1:454–55): "Superfluous, too, in that case is His descent into Mary; for why did He come down into her if He were to take nothing of her? Still further, if He had taken nothing of Mary, He would never have availed Himself of those kinds of food which are derived from the earth, by which that body which has been taken from the earth is nourished; nor would He have hungered, fasting those forty days, like Moses and Elias, unless His body was craving after its own proper nourishment; nor, again, would John His disciple have said, when writing of Him, 'But Jesus, being wearied with the journey, was sitting [to rest]'; nor would David have proclaimed of Him beforehand, 'They have added to the grief of my wounds'; nor would He have wept over Lazarus, nor have sweated great drops of blood; nor have declared, 'My soul is exceeding sorrowful'; nor, when His side was pierced, would there have come forth blood and water. For all these are tokens of the flesh which had been derived from the earth, which He had recapitulated in Himself, bearing salvation to His own handiwork."

45. Tertullian, *The Flesh of Christ* 20 (*Ante-Nicene Fathers* 3:538). See also the long, quite illuminating passage: "in your attempt to rob the syllable *ex* (*of*) of its proper force as a preposition, and to substitute another for it in a sense not found throughout the Holy Scriptures! You say that He was born *through* a virgin, not *of* a virgin, and *in* a womb, not *of* a womb, because the angel in the dream said to Joseph, 'That which is born in her' (not of her) 'is of the Holy Ghost' [Matt 1:20]. But the fact is, if he had meant 'of her,' he must have said 'in her'; for that which was of her, was also in her. The angel's expression, therefore, 'in her,' has precisely the same meaning as the phrase 'of her.' It is, however, a fortunate circumstance that Matthew also, when tracing down the Lord's descent from Abraham to Mary, says, 'Jacob begot Joseph the husband of Mary, *of whom* was born Christ' [Matt 1:16]. But Paul, too, silences these critics when he says, 'God sent forth His Son, made of a woman' [Gal 4:4]. Does he mean *through* a woman, or *in* a woman? Nay more, for the sake of greater emphasis, he uses the word '*made*' rather than *born*, although the use of the latter expression would have been simpler. But by saying '*made*,' he not only confirmed the statement, 'The Word was made flesh' [John 1:14], but he also asserted the reality of the flesh which was made of a virgin" (*The Flesh of Christ* 20 [*Ante-Nicene Fathers* 3:538]).

46. Origen, *Commentary on the Epistle to the Romans* 3.10.5; see Origen, *Commentary on the Epistle to the Romans Books 1–5*, trans. Thomas P. Scheck, Fathers of the Church 103 (Washington, DC: Catholic University of America Press, 2001), 232–33.

according to the flesh *from her womb.*"[47] Bernard of Clairvaux hymns, "He who comes from the bosom of the Father into your womb will not only overshadow you, he will even take to himself something of your substance."[48] Modern theologians receive this point as the tradition in which they stand. Thomas F. Torrance asserts, "we cannot say that his flesh was created out of nothing and absolutely *de novo*, it was created out of fallen humanity."[49] Torrance states the idea even more elegantly: "not a creation *creatio ex nihilo* but a *creatio ex virgine.*"[50] With varying space left to mystery, the Christian position has consistently affirmed that the divine hovered over, utilized, and dwelt within *a female body* to bring about the pinnacle of divine revelation, the Word of God *made flesh*. If the Christian God really disdained the female body, the Son would have found another way to achieve the reconciliation of all things.

Birth and Mothering

The gospels attest not only to God's conception from Mary but also to the Son of God's birth from and infancy with Mary, which continues the divine affirmation of female embodiment even as it connects Mary and Jesus's experience to the purity laws in surprising ways.

Matthew

Mary's actions as a mother are a vital feature of Matthew's birth narrative. After the genealogy, Matthew keeps his focus upon Mary. He restates her name, her relation to Jesus, and her relation to Joseph (Matt 1:18). *She* was discovered as being pregnant before the consummation of the marriage, which is an act of the Holy Spirit upon *her*. Joseph is *her* husband.

At verse 19, however, Matthew turns his attention to Joseph's motivations, visions, and actions. He is righteous, and as such, he desires to follow the

---

47. Cyril of Alexandria, *Selected Letters*, ed. and trans. Lionel R. Wickham (Oxford: Clarendon Press, 1983), 29.

48. Bernard of Clairvaux, *Homilies in Praise of the Virgin Mary*, trans. Mary-Bernard Saïd, Cistercian Fathers Series 18a (Kalamazoo, MI: Cistercian, 1993), 50.

49. Thomas F. Torrance, *The Doctrine of Jesus Christ* (Eugene, OR: Wipf & Stock, 2002), 122.

50. Thomas F. Torrance, *The Incarnation: Ecumenical Studies in the Nicene-Constantinopolitan Creed A.D. 381* (Eugene, OR: Wipf & Stock, 1998), 100.

law, but in such a way that protects her as much as is possible.[51] He accepts the message in the dream and responds with obedience in taking Mary into his house.

The angel of the Lord does speak of Mary's action, that of bearing a son (Matt 1:21), reiterated by Matthew in his fulfillment citation of Isa 7:14 (Matt 1:23) and again in his narration (1:25). This really is all readers know about Mary initially. She bore a son.

Mary appears again in the magi encounter. When they enter the house, they saw the child king with his mother Mary (Matt 2:11). Their coming stirs the vicious pride of Herod. In response to a dream, Joseph acts again and takes Mary and the child to safety in Egypt. Herod inflicts his wrath on the families of Bethlehem. Once Herod has met his end, Joseph takes Mary and the child again back to Israel (2:21). From beginning to end, Mary appears rather passive in this birth narrative, at least grammatically. She is moved along by Joseph, not unlike her small child.

But she is not a child. She is, as Matthew says six times (Matt 1:18; 2:11, 13, 14, 20, 21), his mother. She may be being acted upon,[52] most directly by the self-sacrificial and costly protectorate of Joseph,[53] but she is also acting. She

51. William R. G. Loader, *The New Testament on Sexuality* (Grand Rapids: Eerdmans, 2012), 251–52.

52. Beverly Roberts Gaventa notes, "Although she speaks not a single word and is the subject of an active verb only as she gives birth (Matt 1:21, 25), she remains constantly in view" (*Mary: Glimpses of the Mother of Jesus*, Personalities of the New Testament [Minneapolis: Fortress, 1999], 42).

53. Writing about Joseph's exemplary character, Hoon Choi looks to Joseph as an example of "persistence and patience, warmth and attentiveness (Jasang-ham), and confidence and courage (Jashin-gam)" for Korean men ("Encouraging Male Participation in the Life of the Church," *New Theology Review* 31 [2018]: 2). Eugene Hensell, O.S.B., states, "Not only is he just and righteous, he is also merciful and compassionate" ("The Annunciation to St. Joseph: Reflections on Matthew 1:18–25," *Priest* 74 [2018]: 41). Noting the difficulty he faces, Balthasar states, "It must have been a sorry state of affairs if Joseph could find no better way out than to divorce his bride quietly." See Hans Urs von Balthasar and Joseph Cardinal Ratzinger, *Mary: The Church at the Source*, trans. Adrian Walker (San Francisco: Ignatius, 2005), 156. Elizabeth Johnson comments, "Joseph's action regarding Jesus came as a saving grace, providing a home and long-term provision for this young mother and her child" (*Truly Our Sister: A Theology of Mary in the Communion of Saints* [New York: Continuum, 2003], 193). Gaventa notes that Joseph's marriage to Mary "removes from her and her child the threat of scandal or even death" (*Mary,*

does two things in Matthew's Gospel. She bears a child (repeated five times: 1:16, 21, 23, 25; 2:4) and mothers him, and these are no small things indeed.

The power of such mundane acts only increases in intensity as Matthew portrays the storms swirling around her. Mary is not removed from the dangers of real life; instead she is in dire need of protection. She is vulnerable. Matthew brings attention to the ways in which God enacts power to protect, bringing the providential plan to fruition despite the great threats against it. The forty-two names in the genealogy at Matthew's opening testify that on forty-two occasions God allowed conception, protected the mother through pregnancy, and preserved the baby through delivery. Such a track record gives assurance that God will do the same for this child, Jesus, the focus of the account.[54]

It will be even more necessary because with such threats as divorce and murder, God's hand of protection intervenes explicitly by protecting Mary and Jesus through dreams and angelic visitations. The first threat appears when Joseph considers dismissing Mary. Were Mary's betrothal to Joseph ended, even quietly (Matt 1:19), her and her child's position would be very precarious. It would appear to her community that she had violated the terms of their betrothal,[55] leaving her open to the punishments and shame of a woman who had committed adultery.[56] If Joseph did not want to live with her, her family

---

42). See also Amy Peeler, "Joseph, Husband of Mary," *Bible Odyssey*, http://www.bibleodyssey .org/en/people/related-articles/joseph-husband-of-mary.

54. Candida R. Moss and Joel S. Baden call attention to the reality that Mary's fertility "is by no means assured" (*Reconceiving Infertility: Biblical Perspectives on Procreation and Childlessness* [Princeton: Princeton University Press, 2015], 162).

55. See Gaventa, *Mary*, 40–41. It is important to note that there seemed to be disagreement on whether a betrothed couple would have been shamed for having sexual relations before the final consummation of the marriage. See Joseph and Aseneth 21.1/20.8 (*Old Testament Pseudepigrapha*, ed. James H. Charlesworth [New York: Doubleday, 1983], 1:235). But certainly a woman who had sexual relations with a man *other than her betrothed* would have been shamed. Since Matthew portrays Joseph as knowing this child is not his, that puts Mary into the shamed category. See discussion in Cohick, *Women in the World of the Earliest Christians*, 153.

56. Sirach 25:16 may be a fitting comment here: "I shall be content to live with lion and dragon, rather than to live with a wicked woman." See Craig S. Keener, "Adultery, Divorce," in *Dictionary of New Testament Background* (Downers Grove, IL: InterVarsity Press, 2005), 6–16, esp. 8–10. Tal Ilan notes that while the Scriptures of Israel demand capital punishment (Deut 22:23–24), "the proper punishment for the adulterous woman was the subject of controversy in the Second Temple Period," ranging between death and divorce (*Jewish Women in Greco-Roman*

of origin might have felt the same. It seems a live narrative possibility that
Matthew intended his reader to wonder whether Mary might have ended up
much like those women in the genealogy, employing the oldest profession in
the world for survival.

The need for protection remains after Jesus is born. Were the magi to honor
Herod's request (Matt 2:8), his murderous pride would have discovered Jesus's
precise location, and were Joseph not warned to flee suddenly in the dead
of night (2:13), the family would not have escaped Herod's soldiers of death.
Many are the threats on her and her child in this short story.[57]

Even in the midst of this, she is steady. She conceives and carries while
Joseph contemplates her fate. She bears and raises while Herod searches to
kill. While the slaughter of the innocents may display Herod's evil and fulfill
Scripture's lamentation, it also discloses Mary's tenacity. The children slain
would have been playmates of Jesus, the sons of her friends.[58] The narrative
portrays her keeping about the business of loving her child when none of her
townswomen can do the same.[59] In grief, in fear, in travel, in displacement,

---

Palestine [Peabody, MA: Hendrickson, 1996], 136). Scot McKnight describes the test for adultery
if a woman claimed to be innocent: "She would have been required to drink bitter waters, her
clothes would have been torn enough to expose a breast, her hair would have been let down,
and all her jewelry would have been removed. And passersby, especially women, would have
been encouraged to stare at the publicly shamed woman in order to make an object lesson of
her" (*The Real Mary: Why Evangelical Christians Can Embrace the Mother of Jesus* [Brewster, MA:
Paraclete, 2007], 11). Ilan reads the evidence to conclude that this practice was active during the
Second Temple period (*Jewish Women in Greco-Roman Palestine*, 136–41).

57. Gaventa awakened my attention to the danger present in Matthew's birth narrative,
published in "Threatened and Threatening: Mary in the Gospel of Matthew," in *Mary: Glimpses
of the Mother of Jesus*, Personalities of the New Testament (Minneapolis: Fortress, 1999), 29–48.

58. See the arresting account of an imagined interaction between one of these women and
Mary years later, in Serene Jones, *Trauma and Grace: Theology in a Ruptured World*, 2nd ed.
(Louisville: Westminster John Knox, 2019), esp. part 3, "Ruptured Redeemings," 99–166.

59. On the lack of historical attestation of the slaughter of the innocents outside Matthew,
Hagner comments, "The fact that there are no other unquestionable references among contemporary historians to the killing of the infants may not be surprising if, as seems probable, the
number killed was around twenty. Among the atrocities of Herod, this event in a small unimportant village would hardly have demanded the attention of historians" (*Matthew 1–13*, 35). For
an analysis of Herod's psychological state as reconstructed from historical sources, see Aryeh
Kasher and Eliezer Witsum, *King Herod: A Persecuted Persecutor; A Case Study in Psychohistory
and Psychobiography* (Berlin: de Gruyter, 2007).

she mothers the miraculous yet vulnerable child. In the midst of wild and life-threatening extremes, she is the steady support most intimately close to him. Matthew's words about her may not be many, but they are powerful. She does, like countless millions have done before and since, the simply profound, steady work of motherhood, and she does it like countless millions have done before and since, under the threat of death. Matthew's narrative leads his readers to contemplate how terrifying it must have been to bear and raise this child.[60] She and her child, and Joseph as well, were in need of protection. God ensured that it was always provided. By the end, the reader can breathe a sigh of relief because no threat, arising from either righteousness or pride, was able to prevent God's Messiah's birth and growth. God entrusted the care of the Son to Joseph and to Mary. Joseph plays a vital and costly role here, but the most proximate care for the Messiah comes from Mary herself. As a fixed point, around which energy swirls, she is steady at the center of this tumultuous drama. She may not be the focus of the action, but without her constant care for the child, without her motherhood, the drama could not unfold at all.

Luke

Luke's account is not quite as ominous, but Mary's care for the Son is no less vital. When Joseph and Mary travel to Bethlehem, she is both betrothed and pregnant (ἐγκύῳ [*enkyō*] Luke 2:5). The days are fulfilled for her to give birth (τοῦ τεκεῖν [*tou tekein*] 2:6), and then she does so (ἔτεκεν [*eteken*] 2:7). Jesus is a firstborn son (πρωτότοκος [*prōtotokos*] 2:7), and that invites reflection upon the fact that this is her first experience of the birthing process. Inauguration—whether one embraces a tradition that this birth was painless or painful[61]—brings a certain unsettledness because she has no experience from which to draw.[62] Moreover, as Luke tells the story, Mary finds herself not only away from the familiar setting of their home but also without easy access to a

---

60. "Among the points Matthew underscores is that Jesus is already, even before his birth, threatened by those who do not understand him properly and whose own power is threatened by Jesus. The treatment of Mary in this narrative depicts her as posing a threat to Joseph and as being threatened in return" (Gaventa, *Mary*, 44).

61. See Jennifer Glancy's treatment of Mary's pain or lack thereof in childbirth, in *Corporeal Knowledge: Early Christian Bodies* (New York: Oxford University Press, 2010), 85–106.

62. Courtney Hall Lee comments, "A first pregnancy is scary, physically and emotionally. A great

place to stay. There was no place for them (2:7). Scholars have debated whether this means that they were denied access to an "inn." It could simply be a matter of limited space, or it could be their class or their story that would cause those who do agree to house them to put them in the liminal spaces.[63] Alternatively, others have suggested that they were given a place by extended family but not the normal guest room; instead, they were put in the animal quarters.[64] Either way, they are in an unfamiliar and liminal space.[65]

After giving birth in this place, it is she who swaddles (σπαργανόω [*sparganoō*]) him. In the writings of Israel, to do so demonstrates the common care of parents (Wis 7:4),[66] and its absence demonstrates an unnatural lack of care (Ezek 16:4–5).[67] She also lays him in the manger, a feeding trough (φάτνη [*phatnē*]).[68] This act is a tangible expression that Mary's motherhood is not

responsibility has been given, and we have no real idea what it will be like until it happens" (*Black Madonna: A Womanist Look at Mary of Nazareth* [Eugene, OR: Cascade, 2017], xii).

63. Raymond E. Brown cannot ultimately decide between the three options of a private home, a room in a home, or a traveler's inn. His description of crowded condition of the inn helps the reader visualize Luke's point of Jesus's lowly birth: "They were closer to a type of khan or caravansary where large groups of travelers found shelter under one roof; the people slept on cots or on a terrace elevated by a few steps from the floor, with the animals on the floor in the same room" (*The Birth of the Messiah: A Commentary on the Infancy Narratives in the Gospels of Matthew and Luke*, new updated ed. [New York: Doubleday, 1993], 400). Kent Annan discusses the suggestion that there being "no room" arises not from logistics but shame in "Reading Luke's Christmas Story with Those in Haiti" (*Global Perspectives in the New Testament*, ed. Mark Roncace and Joseph Weaver [Boston: Pearson, 2014], 8–10).

64. Joel B. Green, *The Gospel of Luke*, New International Commentary on the New Testament (Grand Rapids: Eerdmans, 1997), 128–29.

65. See discussion in Nicholas King, "The Significance of the Inn for Luke's Infancy Narrative," in *New Perspectives on the Nativity*, ed. Jeremy Corley (London: T&T Clark, 2009), 67–76.

66. Jody Vaccaro Lewis explains, "That Mary swaddles her newborn baby, then, is to be expected. It is not a sign, as some readers see it, that the Holy Family is poor. All babies were swaddled, rich and poor alike, dictated by maternal care and cultural custom" ("The Inn, the Manger, the Swaddling Cloths, the Shepherds, and the Animals," in *The Oxford Handbook of Christmas*, ed. Timothy Larsen [Oxford: Oxford University Press, 2020], 230). See also Job 38:1–9 when God describes creation as his child, including God's act of swaddling the sea.

67. This normal activity of swaddling stands as a paradox for a child who is not normal. Ephrem the Syrian captures the paradox in his hymn (5.24) that gives voice to Mary: "How shall I approach with swaddling clothes the One arrayed in streams [of light]?" (*Hymns*, trans. Kathleen E. McVey, The Classics of Western Spirituality [New York: Paulist, 1989], 109).

68. F. Scott Spencer makes the insightful connection with a manger in Isa 1:3: "The ox knows

going according to any ideal plan. She is picked to have a miraculous child, but then she has to put that child in a space normally used by animals.⁶⁹ This is not a comfortable situation. Luke makes no comments on her feelings or thoughts in this particular section, but it only seems fitting that she and Joseph would have felt the dissonance of the claims about this child and his uncomely beginning. They, like every caring parent in situations of oppression and displacement, would have wished for better for their child.

Her normal yet difficult actions (bearing, swaddling, laying in the trough) are what the angel refers to when directing the shepherds to the new king's location (Luke 2:11–12). They are not, however, told precisely where to go by the angelic choir, so they must search (ἀνευρίσκω [*aneuriskō*] 2:16). When they do, they find Mary and Joseph, and also the baby, sleeping—as brand-new infants are wont to do—in his makeshift bed. In the exhausted bliss of that first day, Mary and Joseph welcome these visitors to the room. The shepherds share the miraculous angelic event of the night with all who are there, causing everyone to marvel, the first of what will become a common reaction to Jesus (2:33; 4:22; 7:9; 8:25; 9:43; 11:14). Luke also tells the reader specifically how Mary reacted. She holds these words close (συντηρέω [*syntēreō*]) and tumbles them around (συμβάλλω [*symballō*]) in her heart.⁷⁰ She does so possibly as confirmation that the encounters and visions she and Joseph experienced are not delusions but now have been attested, not just by supportive family members but by strangers as well. The honor for her child, and therefore for her and Joseph as well, is beginning after all, but it comes from the lips of the humble, just as Mary proclaimed that it would (1:46–48).

---

its owner and the donkey its master's crib [or lord's manger (φάτνην τοῦ κυρίου, *phatnēn tou kyriou*)]. But Israel did not know [its Lord], my people do not understand." He states, "Through the manger born Savior and Lord, God's wayward people will come to know and understand their divine Master/Lord anew" (*Salty Wives, Spirited Mothers, and Savvy Widows: Capable Women of Purpose and Persistence in Luke's Gospel* [Grand Rapids: Eerdmans, 2012], 83).

69. Green sees this as an indication of the crowded conditions in which they find themselves (*Gospel of Luke*, 129).

70. Ratzinger's poetic description is worth hearing; "Mary 'puts together', 'holds together'— she fits the single details into the whole picture, compares and considers them, and then preserves them. The word becomes seed in good soil. She does not snatch at it, hold it locked in an immediate, superficial grasp, and then forget it. Rather the outward event finds in her heart a space to abide and, in this way, gradually to unveil its depth, without any blurring of its once-only contours" (Balthasar and Ratzinger, *Mary*, 71).

Mary is mothering the Son of God of whom angels sing, but she still mothers him as others do. She cares for his basic and many needs in the stage of infancy and uses those long hours full of new things to ponder the new life she can now touch. Yet also at a disadvantage in comparison with many mothers, she cares for her son in a situation of displacement and oppression, where she and her husband must make the best with what they have.

First Temple Visit

Their first visit to the temple also points to the reality of her motherhood. The family's encounter with Simeon when they arrive at the temple invites the reader to consider her tangible experience of mothering Jesus. In the midst of their faithful errand to the temple, they cross paths with Simeon, who grabs Jesus (Luke 2:28).[71] He, like the shepherds, confirms the angelic message that this child is like no other, and through him, God will bring about the prophetic promises. At this, his parents marvel at what is said of him. This need not imply doubt or new knowledge, only awe, at the fact that the child in their care is the fulfillment of the hope of Israel and, therefore, all people.[72]

In this exchange, readers might wonder how long he might be in the care of his parents. Simeon's words could raise alarm at this point. The reader knows that Simeon is blessing God for the fulfillment of God's promises to him, but Mary and Joseph do not know this. She only knows that an older gentleman has taken her infant and said, "And now, Lord, send away your servant in peace according to your word" (Luke 2:29).[73] Jesus's parents might imagine that he is speaking of Joseph, who has served God by obeying God's words/laws in bringing Jesus to the temple. An even closer narrative connection is Mary, who has called herself the servant of the Lord (Luke 1:38). As Hannah, whose song Mary's evokes,

71. McKnight colors the story with a contemporary parallel: "How would it strike you if, when leaving the hospital after a birth or when leaving the church after your child's baptism or dedication, some aged stranger grabbed your infant into his arms . . . ?" (*Real Mary*, 49).

72. So also Green: "Amazement is neither negative nor necessarily positive (cf. 2:18). It is an expected reaction to the miraculous but does not promise correct understanding or faith in the present or future. That such a response is credited to Mary and Joseph—especially Mary, who has been portrayed so positively—should encourage us to pause for reflection. What Simeon has asserted in his prayerlike hymn is so extraordinary that even Mary and Joseph are amazed" (*Gospel of Luke*, 146).

73. Translations are my own unless otherwise noted.

had to leave her son in the service of the temple (1 Sam 1:28), Mary and Joseph might imagine that they are not only presenting their son to the Lord but will also leave him there. Nothing in what Gabriel has told her or what the shepherds reported to her or what Simeon has just stated guarantees that she and Joseph will raise Jesus.

Though the Hannah/Samuel echoes and the initial impression of Simeon's words may open this possibility, maternal realities provide the controls. Mary would have been nursing a six-week-old infant.[74] No one would contemplate, least of all her, the separation of mother from child. Simeon may have grabbed Jesus, but, for everyone's sake, he must hand him back before the next feeding time.

When he hands Jesus back, Simeon blesses his parents, too, imploring God's goodness as they continue to care for this child. Then he addresses Mary alone, "Look at this child, he is set for the falling and rising [ἀνάστασις (*anastasis*)] of many in Israel" (Luke 2:34).[75]

Simeon's continued speech to her about her child then includes a barb aimed directly at Mary. His emphatic aside to her stands out in content even as it does by its disjunctive grammar. "Also a sword will go through your soul itself" (Luke 2:35). She has already declared her life as positioned toward God's praise, and Simeon indicates that, because she has pledged herself to God to bear this son, because she has already declared the dynamic of his kingship, because she has borne him and cared for him, when he is opposed, it will be like a sword in her own being as well. What she has learned in this exchange is that her heart, too, will be exposed for all to see, that she will suffer at his suffering.[76] When

---

74. Ilan's discussion on Jewish views of nursing is illuminative. In such an early stage, the infant is completely dependent upon the milk of his or her mother. While authors discuss wet nurses, and contracts for this employment exist, Ilan concludes, "a wet-nurse was a luxury . . . most mothers in the period nursed their own infants for lack of other means to maintain them." The period for nursing ranged from eighteen months to five years (*Jewish Women in Greco-Roman Palestine*, 119–21). Cohick recounts the preference among Roman philosophers for mothers nursing their own children but cautions that the use of wet nurses might not have been a major concern to many Roman men. Again, however, she notes that the use of wet nurses is an option for the elite (*Women in the World of the Earliest Christians*, 144–48).

75. Luke employs ἀνάστασις as a reference to the resurrection in all other occurrences of the word (Luke 14:14; 20:27, 33, 35–36; Acts 1:22; 2:31; 4:2, 33; 17:18, 32; 23:6, 8; 24:15, 21; 26:23).

76. It is an unexpected silence that Luke does not mention Mary specifically at the cross (23:49), yet, because he mentions those who know him, specifically women, who have fol-

they take him home, she knows that raising such a son will bring her pain. She does it anyway, accepting her motherhood of him with all it entails.

God Is Born

Matthew's and Luke's affirmation of Mary's conception, pregnancy, birth, and care of Jesus the Son of God provides powerful implications for women within the Christian community. These implications become clear when one attends to the provocative proclamation, "God is born."

Despising birth is rather self-destructive. To view it as shameful is, of course, to disparage one's own humanity; for everyone was born.[77] Nevertheless, birth was regarded in cultures of the first century as a dirty and dangerous process. Plutarch notes the gracious love of the gods and how they attend birth, as it "with its accompaniment of blood and travail is no lovely thing."[78] He praises Nature who has so designed humans to love their offspring even when humans come as they do:

> For there is nothing so imperfect, so helpless, so naked, so shapeless, so foul, as man observed at birth, to whom alone, one might almost say, Nature has given not even a clean passage to the light; but, defiled with blood and covered with filth and resembling more one just slain than one just born, he is an object for none to touch or lift up or kiss or embrace except for someone who loves with a natural affection.[79]

---

lowed him from Galilee, and Mary fits those descriptions, it is not impossible that Simeon's pronouncement finds fulfillment in chapter 23 at Jesus's death. Gaventa provides examples of the sword as a trope in Greco-Roman literature describing the grief of a mother over the loss of a child (*Mary*, 65).

77. Mayra Rivera captures the irony: "Rejecting Jesus's flesh as unworthy implies rejecting their own flesh. But how can they distance themselves from their own birth. . . . Those who are ashamed of flesh are put to shame" (*Poetics of the Flesh* [Durham, NC: Duke University Press, 2015], 45). Her conclusion captures the beautiful vitality of affirming the way in which the Savior came: "Unless I can embrace my own flesh, and its beginnings in the flesh of another, I cannot love other fleshly beings—nor can I understand the incarnation. What is at stake for them is nothing less than the possibility of love" (*Poetics of the Flesh* 155).

78. Plutarch, *Moralia* 758a (*Dialogue on Love* 15).

79. Plutarch, *Moralia* 496c (*On Affection for Offspring* 3).

Gore that accompanies birth shows close association—as the quotations of Plutarch show—with death. Although numbers vary,[80] the possibility of death for either the mother or the infant, or for both, intensified during birth.[81] There were few other times in life in which the gripping power of the fear of death must have pervaded the thoughts of the family of the baby.[82]

Hence, if it would be an act of grace for the gods to attend and preserve birth, how much more so would it be an astounding act for the God of Israel, God above all gods, to be born, to journey through this messy brush with death. To assert that Jesus the Son of God is human is to assert that he, as God, willingly humbled himself not only even to the point of a shameful death on a cross but also even to the point of shameful birth. Tertullian, in *The Flesh of Christ*, makes this point with power in an invective against Marcion:

> Come now, beginning from the nativity itself, declaim against the unclean-ness of the generative elements within the womb, the filthy concretion of fluid and blood, of the growth of the flesh for nine months long out of that very mire. Describe the womb as it enlarges from day to day—heavy, trou-blesome, restless even in sleep, changeful in its feelings of dislike and desire. Inveigh now likewise against the shame itself of a woman in travail which, however, ought rather to be honoured in consideration of that peril, or to be held sacred in respect of (the mystery of) nature. Of course you are horrified also at the infant, which is shed into life with the embarrassments which ac-company it from the womb; you likewise, of course, loathe it even after it is washed, when it is dressed out in its swaddling-clothes, graced with repeated anointing, smiled on with nurse's fawns. This reverend course of nature, you, O Marcion, (are pleased to) spit upon; and yet, in what way were you born? You detest a human being at his birth; then after what fashion do you love anybody? . . . Christ, at any rate, has loved even that man who was condensed

---

80. Edith Gillian Clark, "Childbirth," in *The Oxford Classical Dictionary*, ed. Simon Horn-blower and Antony Spawforth, 4th ed. (Oxford: Oxford University Press, 2012), 309.

81. Christian Laes, *Children in the Roman Empire: Outsiders Within* (Cambridge: Cambridge University Press, 2011), 50–56.

82. Laes quotes the sentiment: "Will my wife give birth to a child? And if she does, will the child live? These are some of the questions that appear in the Lots of Astrampsychus, a kind of do-it-yourself oracle book that was extremely popular during Antiquity" (*Children in the Roman Empire*, 56).

in his mother's womb amidst all its uncleannesses, even that man who was
brought into life out of the said womb, even that man who was nursed amidst
the nurse's simpers. For his sake He came down (from heaven), for his sake
He preached, for his sake He humbled Himself even unto death—the death
of the cross [Phil 2:8]. He loved, of course, the being whom He redeemed
at so great a cost. . . . Well, then, loving man He loved his nativity also, and
his flesh as well.[83]

In the perception of many, birth remained shameful. The punch of the argument resides in this perception. God was willing, because of a loving desire
to reconcile with humanity, to undergo this process oft viewed as shameful.
It must be named that assertions of the shamefulness of gestation in a
woman's body and birth through a woman's body are evidence of a deep-
seated pancultural misogyny.[84] Women's perceptions are much more varied.
Some experience pregnancy and birth as difficult and ugly; some experience
it as empowering and beautiful, and probably most women who experience
pregnancy resonate with both sides of that spectrum at some point along the
journey. The sparse affirmations of the biblical text and the early creeds—that
Mary gave birth to Jesus—proclaim that God did something that was beautiful
by undergoing something that many regarded as shameful. It should not be
missed that God *chose* to do so. One cannot hold that pregnancy and birth—
in other words, the female body—is so deformed and shameful as to remain
untouchable by the divine. As the ancient liturgy says, he abhorred not the
virgin's womb.[85]

83. Tertullian, *The Flesh of Christ* 4 (*Ante-Nicene Fathers* 3:524). See Tina Beattie, "Mary in
Patristic Theology," in *Mary: The Complete Resource*, ed. Sarah Jane Boss (London: Continuum,
2007), 97. Virginia Burrus comments that theologians like Tertullian "positively rejoice in the
scandal of divine incarnation" ("An Embarrassment of the Flesh," in *Saving Shame: Martyrs,
Saints, and Other Abject Subjects* [Philadelphia: University of Pennsylvania Press, 2008], 45).
Rivera notes, "Rather than downplaying his opponents' disgust for the flesh, he repeatedly in-
tensifies it, only to move ever more deeply and ardently toward flesh—to the depths of its origins
in the womb" (*Poetics of the Flesh*, 44). See also Glancy's analysis of Tertullian's comments on
Mary's body (*Corporeal Knowledge*, 117–33).
    84. It is a sad reality that even with his robust affirmation of Jesus's nativity in Mary's womb,
Tertullian, at other times, shames women. See Rivera, *Poetics of the Flesh*, 45–46.
    85. This is a line in the *Te Deum* (*non horruísti Vírginis úterum*), an ancient hymn utilized still

The Christian confession contains this immovable fact: God was willing to touch the female body. In the shamefulness of seemingly unending examples of misogynistic patriarchy, the Christian story has never ceased to affirm that God invited Mary, in an embodied way, to participate singularly in the salvific plan of the divine life. This has not been enough to elevate women as much as many desire, but neither does it allow them to be shamed to the point of exclusion. Those who do so have put themselves outside the deep logic of the Christian narrative. Divine cultivation, residence, and birth prohibits any despising of the female body.

Purity Reconsidered: God Is Handled

A brush with these realities of birth, gore and death, could be the reason why ancient cultures viewed birth as polluting for those who experienced it and attended it.[86] Greek religion demanded a sacrifice after birth,[87] and Roman culture recommended washing for the mother after birth.[88] As mentioned, in Lev 12, the law lays out the purification rituals following birth. It is no moral

today by many Christian groups in liturgy. The line is replicated in Frederick Oakeley's English translation of a Latin hymn, "O Come All Ye Faithful."

86. In presenting the various reasons why "Leviticus excludes new mothers from sancta," Matthew Thiessen concludes, "Either interpretation suggests that the mortality of humanity is the issue and that it is such mortality that cannot approach God" ("Luke 2:22, Leviticus 12, and Parturient Impurity," *Novum Testamentum* 54 [2012]: 20n121). Pamela M. Eisenbaum also discusses the connection between childbirth impurity and death ("A Remedy for Having Been Born of Woman: Jesus, Gentiles, and Genealogy in Romans," *Journal of Biblical Literature* 123 [2004]: 678–79), as does Tina Beattie in her analysis of Irigaray, stating, "Many of Irigaray's writings seek to expose the hidden connection between the fear of the sexual female body as a source of corruption and pollution, and the fear of the maternal body as a source of death" (*God's Mother, Eve's Advocate: A Marian Narrative of Women's Salvation* [London: Continuum, 2002], 131).

87. Maurizio Bettini, *Women and Weasels: Mythologies of Birth in Ancient Greece and Rome*, trans. Emlyn Eisenach (Chicago: University of Chicago Press, 2013), 51–53; Eisenbaum, "Remedy for Having Been Born of Woman," 677.

88. Elaine Fantham, "Purification in Ancient Rome," in *Rome, Pollution and Propriety: Dirt, Disease and Hygiene in the Eternal City from Antiquity*, ed. Mark Bradley (Cambridge: Cambridge University Press, 2012), 62.

failure to have a child, but it is unclean. My argument now comes full circle, returning to the laws of Judaism most ripe for the charge of gender disparity. It is here within the practice of these laws that God, in divine vulnerability after birth, meets Mary. This view appears most clearly in Luke's retelling. On the eighth day, Mary does what other Jewish mothers did; she circumcises her son (Luke 2:21). The point of the visit to the temple after this ritual is to offer a sacrifice for purification after the correct number of days following the birth (2:22; based on the law in Lev 12). The best manuscripts include a plural pronoun—the family travels for *their* purification—a confusing statement that creates much debate in the interpretive tradition.[89] No matter who else is included in the pronoun,[90] Mary certainly is, since the law cited in this section of Leviticus focuses upon the purification of the woman (Lev 12). Opposing sides in the later debate concerning Mary's experience of pain or lack thereof in childbirth as evidence of her sinlessness[91] must agree that she joins with other mothers in the ritual act of purification after childbirth.[92] This act shows that Luke does not picture her as exempt from this common act of obedience.

Within the parturient laws of Lev 12, it is clear that a woman is most impure in the first week after the birth of a son. Then she continues in impurity for another thirty-three days. Leviticus 12:4 states, "She shall not touch any consecrated

89. See Thiessen, "Luke 2:22, Leviticus 12, and Parturient Impurity."

90. I find Thiessen's argument that Jesus is included persuasive. The possibility of Jesus sharing in Mary's impurity is based upon the closeness of their bond, via nursing, during this time.

91. Sarah Jane Boss summarizes the position of those who see this as the result of Mary's redemption from sin: "[Pain in childbirth] is one of the most obvious signs of a fall from grace, so that painless childbearing is a corresponding sign of preservation or redemption from the effects of that Fall" (*Empress and Handmaid: On Nature and Gender in the Cult of the Virgin Mary* [London: Cassell, 2000], 78).

92. She does so either because she herself needs to be purified from a normal birth process or because she stands in solidarity with those, unlike herself, who do. Bede wrote, "Mary, God's blessed mother and a perpetual virgin, was, along with the Son she bore, most free from all subjection to the law. . . . But as our Lord and Savior, who in his divinity was the one who gave the law, when he appeared as a human being, willed to be under the law . . . so too his blessed mother, who by a singular privilege was above the law, nevertheless did not shun being made subject to the principles of the law for the sake of showing us an example of humility" (*Homilies on the Gospels* 1.18; see Arthur A. Just Jr., ed., *Luke*, Ancient Christian Commentary on Scripture [Downers Grove, IL: InterVarsity Press, 2003], 47). Luther also affirms her *in partu* virginity and so praises her obedience of faith in going through with the ritual ("Freedom of a Christian," in *Luther's Works*, ed. Jaroslav Pelikan et al. [Saint Louis: Concordia, 1955], 31:368).

thing nor enter the sanctuary until the days of her purification are completed." Menstruation, which is comparable to the bleeding a woman experiences after pregnancy, is viewed, not as sinful, but as defiling of the holy tabernacle of God among the people (Lev 15:31). The Christian story does not have its God disregard these purity laws. Mary is not allowed into the temple in the weeks after giving birth. To reiterate, Luke, without any defensiveness, shows that Mary follows the laws for refraining from the sacred space during her forty days.

It is during this time that God works in surprising ways. In the weeks after the birth, in the very time in which she was perceived to be in her greatest impurity, God is with her. The same God who set the laws for female purification and exclusion from the temple met this woman when she was existing faithfully within those laws. God does not abrogate those laws and invite Mary to the temple before the time of her purification. Divine action respects the laws. At the same time, God performs a radical act within the laws. The separation between impure humanity and holy God has been breached. The law, with its "pedagogy of human alienation,"[93] has prepared for a moment in which God has not asked Mary to transgress the boundary line, but God the Son has done so himself. God honors the realities of female embodiment not by taking her out of her life to go to the temple as a priest but by keeping her in her life to remain at home as a mother and there to handle the holiest of all things. Instead of bringing her into the holy space, God has made her the holy space.[94] In the incarnation, God has deemed the female body—the impure, bleeding female body—worthy to handle the most sacred of all things, the very body of God.[95]

Conclusion

With bold simplicity, the incarnation of Jesus through Mary affirms the confluence of holiness and female bodies in a radically powerful way. The incar-

---

93. Thanks to David Luy for this phrase and insight.

94. Elisabeth Behr-Sigel comments, "Mary's holiness therefore surpasses that of the Jerusalem Temple. Her holiness situates her beyond the sacred that is signified by the temple" (*Ministry of Women in the Church* [New York: St. Vladimir's Seminary Press, 2004], 201).

95. Aquinas notes that at this time "she did have the very Author of grace with her" (Thomas Aquinas, "Whether It Was Fitting That the Mother of God Should Go to the Temple to Be Purified?," III, q. 37, a. 4, obj. 3 in *Summa Theologica*, trans. Fathers of the English Dominican Province [New York: Benziger Brothers, 1947], 2:2222).

nation, in continuity with a positive view of the Levitical purity laws, puts misogyny out of bounds. The sinful fruit of patriarchy may cause some to despise the female body, but the God of Judaism and Christianity did not. To redeem humanity, God cultivated and dwelt within the flesh of a woman. The Son of God is then born, which, no matter how this happens, with pain or not, by separating the hymen or not, means that the embodied God passes through the birth canal of a woman.[96] Because he is completely human and was born in the time before formula and bottles, he nursed at the breast of a woman. From that moment until he was grown, her hands held him; her arms enveloped him; her lap gave him a place to rest. God's choice to allow the body of a woman, even the most intimate parts of herself, to come into direct contact with the body and blood of the Son stands against any who would deny women *by virtue of the fact that they are women* access to the holy.

The incarnation says a clear and singular no to misogyny, but the affirmations it allows are multifaceted and therefore more complicated. God's incarnate holiness provides inestimable honor to motherhood. Those who find themselves either by choice or necessity bearing the mundane tasks of pregnancy, nursing, and childcare can know that God did not demand that women deny these unique bodily realities, but instead, in midst of their ritual impurity and physical messiness, God came to them. Instead of demanding they separate from their female embodiment to approach the holy, God's holiness came to them in the midst of their female embodiment. God had said of the female body at creation that it was good. God said so again in the incarnation, good enough for the residence and handling of God. For those who choose to or must remain in exclusive women's spaces, God has met them there.

At the same time, the incarnation validates women who respond to a call to handle the holy. This seems especially pertinent for the Eucharist. Any of those who affirm real presence could agree that "the eucharistic body is, in

---

96. Some early traditions, like the Protevangelium of James, hinted that Jesus's birth was different from all others. In the tradition, these narrative hints developed into the assertion that Mary remained a virgin—her womb remained unopened—even during the birth of Jesus, *in partu* virginity (19.3). Without description of the process, the canonical account, under certain anthropological and theological commitments, allows for this reading. Even if, however, Jesus's birth was not as messy as every other human birth, even if the process was miraculous at both conception and parturition, it remains true that he gestated in and somehow passed through the body of a woman. See discussion in Gaventa, *Mary*, 100–125, and Glancy, *Corporeal Bodies*, 81–136.

some sense, the very same body that was born of the Virgin Mary."[97] This is the body that the Holy Spirit prepared from the flesh of Mary alone and the body that entered the world through Mary, the body that was sustained by Mary's milk and handled by Mary's arms. God's decision for this mode of the incarnation, that in the fullness of time God sent forth his Son born of a woman, to be raised by a man *and a woman,* suggests God's decision for who now can facilitate the consecration of the extension of that same body. God has already made a call on women handling this body and this blood, and God's answer was yes.[98] An incarnational model of the Eucharist opens the possibility of the extension of Mary's embodied role in the incarnation to women's role in the administration of the Eucharist.[99] Saint Francis's comparison between Mary and the priest is instructive: "If the Blessed Virgin is so honoured as is right, since she carried him in her most holy womb . . . , how holy just and worthy must be the person who touches him with his hands, receives him in his heart and mouth, and offers him to others to be received."[100]

Some may counter that God's interactions with Mary are unique for her and would not apply to any other woman. Wide streams of the Christian tradition have asserted that Mary could bear God because she was so captured by God's grace even before her own birth so that she was untainted by sin. However, if Mary was preserved from sin, then her example of a tangible engagement with the body of Christ could not apply to any other human, male or female, because no one else was immaculately conceived free from sin. If her purity would distinguish her from sinful women, and thus disqualify them from presiding over the Eucharist because they do not share her charisma, her

97. James Arcadi, *An Incarnational Model of the Eucharist* (Cambridge: Cambridge University Press, 2018), 234.

98. My statement about a man and a woman is intended to point to the inclusion of women in the Eucharist and is in no way meant to exclude intersex persons.

99. See the analysis of the textual and artistic tradition that portrays Mary as a priest and bishop in Ally Kateusz, *Mary and Early Christian Women: Hidden Leadership* (Cham: Palgrave MacMillan, 2019).

100. Cited in John Saward, *Redeemer in the Womb: Jesus Living in Mary* (San Francisco: Ignatius, 1993), 80. For an analysis of Francis and his relation to the feminine, see Jacques Dalarun, *Francis of Assisi and the Feminine* (Saint Bonaventure, NY: Franciscan Institute, 2006). Through his relationship with Clare of Assisi, Dalarun argues, Francis "plays a role in the respective evolution of the two genders in regard to religion and hence the relationship of the genders with one another" (*Francis of Assisi and the Feminine,* 14).

purity would similarly disqualify men. Hence, Mary's sinlessness could not be used to bar other sinful women from the Eucharist any more than it could be used to bar sinful men. With this logic, no one save her could handle the body and the blood. Clearly, however, that is not the direction the tradition went.

Another counterargument could be that Mary handles Christ but does not *sacrifice* Christ, and, if the Eucharist is a priestly sacrifice, it traces its roots to the male Levitical priesthood. Just as some were chosen for priesthood then (Levites), some are chosen for priesthood now (some men), and that is the mysterious prerogative of God.[101] I worry, however, that the selection of men and not women is not always so respectfully left to divine mystery but argued, as I will present in the following chapters, on the basis of an errant masculine picture of God. Other points in the debate about women's ordination to the priesthood certainly demand consideration, and those of good faith may reach different conclusions, but the holy God's embodiment in, through, and with the care of a female body should be a significant—and because it has to do with the incarnation, I would even say a *central*—part of the conversation.

Having considered the body of Mary, I now turn to her will and the very serious questions that arise in the moment she is told of the role her body would play in God's story.

---

101. I am grateful to Tim Pawl for articulating this reasoning to me.

three

Honor and Agency

The engendering spirit did not enter her without consent
God waited.

—Denise Levertov, "Annunciation"

A number of interpreters on opposite sides of the theological spectrum share a similar caricature of the annunciation in Luke's birth narrative: God is cast as the strong male opposite Mary the coerced female. She plays the negative gender stereotype of femininity. In this chapter, I draw particularly from interpreters who have called attention to the scandal in this exchange, a divine proclamation of pregnancy received by a young girl who calls herself a slave. All readers benefit from this frankness. To ignore these problematic elements is to fail to hear this text in its fullness.

To respect the presence of the problematic elements in the text, however, does not demand surrender to disdain for the text. Attending to the hard questions reveals that only two of the four elements of the caricature—strong male/coerced female—are fitting. God is strong, and Mary is female. Utilizing narrative tropes that very easily could have proceeded down a diabolical path, I will argue that Luke does not follow it. With attention to that evangelist's narrative prowess, I attend to each section of the annunciation: Gabriel's approach, Mary's hesitancy, Gabriel's explanation, and finally, Mary's acceptance.

The narrative comprises only twelve verses (Luke 1:26–38), but even in its brevity, it offers seemingly inexhaustible riches to contemplate the character of both God and Mary. The powerful God approaches Mary with honor and blessing and waits for her response. She, the young circumspect female, with grit and self-respect, accepts.[1] The exchange then is not between one strong and one weak, one forceful male and one forced female, but between one God and one human woman, who both act for her honor from the place of strength.

Approach (Luke 1:26–27)

From panorama to portrait, Luke telescopes from God's heavenly realm to an individual. God sends the angel Gabriel to Nazareth in Galilee, to a young, engaged woman. God's messenger comes to *her*. While such an approach is not unique, as God's messengers come to others throughout the Scriptures of Israel,[2] Luke's narration highlights the fact that God does not summon Mary to a meeting point. Rather, God sends the angelic messenger directly to her. The heavenly deigns to come to Mary's particular space. Moreover, God's instructions to Gabriel are quite personalized. To show the messenger where to go, God relays precise coordinates. God provides the name of the young woman as well as her family connections, the name of her fiancé, and her house. The reader is not told whether she rests in her room, stands in a garden, or is working at a well (all imagined in Christian art and story),[3] but the direction of the

1. Readers will note how my method is informed by Sarah Coakley's work. She states, "The profound paradox of an inalienable surrender ('submission') to God that—as I argue—must remain the secret ground of even feminist empowerment" (*Powers and Submissions: Spirituality, Philosophy and Gender* [Malden, MA: Wiley-Blackwell, 2002], x).

2. To Hagar (Gen 16:7–11), to Lot (Gen 19), to Eleazar (Gen 27:4, 40), to Jacob (Gen 32:1), to Moses (Exod 3:2), to the people of Israel (Exod 14:19; 23:20, 23; 32:34; 33:2; Num 20:16), and to Balaam (Num 22:22–35; Zech 1:9; Dan 3:49 LXX).

3. For example, the Protevangelium of James (11.1), penned around AD 150, places Mary at a well. See Bart D. Ehrman, ed., *After the New Testament: A Reader in Early Christianity* (New York: Oxford University Press, 1998), 251. *The Life of the Virgin* (2.19), attributed to Maximus the Confessor, also has her near a fountain. See Stephen J. Shoemaker, trans., *The Life of the Virgin: Maximus the Confessor* (New Haven: Yale University Press, 2012), 50. The earliest image of the annunciation, dated to the seventh century, places her near a source of water with a pitcher. For

movement—from heaven to earth—could not be clearer. God knows who Mary is and sends an emissary directly to her.

The setting is striking, particularly when contrasted with Gabriel's parallel announcement to Zechariah that immediately precedes it.[4] Luke's story opens with a couple, a priest named Zechariah, from Abia, one of the priestly divisions (1 Chr 24:10), and his wife Elizabeth, herself from the daughters of Aaron. This daughter of a priest marries a priest, resulting in the ideal marriage for a Levitical family.[5] They are a couple of valor, righteous before God by keeping the commandments and being blameless in the ordinances. Their faithfulness, however, had not been rewarded with a child. Elizabeth was barren, and by the time the story begins, both Zechariah and Elizabeth are older. The biographical details provide the backdrop for his angelic encounter.

It has come time for Zechariah to serve in the temple. If he followed the model as laid out in Chronicles, and reiterated in Josephus (*Jewish Antiquities* 7.365) and the Mishnah (Sukkah 5:6), this was one of the two weeks a year that he came to the temple.[6] In this particular story, he is granted a rare chance, in all likelihood a once-in-a-lifetime opportunity.[7] It appears Zechariah was

---

summary, see Michael Peppard, who identifies a third-century house church in Dura-Europos as Mary Annunciate (*The World's Oldest Church: Bible, Art, and Ritual at Dura-Europos, Syria*, illustrated ed. [New Haven: Yale University Press, 2016], 155–201). Jaroslav Pelikan comments, "among all the scenes in the life of the Virgin Mary that have engaged the piety of the devout and the creativity of the artists, the Annunciation has been predominant" (*Mary through the Centuries: Her Place in the History of Culture* [New Haven: Yale University Press, 1996], 81–85, here 81).

4. Zechariah's encounter with Gabriel has a different outcome, of course. Interpreters cannot responsibly ignore his story, however, because Luke very intentionally weaves them together. See Robert C. Tannehill, *The Gospel according to Luke*, vol. 1 of *The Narrative Unity of Luke-Acts: A Literary Interpretation* (Philadelphia: Fortress, 1986), 15–25. Luke narrates that Gabriel approaches Mary in the sixth month (1:26), that is, the sixth month of Elizabeth's pregnancy. Readers recall Elizabeth's story again when Gabriel shares her gestational calendar with Mary (1:36).

5. Joachim Jeremias, *Jerusalem in the Time of Jesus: An Investigation into Economic and Social Conditions during the New Testament Period*, trans. F. H. and C. H. Cave (Philadelphia: Fortress, 1969), 198–207. E. P. Sanders quotes Josephus (*Against Apion* 1.32), who notes the close accounting of priestly marriages (*Judaism: Practice and Belief, 63 BCE–66 CE* [London: SCM, 1992], 52).

6. Sanders states, "Sacrificing was both a privilege, since it served God, and a benefit, since it provided the priest with meat" (*Judaism*, 78).

7. I. Howard Marshall, *The Gospel of Luke*, New International Greek Testament Commentary (Grand Rapids: Eerdmans, 1978), 54.

afforded the right, by lot, to enter the holy place.[8] If priesthood can be understood as mediation between God and humanity, Zechariah fulfills his vocation by crossing at last into the precinct where God's presence dwells, and there one mediator is met by another. Zechariah encounters an angel.[9] Gabriel declares that he was sent by God to speak with Zechariah (Luke 1:19). Contrast by comparison becomes clear. Whereas Zechariah has approached God's realm, God's messenger has approached Mary's realm.[10] One might imagine it this way: while Zechariah is invited to a state banquet at Buckingham Palace, the royal family themselves pay a formal visit to Mary's home address.

Favor Resisted (Luke 1:28–33)

Upon arrival, Gabriel greets Mary with the positive statement that she has been given grace (κεχαριτωμένη [kecharitōmenē]) and that the Lord is with her. This initial statement of Gabriel lacks any parallel with Zechariah's angelic conversation. While the narrator has described both Zechariah and Elizabeth as righteous, walking without blame in all the commandments and requirements of the Lord (Luke 1:6), Gabriel says nothing about Zechariah's relationship with God when speaking to him. One wonders whether Luke intends to draw a comparison between the good of obeying God's commandments and the even greater good of the Lord's gracious presence with Mary without justification from any previous performance.[11]

---

8. Robert C. Tannehill, *Luke*, Abingdon New Testament Commentaries (Nashville: Abingdon, 1996), 44.

9. Here "the priest would be as close to the Holy of Holies as anyone other than the high priest would ever come" (Tannehill, *Luke*, 44).

10. Deborah F. Middelton notes, "By contrast, Gabriel's second visit is to the northern province of Galilee, a long way from the Temple, and the recipient is not a priest, not even a man, but a young woman" ("The Story of Mary: Luke's Version," *New Blackfriars* 70 [1989]: 557).

11. A theme ripe for the Reformers. See Martin Luther, *Luther's Works*, ed. Jaroslav Pelikan et al. (Saint Louis: Concordia, 1955), 32:157; 21:329, and John Calvin, *A Harmony of the Gospels* (Grand Rapids: Eerdmans, 1972), 1:22, 35, as well as theologians in the Reformed tradition: Nancy J. Duff, "Mary, the Servant of the Lord," and Daniel L. Migliore, "Woman of Faith: Toward a Reformed Understanding of Mary," in *Blessed One: Protestant Perspectives on Mary*, ed. Beverly Roberts Gaventa and Cynthia L. Rigby (Westminster John Knox, 2002), 59–70 and 117–30, respectively. Jerusha Matsen Neal notes, "Mary's description tells us nothing that

Gabriel's initial word to Mary shows that this is not the entrance of a strange and foreign power. He addresses her with the common greeting, χαῖρε (*chaire*), a term related to both χάρις (*charis*), "grace," and χαρά (*chara*), "joy,"[12] showing that the cause for rejoicing is the favor of the Lord whom she and her family have known for generations. God has already been with her and has already shown her favor; κεχαριτωμένη (*kecharitōmenē*) is in the perfect tense, speaking of a previously established reality. Jon Levenson's reflection on God's communication with Israel works as a parallel example and captures my point: "Because [God's words] are grounded in the history of redemption, they are not the imposition of an alien force, but rather the revelation of a familiar, benevolent, and loving God."[13] She is favored because the Lord has been with her and is now presenting divine presence to her in a palpable way.

This act of honor from a deity known to be good elicits in Mary—surprisingly—hesitancy. She does not immediately rush head long, unthinkingly, into this conversation. She is unsettled, and so she pauses the rhetorical progress of the divine emissary.

Luke describes her reaction by noting that Mary is disturbed (διαταράσσω [*diatarassō*]). Her unease may have arisen from the simple presence of an angel, which is the widespread response from other biblical figures to such visitations as well.[14] Luke, however, adds further comment that her sense of disturbance emerges from her distinctly interrogative character. She considers what kind of greeting this might be (Luke 2:29).[15] It is not only the presence

---

would distinguish her as particularly worthy of the calling she will receive" (*The Overshadowed Preacher: Mary, the Spirit, and the Labor of Proclamation* [Grand Rapids: Eerdmans, 2020], 97). This is also affirmed in different ways by the Catholic and Orthodox traditions. See John Paul II, "Redemptoris Mater: Ioannes Paulus PP. II on the Blessed Virgin Mary in the Life of the Pilgrim Church" (1.7–11), The Holy See, https://www.vatican.va/content/john-paul-ii/en/encyclicals/documents/hf_jp-ii_enc_25031987_redemptoris-mater.html; Sergius Bulgakov, *The Burning Bush: On the Orthodox Veneration of the Mother of God*, trans., ed., and intro. Thomas Allan Smith (Grand Rapids: Eerdmans, 2009), 7–10. All affirm that it is God and God alone who grants Mary grace.

12. Warren C. Trenchard, "Χαίρω" (*Chairō*), in *The Complete Vocabulary Guide to the Greek New Testament*, rev. ed. (Grand Rapids: Zondervan, 1998), 121.

13. Jon D. Levenson, *Creation and the Persistence of Evil: The Jewish Drama of Divine Omnipotence* (Princeton: Princeton University Press, 1994), 144.

14. Gen 21:17; Matt 1:20; 28:5; Luke 1:13; 2:9–10; Acts 27:23–24.

15. Joshua D. Genig calls attention to the weight of the proclaimed word to Mary. About the

of a supernatural being but *the words* that grab her attention and cause her distress. Possibly she suspects concealed contractual details in the fine print: "I've been given grace to do *what* exactly?"

Mary's considering (διαλογίζομαι [*dialogizomai*]) is a rather general word for thinking, but in Luke's writings, the majority of uses carry the more negative connotation of doubting.[16] Which is to say, Mary's initial response seems very similar to that of Zechariah. Both Mary and Zechariah are disturbed when they see the angel. Zechariah was shaken (ταράσσω [*tarassō*] Luke 1:12) and fear (φόβος [*phobos*] 1:12) falls upon him. Mary is also disturbed (διαταράσσω [*diatarassō*] 1:29) and considers (διαλογίζομαι [*dialogizomai*]) the greeting. Gabriel's first words to both are also the same, "Do not fear" (μὴ φοβοῦ [*mē phobou*] 1:13, 30b). If Luke intended to draw a stark comparison between the two based on their initial interactions with Gabriel, that contrast remains opaque.[17] In both cases, Gabriel is met with questioning concern, even agitation, rather than robotic compliance.

Birth Questioned

Perceiving her less than jovial reaction, Gabriel reiterates God's graciousness toward her: "You have found favor with God" (Luke 1:30b). He then specifies the shape this grace will take: a child, a son—that she will call by the name Jesus. In the midst of verse 32, the news transforms from a common hope for a healthy son into something unique, a cause for even greater rejoicing. Gabriel tells Mary that she has been chosen to bear the Messiah, the ruler of Israel, the heir to David's kingdom, the possessor of God's long-ago and as yet unfulfilled promise for a perpetual throne. God's grace toward her is a grace to remove any specter of barrenness, any fear of death in pregnancy or delivery. God's

---

annunciation, he states, "The word was the sermon of the angel, combined with the overshadowing of the Holy Spirit, which, when it was added to the material element of Mary's ear, brought to reality that of which it spoke: the person of Jesus Christ" (*Viva Vox: Rediscovering the Sacramentality of the Word through the Annunciation*, Emerging Scholars [Minneapolis: Fortress, 2015], 158).

16. Luke 2:35; 3:15; 5:21–22; 6:8; 9:46–47; 12:17; 20:14; 24:38.

17. See the discussion of the similarities between the two encounters in Brittany E. Wilson, *Unmanly Men: Refigurations of Masculinity in Luke-Acts* (Oxford: Oxford University Press, 2015), 79–94.

grace is to bless her with the honor of a son, and most spectacularly of all, to bless her with the honor of bearing the Messiah. The scriptural language he uses (with allusions to 2 Sam 7, Isa 9, and Mic 4) would have resonated with a first-century Jewish person.[18] Which is to say, by announcing God's particular grace to Mary, at the same time, Gabriel proclaims God's general graciousness of keeping promises to her entire people and, through them, the world. God is gracious to descend, to preserve, and to honor Mary, and in so doing to elevate her by keeping the ancient promises to Israel and the nations through her. She has reason to rejoice indeed, for Gabriel has brought her good news, that is, gospel (εὐαγγέλιον [*euangelion*]).

Although such tidings would likely be welcome, it needs to be asserted again that Luke's report emphasizes Mary's hesitancy and thoughtfulness. She does not immediately embrace the statement with a giddy celebration; instead, she inquires. It is an odd question for an engaged young woman. Gabriel has told her of events that will happen in the future: you *will* conceive, you *will* bear, you *will* name.[19] The natural thing would be for Mary to assume that this will happen when she consummates her marriage. But she makes no such assumption.

Something about what Gabriel has said makes her ask about the mechanics of this good news. In her own voice, she states what the narrator has already stated twice in one sentence (Luke 1:27)—she has not known a man (1:34).

18. Matthew V. Novenson threads the needle between idealized messianic hope and diffuse messianic meaninglessness to assert, "The meaningfulness of ancient messiah language derives neither from the self-expression of a reified messianic idea nor from the mass psychological phenomenon of a shared hope for redemption. Popular hope may have been more or less current at different times and places in early Judaism, but the meaningfulness of the language is independent of the fervency of the popular hope. People could know what the words meant whether or not they shared the sentiment expressed. In short, messiah language could be used meaningfully in antiquity because it was deployed in the context of a linguistic community whose members shared a stock of common linguistic resources" (*Christ among the Messiahs: Christ Language in Paul and Messiah Language in Ancient Judaism* [New York: Oxford University Press, 2012], 47). Gabriel's words appeal to messianic texts, including those that are most common among messiah texts. His words therefore affirm "a promise . . . of an indigenous ruler for the Jewish people" (57–58).

19. Some translations (NRSV) have the word "now" in 1:31 as the rendering of ἰδού (*idou*). If this is the meaning, it would lead to Mary wondering how she could conceive in that moment without having had intercourse. Most translations render it as "behold," in the sense of "pay attention to my words!" which would demand another explanation for her question.

How then, she queries, will this be possible?[20] Her question reveals that she has already perceived that he is not speaking about a typical pregnancy because he is not speaking about a typical son.

An angel has been sent to her to say that her son will reign over the house of Israel *forever*, that his kingdom will never come to an end. The language of Gabriel's pronouncement draws from numerous occasions in Israel's Scriptures where the heir of David is said to possess an eternal throne. The statements are made in reference to David's seed.[21] That applies first to Solomon, but the text does not indicate that the audience at his coronation or the readers of Samuel/ Chronicles imagined that Solomon had been given the miraculous gift of eternal life. The "seed" would reign over the house of Israel forever. Although the "seed" would have initially referred to Solomon, at his natural, expected death, the seed was embodied by his son, then grandson, and so on. The singular "seed" indicates a succession of many people. It is the seed, the throne, or the reign that is forever (2 Sam 7:16; 1 Kgs 9:5; 1 Chr 17:14; 22:10; 28:7; 1 Macc 2:57; Ps 44:7 LXX; Isa 9:7; Dan 2:44), not the individual.

Gabriel's words echo the royal promises, but they are also slightly different, and the difference centers on the singularity of the one who will sit on David's throne. He and he alone will reign over the house of Israel forever. He will not reign as one among many in a continuing line, but his kingdom—not his son's or grandson's but *his*—will have no end. This "seed," referring to a descendant of David who receives the royal promises, is not a collective noun but is puzzlingly, defiantly singular.[22] In this way, his reign sounds much more like the rulership of God, the only one in Israel's Scriptures who is the subject of *eternal* reigning (Pss 9:37; 145:10; Mic 4:7; Wis 3:8).

Luke's Mary seems privy to these crucial details, the distinction of her son from previous sons of David and also his similarity to God. This is why she asks

---

20. F. Scott Spencer interprets this as a sign of her agency: "She does not immediately give herself over to the angel's plan, however much he claims divine authorization. This is her body, and she would like to know exactly how it's going to be appropriated" (*Salty Wives, Spirited Mothers, and Savvy Widows: Capable Women of Purpose and Persistence in Luke's Gospel* [Grand Rapids: Eerdmans, 2012], 70).

21. Michael Pope makes this connection as well, noting Ps 88:36–37 LXX as well as 3 Kgdms 2:33 ("Luke's Seminal Annunciation: An Embryological Reading of Mary's Conception," *Journal of Biblical Literature* 138 [2019]: 797).

22. Not unlike Paul's grammatically clever reading of Abraham's seed in Gal 3:16.

about the nature of the pregnancy of this uniquely enduring son. Luke presents her as a quick study, a few steps ahead of the class. Her question is not a non sequitur; she is not being obtuse.[23] Instead, she is leading the angelic witness, questioning so that Gabriel can say explicitly what she has already begun to guess.[24] Her question indicates that she has already begun to perceive that her son will be called Son of the Most High in a way never true of any other king. As far as Luke is concerned, Mary's is the first human mind to begin to fathom the unexpected nature of God's long-anticipated reign. It is not that she and her husband will soon give birth to the "son of God"—the political leader for the nation of Israel—instead, she and she alone will conceive and give birth (Luke 1:31) to the one who is truly God's Son.

The dawning of understanding betrayed by her question solves a conundrum that has long plagued interpreters of Luke's birth narrative. After Zechariah hears the good news of the forerunner's birth, he asks, "According to what will I know this?" Likewise, after receiving Gabriel's tidings, Mary asks, "How can this be?" Furthermore, following these questions, both Mary and Zechariah name a logistical problem: in his case, the age of him and his wife (Luke 1:18b), and, in her case, virginity.[25] Nothing in the angel's reply to Mary's question, however, carries a hint of reproach. In contrast, after Zechariah asks a seemingly similar question, he is sentenced to silence because, as the angel says plainly to Zechariah, "You did not believe my words" (1:20). This is out of character for Zechariah, whom Luke has described as righteous (1:6). Both Zechariah and Mary may have been startled by their vision of the angel, but the narration suggests that they reacted differently to his speech. Zechariah did *not* believe the angel's extensive message of good news (1:20).[26] The contrast

23. Interpreters note that the question is "unnatural," as the reader might expect Mary to assume the child will come when she consummates her marriage. See John Nolland, *Luke 1:1–9:20*, Word Biblical Commentary 35A (Dallas: Word, 1989), 53, and Joel B. Green, *The Gospel of Luke*, The New International Commentary on the New Testament (Grand Rapids: Eerdmans, 1997), 89. I suggest that her question is, instead, intuitive.

24. Luke has crafted the narrative in such a way that her question prompts the amazing answer. See discussion in Nolland, *Luke 1:1–9:20*, 53.

25. "Overall, it is difficult to parse the differences between the objections, because both objections follow a similar narrative pattern" (Wilson, *Unmanly Men*, 88).

26. Spencer finds another possible reason for Zechariah's punishment: "Perhaps if Zechariah had been more concerned about Elizabeth's involvement than his own uncertainty—after

with Zechariah reveals Mary to be the exception to the wider lexical pattern of doubt.[27] Her question shows evidence of a certain kind of trust, an assumption that the proclamation will happen, but one that moves to ask about the mechanics. Hers is a faith that listens well and then clarifies the seemingly impossible. Luke has used her question to underline a key point in the narrative: if her son was going to reign forever because he was truly the Son of the Most High, not the son of any man,[28] she wanted confirmation that her virginity played an important role in the fulfillment of that promise. Her question demands clarity, and Gabriel provides it.

"You do not know a man?" Precisely. That does not disqualify you from bearing this child, it actually qualifies you. You will conceive this child as a virgin because this child will not be the son of Joseph or any man.

Overshadowing Accepted (Luke 1:35–37)

Mary's faithful questioning opens the way for Gabriel to answer in a way that shows the miraculous nature of God's honoring favor toward her. God's grace has been with her, but now it will become tangible in an embodied way. The Holy Spirit, as indicated by the parallel statement "the power of the Most High," is for Luke a manifestation of the God of Israel.[29] God will visit Mary, and through that act, the conundrum of her virginal maternity is solved. Zech-

---

all, it was *her* body that would be most affected—he would have merited a more sympathetic response" (*Salty Wives*, 7).

27. Nolland similarly concludes, "In the context (esp. v. 45), Mary's question is not understood to be colored by doubt in the way that Zechariah's had been" (*Luke 1:1–9:20*, 54).

28. Similarly, Green clarifies, "Jesus is 'Son of God' not as a consequence of his assuming the throne of David (as in Ps 2:7), but as a result of his conception, itself the result of the miraculous work of the Spirit" (*Gospel of Luke*, 91).

29. See also Luke 3:22, where the Holy Spirit's coming is followed by a paternal voice from heaven; 11:13, where the Holy Spirit is the gift from God to the children who ask for good things; 12:10, where blasphemy against the Holy Spirit is unforgivable; Acts 2:33, where the Holy Spirit is given by God the Father to the Son; 4:31, where being filled with the Holy Spirit results in speaking the word of God; 5:32 and 15:8, where the Holy Spirit is a gift to the believers; 7:55, where the Holy Spirit allows a vision of God and Jesus; and 10:38, which recounts that God anointed Jesus with the Holy Spirit.

ariah had been given the privilege of entering the holy of holies; but now the presence in the holy of holies is poised to enter Mary herself.

The danger for Mary is that the statements of Gabriel are proclamations in the indicative: You *will* conceive; you *will* bear a son; you *will* name him Jesus; the Holy Spirit *will* come upon you; the power of the Most High *will* over-shadow you. It does not sound like the messenger is asking, but rather *telling*. As the story continues, however, Luke moves through the danger to show that God honors Mary, not only by giving grace and blessing in a nonviolating way but also by creating space for her willing agency.

Familial Example

Such a proclamation about virginal conception may be too hard to believe, so Gabriel provides a categorically different though related example. He provides a sign even though, and perhaps maybe because, Mary does not ask for one. It is a further example of honoring grace.[30] Mary's relative Elizabeth, known as the barren one, now in her old age is six months pregnant.[31] She had two strikes against her, previous sterility and age, and Mary knows the story because she is a family member. Now Elizabeth has conceived a son with Zechariah, and, at six months pregnant, she is past several points of gestational danger.

God has answered Elizabeth's desires, but in such a way that also facilitates Mary's acceptance of her miraculous call. The messenger presents the story of Elizabeth to aid Mary's apprehension of the proclamation made about her future. If things had already been decided for Mary, no need would exist to present the experience of her relative. Elizabeth's conception certainly testifies to the power of God, but Gabriel testifies to God's miraculous power at this moment in order to encourage Mary. Coercion need not explain itself, but Gabriel does. Gabriel does so by showing that God has been at work already in Mary's family. In Jewish tradition, the coming of the Lord was preceded by

---

30. Thanks to Brittany Wilson for calling attention to this point.

31. Lukan scholars have come to see the two stories as more of a contrast than a parallel. See Andrew T. Lincoln, *Born of a Virgin? Reconceiving Jesus in the Bible, Tradition, and Theology* (Grand Rapids: Eerdmans, 2013), 99.

a forerunner (Mal 4:5 [3:23 MT]; Isa 40:3), but there is nothing in the Elijah/Messiah tradition that demands John and Jesus, as the forerunner and inaugurator of God's reign, be a part of the same family. The familial connection serves no other purpose in Luke's narrative than to support Mary's acceptance.

Mary's Speech

The reality of Elizabeth's pregnancy is evidence, Gabriel says, that every word of God is possible, no matter how impossible it seems (Luke 1:37). Such a proclamation of God's unlimited power proves an ominous statement in a narrative haunted by the threat of (male?) divine coercion. The account could have ended there—God has said it, so it will happen—but it does not. Had the narrative ended with Gabriel's words, the reader would be forgiven for wondering whether the pregnancy was forced upon Mary. Gabriel has made clear that nothing can stand in the way of the word of God, and yet God waits to enact this word until Mary accepts it.

Luke gives the clearest picture of Mary's agency through her verbal assent to Gabriel. She has considered and questioned and been provided with answers and encouragement. Mary does not know everything that will happen with this son, but her hesitant inquisitiveness has allowed Gabriel to disclose enough to her so that she can make an informed decision.

It is vital to note—first of all—that Mary speaks. Not all traditions present her as so vocal. In the Qur'an's account of the annunciation, Mary never replies to Gabriel.[32] Closer at hand, Luke's narrative twin—the annunciation to Zechariah—presents him offering no acceptance. After he asks a question similar to Mary's, Gabriel strikes him mute (Luke 1:20). He never has a chance to respond. Zechariah and Elizabeth prepare the one who will prepare the way of the Lord without verbally agreeing to the invitation—an honor to be sure, but a challenging one. Conversely, Mary does agree—verbally—to the word that has been spoken to her,[33] and her agreement demonstrates a thoughtful self-respect.

32. She does ask the question, and readers should not make too much of silence. She could have spoken, but it is not recorded. See Qur'an 3:44 and 19:21–22.

33. "At the end of the birth announcement, Mary—not Gabriel—is even the one to have the last word" (Wilson, *Unmanly Men*, 88).

She begins by calling attention to herself. Behold (ἰδού [*idou*])! Luke employs this attention-getting term throughout his gospel narrative,[34] but here it functions not as narration but as her speech. *She* calls attention to *herself.* From the beginning, the account has involved her: her story, her family, her body, and so she identifies herself as the focal point. Look at me.[35]

Slave of the Lord

Attention to herself, however, is then shaped (or is that negated?) by the next term she uses. She refers to herself as the δούλη (*doulē*), a female slave, of the Lord. Such self-naming might only be evidence of a woefully commonplace example of female acquiescence to oppression.[36] Several dynamics of the re-

---

34. Luke 1:20, 31, 36, 38, 44, 48; 2:10, 25, 34, 48; 5:12, 18; 6:23; 7:12, 25, 27, 34, 37; 8:41; 9:30, 38–39; 10:3, 19, 25; 11:31–32, 41; 13:7, 11, 16, 30, 32, 35; 14:2; 15:29; 17:21, 23; 18:28, 31; 19:2, 8, 20; 22:10, 21, 31, 38, 47; 23:14–15, 29, 50; 24:4, 13, 49.

35. Courtney Hall Lee states this well: "Without the interference of male aggression or seduction, this Mary can concentrate on her worth as a highly favored, God-created being" (*Black Madonna: A Womanist Look at Mary of Nazareth* [Eugene, OR: Cascade, 2017], 125).

36. Several scholars argue that her story indicates that "suffering is natural and that their meek and mild acceptance of all the world throws at them is holy and reflects the example of the Virgin." See Lisa Isherwood, *Introducing Feminist Theology*, 2nd ed. (Sheffield: Sheffield Academic, 2001), 70. Sarah Jane Boss names the danger in this use of Mary's narrative: "Under social conditions of domination she frequently signifies the object of domination when it is in the condition of accomplished subordination (whatever that may be at a given time and place), and not when it is in a state of rebellion. It is for this reason that Mary can be used as a tool of the dominator against the oppressed . . . she is the subordinate who accepts her lot and not the one who resists. In this way, Mary can be brought into play in the drama of dualistic domination, on the side of the powerful rather than the subordinate" (*Empress and Handmaid: Nature and Gender in the Cult of the Virgin Mary* [London: Cassell, 2000], 170). Sally Cunneen catalogs the experiences of women who would agree that "Mary has been turned into a model of passive obedience and artificial goodness that has often served to keep women from exercising their freedom and developing their strength" (*In Search of Mary: The Woman and the Symbol* [New York: Ballantine Books, 1996], 278). Even Joseph Ratzinger acknowledges the critique: "The veneration of the Virgin and Mother, the obedient and humble servant has been, so it is said, a means of fixing the woman's role for centuries. It has glorified her in order to suppress her." See Hans Urs von Balthasar and Joseph Cardinal Ratzinger, *Mary: The Church at the Source*, trans. Adrian Walker (San Francisco: Ignatius, 1997), 37. Previous misuse should not prohibit close attention, which can result in beneficial rather than oppressive employment of her story.

lationship between Mary and the Lord complicate and eventually rule out that conclusion, however. Mary's language of "handmaid"—or less genteel, "female slave"—not only avoids but actively works against the worries about oppression its connotations certainly elicit.

It must be stated plainly that to be a slave is to exist in a degrading position of subservience. In the ancient world, a slave was simply a body to be used as the master desired, affording the slave little to no hope for self-control or societal honor with respect to free people.[37] The low position of the slave, however, was not homogenous. One's slave status depended on the job the slave did as well as on the master the slave served. The slaves of Caesar, for instance, were afforded greater power and influence.[38] Luke's language works along the grain of this comparison. If there was a certain desirability in being a slave of Caesar, to be a slave of the Most High God is to claim a position of unparalleled importance. Such a statement is congruent with the system of reversal about which Mary will soon sing: in the economy of this Lord, to be low is to be raised high (Luke 1:48). To be servant of this Lord, then, is to grant one access to the sovereign of all creation.[39] Moreover, with Luke's ambiguous use of κύριος (kyrios), she is also placing herself as the servant of the coming eternal King of Israel. She has gained access to the court, and an unrivalled proximate access at that.[40] Ephrem the Syrian captures the paradox beautifully in his poetry penned in the voice of Mary: "The day when Gabriel entered

37. See Jennifer A. Glancy, *Slavery in Early Christianity* (Minneapolis: Fortress, 2006).

38. S. Scott Bartchy concludes, "Perhaps most surprising is the power exercised by the emperor's personal slaves and freedman, the *familia Caesaris*, who were given top administrative positions, a practice that dismayed both Tacitus (*Ann.* 12) and Pliny the Younger (*Ep.* 8.6). Claudius drew from his more than twenty thousand slaves and freeman to create an imperial bureaucracy" ("Slaves and Slavery in the Roman World," in *The World of the New Testament*, ed. Joel B. Green and Lee Martin McDonald [Grand Rapids: Baker, 2013], 173).

39. Joel B. Green states, "When Mary asserts her position as a servant of the Lord, we recognize that she derives her status from him" ("The Social Status of Mary in Luke 1:5–2:52: A Plea for Methodological Integration," *Biblica* 73 [1992]: 468).

40. Levenson describes a similar dynamic in the covenant of Israel. Although his words here concern the nation, they seem just as applicable to Mary: "Her obligation to serve does not compromise her majesty; indeed, it defines it. . . . No statement of the autonomy and dignity of humanity can be adequate to this ancient Jewish theology if it fails to reckon with the difference made by the God who commands" (*Creation*, 141, 148).

my poor presence, he made me immediately a free woman and a servant . . . suddenly a handmaiden has become daughter of the King."[41]

In this position of honored subservience, she is not alone. In the first-century cultural setting, by putting herself in the place of a servant, a maid slave of this Lord, Mary's words agree with those throughout the New Testament. This is what Jesus asks of his disciples (Matt 20:27; Mark 10:44; Luke 17:10). In Luke's two-volume narrative, this is the same position that Simeon owns for himself (Luke 2:29), as well as Peter and John (Acts 4:29). Other New Testament authors adopt this as a self-description, including James (Jas 1:1), Peter (2 Pet 1:1), and Jude (Jude 1). Both the Petrine (1 Pet 2:16) and Johannine (Rev 1:1; 7:3; 10:7; 11:18; 15:3; 19:2, 5; 22:3, 6) literature describes God's people in this way. Paul names himself and his coworkers as God's slaves (Rom 1:1; 2 Cor 4:5; Gal 1:10; Phil 1:1; Col 4:12; Titus 1:1) and urges his readers to do the same (Rom 6:19; 1 Cor 7:22; Eph 6:6; 2 Tim 2:24). Both Abraham and David, in Jesus's line, are called slaves of God (2 Sam 3:18; Ps 104:42). The list here indicates that servitude is not a gendered issue; both men and women in the early Christian movement own this identity.

These people do so because they are following a Lord who himself became a servant. This is a central assertion of Pauline Christology—Jesus Christ took on the form of a δοῦλος (*doulos*) (Phil 2:7)—expressed practically in the gospel tradition when Jesus proclaims his goal of service (Mark 10:45; Luke 22:27) and washes the feet of his disciples (John 13).[42] All those who take on this mantle do so because they are following the pattern set by the Lord to whom they pledge their service.[43] To be a handmaid of this Lord is to stand in a position

41. *Hymns* 5.20; see Ephrem the Syrian, *Hymns*, trans. Kathleen E. McVey, The Classics of Western Spirituality (New York: Paulist, 1989), 108–9.

42. Luke, however, never calls Jesus a δοῦλος (*doulos*) but instead a παῖς (*pais*) (Luke 2:43; Acts 3:13, 26; 4:27, 30), which was also employed to indicate young slaves. See "παῖς," in Frederick W. Danker et al., *Greek-English Lexicon of the New Testament and Other Early Christian Literature*, 3rd ed. (Chicago: University of Chicago Press, 2000), 750.

43. In disagreement with Michael Pope's argument, δούλη (*doulē*), though a feminine form, connects Mary with other slaves of God more closely than it connects her with examples of slave women impregnated (Παιδίσκη [*Paidiskē*], Gen 16:3–4; 30:4–5, 9–10) ("Gabriel's Entrance and Biblical Violence in Luke's Annunciation Narrative," *Journal of Biblical Literature* 137 [2018]: 708). Spencer makes a similar point this way: "the role of servant/slave/minister . . . represents for Luke the quintessential, 'greatest' vocation for all of God's people—highborn or lowborn, male or female—including Jesus" (*Salty Wives*, 78). John Macquarrie concurs: "Humility is a

of blessing and honor among all other believers who follow the one who took this position of service himself.

Although this places her among the other slaves, in the texts of the New Testament, Luke is the only New Testament author to employ the feminine form of this term. Mary speaks it twice (Luke 1:38, 48), and Peter speaks it in his quotation of Joel 2:29 (Acts 1:18). This connection affirms the blessing and honor of her role. She foreshadows Peter's appeal to the promise of Joel (Joel 2:29) that women and men will have vital roles because they have been blessed by God in the new era her son inaugurates. In the age of the Messiah, she is the first slave upon whom God pours out the Spirit.[44] As a maidservant of this κύριος (kyrios), she is first in line to reap the eschatological benefits and demonstrates that with her own prophetic speech (Acts 2:17–18) in the song she will soon sing, the Magnificat. Luke makes this radical and even disturbing attribution to Mary not to oppress her, but in his theologically shaped narrative focusing on the God of Israel, Luke does so to honor her.

It must be recognized, however, that slavery language of the New Testament has been used in reprehensible ways, and its problematic nature has been named and discussed, especially by theologians sensitive to racialized communities.[45] As a person who has been racialized as "white," this language does not impact me in the same way that it strikes others.[46] It is vital to hear

---

Christian virtue not confined to Mary and not recommended only to women. Christ was also meek and humble. Indeed, one might say that this is the very heart of the revelation of God in Christ. God has come among us in meekness and humility not in power and overwhelmingness" (*Mary for All Christians*, 2nd ed. [Edinburgh: T&T Clark, 2001], 8).

44. Turid Karlsen Seim notes, "The Spirit marks out God's total right of disposal, but it does not reduce humans to puppets. Individuals can choose to respond positively or negatively, but the Holy Spirit is given only to 'those who obey God' (Acts 5.32)" ("The Virgin Mother: Mary and Ascetic Discipleship in Luke," in *A Feminist Companion to Luke*, ed. Amy-Jill Levine, Feminist Companion to the New Testament and Early Christian Writings 3 [London: Sheffield Academic, 2002], 102).

45. See Lee, *Black Madonna*, 112, and James Albert Harrill, *Slaves in the New Testament: Literary, Social, and Moral Dimensions* (Minneapolis: Fortress, 2006).

46. See the treatment of metaphor's impact on different readers in Marianne Bjelland Kartzow, *The Slave Metaphor and Gendered Enslavement in Early Christian Discourse: Double Trouble Embodied* (New York: Routledge, 2018). Thankfully, the biblical texts give other images and word pictures to describe the God/human relationship, and this one need not be adopted if the problems outweigh the benefits.

the word Luke writes—female slave—and not sanitize it, both to name the horrendously oppressive system from which it comes as well as to hear Mary's relationship with the God who is destroying those same systems.[47]

Let It Be

It is true that Mary did not seek out this situation, this honor; she did not ask to be the "Mother of the Universal Lord." Instead, God sent the messenger with the invitation to her. She does not ask for this role. Instead, God asks her whether she will receive it. In response, Mary continues, "Let it be unto me according to your word" (Luke 1:38). This could be hopeless resignation or an unnecessary yes, a verbal rubber stamp because such acquiescence is the only option open in the face of the proclamation of the powerful deity. Such a criticism easily fits the behavior of a god like Zeus toward his many female victims,[48] but it does not apply to this passage for two reasons.

First, as I've already argued in the first chapter, the *ethos* of the divine in Luke is necessary to a redemptive reading of this story.[49] Luke's reader approaches the God of Israel neither with disdain nor even uncertainty, but in trust. Theophilus, representative of the ideal reader, has already been instructed in and experienced the work of God (Luke 1:1–4). Not dissimilar to readers shaped by the Christian faith today, Luke's reader would not assume the worst simply because she knows the Christian God would not act in any inappropriate way. Moreover, as the narrative develops, the Lord of whom Gabriel speaks is revealed not to exercise his power in oppressive dominion but instead in honoring, if demanding, service. The tone for Lordship is set by the Isaianic prophecy of redemption, recovery, and release (4:18–19) and con-

---

47. Raquel S. Lettsome argues that by reading "slave," we see "the narrative turnabout that flips the slave language in the text on its head. Such is the case of Mary's self-identification as *doulē* (slave) in Luke 1:38, 48." The author honestly names all the problems of this language but asserts that Mary's slave relationship with God is one of mutualism resulting in her benefit, concluding, "Mary's slave language is the modified dose of the disease of slavery. Mary's narrative depiction rallies against it" ("Mary's Slave Songs: The Tensions and Turnarounds of Faithfully Reading *Doulē* in the Magnificat," *Interpretation* 75 [2021]: 11, 18).

48. See discussion of divine conceptions in ancient literature in chapter 1, pp. 21–22.

49. See full discussion of the character of God the Father, both in Luke, and throughout the New Testament, in the appendix.

tinued through acts of healing and compassion. This Lord certainly demands no less than complete allegiance (Luke 9:23–25) but does this so that his followers can join him in acts of restorative service.

Second, the interpretation of a forcefully maleficent god is equally unsatisfying if the human accepts not out of weakness but out of strength, if the human speaks *for herself*. Throughout the account, Luke has displayed Mary as thoughtful. She was hesitant at the proclamation of God's favor. She questioned the promise of a birth. Her acceptance at the close of the conversation has not come flippantly.

As Gabriel has announced to her, the birth of this child carries both honor and cost. On one hand, she is saying yes to something that is good *for her*. In other words, her agreement arises not only from self-sacrifice but also from self-respect. It makes sense that she would want this. She assents to the ability to have a healthy child. She agrees to bear a great son. Most powerfully, she accepts for herself the honor of being the mother of the Messiah who will reign forever. To recall the comparison with Zechariah: Gabriel offers to him as well the blessing of conception, but he will have the less valued honor of being related to the forerunner of the Messiah (Luke 1:17). Even so, he is incredibly grateful as he expresses in his own song of praise (1:68–79). Viewed from this angle, her words give evidence that she accepted God's call with excitement: "The word I have heard is *good*, and I embrace it."[50] She does not let this honor pass her by. The grace that is being offered to her she takes for herself, embracing the favor of God that Gabriel proclaimed at the outset.

Lest the portrayal of Mary tip from self-respect toward an insinuation of selfishness, the historical situatedness of the narrative joins her embrace of honor with a mature acceptance of the cost. It is clear to her now, based on Gabriel's explanation in verse 35, that nothing about this pregnancy will be normal. Moreover, because it will not be within the bounds of appropriate scripts for women, it will cause her shame and danger, a theme that Luke leaves undeveloped but one available to readers, as evidenced by Matthew's treatment. Being old enough to know the ramifications of being betrothed—that she should not yet have a child—she is old enough to know the consequences

---

50. In the words of Boss, "She does not have to 'knuckle under' and do as she is told, because it is her own desire which is about to be realized. She is to be the bearer of her own Saviour, who is also the Redeemer of the world" (*Empress and Handmaid*, 218).

that will come to those who transgress the boundaries of respectability.[51] Emphasizing the cost rather than the blessing, John Chrysostom postulated that she might have even contemplated suicide at this moment: "For it were likely that she, not knowing the certainty, might have even devised something amiss touching herself, and have gone on to strangle or to stab herself, not enduring the disgrace."[52] To possess the honor of bearing the Messiah, she must be willing to walk through the shame of bearing a "bastard." If she is aware of what it means to be betrothed, and her question suggests that she is, her answer indicates that she had counted the cost, and then she agreed. She consented to the negative consequences of the words Gabriel prophesied about her. To put oneself in that place of humility in order to play such a key role in God's story requires incredible strength.

The grammar of her response itself illuminates the dynamics. γένοιτο (*genoito*), "let it be," is a verb in the middle voice, a territory that is neither active nor passive. It is, instead, reflexive. The action is initiated by God, and yet Mary permits its impact. The mood of the verb is an optative. Optatives express a wish, as in "Might this be true."[53] Such language is not resignation. It is agreement to an invitation, an agreement motivated by desire.

In both of her statements, "Behold the handmaid of the Lord!" and "Let it be unto me according to your word," Luke presents the delicate balance of both self-respect and humility. Look at *me*! I am a *slave* of the Lord. Let the *good* and *hard* word happen to me.

Luke has portrayed Mary as a complex character offering a self-involved response. He indicates her feelings and thoughts (Luke 1:29). She articulates questions (1:34). Then, in her own voice, she responds (1:38). In so doing, she demonstrates an unblinking and willing resolve. However catchy it may be, the

51. Age at marriage varied depending on social class and location, but mid to late teens seems a safe assumption. See M. K. Hopkins, "The Age of Roman Girls at Marriage," *Population Studies* 18 (1965): 309–27, and B. Shaw, "The Age of Roman Girls at Marriage: Some Reconsiderations," *Journal of Roman Studies* 77 (1987): 28–46. See also Ross Shepherd Kraemer, "Jewish Religion in the Diaspora World of Late Antiquity," in *Jewish Women in Historical Perspective*, ed. Judith Reesa Baskin, 2nd ed. (Detroit: Wayne State University Press, 1998), 58–59.

52. *Homilies on Matthew* 9 (*Nicene and Post-Nicene Fathers*, Series 1, 10:224).

53. Herbert Weir Smyth presents the aspect of desire present in the optative throughout Greek literature (*Greek Grammar*, rev. ed. Gordon M. Messing [Cambridge: Harvard University Press, 1984], 406–7).

sweet, surrendering cadence of the Beatles's song "Let It Be" is a bit too soft to do justice to the biblical account. Mary's yes has grit.

Denouement

A more elegant drama would end here. Luke, however, adds one more seemingly inelegant mundane phrase: "And the angel departed from her." The narrative addendum after the most powerful of speeches underlines the necessity of her response. The angel Gabriel has waited to hear her reply. Only then—after she has agreed—can the encounter come to an end. The divine messenger, the one who relays messages from God, will now carry a message back. A final proof of Mary's agency, the narrative conclusion affirms that even Gabriel cannot be dismissed until her assent is confirmed.[54]

The consensus of Christian tradition is therefore on solid footing. God has not oppressed Mary with the birth of the Messiah; instead, God has presented her with a great honor. Equally important, it is an honor she has accepted willingly. Therein lies the paradox; in her humility before God, Mary is active and even esteemed.

From the Orthodox tradition, Elisabeth Behr-Sigel quotes Nicolas Cabasilas's homily: "The incarnation was, however, also the work of the will and the faith of the Virgin." In contrast to God's work with Adam who had no say in the creation of Eve, with Mary, God "borrowed the flesh of a conscious and consenting woman so that just as he was conceived because he wanted to be, Mary conceived by an act of her free will and became mother by a free choice. She rather offered herself and become the co-worker with God for the providence of mankind."[55] From liturgical texts such as these, she concludes: "The

54. Levenson's analysis of the founding moment of the people of Israel, as this is the founding moment of the Christian expression of that story, provides an illuminating comparison: "That moment of choice keeps alive the element of human autonomy in the dialectic of divine suzerainty. This is the element that distinguishes covenantal theonomy from theocratic tyranny" (*Creation*, 141). Ernest W. Nicholson states similarly about the covenant, "God's choice of his people and their 'choice' of him, that is, their free decision to be obedient and faithful to him. This understood 'covenant' is the central expression of the distinctive faith of Israel" (*God and His People: Covenant and Theology in the Old Testament* [Oxford: Clarendon, 1986], 215–16), quoted in Levenson, *Creation*, 147.

55. N. Cabasilas, *Bulletin of the Crypt* 131, March 1985; cited in Elisabeth Behr-Sigel, *The Ministry of Women in the Church* (Crestwood, NY: St. Vladimir's Seminary Press, 1999), 195.

Orthodox tradition in particular has always insisted on the liberty of Mary's *fiat*, a liberty that is the inalienable image of God in humanity."[56] Mary B. Cunningham concurs: "This was not a passive process, however; Orthodox tradition stresses the fact that Mary freely chose to accept this role when she gave her answer to the archangel Gabriel."[57]

Catholic theologians are no less insistent on this point. Joseph Ratzinger states, "Without this free consent on Mary's part, God cannot become man."[58] Karl Rahner makes her active assent the prime point of Marian reflection: "Mary occupies this central place precisely not in so far as she *is* the Lord's mother passively, but in so far as she *becomes* his mother actively, in so far as she says 'yes' to God's decisive act. If therefore we wish to determine the theological starting point for all we must say about Mary, we shall have to begin with this fact."[59] Feminist Catholic theologian Elizabeth Johnson sets Mary's activity as the example: "Listening to the Spirit, rising to the immense possibilities of her call, she walks by faith in the integrity of her own person. Inspired by Spirit-Sophia, women who make their own decisions before God claim her into their circle."[60]

Protestant theologians agree with this assessment. Beverly Gaventa notes the distinction between choosing and being chosen yet retains a commitment to Mary's active role: "Mary has not chosen this task for herself, any more than the apostles will later choose their own roles, but she does consent to it."[61] She is in line with Richard Bauckham, who writes of Mary as "the active and responsible subject of her own story, when she acts as the Lord's servant, taking God at his word and taking responsibility for acting with trust in that word."[62]

56. Behr-Sigel, *Ministry of Women in the Church*, 59.

57. Mary B. Cunningham, *Gateway of Life: Orthodox Thinking on the Mother of God*, Foundations Series 7 (Yonkers, NY: St. Vladimir's Seminary Press, 2015), 14.

58. Balthasar and Ratzinger, *Church at the Source*, 89.

59. Karl Rahner, "The Fundamental Principle of Marian Theology," trans. Philip Endean in *Mary: The Complete Resource*, ed. Sarah Jane Boss (Oxford: Oxford University Press, 2007), 296.

60. Elizabeth A. Johnson, *Truly Our Sister: A Theology of Mary in the Communion of Saints* (New York: Continuum, 2003), 258.

61. Beverly Roberts Gaventa, *Mary: Glimpses of the Mother of Jesus*, Personalities of the New Testament (Minneapolis: Fortress, 1999), 54.

62. Richard Bauckham, *Gospel Women: Studies of the Named Women in the Gospels* (Grand Rapids: Eerdmans, 2002), 73.

Scot McKnight says succinctly, "Mary's 'may it be' was an act of courageous faith."[63] Cynthia L. Rigby notes that Mary responds "out of the context of her relationship with God" and does not make a "choice" alien to herself but, like an artist, celebrates who "she herself claims to be," a servant of God included in the divine plan.[64] Sarah Jane Boss summarizes:

> The catholic, orthodox and ancient eastern churches have invariably held that Mary gave her free assent to the conception of Christ. If she had not consented to Gabriel's message, then the world's redemption would not have come about in precisely the manner in which it did: the redeemer would not have been the Jesus of Nazareth who is in fact God incarnate. So Mary is not only a physical but also a moral agent in the world's salvation.[65]

In the annunciation, God has respected the faithful will of the young woman Mary.

Conclusion

The annunciation resonates with the delicate dance of divine and human agency affirmed throughout the Christian faith. Nothing stands outside the efficacy of God's word. This powerful word proclaims what will be, yet it does so by approaching its recipient, preparing its recipient to accept, and waiting to hear her acceptance. God speaks what is true, and humans, having been granted the favor of God, are invited and allowed to accept the true word. Divine initiative. Divine statement of reality. Divine patience that waits to hear human acceptance of said reality. There is an indicative statement, "You will bear a son," but also embrace of the indicative, "Let it be unto me."[66] This costly honor is not forced; it is offered.

63. Scot McKnight, *The Real Mary: Why Evangelical Christians Can Embrace the Mother of Jesus* (Brewster MA: Paraclete, 2007), 9.

64. Cynthia L. Rigby, "Mary and the Artistry of God," in Gaventa and Rigby, *Blessed One*, 148–49.

65. Sarah Jane Boss, "The Title Theotokos," in Boss, *Mary*, 53.

66. It is not a situation in which it is either God's act or human response. Instead, "only

Critics have charged that not only does Mary make weak women weaker, she leaves powerful women without any support. "She cannot function as a true role model to women who . . . seek both personal power to run their own lives, and corporate strength to engage with other men and women in improving their lot."[67] On this point, I agree. Mary offers nothing to women or men who seek to run their own lives. Without question, Mary is subservient. There remains a hierarchy—not between Romans and Jews, rich and poor, or men and women but between God and humanity—and Mary stands in the place of the slave rather than the master. The terms of the relationship elicit resistance, understandably and rightfully so. Yet the nature of her submission *to God*, her free decision to submit, I argue, not only avoids but even overturns the implications of oppressive force. She thoughtfully and willfully humbles *herself*; she is not lowered. In this place, as *this* handmaid, Mary is not oppressed; instead, she is blessed. As the God of Israel, the God of her son, remains sovereign over her, she is honored beyond measure. She finds that empowerment only insofar as she is submissive to God.[68] In so doing, she complicates to the point of destroying the negative feminine stereotype. She is not weak. Instead, in her strong submission, she sets the template for all disciples, female and male.

God honors her, grants her agency, and she says yes. It is her yes that changed the fabric of the universe. Somewhere in the empty spaces on the page between her yes (Luke 1:38) and Elizabeth's recognition of the babe (1:42), the Holy Spirit transforms the willing flesh of Mary to form the body of God.

---

when the opposition of dichotomy yields to the subtlety of dialectic can we begin to grasp the Jewish dynamics of lordship and submission. . . . Chosen for service, they must choose to serve" (Levenson, *Creation*, 144, 148).

67. Isherwood, "Mary," 57.

68. I recognize the unsettling and provocative nature of the term "submissive." I see Luke's narrative of Mary affirming submission as "a very subtle, and one might say *sui generis*, response to the divine allure" (Coakley, *Powers and Submissions*, xviii). Medieval Christian women heavily influenced by the story of Mary found strength in the same way. Barbara Newman argues, "It was not because of their commitment to feminism, self-empowerment, subversion, sexuality, or 'the body' that [medieval women] struggled and won their voices; it was because of their commitment to God" (*From Virile Woman to Woman Christ: Studies in Medieval Religion and Literature*, Middle Ages Series [Philadelphia: University of Pennsylvania Press, 1995], 246).

Before I can consider the unique nature of the body of her son, I will return to the character of God the Father. Having argued that God is neither male nor oppressive, I now posit that just as the incarnation as depicted in the New Testament rejects the negative *feminine* stereotype, so too does it prohibit a masculine gendered conception of God.

four

God Is Not Masculine

From Mary, the bearer of the Word, we learn the meaning of our words.

—Blanche Jenson, "Movement and the Story"

Christian theology has rejected the idea that God the Father is male. In the first chapter, I argued that this denial finds support in the birth narratives, vital texts for constructing the shape of the central doctrine of the incarnation. This orthodox agreement that God is not male has not prevented an insidious corollary, however, namely, that males are more like God. Readers might call to mind John Piper's assertion that Christianity has a "masculine feel."[1]

Previous generations might be excused for such associations between men and God because of the cultures in which they existed, cultures infected by

---

1. John Piper, "'The Frank and Manly Mr. Ryle': The Value of a Masculine Ministry," Desiring God, https://www.desiringgod.org/messages/the-frank-and-manly-mr-ryle-the-value -of-a-masculine-ministry. Piper begins with the revelation of God the Father and the maleness of the Son to then argue for the masculine leadership in the church. Piper does not fall into the inappropriate descriptions of God I catalog here, although his preference for male leadership may imply proximity between men and God not shared by women. He responds to critiques against this statement in a video discussed here by David Mathis, "More on the Masculine Feel of Christianity," Desiring God, https://www.desiringgod.org/articles/more-on-the-masculine -feel-of-christianity.

the pervasive belief that women, typically with smaller bodies, were, in fact, weaker in body, mind, and spirit. Women were viewed as passive material, whereas ideal men were lauded as powerful actors, and this opposition began at the moment of conception. Many believed that men provided the energy, and women provided the material of a new human, and if the warm power fully energized the cold material, a boy was born. If the process went awry, the result was a girl.[2] Even linguistic connections reveal the correlations between being male and achieving excellence. In Greek, ἀρετή (aretē), "virtue," is etymologically related to ἄρρην (arrēn) and ἄρσην (arsēn), "male,"[3] and in Latin, "virtue" is created from the base word vir, meaning "male." The dominant assumption was that men were more naturally inclined to reason, justice, self-control, wisdom, and manly courage.[4] In a belief system where men were

2. Aristotle infamously calls the female a "deformed male" (Generation of Animals 737a18). See also Hippocrates of Cos: "And as the male sex is stronger than the female, it must follow that it is engendered from stronger semen. The matter is like this: if stronger semen comes from both parents, a male is engendered, if weaker, a female" (Genitals 6.478). See the summaries in Alicia D. Myers, Blessed among Women? Mothers and Motherhood in the New Testament (New York: Oxford University Press, 2017), 18–57; L. Stephanie Cobb, Dying to Be Men: Gender and Language in Early Christian Martyr Texts (New York: Columbia University Press, 2008), 26–33; and Nancy Tuana, "The Weaker Seed: The Sexist Bias of Reproductive Theory," Hypatia 3 (1988): 35–59. Thomas Laqueur's Making Sex: Body and Gender from the Greeks to Freud (Cambridge: Harvard University Press, 1990) influentially argued for a one-sex model in the ancient world, in which all humans were male, some only deformed. This model, however, is not applicable to all ancient writers. See Helen King, The One Sex Body on Trial: The Classical and Early Modern Evidence (New York: Routledge, 2013).

3. ἀρετή (aretē) can be applied to women, gods, and men, yet the first definition notes, "goodness, excellence, of any kind, in Hom. esp. of manly qualities." See "ἀρετή" (aretē) in Henry George Liddell, Robert Scott, and Henry Stuart Jones, A Greek-English Lexicon, 9th ed. with revised supplement (Oxford: Clarendon, 1996), 238.

4. Brittany E. Wilson summarizes, "Manliness, for instance, was the standard for morality among Roman and Greek authors, with the Latin word often translated as 'valor' or 'virtue' (virtus) etymologically related to the word 'man' (vir) and the Greek word often translated as 'courage' (ἀνδρεία) likewise etymologically related to the word 'man' (ἀνήρ). Both these qualities were central concepts in ancient articulations of morality and were also qualities fundamentally bestowed on men" (Unmanly Men: Reconfigurations of Masculinity in Luke-Acts [Oxford: Oxford University Press, 2015], 44). See also Cobb, Dying to Be Men, 27–30. In her analysis of the world of early Christians, Lynn Cohick summarizes, "a well-attested belief . . . among both Jews and gentiles that women at any age are unable to practice virtues fully or adequately" (Women in the World of the Earliest Christians: Illuminating Ancient Ways of Live [Grand Rapids: Baker, 2009], 49).

so clearly superior, it is no surprise that the superior being, God, would favor men and not women. With scientific advancement, in particular a growth in understanding the process of conception, as well as broad cultural shifts toward more respect for women, one would imagine that arguments for a malelike God would disappear. This, sadly, has not been the case. Such a long and deeply held preference for the male dies hard.

The assumption that God is more like men than women still thrives. No longer explicitly supported by the myth of superior male virtue or ancient incorrect biology (although those theories are sometimes not far below the surface, as I will demonstrate), the modern argument in theological literature that the divine is masculine often rests upon the concept of transcendent initiation, in other words, that God is sovereign over creation and that God moves first to establish relationship with creation. Many theological branches may deny that God is male, but by insisting that God's actions are masculine ones they assert that males have an advantage to be more like "him" than females.[5]

The claim of divine masculinity has shown itself most clearly in discussions about theological language, how the faithful should address God. These debates are certainly not as intense as they were several decades ago.[6] Denominations and theological groups have largely made their decisions on what they will and will not call God and have continued those practices in their own like-minded affinity groups. Although the conversation has not continued

5. Grace Jantzen comments, "Men . . . have been slow to recognize that the classical concept of God is bound up with their ideas of masculinity" (*Becoming Divine: Towards a Feminist Philosophy of Religion*, Manchester Studies in Religion, Culture and Gender [Manchester: Manchester University Press, 1998], 90). As the following examples will show, it is not only men who have struggled with this recognition.

6. For example, the National Council of Churches issued *An Inclusive Language Lectionary* in 1982 (Atlanta: John Knox). The Vatican Council for Doctrine has affirmed the sole use of "Father, Son, and Holy Spirit" in baptism several times in recent decades ("Blessed Be the Name of the Lord: Why 'Creator, Redeemer, Sanctifier' Is Somewhere between Heresy and Idolatry," *Christianity Today* 52 [2008]: 21). A series of books captures the debates in the 1980s and 1990s, including Donald G. Bloesch, *The Battle for the Trinity: The Debate over Inclusive God-Language* (Ann Arbor: Servant, 1985); Alvin F. Kimel Jr., ed., *Speaking the Christian God: The Holy Trinity and the Challenge of Feminism* (Grand Rapids: Eerdmans, 1992); Kimel, ed., *This Is My Name Forever: The Trinity and Gender Language for God* (Downers Grove, IL: InterVarsity Press, 2001); Paul R. Smith, *Is It Okay to Call God Mother? Considering the Feminine Face of God* (Grand Rapids: Baker, 1993).

with the same fervor, the influence has, and therefore the arguments utilized in those debates stand in need of reconsideration. Evidence from a broad ecumenical spectrum demonstrates the pervasiveness of the assumption of God's transcendent and initiating masculinity, and I will discuss its appearance in three forms: God as the source of life, God as sovereign initiator, and Jesus's maleness. I discuss the first two in this chapter; the third necessitates its own. These supports for a masculine God are both insufficient and dangerous, insufficient because masculinity is a concept projected upon God not found in the text, and dangerous because all humans suffer when God is more like some than others.

Insufficient Arguments

The theological positions that the living God is the source of all life and that the living God initiates reconciliation find wide and deep support in Christian thought. That these positions demand that the living God is more like males than females is a false conclusion because neither the biblical text, the consensus tradition, nor scientific knowledge support that conclusion.

God the Father as the Source of Life

In three respects, God as the fount of all life is revealed and understood to be as similar to female procreation as to male. God's creation of the world is radically different from anything in the human arena; neither male nor female is favored above the other. Conversely, God the Father's begetting of the Son and subsequent relationship with those who confess the Son finds analogy in both. The Creator and Begettor God offers no safe haven for those whose theological view favors males and ideal masculinity.

Creation

The widespread assumption of a masculine God frequently rests on a particular vision of God as the source of created life. Because God causes creation and stands distinct from it, it is more fitting to speak of and therefore think of God in masculine terms, so the arguments go. Consequently—they insist—

God, the first person, is best named "Father," rather than "Mother." Proponents recognize that the analogy is not exact. Nonetheless, they do find ground for the fittingness of analogical paternal language by arguing that similarities exist between human fathers' role in procreation and divine creative actions.

One line of this argument suggests that God is best called "Father" because it is fathers who are most responsible for causing human life. Orthodox theologian Christos Yannaras affirms that the term "Father" "expresses in the most profound way the hypostasis of God, what God really *is*: He is one who begets, a life-giving principle."[7] Yannaras associates the "life-giving principle" with the male:

> In the language of archetypes of life which the Scripture uses . . . the woman is the image of *nature*, in contradistinction to the man who is symbol of the *essential principle* (*logos*). This contrast of nature and essential principle, feminine and masculine, does not represent an evaluative distinction, but portrays the experience which man [*sic*] has of the way in which physical life is realized: nature has a 'feminine' readiness to incarnate the event of life, but it needs the seed of the essential principle in order that this incarnation be realized. Without the intervention of the constitutive principle, nature is only a potential, not an existential event. And without its incarnation in nature, the existential principle is just an abstract concept, without substance.[8]

God is fittingly the Father because God is like males in "the way in which physical life is realized" in that both provide the "principle" of life. Similarly, Catholic Old Testament scholar Paul Mankowski argues that fatherhood language for God "marks him as definitively masculine."[9] In the formation of the covenant people, "YHWH's activity in the election of Israel is masculine because it is fatherly; it is fatherly because the initiative, the prerogative, and the motive power of creation are his and his alone," and "as a potter YHWH takes the active and intentional (and to that extent paternal) role in the genesis of his people."[10]

---

7. Christos Yannaras, *Elements of Faith: An Introduction to Orthodox Theology* (Edinburgh: T&T Clark, 1991), 32.

8. Yannaras, *Elements of Faith*, 79.

9. Paul Mankowski, "The Gender of Israel's God," in Kimel, *This Is My Name Forever*, 39.

10. Mankowski, "Gender of Israel's God," 44.

Finally, in an essay published in 1983, Deborah Belonick draws from Gregory of Nyssa to show that the fathers saw in the name "Father" a connotation of "the initiator of a generation, the inaugurator of all, the one who begets life rather than bringing it to fruition in birth. This is the mode of existence (the way of being) of the first person of the Trinity." By the 1980s, she is aware of sperm and ovum and asserts that the church also knew that it "took male and female cells to create life." Nonetheless, she claims that the male cell is "the generator, inaugurator, and impregnator; there are distinctions in the biological act of creation."[11]

Strikingly similar to ancient biology, these authors attribute a more significant cause for the creation of life to fathers rather than mothers. Both men and women are necessary for procreation, of course, but they claim that the dominant energizing principle of life is located with the male. Hence, God is better called "Father." Ancient biological understandings in which males are the true source of life may not, it seems, be so ancient. If God is named "Father" *because* God is "active creator,"[12] then fathers are afforded more of a role than they truly play in human conception. Men are no more active and creative than are women. Both are absolutely necessary to contribute to the formation of a new human.[13] Incorrect biology offers a very precarious foundation for masculine, specifically paternal, language for God.

---

11. Deborah Belonick, "The Spirit of the Female Priesthood: Women and the Priesthood," in *Women and the Priesthood*, ed. Thomas Hopko (Crestwood, NY: St. Vladimir's Seminary Press, 1983), 159, citing *Against Eunomius* 2.9. I recognize that this quotation comes early in Belonick's work, from a masters' thesis, and I do not seek to put forth a young scholar as a straw-man argument. I bring this forward because she is engaging directly with a more advanced biological understanding and yet denies it by preferring the primacy of male activity in procreation.

12. Mankowski, "Gender of Israel's God," 44.

13. A biological textbook puts it this way: "Some of the most remarkable cases of translational regulation of gene expression occur in the oocyte. Prior to meiosis, while the oocyte is still within the ovary, the oocyte often makes and stores mRNAs that will be used only after fertilization occurs.... The stored mRNAs and proteins are referred to as maternal contributions (produced from the maternal genome), and in many species . . . maintenance of the normal rate and pattern of early cell divisions does not require DNA—or even a nucleus! . . . So at some point, each of us should give a shout-out to our biological moms for giving us those transcripts early on." See Michael J. F. Barresi and Scott F. Gilbert, *Developmental Biology*, 12th ed. (Oxford: Oxford University Press, 2019), 83. Not only do women provide material, they also provide transcripts for cell action, all of which need the catalyst of the entrance of the sperm. Any sense that one parent is more the cause of life than another fails in light of the discoveries of science.

A second approach is to make a distinction between the body of a fetus with respect to its mother and father. In response to calls for the feminization of God-language, many scholars—rightly, in my opinion—demonstrate the problems that arise. If God is imagined as Mother, so they argue, then creation is too intimately associated with God. God's transcendence suffers in favor of God's immanence as God is brought down to the level of creation. So too, creation can imagine itself not just in God's image but innately divine. Creation is elevated to the level of God. Such a path has led some to cast off submission to God and argue for making humans themselves into gods.[14] Such are the dangers that consistently propel advocacy for masculine language for God. Elizabeth Achtemeier critiques divine maternal language in this way: "If creation has issued forth from the body of the deity, it shares in deity's substance; deity is in, through, and under all things, and therefore everything is divine."[15] Feminine God-language can lead to various forms of pantheism, that God inheres in all.[16] Masculine language, in Achtemeier's view, avoids these problems: "the Bible's language for God is masculine, a unique revelation of God in the world. The basic reason for that designation of God is that the God of the Bible will not let himself be identified with his creation . . . it is that holiness, that otherness, that transcendence of the Creator which also

14. Jantzen's feminist philosophy argues against submission to the law of God (*Becoming Divine*, 44) and rejects a hierarchy between God and human, preferring instead that "the transcendent and the immanent are not to be seen as opposites. Rather, the sensible transcendental, the pantheistic projection of the female divine, opens out what has hitherto been seen as a set of polarities into a play of diversities, 'bringing the god to life through us'" (*Becoming Divine*, 272). She is quoting from Luce Irigaray, *An Ethics of Sexual Difference*, trans. Carolyn Burke and Gillian C. Gill (Ithaca, NY: Cornell University Press, 1993), 144. For examples of this rejection, Achtemeier cites Virginia Ramey Mollenkott, *The Divine Feminine: The Biblical Image of God as Female* (New York: Crossroad, 1983), and Zsuzsanna E. Budapest, "Self-Blessing Ritual," in *Womanspirit Rising: A Feminist Reader in Religion*, ed. Carol P. Christ and Judith Plaskow (San Francisco: Harper & Row, 1979), 271–72, in "Exchanging God for 'No Gods': A Discussion of Female Language for God," in *Speaking the Christian God: The Holy Trinity and the Challenge of Feminism*, ed. Alvin F. Kimel Jr. (Grand Rapids: Eerdmans, 1992), 9.

15. Achtemeier, "Exchanging God for 'No Gods,'" 9.

16. Jantzen connects an acceptance of pantheism with a rejection of masculine superiority (*Becoming Divine*, 266–68). I counter that the incarnation threatens much of the "binary dualism" her project seeks to dismantle, while retaining God's sovereignty over creation.

distinguishes biblical religion from all others."[17] For Mankowski as well, "the clay is not the same stuff as the potter but outside him and wholly passive to him, similarly YHWH's people is not split off from YHWH and does not issue from him."[18] Fathers cause a child but do not grow a child in their bodies. So too, God causes creation, but creation did not proceed from the body of God like a child is birthed from its mother. Precisely the opposite, creation stands distinct from God on the other side of an infinite qualitative divide.

Although genetics makes this common knowledge today, as noted previously, even the ancients believed that both male and female contributed *something* from their bodies for the issuance of a new human. Either both contributed seed or only the male contributed seed to the female blood, but no matter the theory, the male contributed *something from his body*.[19]

Speaking of God as "Father," however, when *based on the analogy of human procreation, ancient or modern*, falls prey to the very same mistakes. If human procreation is the lens, then "father" language is just as susceptible to blurring of the Creator/creation distinction as is "mother" language. The Scriptural witness, the theological tradition, and modern science affirm that God does not create like men procreate. Affirming the distinction between God the Creator and creation is a vital tenet of both Judaism and Christianity. (And this is what makes the incarnation *so arresting!*) The descriptions of God as Creator throughout Israel's Scriptures and the New Testament make a sharp distinction between God and the creation such that it would be incorrect to describe creation coming forth from God.[20] The Christian tradition departed

17. Achtemeier, "Exchanging God for 'No Gods,'" 8.

18. Mankowski, "Gender of Israel's God," 44.

19. In his introduction to Aristotle's *Generation of Animals*, A. L. Peck comments, "With regard to his famous doctrine that the male supplies the Form and the female the Matter of the embryo, some misunderstanding may easily arise . . . consider the 'residue' contributed by the male. Aristotle . . . held that Form is not normally found apart from Matter (i.e., body) of some sort, . . . something corporeal must be supplied by the male as well as Form, and this is of course the substance which carries the potential form. . . . Hence it is clear that fundamentally the contributions of both parents in generation are identical; both are potentially a living animal of a certain kind." See Aristotle, *Generation of Animals*, trans. A. L. Peck, Loeb Classical Library (Cambridge: Harvard University Press, 1942), xiii–vi.

20. God's act of creation is not analogous to female participation in the development of new life. I grant, however, that the male/female distinction with regard to *pregnancy* does slot God's role as like that of the man and not the woman in that God stands distinct from creation as a

from the creation narratives of the Greeks to assert that creation was not on-tologically necessary, it was not an emanation from God; instead, "they made being—the existence of the world, existent things—*a product of freedom.*"[21] Thinkers such as Gregory of Nazianzus distinguished God from creation be-cause God created freely out of love not as an emanation of God's "'nature' or by 'essence.'"[22] Conservative theologian Donald Bloesch similarly summarizes the Christian doctrine of creation in this way: "God did not create the world from pre-existing 'matter' or out of God's own divine substance; creation is made, not born."[23] The difference between men and God should be obvious. Very different from God's act of creation, and actually quite similar to wom-en's role in procreation, men issue forth their offspring *from their bodies,* and their offspring shares *in their substance.* They contribute something from their own bodies to create new life. With regard to *conception* of life, then, God is no more like the male than the female because creation does not issue forth from God.

The converse is also true and provides the third and final reason this argu-mentation is faulty. Males do not procreate like God creates. Men always need a partner to procreate, but God did not need a partner to create.[24] Neverthe-less, Mankowski argues that God's fatherhood remains masculine because it is "seen by the Old Testament as a pure and sovereign act of divine will, di-vorced from any external limitation or constraint, including that of a coexistent female consort into which his seed is implanted." He goes on, "The lack of a correlative maternal contribution to YHWH's fatherhood does not make itself felt because there is nothing outside of God's will to be contributed." God's

---

man stands distinct from the fetus during pregnancy. I will speak more about this distinction in the following section.

21. John D. Zizioulas, *Being as Communion: Studies in Personhood and the Church* (London: Darton, Longman & Todd, 1985), 39.

22. Gregory of Nazianzus, *Orations* 38.7 (*Nicene and Post-Nicene Fathers*, Series 2, 7:346–47).

23. Bloesch, *Battle for the Trinity,* 29.

24. In his discussion of the creation of the first human, Karl Barth captures the difference well when he distinguishes God's creation from that of male procreation, beginning even with Adam: "He [Adam] cannot himself divest himself of this part or member of his body. He can-not himself produce woman of himself, not even in the way in which he will afterwards beget" (*Church Dogmatics* III/1, ed. G. W. Bromiley and T. F. Torrance, trans. J. W. Edwards et al. [Lon-don: T&T Clark, 2004], §41.3, p. 296).

complete independence is, for Mankowski, a sign of paternity: "his people are the work of his hands, that is, of his intelligent will. The image does not invite curiosity about a mother or feminine contributor to the process of creation; it is complete in itself." Mankowski asserts that fatherhood imagery should be preeminent because it, and the version of rogue and powerful masculinity incumbent with it, fittingly captures the creative activity of God. No matter what other pictures are employed in the Scriptures of Israel, the masculine image should dominate: "God is tender and compassionate but these qualities do not threaten his sovereign masculinity."[25] For humans though, masculinity is not communicated by male independence in procreation. Such a communication is a natural impossibility. Males cannot procreate on their own. This third and final argument also fails.

It is true that God's interaction with creation is not motherly. Neither, though, is it fatherly. Creation provides no justification for addressing God as "Father." God cannot be called "Father" based on any comparison to human procreation, for God does not create like men, and men do not procreate like God. Men do not cause new life either independently or more so than women. Instead, they must partner—equally—with women to procreate. The analogy from human conception offers nothing similar between men and God. Moreover, a masculine concept of divine creation does no better in avoiding the problems associated with a feminine conception of God. Neither men nor women procreate via an act separated from their own bodies. Instead, men cause their decedents through semen that issues forth from their bodies. A dangerously close association between creation and God adheres to human fathers just as it does to human mothers. How God creates is nothing like how women or men procreate, and so creation offers no justification for a masculine view of God.

The Son

Christian tradition widely agrees that God the Father's relationship with Jesus Christ, the Son, first and foremost motivates paternal language in Christian theology.[26] Followers of Christ relate to God as Father as they do because of

25. Mankowski, "Gender of Israel's God," 40, 41, 44, 58.
26. Gregory of Nyssa, *Against Eunomius* 1.296–298: "The Son's generation is defined solely

the eternal relationship between God and the Son; along with the Holy Spirit, such a relationship constitutes the triune God's eternal being. As the tradition has envisioned the eternal begetting of the Son, it has deemed *both* fatherly and motherly language and processes as fitting descriptions of a mystery no human language could ever fully describe. For example, Clement of Alexandria portrays the Logos as the breast of the Father, thereby casting the first person maternally.²⁷ Gregory of Nyssa envisioned the first person as both the Father and the Mother of the bridegroom.²⁸ The Chalcedonian Definition says that

in terms of relationship with the Father: The Lord was not created [ἐκτίσθη], but came forth [ἐξῆλθε] from the Father, as the Divine Word himself in person attests in the Gospel, by that ineffable and inexplicable manner of his generation [γεννήσεως] or coming-forth [ἐξόδου]. What truer witness could be found than the voice of the Lord, who throughout the Gospel calls his own true Father 'Father' and not 'Creator' [κτίστην] and refers to himself not as 'work of God' but as 'Son of God'?" (trans. Stuart G. Hall in *Gregory of Nyssa: Contra Eunomium I; An English Translation with Supporting Studies*, ed. Miguel Brugarolas [Leiden, Brill, 2018], 126).

Nonna Verna Harrison comments that the language of Scripture indicates that the Son's generation from God the Father and Mary "share[s] the essential character of generation as such, that is coming forth from another in a way that involves sharing the other's nature and remaining in communion with it" ("Gender, Generation, and Virginity," *Journal of Theological Studies* 47 [1996]: 42).

27. *Christ the Educator* 3.12 (*Ante-Nicene Fathers* 2:296). See discussion of this theme in Clement in Verna Harrison, "The Breast of the Father," in *Feminism and Theology*, ed. J. M. Soskice and D. Lipton (Oxford: Oxford University Press), 327–32. She concludes, "Here Christ's flesh and blood are the milk, the Logos is the breast, and the breast belongs to God the Father, who proves to be the ultimate source of the milk and thus the ultimate mother" (331).

28. "Now no one who has given thought to the way we talk about God is going to be over precise about the sense of the name—that 'mother' is mentioned instead of 'father,' for he will gather the same meaning from either term. For the Divine is neither male nor female. (How, after all, could any such thing be conceived in the case of Deity, when this condition is not permanent even for us human beings, but when we all become one in Christ, we put off the signs of this difference along with the whole of the old humanity?) For this reason, every name we turn up is of the same adequacy for purposes of pointing to the unutterable Nature, since neither 'male' nor 'female' defiles the meaning of the inviolate Nature. Hence in the Gospel a father is said to give a marriage feast for a son, while the prophet addresses God, saying, 'You have put a crown of precious stone on his head' and then asserts that the crown was put on the Bridegroom's head by his mother. So there is one wedding feast, and the Bride is one, and the crown is placed on the head of the Bridegroom by one agent. Hence it makes no difference whether God calls the Only Begotten 'Son of God' or 'Son of his love' (Col 1:13), as Paul has it, since whichever name is used it is one Power who escorts the Bridegroom to our marriage." See

the Son is "begotten before the ages from the Father in his divinity," the word "begotten" (γεννηθέντα [gennēthenta]) capturing the procreative act of either the male or female parent.[29] The Eleventh Synod of Toledo named the gendered fullness of begetting in 675: "We confess and believe . . . neither from nothing, nor from any other substance, but from the womb of the Father, that is, from his substance, we must believe that the Son was begotten or born."[30] The Father begets the Son via a womb. From the medieval period, although he was wrong about the mechanics, Aquinas recognized that both men and women contributed to conception; with that knowledge, he says of the begetting of the Son, "the things which belong distinctly to the father or to the mother in fleshly generation, in the generation of the Word are all attributed to the Father by Sacred scripture: for the Father is said not only 'to give life to the Son' (John 5:26) but also 'to conceive and to bring forth.'"[31] The patristic tradition displays a gendered breadth, rather than gendered exclusivity, in the way in which the authors discuss the eternal begetting of God.

More recent theologians continue to affirm this multivalent way of describing the eternal relationship of the Father and Son. Jürgen Moltmann states, "A father who both begets and gives birth to his Son is no mere male father. He is a motherly father. He is the motherly father of his only born Son and at the same time the fatherly father of his only begotten Son." He calls these affirmations

---

Gregory of Nyssa, Homilies on the Song of Songs, trans. with introduction and notes by Richard A. Norris Jr. (Atlanta: Society of Biblical Literature, 2012), 225. I disagree with his assessment of the elimination of sex for humans in the eschaton, but his statements on the nonsexed nature of God show my argument's alignment with tradition. See discussion in Harrison, "Gender, Generation, and Virginity," 38–68.

29. Jaroslav Pelikan and Valerie R. Hotchkiss, eds., Creeds and Confessions of Faith in the Christian Tradition, vol. 1 (New Haven: Yale University Press, 2003), 180–81. Harrison comments, "In classical and Christian Greek generally, γέννησις names the engendering of offspring by either a male or a female parent, so with a father as subject it is usually translated begetting, but in the case of a mother it is often rendered bearing or giving birth" ("Gender, Generation, and Virginity," 38). See "γεννάω" (gennaō) and "γέννησις" (gennēsis) in G. W. H. Lampe, ed., A Patristic Greek Lexicon (Oxford: Clarendon, 1961), 311–12.

30. Discussed in Janet Martin Soskice, "Can a Feminist Call God Father?," in Kimel, Speaking the Christian God, 93. For the text, see Pelikan and Hotchkiss, Creeds and Confessions, 716.

31. J. A. DiNoia, "Knowing and Naming the Triune God: The Grammar of Trinitarian Confession," in Kimel, Speaking the Christian God, 187, quoting Aquinas, Summa Contra Gentiles 4.11.19 (O'Neill).

a "radical denial of patriarchal monotheism."[32] It is upheld as well by Catholic theology in the encyclical *Mulieris Dignitatem*. About the "mystery of the eternal 'generating,'" John Paul II states, "Thus every element of human generation which is proper to man, and every element which is proper to woman, namely human '*fatherhood*' and '*motherhood*,' bears within itself a likeness to, or analogy with the divine 'generating' and with that 'fatherhood' which in God is 'totally different.'"[33] Kathryn Tanner notes, "The potential for gender-bending use of gendered imagery—a Father with a womb—might very well present the best hope for avoiding theological reinforcement of male privilege."[34] Hence, exclusive use of paternal language for God cannot be justified on what Scripture and the ancient and widespread theological tradition point to concerning the eternally begotten relationship in God. Addressing the personal and eternal divine source of the Son as "Parent" rather than "Father" may more correctly name this relationship.

The Son's Siblings

This attribution is confirmed by Scripture and tradition's recognition that God acts toward the Son's community, the many sons and daughters, in ways described as both fatherly and motherly. Feminine images for the God of Israel are well known.[35] For example, God "nursed" Israel (Isa 49:15), and God comforts Israel as a mother would (Isa 66:12–13). Standing alongside the many masculine descriptions, the text depicts the God of Israel as personal and relational, in ways similar to fathers and mothers, without appearing as a fully

32. Jürgen Moltmann, "The Motherly Father: Is Trinitarian Patripassianism Replacing Theological Patriarchalism?," in *God as Father?*, ed. Johann Baptist Metz, Edward Schillebeeckx, and Marcus Lefébure, trans. G. W. S. Knowles (Edinburgh: T&T Clark; New York: Seabury, 1981), 53.

33. John Paul II, "Mulieris Dignitatem: Apostolic Letter of the Supreme Pontiff John Paul II on the Dignity and Vocation of Women on the Occasion of the Marian Year" (3.8), The Holy See, https://www.vatican.va/content/john-paul-ii/en/apost_letters/1988/documents/hf_jp-ii_apl_19880815_mulieris-dignitatem.html.

34. Kathryn Tanner, *Christ the Key*, Current Issues in Theology (Cambridge: Cambridge University Press, 2010), 215. See also Sarah Coakley's treatment of Christian art that both affirms and resists a crude male anthropomorphism for God the Father (*God, Sexuality, and the Self: An Essay 'On the Trinity'* [Cambridge: Cambridge University Press, 2013], 190–265).

35. See L. Juliana M. Claassens, *Mourner, Mother, Midwife: Reimagining God's Delivering Presence in the Old Testament* (Louisville: Westminster John Knox, 2012).

bisexual being, since God as God transcends that category.[36] The motherly portrayals of God continue into the New Testament.[37] God is the woman searching for the lost coin (Luke 15:8–10), and Jesus as the Son of God describes himself as the mother hen who longs to gather Jerusalem under her wings (Matt 23:37 // Luke 13:34). Julian of Norwich's rich and multivalent images of all three triune persons as Father and Mother attest to this allowance,[38] an "excess" of gender Janet Soskice says "keeps in place the symbols of desire, fecundity, and parental love, while destabilizing any over-literalistic reading."[39] For Soskice, Gen 1:27 indicates that when humans are in relationship with God, they are in relationship with "the Other, who is both maternal and paternal."[40] God treats creation, and humans in particular, in ways typically associated with both fathers and mothers. The result is that, in full alignment with the biblical text, God may be called upon metaphorically as Father just as God may be addressed metaphorically as Mother.[41]

God is the source of life, but neither in relationship with creation nor with the Son and the Son's siblings are God's actions more like those of men rather

---

36. Mark Smith summarizes Israel's perception of their God: "the male language for Yahweh stood in tension both with less anthropomorphic descriptions for the deity and with metaphors occasionally including female imagery or comparing it with male imagery. This state of affairs resembles neither a Greek philosophical notion of Deity as nonsexual Being nor some type of divine bisexuality. Rather Israelite society perceived Yahweh primarily as a god, although Yahweh was viewed also as embodying traits or values expressed by various gendered metaphors and as transcending such particular renderings" (*The Early History of God: Yahweh and the Other Deities in Ancient Israel*, 2nd ed., The Biblical Resource Series [Grand Rapids: Eerdmans, 2002], 103).

37. Paul sets this imagery for himself as well. See Beverly Roberts Gaventa, *Our Mother Saint Paul* (Louisville: Westminster John Knox, 2007).

38. See Julian of Norwich, *Showings: Authoritative Text, Contexts, Criticism*, ed. Denise Nowakowski Baker (New York: Norton, 2005). Geoffrey Wainwright comments, "Julian of Norwich, when speaking of the maternal characteristics of God manifested in Christ, should have in mind the attitudes and acts of the Godhead as such *toward us*—'*our* Mother'" ("Trinitarian Worship," in Kimel, *Speaking the Christian God*, 216).

39. Janet Martin Soskice, *The Kindness of God: Metaphor, Gender, and Religious Language* (Oxford: Oxford University Press, 2008), 115.

40. "Can a Feminist Call God Father?," 94. Stanley J. Grenz agrees: "God's relationship to creation—even the matter in which God nurtures God's people—takes on both masculine and feminine dimensions . . . the masculine does not exhaust the divine reality" ("Is God Sexual?," in Kimel, *This Is My Name Forever*, 203).

41. DiNoia, "Knowing and Naming the Triune God," 185.

than women. With regard to creation, God is God and not human; and, hence, God does not create in a way similar to the process by which either a woman *or a man* conceives life. With regard to the Son, God begets in a way that both male and female procreation attest to that eternal relationship. With regard to the many followers of the Son, they may, in ways faithful to the text and tradition, imagine their relationship with God as that with a father or a mother. God the Father begets the Son and treats the many children in ways *similar to* the way a man and woman conceive and care for life. Neither the doctrine of creation nor the Trinity nor salvation necessitate exclusively masculine paternal language for the first person. In fact, they all prohibit it.

God the Father as the Sovereign Initiator

If life offers no justification for paternal language for God, then possibly the masculine vision of God finds support in a commitment to males as initiating leaders. Because some believe that men should lead and initiate in relationships, they argue that it is more proper to think of God, who is the most sovereign and the first mover, as masculine. This line of argument appears in each of the major branches of the Christian church.

Orthodox theologian Alexander Schmemann in his *For the Life of the World* casts the divine-human relationship as broadly as possible. In response to God, all "creation is female in its acceptance and response."[42] If all creation is cast as the female, that suggests then that God is best viewed as "the male" to whom humanity responds. Elisabeth Behr-Sigel provides another example of an Orthodox thinker who, though she recognizes the complexity of gender on the anthropological side,[43] at times, falls prey to this masculine picture of God.

42. Alexander Schmemann, *For the Life of the World: Sacraments and Orthodoxy* (Crestwood, NY: St. Vladimir's Seminary Press, 2004), 85.

43. She argues that humans exist on a spectrum: "every human person is in reality a composite being having either a masculine or feminine dominance which has been more or less accentuated, formed or deformed by education and cultural influences." See Elisabeth Behr-Sigel, *The Ministry of Women in the Church*, trans. Steven Bigham (Crestwood, NY: St. Vladimir's Seminary Press, 1991), 131. She also frequently calls attention to the problems with sexism and oppressive gender roles. For an insightful analysis of her life and work see Sarah Hinlicky Wilson, *Woman, Women and the Priesthood in the Trinitarian Theology of Elisabeth Behr-Sigel* (New York: Bloomsbury T&T Clark, 2013).

When focusing on the relationship between humans and God, she suggests that the "feminine" is a spiritual principle and basic category of human existence. She defines "femininity" in this way: "In their relation to God the source and giver of life all persons and mankind in general are called upon to adopt an attitude of openness and altruistic self-abandonment which makes them transparent to the radiance of the Other."[44] And again, "we are all called, men and women, to a 'feminine' attitude of welcoming grace, of giving and offering ourselves so that the new man, the total Christ, *totus Christus*, can be born in the Spirit in each one of us and in all of us together in the Church."[45] She resists gender stereotypes for humans but in some of her writings inscribes them for humans in relationship with a male-like God.

Catholic scholar Hans Urs von Balthasar argues that this is the relationship God has with the church: "The Church is primarily feminine because her primary, all-encompassing truth is her ontological gratitude, which both receives the gift and passes it on. And the masculine office, which has to represent the true giver, the Lord of the Church (albeit within the Church's feminine receptivity), is instituted in her only to prevent her from forgetting this primary reality, to ensure that she will always remain a receiver and never become self-assertive possessor and user."[46] The latter phrase raises another element to the concern of a masculine God. Certainly, Christians affirm that God is Lord of the church and is glorified by the church, but the negative connotations of these terms "possessor and user" show the dangerous slippage that can happen when God is cast as the male. Balthasar colors God intentionally and positively as the giving male but, in introducing what the feminine church cannot be, raises concern that the masculine God could be cast as the "user." Catholic theologian Tina Beattie agrees that the theme is widespread in her tradition: "masculinity symbolizes God and femininity symbolizes the creature," or put differently, "masculinity defines godliness and femininity defines creatureliness."[47] Beattie concludes that Catholic theology and practice suggests "masculinity as a non-negotiable feature of God's fatherhood."[48]

44. Behr-Sigel, *Ministry of Women*, 131, 212.
45. Behr-Sigel, *Ministry of Women*, 24.
46. Hans Urs von Balthasar and Joseph Cardinal Ratzinger, *Mary: The Church at the Source*, trans. Adrian Walker (San Francisco: Ignatius, 1997), 140.
47. Tina Beattie, *God's Mother, Eve's Advocate: A Marian Narrative of Women's Salvation* (London: Continuum, 2002), 73, 76.
48. Beattie, *God's Mother, Eve's Advocate*, 81.

Anglican C. S. Lewis argues that male and female are not interchangeable; they are the "live and awful shadows of realities utterly beyond our control and largely beyond our direct knowledge." These realities are "dealing with us."[49] On the anthropological level, I, too, assert the goodness in the created givenness of male and female, but his arguments about humans are grounded in a particular conception of God. In *That Hideous Strength*, the character Ransom speaks to this, saying that there exists "a masculine none of us can escape. What is above and beyond all things is so masculine that we are all feminine in relation to it."[50] All humans are feminine in relationship to an unassailably masculine God. This was affirmed in the late 1980s by the Church of England: "In terms of our relationship to God we are essentially 'female-like' and feminine and he is 'male-like' and masculine. God always has the initiative, and our duty is to respond. Because, psychologically and symbolically and, to an important extent, biologically, taking the initiative is male, it was therefore appropriate that the Word was incarnate as a male human being and not as a female human being. The particularity of maleness assumed in the incarnation and taken into the Godhead signifies divine initiative."[51] In the reprinted edition of *Recovering Biblical Manhood and Womanhood*, John M. Frame argues that the "overwhelming preponderance of imagery" for God is male because "Scripture wants us to think of God as Lord, and lordship, in Scripture, always connotes authority." It is males who hold authority, so "unisex or female language for God is wrongheaded."[52] He immediately acknowledges that the sub-

49. C. S. Lewis, "Priestesses in the Church," in *God in the Dock*, ed. Walter Hooper (Grand Rapids: Eerdmans, 2014), 262.

50. C. S. Lewis, *That Hideous Strength* (New York: Scribner, 2003), 312.

51. Central Board of Finance of the Church of England, *The Ordination of Women to the Priesthood: A Second Report by the House of Bishops of the General Synod of the Church of England* (London: General Synod of the Church of England, 1988), 27. A stark version of this appears in the writings of Protestant scholar Thomas Schmidt, who argues that "revelation from heaven to earth could be read as a cosmic barrier penetration, a 'phallocentrism' in the gospel, evidence that 'patriarchalism' of the Gospel narrative is deeper than accommodation to the first century expectations of a male messiah" ("The Christological Phallicy in the Gospels," in Kimel, *This Is My Name Forever*, 105). It is not just Jesus, the male Messiah, but God from above who breaks through to creation, in Schmidt's words, "penetrates," setting all humanity in "feminine" relationship with a masculinized God.

52. John M. Frame, "Male and Female in the Image of God," in *Recovering Biblical Manhood and Womanhood: A Response to Evangelical Feminism*, ed. Wayne Grudem and John Piper (Wheaton, IL: Crossway, 2006), 229–30.

mission of women also images God who is not too proud to be our "helper," but God is still the "Lord," who is preponderantly and better imaged with male language.

These arguments provide examples of anthropological projectionism. God the Father as the masculine sovereign initiation is also built upon debated premises. Not all the faithful interpret the biblical text to demand that only men should lead. Hence to demand that God's sovereign initiation be described as masculine is to assume a consensus that does not exist.

Nowhere is this assumption more prominent than in the interpretation of Mary's story. The narrative of the incarnation is frequently used to reinforce these masculine conceptions of God. Mary stands for "feminine" receptivity to the initiating "masculine" God.[53] As argued in the previous chapter, the scriptural account of the incarnation does not demand and in fact rejects that these actions be so gendered. The fulcrum between Mary and God, and hence creation and God, need not be viewed as the meeting between feminine and masculine, emphasizing motherhood and a masculine idea of initiation, but is more aptly described as the meeting between an insufficient human and an all-sufficient God. The binary is not male-female or masculine-feminine but Creator and creature.[54]

Moreover, the masculine projectionism cataloged here is of a particularly dangerous kind. A masculinized God unleashes false and, dare I say, even heretical theology. Masculinizing God's transcendent initiation results in a particular blasphemy. To say that God initiates and that humans' role is to respond, *and that these are masculine and feminine actions*, posits God as an aggressive sexual human male. In no other relationship is initiation *necessarily* the role of the male. Women may (even if some think it untoward) cast the vision

53. Sarah Jane Boss describes how the dyad of male/self/master/culture/intellect, on the one hand, and female/other/subordinate/nature/feeling, on the other, has had a bearing on the understanding of God and the Virgin Mary. Mary can signify creation, which can be subordinated to the God who is like a male (*Empress and Handmaid: Nature and Gender in the Cult of the Virgin Mary* [London: Cassell, 2000], 170).

54. Although she speaks of the "masculine" divine, Humphrey then switches to the language of "Creature" and "Creator" in the next sentence, showing that "masculine" and "feminine" categories are not the only way to describe God's relationship with humanity. See Edith M. Humphrey, *Further Up and Further In: Orthodox Conversations with C. S. Lewis on Scripture and Theology* (Crestwood, NY: St. Vladimir's Seminary Press, 2017), 261.

and take the lead in public and private spheres: in business, politics, groups of friends, or in families. Even in courtship, and sex, women may initiate the relationship or the encounter just as men can. One may even view heterosexual genital intercourse as the woman enveloping the man. The only interchange between men and women in which men must initiate and women must receive is forcible genital intercourse. Rape by a man of a woman is the only time when initiation must be from the male. Theologians who assert that God's initiation is masculine have embraced what Israel's Scriptures, the New Testament, and conciliar Christianity adamantly denies: the crude male sexualization of God. Even worse, this theory assumes what the evangelists worked so hard to deny: rape by a male god.

One can, and should, in my opinion, affirm with Scripture and the orthodox tradition that God is the transcendent initiator. One need not and, as these problems attest, should not deem divine transcendent initiation as more similar to male acts than female. The initiation is from the Creator to the creature, not from male to female or even masculine to feminine. In other words, one can affirm the triune God's supremacy without calling that masculinity.[55]

Those interlocutors comfortable with masculine language for God may counter that this gendered framework is more poetry than science, the arena of symbol rather than reality. Masculinity, as gender studies has taught, is "something one achieves rather than a gender into which one is born."[56] Possibly, anyone could be masculine like the masculine God.

As is evident, however, this symbolism is not utilized in such a fluid and

---

55. Jantzen argues for a similar move with regard to language: "Although in western modernity [semiotic and the symbolic] have been conceptually linked with the feminine and masculine respectively, this is not a necessary or 'natural' linkage, but one which can be subverted" (*Becoming Divine*, 203). More pointedly, this appears in her engagement with Lacan and his description of language. Building upon Freud, he argued that all language is masculine, oriented to the ultimate signifier of desire, the "Phallus." Jantzen, in order to challenge the "necessary maleness of language and subjectivity," counters, "there is no need to construe desire in strictly masculine terms: though he shudders at the very idea, Lacan could have used 'breast' as easily as 'Phallus' to designate desire as such." He has, she says, "helped himself . . . to the master's tools, to language, and to women, but he has done so by theft and by decree, not by entitlement" (*Becoming Divine*, 51). I, too, assert that the masculinization of God is neither a necessity nor an entitlement.

56. Colleen M. Conway, "Masculinity Studies," in *The Oxford Handbook of New Testament, Gender, and Sexuality*, ed. Benjamin H. Dunning (Oxford: Oxford University Press, 2019), 79.

inclusive way. This sampling of theologically conservative theologians, represented across the major traditions, categorizes God's transcendence, including God's act of creation and sovereign initiative, as masculinity most naturally achievable by men. In this widespread presentation, God is acting in ways more similar to the actions of men than of women. The assertion that God is more masculine than feminine is based upon biological or cultural exigencies (or hopes) that privilege males over females. Their presentation is not crude, the eternal God is not a grand male in the sky, but at the same time, it is consistently true that men by virtue of their bodies or societal roles are *more* like God. It should not be surprising that the critique can still arise that much theology has failed to "undo the masculinity of God."[57] This argument for "Father" language does not acknowledge God's sole sovereignty on the throne of the universe and prevent humans—especially males—from putting themselves on it.

Dangerous Arguments

Not only does the argument for a masculinized God the Father lack scientific, exegetical, and doctrinal support, but it also wreaks havoc. The problems with this theological framework run deeper than any progressive allergy to inequality. When God's transcendence is masculinized, as God is blasphemed, humans are damaged.

When God's transcendence is deemed "masculine," all humans suffer.[58] Instead of all standing in the confidence of being in the image of God, some are invited to identify with and represent God more naturally than others.[59] When God imagined to be male-like enters into relationship with humanity who takes a feminized role, then this gendered divine(male)-human(female) relationship impacts how one views all human males and females. Linn Marie Tonstad puts it this way: "If the fundamental difference between male and female analogically encodes the God-world relation, then the difference be-

57. Soskice, *Kindness of God*, 16.

58. Jantzen names some of the same consequences of a masculine God: men domineering women, women's agency thwarted, and men's fears and insecurities flamed (*Becoming Divine*, 173).

59. Behr-Sigel wonders, "Is it not dangerous to turn the masculine and the feminine principles into personal realities to the detriment of the basic category of *person* as the image of God in man (*anthropos*)?" (*Ministry of Women*, 209).

tween male and females becomes a difference of unequals."[60] If God is like a male in relationship with the world who is like a female, and God is clearly superior to the world, then that image suggests that males are superior to females. When women are considered less like God, they cannot be fully human, because they cannot bear the *imago Dei* in the same way as do men. At the same time, what a burden this association between God and masculinity places upon men, who fall prey either to despair over their failure to rise to this divine-like superior position or to the lust for power itself over women and less manly men.[61]

Those who argue for, or assume, a male-like first person of the Trinity fall short of the truth and goodness of the God revealed in the biblical text. God as both Creator and sovereign resists masculinization. When that resistance is ignored, great harm comes to humans, females as well as males. A theological assumption that is both false and damaging should be put to rest.

God Talk

Nevertheless, I still assert that it is both right and good to call God "Father." Many and serious are the problems with paternal language for God, leading some to advocate for the dismissal of this theological language. In light of that,

---

60. Linn Marie Tonstad, *God and Difference: The Trinity, Sexuality, and the Transformation of Finitude* (New York: Routledge, 2016), 4.

61. Howard Eilberg-Swartz notices the same struggle: "A masculine god, I suggest, is a kind of male beauty image, an image of male perfection against which men measure themselves and in terms of which they fall short" (*God's Phallus: And Other Problems for Men and Monotheism* [Boston: Beacon, 1994], 17). He also explores other challenges for men, including homoeroticism/the feminization of men and the pressure to procreate. Studies on masculinity highlight the threat that men in the ancient world could slip into femininity. See Maud W. Gleason, *Making Men: Sophists and Self-Presentation in Ancient Rome* (Princeton: Princeton University Press, 1995), and Erik Gunderson, *Staging Masculinity: The Rhetoric of Performance in the Roman World* (Ann Arbor: University of Michigan Press, 2000). Wilson states it this way: "According to elite Greek and Roman authors, however, not all men were situated at the top of this vertical axis of power, for not all biologically marked males qualified as 'true,' or 'manly,' men. Simply having the necessary anatomical features did not guarantee that a specifically sexed man would have been considered a true man in the ancient world. Instead, true men were those of high social status who also embodied the requisite 'manly' characteristics" (*Unmanly Men*, 41).

the conclusion of this chapter may take readers by surprise. Having argued
that Christian doctrine, and, centrally, the incarnation, offers no support for
the belief that God is male or even masculine, I do argue that it is fitting to
address God as "Father." In addition to reviewing the common and general
arguments in support for this paternal terminology, I offer a fresh presentation
of the particular benefits of this language for *women*. No other name for God
grants women such value in the Christian story.

Many theologians agree that this term, "Father," joined with Son and Holy
Spirit, as opposed to functionally cast suggestions like Creator, Redeemer,
Sustainer, retains the personal nature of God.[62] Although the divine persons
are not the same as human persons, the descriptions and actions of Father,
Son, and Holy Spirit in Scripture are undeniably *personable*,[63] both in relation
to one another and in relation to creation.[64] If humanity ceases to relate to a
personal God, it ceases to relate to the Christian God.[65]

Familial language asserts more, however, than the personal nature of God;
it specifies the *type* of relationship that exists. The relations in God are mutually
dependent. Barth states it this way: "The Christian God is not, never has been,

62. Recognizing that the tradition has not recognized God as the best "person" in the same class
as all other persons—God is the "Being beyond all being"—nonetheless, God is personal. Orthodox
theologian Christos Yannaras states it this way: "We do not know what God is in his Essence, but we
do know the mode of his existence. God is a personal existence, three specific personal existences
of whose personal difference the Christ has direct historical experience" (*Elements of Faith*, 18, 29).

63. Tonstad states, "As characters or actors the narrated relationships between the persons
cannot help but generate thickly personal impressions" (*God and Difference*, 228).

64. See Matthew W. Bates, *The Birth of the Trinity: Jesus, God, and Spirit in New Testament
and Early Christian Interpretations of the Old Testament* (Oxford: Oxford University Press, 2015),
and Madison N. Pierce, *Divine Discourse in the Epistle to the Hebrews: The Recontextualization
of Spoken Quotations of Scripture*, Society for New Testament Studies Monograph Series 178
(Cambridge: Cambridge University Press, 2020), for ways in which divine speech in the New
Testament resulted in Trinitarian formulations in the early church. Thomas F. Torrance states,
"the trinitarian formula—Father, Son, and Holy Spirit—gives expression to God's *personal self-
revelation*, one in which, what he is toward us in the persons of the Father, the Son, and the
Holy Spirit, he is inherently and eternally in himself, three persons in one divine being" ("The
Christian Apprehension of God the Father," in Kimel, *Speaking the Christian God*, 141).

65. "A non-personalist theology would turn God into a natural object and would have noth-
ing to do with the living God of the Bible and the worshipping Church" (John D. Zizioulas,
Communion and Otherness: Further Studies in Personhood and the Church, ed. Paul McPartlan
[London: T&T Clark, 2006], 29).

and never will be a solitary God."[66] One cannot be a parent until one has a child. Perhaps one could say something similar about the mutual dependence between other relations like teacher and student or leader and follower, but these do not convey the divine cost inherent in the gospel message: "For God so loved the world, that he gave his only begotten Son" (John 3:16). A teacher giving up a student or a deity giving up a prophet pales in comparison to the pathos of a parent giving up a child.[67]

Moreover, no other picture conveys the necessary sameness yet distinction as is present in a familial framework. A parent and child are related and therefore, though they are distinct beings, share many things in common. Familial language, built upon a triune foundation, also differentiates the Son from creation. God made (ποίησις [*poiēsis*]) creation; but the Son is begotten (γέννηθεις [*gennētheis*]), not made. Hence this language connects the Son to God at the same time that it distinguishes the Son from all created things as the only one who has come from God.[68] Unlike creation, the Son *does* come from the very being of God. Parental language, therefore, *is* fitting for this relationship. God has given a signpost for it. In the very process of life in which all humans participate, namely, birth, they are given the embodied picture that points toward the spiritual reality at the very fount of life itself, the begetting of the Son.[69] In the conception and birth of every infant is a beautiful image of the very nature of God.

---

66. *Church Dogmatics*, III/2, ed. G. W. Bromiley and T. F. Torrance, trans. H. Knight et al. (London: T&T Clark, 2001), §45.3, p. 324.

67. Interpreters have raised weighty questions about the picture this paints of God, a Father who would give up a Son, but I counter that the texts and Trinitarian theology displayed by them withstand these critiques. See the appendix.

68. David A. Scott states, "the language of 'begetting' or 'generating' was considered important as contrasted with 'reducing,' which was simply a creation out of nothing by the will of God" ("Creation as Christ: A Problematic Theme in Some Feminist Theology," in Kimel, *Speaking the Christian God*, 245).

69. "A parent's communication of their human nature to their child is but a pale and second reflection of this act" (Scott, "Creation as Christ," 245).

Privileging Paternal Language

Because familial language for the Christian God is theologically beneficial, but masculine conceptions of God are deeply problematic, I must offer a way through the impasse by providing a final argument for continuing and even privileging the practice of addressing God not only as "Parent" but also as "Father."

God does exhibit both masculine and feminine characteristics. The language for God in both Scripture and tradition, however, is not balanced. It tilts overwhelmingly toward the masculine.[70] Patriarchal societies provide explanation, certainly, but many interpreters are unsatisfied with this as the sole reason. In other ways, the texts of Israel and the early Christians push against the grain of accepted norms in the societies in which they were written. Moreover, female, even maternal gods existed, so this, too, was an option.

The answer must lie not only in their society but more importantly in their movement. Christians call God "Father" because, according to the documents of the New Testament, Jesus did so.[71] The tradition appears in the earliest writings of the New Testament, the letters of Paul.[72] If God's fatherhood is not general but defined in relationship with the Son of God Jesus Christ, then Jesus's terminology for God should take precedence.[73] The revelation of God culminating in and confirmed by the incarnation is the reason why followers

70. Humphrey puts it this way: "Why is it that the Bible, while it sometimes uses the feminine imagery for a God who transcends human sexuality, never addresses God in feminine terms?" (*Further Up and Further In*, 269). After an analysis of twenty-two of the female-metaphor passages, David J. A. Clines concludes, "There is not a single instance of female language about the deity in the Hebrew Bible in the sense of language suggesting that the deity is viewed as a female" ("Alleged Female Language about the Deity," *Journal of Biblical Literature* 140 [2021]: 248).

71. Garrett Green states, "When Christians call God 'Father,' it is always shorthand for 'the Father of our Lord Jesus Christ.' In other words, Christians are not referring generally to God as *a* father but rather are addressing him in solidarity with Jesus as '*our* Father.' The meaning of the metaphor is accordingly to be sought in the story of the one whom Jesus calls Father" ("The Gender of God and the Theology of Metaphor," in Kimel, *Speaking the Christian God*, 59).

72. For example, 1 Thess 1:1, 3; 3:11; Gal 1:1; 4:6; Rom 8:15.

73. See Marianne Meye Thompson, *The Promise of the Father: Jesus and God in the New Testament* (Louisville: Westminster John Knox, 2000), 1–34. Ray Anderson notes, "It is this essential core of divine love that the terms *Father* and *Son* are meant to convey. . . . One might also say that God loves as Mother loves Daughter, but then there would be no ontological and semantical link with these terms to the incarnation of God that took place in Jesus the historical person

of Jesus can and do speak of God in the ways that God has given. Athanasius argued, "Therefore it is more pious and more accurate to signify God from the Son and call Him Father, than to name Him from his works and call him Unoriginate . . . the title Father has its significance and its bearing only from the Son."[74] If Christians want to speak of God rightly, they must always start with Jesus. Sarah Coakley says it this way: "We follow Jesus into an exploration of the meaning of 'Fatherhood.'"[75] For Christians, the Word must teach us the meaning of our words.

In the early tradition of the church, theologians built upon Jesus's language to assert that the name "Father" is a name and not an adjective. The divine-name tradition asserts that "Father" is a proper name, revealed in the incarnation and not deduced logically from creation or a characteristic description of God's nature,[76] although the texts portray God as an exemplary Father.[77] The first falls prey to biological error, the second to cultural stereotypes. Instead, "Father" is the name of God the first person of the Trinity as revealed by Jesus

---

who called God his Father" ("The Incarnation of God in Feminist Christology: A Theological Critique," in Kimel, *Speaking the Christian God*, 310).

74. *Orations against the Arians* 1.9.34 (*Nicene and Post-Nicene Fathers*, Series 2, 4:326).

75. Coakley, *God, Sexuality, and the Self*, 326.

76. John D. Zizioulas states, "We can see this in the case of our notion of God as Father, which is where the problem of anthropomorphism most frequently appears. . . . They identify their father with certain attributes: he can do things that they cannot, perhaps, such as protecting or providing for them, and through these attributes the child receives an idea of God . . . where authority is contrasted with freedom, the idea of God is discarded. It has to be put aside because we came to 'know' God on the basis of experiences and attributes that we acquired from our own family and wider relationships" (*Lectures in Christian Dogmatics*, ed. Douglas H. Knight [London: T&T Clark, 2008], 20).

77. Characteristics of any fathers, human or divine, cannot be projected up to God because, as Pseudo-Dionysius the Areopagite states, "the Father and the Son . . . supremely transcend all divine Fatherhood and Sonship. In reality there is no exact likeness between caused and cause, for the caused carry within themselves only such images of their originating sources as are possible for them, whereas the causes themselves are located in a realm transcending the caused" (*On the Divine Names* 2.8; see Pseudo-Dionysius the Areopagite, *The Complete Works*, trans. Colm Luibheid and Paul Rorem, The Classics of Western Spirituality [New York: Paulist, 1987], 64). So also Zizioulas: "God is the particular person whom we may know by the name of 'Father'" (*Lectures in Christian Dogmatics*, xii).

Christ.[78] Because Jesus called God "Father," not only can Christians do so, but they should.

Some let this reasoning for paternal language remain at the level of "Jesus says so." Gerhard O. Forde claims, "There is no exhaustively necessary reason we can cite to show why Jesus should have used this language."[79] Alvin F. Kimel Jr. states, "If the Father is constituted by Jesus Christ's invocation of him, then we can see the impossibility of substituting 'Mother' (or some other variant) as a term of filial address. Perhaps Jesus could have addressed God as his Mother (though cogent reasons might be offered in explanation or support of his choice not to do so), in which case the first person of the Godhead would likewise be constituted as Mother."[80] Kimel does not offer any of those reasons, but I will. If speaking of the paternal God finds no justification from God's relationship with creation or from eternal generation, then the reasons must lie in Jesus's decision to speak in this way.

Many have inferred that it is impossible to retain the traditional language without falling prey to this divine-as-masculine heresy. I offer the incarnation as a way to retain orthodox Christian tradition while at the same time not just avoiding the heresy of divine masculinity and the oppression that so often follows but also dismantling it.

In her essay arguing against employing maternal language for God, Elizabeth Achtemeier perceptively observes, "If God is portrayed in feminine language, the figures of carrying in the womb, of giving birth, of suckling immediately come into play."[81] Earlier I noted that God does not create like men conceive, but God's distinction from creation *is* aptly pictured in the difference between men and women *with regard to pregnancy*. God, like a father, does, stood distinct from creation and did not carry it within the divine being.

That which God did not do to creation, however, God allowed creation to

78. Yannaras clarifies, "In the Gospels, Christ reveals that the fatherhood of God is in principle a *unique* character: it corresponds to the *only* Son, who is the 'beloved' (Matt 3.17), the one in whom the Father 'is well pleased' (Lk 3.22), he whom 'he loved before the foundation of the world' (Jn 17.24)" (*Elements of Faith*, 32).

79. Gerhard O. Forde, "Naming the One Who Is Above Us," in Kimel, *Speaking the Christian God*, 118.

80. Alvin F. Kimel Jr., "The God Who Likes His Name: Holy Trinity, Feminism, and the Language of Faith," in Kimel, *Speaking the Christian God*, 207.

81. Achtemeier, "Exchanging God for 'No Gods,'" 9.

do to him. God was carried in the womb. God was birthed, and God suckled at the breast.

Mary the Mother of God has proven a slippery character in the Christian narrative. For some, she has slipped off the page completely, or at least for most of the year, until it is time to set out her figure in the nativity. For others, she has ascended to such an elevation where no effects trickle down to any other woman.[82] Those who miss her and those who misuse her also forget the true nature of her son and the God whom he reveals. It is not only the Word who teaches us the meaning of our words but also the one who bore the Word. A patriarchal society and the few glimmers of God's fatherhood in the Scriptures of Israel do not fully explain the incarnate Son's linguistic expression of his eternal, personal, and begotten relationship with God. If the eternal relationship was the motivation, Jesus should call God "Father," or "*Mother*," or "Parent" even. It must be the incarnation that narrows the fitting choice for divine address. Jesus does not call God "Mother" because he already has one.[83]

Christians can and should address God, the first person, as "Father" not because God is male and not because God is more masculine than feminine but because God the Father as an expression of the triune will sent forth his Son *born of a woman*. There is no God apart from the one who willed to dwell in the womb of Mary.[84] Jesus of Nazareth, with his form of address for God, born out of his unique experience, reveals who God is.[85] This God is indeed Father.

82. Beattie captures the bitterness of such a reality: "A statue or a picture of the Virgin Mary serves to remind men that once upon a time a woman's body was necessary for the story to begin, but her further creatureliness has no further part to play" (*God's Mother, Eve's Advocate*, 81).

83. Credit for this turn of phrase belongs to my colleague Matthew Milliner with whom I teach a delightful undergraduate course entitled Mary: Mother of God. Although coming from a different perspective, Cynthia Bourgeault makes a similar observation: "As Jesus becomes 'son,' so, inevitably, does God become 'father.' And Mary becomes 'mother.' Within the context of this Trinity, it is inappropriate to refer to God as Mother; such a designation blurs the essential mystery of what has just come to pass" (*The Holy Trinity and the Law of Three: Recovering the Radical Truth at the Heart of Christianity* [Boston: Shambhala, 2013], 157).

84. I'm grateful to Keith Johnson for this beautiful articulation.

85. Yannaras puts it this way: "When Jesus manifests himself as the Son of God, he reveals that 'Father' is the name which expresses in the most profound way the hypostasis of God, what God really *is*: He is the one who begets, a life-giving principle. . . . In the Gospels, Christ reveals that the fatherhood of God has in principle a *unique* character: it corresponds to the *only* Son. . . . We say this, not in order to impose our own logical schema on the truth of God, but in order to

Jesus's language also reveals what Christ followers confess *and do not* confess when they address God as Jesus did. Sarah Coakley had stated that "we follow Jesus into an exploration of the meaning of 'Fatherhood'" but goes on to say that the "Fatherhood" is "beyond all human formulations."[86] I agree that God's fatherhood breaks normal conventions and takes confessors into realms of mystery, but it is not a fatherhood beyond *all* human formulations. The incarnation gives us an entry point to the anchor of that divine language, namely, God's relationship with the Son. God is properly addressed as "Father" not because God's is a "fatherhood beyond all human formulations" but because God, as fathers are, was the cause of a Son. At the same time, the *way* in which God is Father shows God to be different from all other fathers. To approach the same point from another perspective, God is addressed as "Father" because Joseph was not. It is the analogical nature of the language, the differences and the similarity, that make this language fitting. Because the Holy Spirit overshadowed the body of Mary so that she conceived and bore and nursed the Son of God, humanity calls the divine person who gives life to all things the "Father." In that event as recorded in the gospels and confirmed in the tradition, the divine Father is revealed as truly beyond sex and gender. Feminist philosopher Grace Jantzen asks pointedly, "How is it that if God is said on all sides to be beyond all naming, nevertheless language about God is firmly masculine?"[87] The answer, I humbly suggest, is that all God-language is interpreted through the lens of the incarnation. The fatherhood of God revealed in the Son determines the meaning of all gendered language for God. If God the Father is not male here, then God is not male.

Calling God "Father" is fitting language. It should ever be included and even privileged, not just because the tradition did so but also because Jesus did so.[88] Jesus's language for God, Jesus's address, "Abba, Father," asserts the mode of the incarnation. When Christians call God "Father" as he did, they

---

express the historical experience of revelation: The Holy Spirit effects in history the revelation of the Word of God, the Incarnation of the Person of the Word" (*Elements of Faith*, 32–33).

86. Coakley, *God, Sexuality, and the Self*, 326.

87. Jantzen, *Becoming Divine*, 173.

88. Tonstad states, "The designations [by which I understand her to mean "Father," "Son," and "Holy Spirit"] are determined by the economy, since God is as God reveals Godself to be" (*God and Difference*, 229). We call God "Father" because in the incarnation, God the Father sent the Son to be born *for us*.

invoke the revelation of the particular way the Son came. This Father is not male. This Father is not masculine. This Father through the work of the Holy Spirit partnered with one human, a woman, to achieve the salvation of all things. Calling God "Father" proclaims the unparalleled role played by the young Jewish girl named Mary, the Mother of God.

Before returning to her story, the many ministries for which God empowered her, however, I must address the nature of her son. God the Father may not be male, but the text of the New Testament says that Jesus is. Christian thinkers have perceived the triune God in a masculine light and privileged males, not only because of their views of God, but also because of Jesus's particular embodiment. The mistake, I will argue, is not that they have focused too much on Jesus but that they have not taken the mode of the incarnation seriously enough.

five

The Male Savior

Can a male savior save women?

—Rosemary Radford Ruether, *To Change the World*

With rare exception, the Christian tradition has understood Jesus of Nazareth to be male. I share this perception.[1] At stake here is not only the nature of the Savior but also the nature of the God whom the Savior represents.

Some theologians work from Jesus's maleness to argue that his particular sex reveals something in God that favors males. Hence, women cannot play the role of Christ in the ecclesial drama because this would fail to communicate these truths about God. Put differently, arguments against women in the priesthood often strongly equate maleness and God, passing through the person of Jesus.

Positions that affirm the full value of women, joined to the conviction that women should be prohibited from certain roles in the home, society, or church, often assert that the prohibitions arise from no lack of talent or virtue among women.[2] If that is the case, then another reason must justify the prohibition. In some instances, the reason is a dissimilarity between women and God.

1. I will present the exegesis of the New Testament texts that lead me to this conclusion as well as suggest authors who have entertained the alternative, namely, that Jesus was intersex.

2. Thomas Hopko says clearly, "The female members of the church community are excluded from holding the sacramental office of bishop and presbyter in the Church not because they are

For example, C. S. Lewis suggested that if a woman can "represent God," then that would involve the assumption that "God is like a good woman," and this assumption, he asserts, would be a religion other than the Christian one.[3] In her comments on that essay, Kathy Keller suggests that God's world is a world in which gender roles, including those in the church, are distinct. "Deep mysteries of revelation hang on our gender and on playing our assigned roles. If God is teaching us something about himself and about our relationship to him (we are all female to God . . .), dare we edit his choice of analogy?"[4] Only men can give the correct image of a masculine God.

In the Orthodox Church, Kallistos Ware quotes Father Maximos Aghiorgoussis: "The ordination of women to the Holy Priesthood is untenable since it would disregard the symbolic and iconic value of male priesthood, both as representing Christ's malehood *and the fatherly role of the Father in the Trinity,* by allowing female persons to interchange with male persons a role which cannot be interchanged."[5] Thomas Hopko states the position with all clarity: "In his actions in and toward the world of his creation, the one God and Father reveals himself primarily and essentially in a 'masculine' way."[6] He goes on to state, "The divine nature is certainly sexless. And certainly all human beings, male and female, are made in the image and according to the likeness of God." Nevertheless, because Jesus is male, only males can represent him. "In the Church, the specific ministry of being the presbyterial/episcopal head of the

---

'inferior' in their humanity to the male members of the Church, or less holy, talented or skilled" ("On the Male Character of Christian Priesthood," in *Women and the Priesthood*, ed. Thomas Hopko [Crestwood, NY: St. Vladimir's Seminary Press, 1983], 123). Deborah Belonick makes the same argument: "The question of women's ordination should not be an endless quarrel about whether women are 'good enough,' 'clean enough' or 'smart enough' to wear vestments, carry chalices, marry, baptize, counsel, preach or theologize as well as men. To be sure, women *are*" ("The Spirit of the Female Priesthood," in Hopko, *Women and the Priesthood*, 137).

3. C. S. Lewis, "Priestesses in the Church?," in *God in the Dock*, ed. Walter Hooper (Grand Rapids: Eerdmans, 1970), 237.

4. Kathy Keller, *Jesus, Justice, and Gender Roles: A Case for Gender Roles in Ministry* (Grand Rapids: Zondervan, 2012), 37.

5. Maximos Aghiorgoussis, *Women Priests?* (Brookline, MA: Holy Cross Orthodox, 1976), 3, 5. Quoted in Kallistos Ware, "Man, Woman and the Priesthood of Christ," in Hopko, *Women and the Priesthood*, 25–26 (emphasis mine). In more recent exchanges on social media, Ware seems more open to dialogue on the issue of women's ordination.

6. Thomas Hopko, "Women and the Priesthood: Reflections on the Debate," in Hopko, *Women and the Priesthood*, 183.

sacramental community . . . is the specific ministry of imaging the person and effecting the ministry of the Son and Word of God incarnate in human form, in his specifically 'masculine' being and activity . . . the priest is . . . the image of Jesus Christ. . . . And this 'image' can only be actualized and effected by certain male members of the Church."[7] Jesus and his representative, the male priest, reflect the way of God wholesale. Women cannot represent Jesus the male because, as male, he is the representation of God the masculine Father.[8]

Hans Urs von Balthasar also provides evidence for this view of God.[9] Similar to the Orthodox theologians, Balthasar also points to Jesus's embodiment as male as a comment upon the masculinity of God the Father: "Jesus must be a man if his mission is to represent the origin of the father in this world."[10] His argument reaches beyond Jesus's status as an embodied male to God's sovereign relationship with the world. Jesus had to be male because that is a better reflection of God.[11] In essays arguing against women in the priesthood, both C. S. Lewis and E. L. Mascall appeal to the Second Person's incarnation as a male, and from there extend back to the nature of God. Mascall states, "the maleness of Jesus cannot be separated from the masculine imagery of revelation. He is the express image of the Father."[12] When only men can stand in for God, then God indeed seems male.

What stands in need of more thought is the particular nature of Jesus the Messiah's maleness, from the perspective of the New Testament through the

7. Hopko, "Women and the Priesthood," 184.

8. Ware, in more recent exchanges on social media, seems more open to dialogue on the issue of women's ordination.

9. Commenting on his work, John Saward summarizes the theme: "God . . . , as the primary actor and initiator, is analogically male with regard to the creature. The creature in its dependence on God is open and receptive and therefore in a certain sense feminine" (*The Mysteries of March: Hans Urs von Balthasar on the Incarnation and Easter* [Washington, DC: Catholic University of America Press, 1990], 67).

10. Hans Urs von Balthasar, *Dramatis Personae: Persons in Christ*, vol. 3. of *Theo-Drama: Theological Dramatic Theory*, trans. Graham Harrison (San Francisco: Ignatius, 1992), 284.

11. Tina Beattie summarizes this point of his work: "Balthasar's Jesus is of necessity a biological male, because he represents God, who is 'the Origin, the Father.' Thus there is—at least implicitly—an identification of the divine fatherhood with masculine sexuality and the male body" (*New Catholic Feminism: Theology and Theory* [London: Routledge, 2006], 113).

12. Quoted in Michael Bruce and G. E. Duffield, eds., *Why Not? Priesthood and the Ministry of Women* (Abingdon: Marcham Manor, 1972), 111–12.

doctrinal tradition that affirms the virginal conception. He is male but a male who became embodied like no other. The process that led to the male Savior's unique embodiment should shape how Christians view him *as well as* the God whom he reveals. I attend to that christological perspective in this chapter by focusing first on the birth narratives in the gospels and the way in which they tell the story of Jesus's beginning. With the clear assertion of the virginal conception in view, I then turn to consider Jesus the Messiah as the image of God and the implications of the virginal conception for that christological affirmation. To frame this analysis of Jesus's unique maleness, I set the stage with the marriage metaphor in Scripture to provide a salient example of the relation between Christ's maleness and God's identity. The incarnation, and particularly the way in which it came to be, should impact everything—Christology, theology, and anthropology, including Christianity's view of women.

Bridegroom

Jesus's identification with the bridegroom wields considerable influence for claims that God is more like a male than a female. For Christian readers of both testaments, the term "bridegroom" most readily denotes Jesus Christ. Ephesians 5:21–31 grounds this schema in the New Testament where the incarnate (male) Messiah serves as the bridegroom of the church.[13] The masculine and feminine imagery makes sense between Jesus Christ and his partner. The picture is certainly complicated, since the church includes many male and female members—yet the images are not reversable. Jesus remains the bridegroom, and the church remains the bride.[14] Interpreters then connect this picture with

---

13. The theme appears in the gospels (Matt 9:14 // Mark 2:29; Luke 5:34–35; John 3:29), Paul (Rom 7:4; 2 Cor 11:2), and Revelation (19:7; 22:17). As I will discuss in what follows, this imagery highlights the gracious humility of God and invites a wealth of reflection on the mystery of the church and marriage. For a powerful reflection, see John C. Clark and Marcus Peter Johnson, *The Incarnation of God: The Mystery of the Gospel as the Foundation of Evangelical Theology* (Wheaton, IL: Crossway), 209–32.

14. So Lewis queries this thought as the culmination of ridiculousness: "Suppose, finally, that the mystical marriage were reversed, that the Church were the Bridegroom and Christ the Bride" (Lewis, "Priestesses in the Church?," 237).

passages in the Scriptures of Israel where God is explicitly the lover, bridegroom, or husband in relationship with Israel (Hosea, Ezek 16:1–14; 23; Isa 54:5; Jer 3) and passages where the marriage relationship appears in the type of Adam and Eve (Gen 2) or Solomon and his bride (Song of Solomon).

From these textual locations, the theological picture comes into focus. In her assessment of Orthodox theologians Bulgakov and Endokimov, Mary Cunningham suggests they see the church offering "a feminine response as bride of Christ to God the Father."[15] Notice the movement from Christ the bridegroom to God the Father. Similarly, the papal encyclical, *Inter Insigniores*, in recognition of Christ's embodiment as a male, states that the symbol of his maleness must be maintained by the representative of Christ because it adheres with the reality of the covenant that takes the "form of a nuptial mystery: for God the Chosen People is seen as his ardently loved spouse."[16] After citing the Catholic catechism that asserts "God is pure Spirit," Christopher West affirms that John Paul II "believes the spousal analogy is the *least* inadequate" way to envision God. The pope said, "There is no other human reality which corresponds more [than marriage], humanly speaking, to that divine mystery."[17] The best way to picture the love of God, according to these interpreters, is to imagine God as a husband. West's commentary on John Paul II's *Theology of the Body* is explicit: "it is of the bridegroom's masculine constitution to *initiate* the gift and of the bride's feminine constitution to *receive* the gift. Hence, in the spousal analogy, God is symbolically 'masculine' as the Heavenly Bridegroom, and man (male and female) is symbolically 'feminine'

15. Mary Cunningham, *Gateway of Life: Orthodox Thinking on the Mother of God* (Yonkers, NY: St. Vladimir's Seminary Press, 2015), 160–61.

16. Paul VI, "Inter Insigniores: Declaration on the Question of Admission of Women to the Ministerial Priesthood," The Holy See, https://www.vatican.va/roman_curia/congregations /cfaith/documents/rc_con_cfaith_doc_19761015_inter-insigniores_en.html.

17. Christopher West, *Theology of the Body Explained: A Commentary on John Paul II's Man and Woman He Created Them*, rev. ed. (Boston: Pauline, 2007), 12. This preference from the leader of the church could be what leads West to make the incorrect assertion that "Scripture uses many images to describe God's love for humanity. . . . But both Old and New Testaments use the image of spousal love far more than any other" (*Theology of the Body Explained*, 10). There is no exegetical data to back up this claim, and so it is not clear upon what the assertion is based, but because God or Jesus as husband occurs only a handful of times, in comparison with the overwhelming New Testament language of God as Father, this appears false.

as the Bride." While all of humanity is intended to be receptive in relationship to God, women display this in a unique way, "woman's particular receptivity to love and to life is her special 'genius.'" In turn, then, God's initiative is cast as the "masculine-bridegroom."[18]

Through these connections, the God of Israel, and not just the incarnate Son, becomes masculinized as the husband. Interpreters would agree that the love of God extends beyond anything possible from a human husband,[19] but nonetheless, through these Scriptures, and especially in light of the connection with Jesus Christ as described in Eph 5, it is deemed fitting to view God the Father in this masculine role.

I counter that the lens through which this picture is shaped, Jesus Christ, dislodges any confidence that God is more closely associated with men, *because this image of God as bridegroom in Israel's Scriptures is, for Christian theologians, funneled through and therefore subservient to the incarnate Son.*[20] His maleness is affirmed in such a way that it prevents any masculine preference for God his Father. To support this claim necessitates an investigation of Jesus the Son's unique embodiment.

The New Testament Witness to the Virginal Conception

The Savior's human beginning is presented explicitly in two of the gospels. Aided by those who have dared to ask difficult questions about the tradition,[21]

18. West, *Theology of the Body Explained*, 180, 195.

19. Barth states, "Yahweh's love and marriage is quite incomparable in this sphere, transcending every comparison with what has ever taken place between husband and wife. For such love and marriage is not the affair of a human husband, but only that of the Husband Yahweh" (*Church Dogmatics* III/1, ed. G. W. Bromiley and T. F. Torrance, trans. J. W. Edwards et al. [London: T&T Clark, 2004], §41.3, p. 318). And again: "the Love of Yahweh is beyond the reach of a human husband" (*Church Dogmatics*, III/2, ed. G. W. Bromiley and T. F. Torrance, trans. H. Knight et al. [London: T&T Clark, 2001], §45.3, p. 298).

20. I am indebted to Barth's reading for illuminating the possibility of this move as will become clear in the section "Revisiting God the Bridegroom."

21. Readers might be aware of the influential work of Jane Schaberg, who argues that Jesus was conceived through an act of rape (*The Illegitimacy of Jesus: A Feminist Theological Interpretation of the Infancy Narratives* [Sheffield: Sheffield Academic Press, 1995]). This is based on

I investigate the exegetical plausibility of the mode of incarnation affirmed in classic theology, namely, conception of the Son of God from the body of Mary. After a brief summary of recent work to investigate the literary and historical traditions in the gospels, I conclude that Matthew's and Luke's texts teach the Son of God's embodiment through God's work with no person other than Mary.

It should be acknowledged that Jesus's supernatural conception through a virgin is not a theological necessity for the doctrine of the incarnation. Human finitude demands the concession that God *could* be present among humanity in another way. In his treatment of the virginal conception, Andrew Lincoln cites a wide swath of theologians, from Schleiermacher to Ratzinger, who concur: "In order to stay in continuity with the distinctive claims of the Christian tradition, it is a basic requirement to maintain that in Jesus God as the eternal Word, that is, Godself and not simply some divinely inspired representative, is encountered by humans. . . . [R]estoration . . . is only effective if God was uniquely and decisively present and active in the life, death and resurrection of Jesus." The texts of Paul, John, and Hebrews hold this affirmation about Jesus of Nazareth without explicit reference to the virginal conception, and so it is possible that "belief in the incarnation is not affected when a literal virginal conception is no longer in the picture."[22] Oliver Crisp, who, against Lincoln, argues for the virginal conception biblically and theologically, puts forth a similar concession:[23] "Strictly speaking, neither the Virgin Birth nor the Virginal Conception is necessary for the Incarnation. . . . Christ could have

a reconstruction of events behind the text, a reconstruction that has not proved convincing to many historians and biblical exegetes. See Beverly Roberts Gaventa, *Mary: Glimpses of the Mother of Jesus*, Personalities of the New Testament (Minneapolis: Fortress, 1999), 9–11. I engage more closely with the work of Andrew Lincoln, because of his close attention to the text as well as thoughtful theological queries (*Born of a Virgin? Reconceiving Jesus in the Bible, Tradition, and Theology* [Grand Rapids: Eerdmans, 2013]).

22. Lincoln, *Born of a Virgin?*, 275.

23. Note that Lincoln does not take this "olive branch" from Crisp because it assumes an analytic theological approach with a "certain view of Scripture and the creeds" along with certain "philosophical and anthropological assumptions" that Lincoln does not share (*Born of a Virgin?*, 273–74). Crisp maintains this position in a later response to Lincoln. See Oliver Crisp, *Analyzing Doctrine: Toward a Systematic Theology* (Waco, TX: Baylor University Press, 2019), 162–78. See Lincoln's further response to Crisp in "The Bible, Theology, and the Virgin Birth: Continuing a Conversation?," *Journal of Theological Interpretation* 14 (2020): 267–85.

been born through natural generation, rather than via the miraculous working of the Holy Spirit. And this is perfectly compatible with a Christology, which, in other respects is entirely in keeping with the catholic faith."[24] Mary, along with Joseph (or someone else), could have conceived a child, and at the moment of conception, "the Word of God assumes [the human nature]."[25] The doctrine of incarnation—God becoming human—is not dependent upon virginal conception.[26]

Some have queried whether the New Testament really includes this doctrine at all and, therefore, have issued an invitation for a closer consideration of the text.[27] Read without the lens of a faith shaped by thousands of years of church tradition, interpreters have suggested that certain sections of Matthew and Luke *could be* read as describing a natural birth. Matthew says that this whole event happened (1:22) to fulfill Isa 7:14, which states that a παρθένος (*parthenos*)—translated as either "young woman" or "virgin"—shall conceive and bear a child.[28] Luke's use of παρθένος (*parthenos*) might indicate that Mary is simply a young woman (Luke 1:26).[29] Moreover, the powerful overshadowing of the Holy Spirit could be the blessing of normal conception rather than the formation of an unusual one. The "coming upon" of the Spirit refers, Lincoln argues, to "empowerment by the Spirit, but in none of the [other] references in Luke is there any suggestion that the Spirit replaces any agency or activity that

---

24. Oliver Crisp, *God Incarnate: Explorations in Christology* (London: T&T Clark, 2009), 77.

25. Crisp, *God Incarnate*, 93.

26. This lack of theological necessity adds even more support for the validity of the evangelists' presentation.

27. See a popularized version of many of these arguments in Kyle Roberts, *A Complicated Pregnancy: Whether Mary Was a Virgin and Why It Matters* (Minneapolis: Fortress, 2017). See also Geoffrey Parrinder, *The Son of Joseph: The Parentage of Jesus* (London: T&T Clark, 1992), or the vitriolic example of Gerd Lüdemann's *Virgin Birth? The Real Story of Mary and Her Son Jesus*, trans. John Bowden (Harrisburg, PA: Trinity Press International, 1998).

28. See "παρθένος" (*parthenos*), in Henry George Liddell, Robert Scott, and Henry Stuart Jones, *A Greek-English Lexicon*, 9th ed. with revised supplement (Oxford: Clarendon, 1996), 1339.

29. Lincoln includes the early work of Joseph A. Fitzmyer, as well as the work of Parrinder, *Son of Joseph*, 31, 35; D. J. Catchpole, *Jesus People: The Historical Jesus and the Beginnings of Community* (London: Darton, Longman & Todd, 2006); Schaberg, *Illegitimacy of Jesus*; Edwin D. Freed, *The Stories of Jesus's Birth: A Critical Introduction* (London: Bloomsbury, 2004); but he notes that "there is far greater agreement that Luke's annunciation story is about a virginal conception" (*Born of a Virgin?*, 99).

humans would normally be expected to exercise."[30] In light of the terms used, both evangelists *could* be read to support a natural, if scandalous, conception. This reading, however, would strain the plain sense of the terms in the context of their narrative. Incarnation through divine virginal conception is the clearest and best interpretation of the story Matthew and Luke tell. Recall that Matthew breaks the rhythm of his genealogy when he asserts not that Joseph begot Jesus, as have all the other fathers, but that Jesus the Messiah was begotten from Mary (Matt 1:16). At the beginning of the story, he asserts that Mary's child is not Joseph's, and while "from the Holy Spirit" could indicate a divine blessing of a natural (and even scandalous) birth, the angel's assurance to the scrupulous Joseph that he should not fear to take Mary into his house suggests that she has done no unrighteousness or had any unrighteousness done to her that would taint Joseph. The child is, righteously, from the Holy Spirit (1:20). Matthew has established this fact even before he brings forth the citation of Isa 7:14 with the ambiguous term παρθένος (*parthenos*). He emphasizes it when he notes that Joseph did not know Mary sexually even after he obediently took her into his home (Matt 1:25). By placing this word in this story's context, Mary is a young woman, but Matthew has shown that she is a young woman who has not had sex and yet has been found with child.

Whereas Matthew ends his account by referring to her as a παρθένος (*parthenos*), Luke begins there, describing her twice as the παρθένος to whom God has sent Gabriel (Luke 1:27). The divine promise of a child prompts her ownership of Luke's description when she replies, "I have not known a man" (1:34), to which Gabriel asserts the overshadowing of the Holy Spirit and the conception of one who will be called the Son of God (1:35). Luke offers no other explanation except to narrate in the scene immediately following that she is expecting (1:42).[31]

Despite raising the possibility of a natural reading, even an interpreter like Lincoln, who is criticial of the virginal conception, reaches the same conclusion

---

30. Lincoln, *Born of a Virgin?*, 104.

31. Lincoln discusses the timing of Luke as well: "Elizabeth is already six months pregnant at the time of the annunciation (cf. 1:36), Mary's visit to Elizabeth lasts for three months and is still before the birth of John" (*Born of a Virgin?*, 106). In other words, Mary did not waste any time in getting to Elizabeth, and when she arrived, she was pregnant.

about the evangelists.[32] After he thoroughly catalogs the possibility of a natural-conception reading in both Matthew and Luke, he ultimately concludes that it is not convincing.[33] Moreover, church tradition continued to read Matthew and Luke in this way, as Lincoln notes: "It would be an unlikely anomaly if, from very early, the Church had completely misunderstood its own Scriptures on this matter and they contained no clear account of a virginal conception."[34] Both tell the birth of Jesus as a divinely enacted virginal conception.

Another line of questioning wonders if Matthew and Luke included a virginal conception because it was part of the expected genre conventions when an author recounted the life of an influential person. Questioning the legitimacy of this conception features prominently in an influential and critical work on the story of Mary by Maria Warner, *Alone of All Her Sex*.[35] In this book, Warner argues that the infancy narratives are later additions that, over the course of eight decades, had accrued more legends than facts.[36] In her interpretation, Luke and Matthew are "intent on revealing to the reader the divinity of Christ, and not to write his biography, as a contemporary historian might."[37] In other words, they are more concerned to say something powerful about Jesus than to say something true. It was not what happened that mattered, but what mattered that they then said happened.

Andrew Lincoln gives voice to similar doubts when he contemplates the influence of Greco-Roman genre on the conception and birth motif in the evangelists' writing. They assert a virgin birth simply because the "genres employed by the biblical authors" shape how they tell that story.[38] If they wanted to say something great about Jesus, virginal conception would have been a ready-at-hand way to do so.

---

32. As does John Dominic Crossan, who is rarely consulted as a repository of theological traditionalism ("Virgin Mother or Bastard Child," in *A Feminist Companion to Mariology*, ed. Amy-Jill Levine and Maria Mayo Robbins [New York: T&T Clark, 2005], 54–55).

33. Lincoln, *Born of a Virgin?*, 97, 105.

34. Lincoln, *Born of a Virgin?*, 99.

35. Maria Warner, *Alone of All Her Sex: The Myth and Cult of the Virgin Mary*, new edition (Oxford: Oxford University Press, 2013).

36. Warner, *Alone of All Her Sex*, 4.

37. Warner, *Alone of All Her Sex*, 8.

38. Lincoln, *Born of a Virgin?*, 240.

Matthew and Luke certainly did not get this idea from the Judaism of their day.[39] The stories of Israel provide many points of connection with Jesus's birth narratives, especially the early days of Moses and Samuel, but these or any other accounts do not suggest virginal conception. Matthew's use of *parthenos* in Isa 7:14 proves the point. If Matthew gives this text a miraculous interpretation, it is because he is reading backward.[40] Isaiah 7:14 did not give him the idea of a virginal conception. Such a thing was not known in Israel.[41]

It is quite common, however, in other cultures of their day.[42] Authors like Warner and Lincoln suggest that Matthew and Luke mined stories from the Greeks, Romans, and Egyptians because they wanted to make a grand point about Jesus. Because of the resurrection, the disciples had come to believe— or, better said, believe with better understanding—in Jesus as the Son of God. The message of the risen and ascended, previously crucified Nazarene became the short form of the message Jesus followers preached.[43] When it was deemed time to write more extensively about his life, they would certainly "interpret the origins of Jesus' life in the light of their post-resurrection beliefs about him."[44] Because no one is usually making records at the beginning of the life of a person who only later becomes influential, birth narratives are "particularly legendary."[45] Lincoln argues that Luke and Matthew employ a common and

39. See Steve Moyise, *Was the Birth of Jesus according to Scripture?* (Eugene, OR: Cascade Books, 2013).

40. I draw the phrase and the insight from Richard B. Hays, especially *Reading Backwards: Figural Christology and the Fourfold Gospel Witness* (Waco, TX: Baylor University Press, 2014).

41. "There is no comparable passage in the Old Testament to the idea of the Holy Spirit 'coming upon' the person who was to give birth to the Messiah" (Edwin D. Freed, *The Stories of Jesus' Birth: A Critical Introduction* [London: T&T Clark, 2004], 67). See also the discussion by John Dominic Crossan, who states, "Virginity is strikingly unusual against the general biblical tradition of extraordinary conceptions where a child is specially marked for future greatness by being born to aged and/or infertile parents" ("Virgin Mother or Bastard Child," 54).

42. "The narrative form" that is "the birth of heroes or great figures in ancient biography . . . lies at hand" (Lincoln, *Born of a Virgin?*, 115).

43. See especially 1 Cor 15:3–8.

44. Lincoln, *Born of a Virgin?*, 41.

45. Lincoln, *Born of a Virgin?*, 64. And again, "Their infancy narratives are the least historical sections of their ancient biographies with their content far more substantially informed than the rest of their narratives by their post-resurrection convictions about the significance of Jesus" (*Born of a Virgin*, 243).

expected genre in which the beginning of a person's life anticipates the kind of person they will become. In Lincoln's words, "The virginal conception was a conventional way of elaborating Jesus' status as Son of God,"[46] and it was penned "under the influence of the cross-fertilization of the stories of the birth of heroes from the gods in the broader culture."[47] In this theory, Matthew and Luke included a virginal conception story similar to these other examples, which were known to them, in order to show God's unique presence with and in Jesus from the beginning.

Certainly, authorial shaping around the theological aim of the gospels inevitably and beautifully colors the way the story runs. It is still worth asking, however, if it is most historically plausible that such coloring results in embellishment to the degree of being legendary.

If Matthew and Luke intentionally created the virginal conception to cast Jesus as Emmanuel/a Son of God from the beginning, the problems they created could have outweighed any honor they bestowed. Chiefly, they risked compromising the exclusive edge of their message. Virginal conception stories appear most often in the milieu of polytheism. Conversely, Luke and Matthew present a theological system, in line with the perceived intransigence of many other Jewish authors of their time,[48] which claims the supremacy of the Most High God.[49] Virginal conception stories, on the basis of their contextual roots,

46. Lincoln, *Born of a Virgin?*, 126.

47. Lincoln, *Born of a Virgin?*, 137, 147.

48. About the Jews Tacitus notes, "Those who are converted to their ways follow the same practice, and the earliest lesson they receive is to despise the gods, to disown their country and to regard their parents, children and brothers as of little account. . . . but their ideas of heavenly things are quite the opposite. The Egyptians worship many animals and monstrous images; the Jews conceive of one god only, and that with the mind alone: they regard as impious those who make from perishable materials representations of gods in man's image; that supreme and eternal being is to them incapable of representation and without end. Therefore, they set up no statues in their cities, still less in their temples; this flattery is not paid their kings nor this honour given to the Caesars" (Tacitus, *Histories* 5.5 [LCL 249], 185).

49. It would be wrong to assume that Greeks and Romans were all polytheists and all Jews were monotheists. Some pagan thinkers asserted the oneness of the divine and some Jewish thinkers acknowledged the existence of other "gods," although the meaning of that term is fluid. See Wilson, *Embodied God*, 98–121. My point is that virginal conception as a trope occurs most often in stories where there is an assumption of multiple gods, an association Matthew and Luke would wish to avoid.

introduce the specter of a pantheon of gods into their accounts with respect to the God of Israel cast as the Father of Jesus. Their God, the only God, ends up playing a similar role to one of the other gods. God ends up looking like one of the many.

This confusion also applies to Jesus. The parallels open wide the suggestion that Jesus was a demigod like many others. The message of the gospels is not that Jesus is like the other gods. It is the precise opposite. Jesus uniquely reveals the one and only God of Israel. He and his Father have no peer. If Matthew and Luke were attempting to increase his honor by showing it at his beginning, the introduction of the virginal conception stories in their particular context could have decreased his honor by making him and his Father God look like the others. Warner describes this difficulty with acuity: "The doctrine of the virgin birth was attacked far more frequently because it was common in pagan belief than because it was unlikely in nature. Its resemblance to the metamorphoses of the gods of antiquity exposed a Christian nerve."[50] This risk applies even if the divine conception is nonsexual. This process, too, was a story of other respected figures and would have decreased Jesus's distinctiveness.

On the other hand, if Jesus is not a demigod, then he very well might be a human who came to be in some unmentionable way. The virgin birth accounts also introduce the question of illegitimacy. If Jesus is not really Son of God like other sons of gods, then there is more to Mary's story left unsaid. Because both narrators make clear that the child is not of her betrothed Joseph, the options that remain are either unfaithfulness or violation. This charge appears as early as the second century, when Origen recounted Celsus's claims that Mary was raped by a Roman soldier named Pantera (*Against Celsus* 1.29). In the 1980s Jane Schaberg built these millennia-old questions into an extensive argument, suggesting that Matthew and Luke inherited and passed down the tradition that "Jesus the Messiah had been illegitimately conceived during the period when his mother Mary was betrothed to Joseph."[51] In her read,

---

50. Schaberg, *Alone of All Her Sex*, 36. So also C. E. B. Cranfield, "The Church may well have sensed the danger that the Virgin Birth, if proclaimed in the Gentile world, would be misunderstood along the lines of the pagan myths, as being like the birth of a Perseus or a Heracles, or as a mere flattering fancy like the stories of the births of Plato, Alexander or Augustus" ("Some Reflections on the Subject of the Virgin Birth," *Scottish Journal of Theology* 41.2 [1988]: 187).

51. For the genesis of her work, see Frank Reilley, "Jane Schaberg, Raymond E. Brown, and the Problem of the Illegitimacy of Jesus," *Journal of Feminist Studies in Religion* 21 (2005): 57–80.

this was not a supernatural but a natural and violent conception that the evangelists saw as redeemed by God's Holy Spirit.[52] Her work is criticized for developing arguments from silence,[53] but these gaps become noticeable because of the things Matthew and Luke *do* say. Schaberg argues that the evangelists were writing these stories apologetically, to dispel the even more scandalous stories of rape that were circulating.[54] Her argument rests on locating rumors documented much later in the time before the writing of Matthew and Luke. The cause and effect could have worked in the other direction: if the evangelists had not brought the issue of Jesus's unusual origin to the fore with the virginal conception stories, far fewer would have wondered (and gossiped) about it.

With human scandal on one hand and superhuman polytheism on the other—and the shame of birth on both—the evangelists had several compelling reasons not to include Jesus's beginning, especially through virginal conception.[55]

Even so, the New Testament teaches it. Suggesting the evangelists told the story of the virgin birth in order to embellish Jesus's story asks interpreters to assume that they would have been either unaware of or undeterred by the myriad of negative implications this account raises. It is unlikely that they

52. In this way her work has borne redemptive fruit for contemporary readers. She notes that in the aftermath of her publication, many came to realize that "the tradition could function to create compassion for the most powerless members of our society" (Jane Schaberg, "A Feminist Experience of Historical-Jesus Scholarship," in *Whose Historical Jesus*, ed. William A. Arnal and Michel Desjardins, Studies in Christianity and Judaism 7 [Waterloo, Ontario: Wilfred Laurier University Press, 1997], 149; cited in Christine Mitchell, "Across Generations: An Interview with Jane D. Schaberg," *Journal of Feminist Studies in Religion* 28.1 [2012]: 66).

53. Gaventa, *Mary*, 38. Lincoln states bluntly, "Indeed all the supporting details Schaberg adduces for her reading of Luke's account (78–144) are dependent for any force on bringing the notion of Jesus' illegitimacy to the text rather than finding it in the text" (*Born of a Virgin*, 118n27).

54. Lynn Cohick argues that the evidence for Jesus's illegitimacy in the gospels is at best thin and more likely absent. People could be known as the son of their mothers without any assumption of illegitimacy, and there is no evidence that Mary was treated as an outsider by her community (*Women in the World of Earliest Christians*, 153–56).

55. John Dominic Crossan's incredulity is illuminating: "Why did anyone coming from that wiser Jewish tradition [divine assistance in normal birth] ever risk the claim of virginal conception, ever risk the almost inevitable rebuttal of bastardy?" ("Virgin Mother or Bastard Child," 54).

would have been unaware of the implications in their own context. Hence, alternatively, they must have been undeterred.

Their boldness arose because, despite the questions it raised, they thought telling the tale was worth it. The positives outweighed the negatives. One possible positive—one reason that might have compelled them—is that they heard that it happened this way and wanted to be faithful communicators of testimony.[56] Differences between historical methods in the past and present do not neatly map onto the creation of legends then and stark objective reporting now. They too would have sensed a responsibility to the tradition, and this provides a reason to include this account even though it raised several difficulties.

Even more weighty theologically, incarnation through virginal conception allows the authors to testify to the greatness of the one whose story they are telling. It does so through highlighting the differences from other stories rather than the similarities. They use a convention to show that he is nonconventional. If they had not included this account, they would have missed an opportunity to show the distinction from the trope. The differences shine forth more brightly on the canvas of the similarities. Jesus is not like other demigods because his Father the God of Israel is not like other gods. The Son of God is born through a nonsexualized process to show his status as Immanuel (Matt 1:23), as Son of the Most High (Luke 1:35), in a unique way.

Taking seriously the questions raised against the tradition allows an even firmer confirmation of the tradition. Matthew and Luke both teach that Jesus was conceived by the power of God and not by the power of any male, through Mary and only through Mary.[57] The exegetical witness of the virginal concep-

---

56. They might have heard their stories from Mary and Joseph (Bauckham, *Eyewitnesses*, 297–98), but this is not necessary to my argument, as they could have heard it from others who heard it from Mary and Joseph. Raymond E. Brown has also concluded: "No search for parallels has given us a truly satisfactory explanation of how early Christians happened upon the idea of a virginal conception—unless, of course, that is what really took place" (*The Virginal Conception and the Bodily Resurrection of Jesus* [New York: Paulist Press, 1973], 65).

57. Candida Moss and Joel Baden reach the same conclusion: "What both authors agree on, however, is that Jesus was not conceived through sexual intercourse.... The important point for our purposes is that Matthew and Luke believe it. The birth of the Son of God took place outside the parameters of ordinary human reproduction" (*Reconceiving Infertility: Biblical Perspectives on Procreation and Childlessness* [Princeton: Princeton University Press, 2015], 151–52).

tion lays the groundwork for the theological and anthropological impact of its christological assertions.

Too Unique?

A pressing concern remains, namely, that Jesus is different from all other humans. Granted, all assertions of the incarnation affirm some degree of Jesus's unique nature. Being God incarnate puts him into a category all his own. The concern is more precise. Some have also worried that Jesus's difference from all other humans *by virtue of his singular maternity* could destroy the aim of the incarnation itself, the recapitulation of the human race. One might respond that accepting the Christian narrative involves accepting truths outside the natural system— the resurrection being the chief example. Dead people do not normally rise, and babies do not normally exist without fathers. Embracing one element of the Christian confession seems to suggest the ability to embrace the other.

Such a retort, however, would be to miss the aim of this critique. Lincoln counters, "This is not an argument about the possibility of the miraculous but about the meaning of the alleged miracle."[58] The question at stake is not whether God *can* do this but whether God would accomplish the redemption of creation if God *did* do this.[59] If Christ is different from all other humans by virtue of the virginal conception, then maybe it is impossible for his unique humanity to redeem any other human.

Tertullian speaks to just this problem in *The Flesh of Christ*: "A word of caution, however, must be addressed to all who refuse to believe that our flesh was in Christ on the ground that it came not of the seed of a human father, let them remember that Adam himself received this flesh of ours without the seed of a human father. As earth was converted into this flesh of ours with the seed of a human father, so also was it quite possible for the Son of God to take to Himself the substance of the self-same flesh, without a human father's

---

58. Lincoln, *Born of a Virgin?*, 262.

59. So also Roberts: "The *primary* (but not only) problem [with virginal conception] is that it conflicts with the logic of the incarnation, the very basis of the gospel itself. A virginal conception is *internally* incoherent with the proclamation that God became a human being in Jesus. A virgin birth gives us a different Christ than the one we really need" (*Complicated Pregnancy*, 183).

agency."[60] He recognizes the disjunct between Christ's beginning and normal human beginning but still asserts that Christ took "our flesh."

From this perspective, Jesus's humanity may not be that different from others.[61] Since all human existence is in some way contingent upon God, then Jesus's contingency upon God's act would be different, but he would still share contingency with all other humans.[62] In relationship with God as well as other humans, he is dependent.[63]

Lincoln agrees with this. If God had to intervene with "a miracle that supplies missing genes, the result could still be human."[64] His objection is that "the resulting human product cannot be said to be either *in solidarity* or *in continuity* with the rest of the human race . . . but a special interventionist creation in which God treats male DNA differently from female and produces it separately." He asserts that if Jesus were conceived without a male father, he would not be human as are other humans.

Lincoln claims that the lack of a male-supplied Y chromosome makes Jesus significantly different from others as to be salvifically ineffective. He appeals to Hebrews, chiefly because it is such a robust text for affirming the humanity of Jesus.[65] In Hebrews, what makes Jesus the fitting high priest is his flesh and blood (Heb 2:14), his experience of suffering and temptation (4:14), and his death (2:12–14). That he has flesh and blood and lives with it and dies in it

60. Tertullian, *The Flesh of Christ* 16 (*Ante-Nicene Fathers* 3:536).

61. See similar critiques of Lincoln's definition of humanity in Daniel J. Treier, "Virgin Territory?," *Pro Ecclesia* 23 (2014): 372–79, esp. 375–76.

62. John Saward also accepts the humanity of Christ, though virginally conceived. In comment upon the writings of Maximus the Confessor and Pope Saint Leo the Great, Saward states, "[Christ's conception]'s virginal and miraculous manner (by the direct operation of the Holy Spirit, without seed) does not make his human nature different from ours. In its 'definition of nature,' Christ's humanity is the same as ours; it differs from ours only in the 'manner of its coming-to-be'. . . . The miraculous *how* of Christ's conception reveals *who* he is; it does not make him any the less *what* we are" (*Redeemer in the Womb: Jesus Living in Mary* [San Francisco: Ignatius, 1993], 11).

63. Stanley J. Grenz says that an argument against the virginal conception "depends on the assumption that 'normal' birth is constitutive of being human." Grenz points to life in community as the definition of humanity, but his point confirms that the definition of "humanity" is not settled (*Theology for the Community of God* [Grand Rapids: Eerdmans, 2000], 321).

64. Lincoln, "Bible, Theology, and the Virgin Birth," 267–85.

65. Lincoln, *Born of a Virgin?*, 261.

makes him the human high priest who opens the way to God. Possessing a Y chromosome that was supplied by God rather than a human male could still afford Jesus this flesh-and-blood humanity that can experience the full human condition.[66] The unique nature of his body by virtue of the virginal conception does not destroy his salvific solidarity. To the contrary, I counter that this is what makes it possible for him to be in solidarity with all.

I sense a fear latent in these kinds of critiques that the virginal conception would leave out males.[67] Birth and especially virginal conception as the mode of the incarnation does elevate women in a way that some interpreters find threatening.[68] Evoking the tradition, Lincoln states it this way: "He cannot be fully human as that is presently understood, since he had no normal male chromosome, and therefore is not fully at one with the humanity that is to be redeemed and that which he has not assumed he has not healed."[69] Such a statement points to a concern that if Jesus, the Savior, has his flesh only from a female, then he might not be able to redeem anyone, including (especially?) males—an ironic turn on a common trope in feminist theology: "Can a male Savior save women?" Lincoln seems to wonder, "Can a female-conceived Savior save men?"

The mode of the incarnation does elevate women. Maria Warner recognized this: "There is no more matriarchal image than the mother of God who bore a child without male assistance."[70] Matthew's and Luke's accounts affirm that

---

66. Hebrews clearly affirms that Jesus suffered death (Heb 2:9), shared in flesh and blood (2:14), was made like his siblings in all things (2:17), had days in the flesh (5:7), arose from the tribe of Judah (7:14), received a body from God (10:5), offered that body (10:10), died on a cross (12:2), and was resurrected from the dead (13:20). See also Crisp, *Analyzing Doctrine*, 162.

67. Roberts points to an exclusion of males in some feminist responses to Mary (*Complicated Pregnancy*, 99–101).

68. Clearly seen in Gerd Lüdemann, who refers to the traditional assertion of the virgin birth as "emasculated church dogmatics" (*Virgin Birth: The Real Story of Mary and Her Son Jesus* [London: Bloomsbury, 2009], xvii). Geoffrey Parrinder, who argues for the natural conception of Jesus, notes what would be missing if Jesus wasn't naturally conceived: "what Jesus would have thought if he had known that down the ages his beloved father [Joseph], who provided him with a favourite model of the divinity, would have been set aside by his followers and his parenthood denied" (*Son of Joseph*, 115). For him, a greater presence of Joseph in the life of Jesus supports and reinforces Jesus's address of God as Father (113).

69. Lincoln, *Born of a Virgin?*, 262, 264–65. He lists D. Minns and A. Peacocke (262n38) as also holding this view of humanity.

70. Warner, *Alone of All Her Sex*, 48. See also Brigitte Kahl, who describes Luke 1 as a "'femi-

when God decided to dwell among God's people, God came singularly from a woman.[71] If Jesus had human flesh, and the texts of the New Testament are rather adamant that he did, that human flesh came from her. Mary supplies what the woman normally supplies in procreation: her genes, her body, her food, her energy, her blood. God's Holy Spirit overshadowed her flesh so that it could do what it could not do on its own, namely, conceive a child. To send the Savior, the Spirit came upon only one human, and that human was a woman.

This way of understanding the incarnation—virginal conception—does indeed have powerful implications for gender. The Christian canonical texts before and after the birth narratives affirm that God has used and will use women for a variety of important roles in the story, but she stands at the story's very heart. The Savior's coming from her alone—more so than any other aspect of the Christian story—confirms that the God of this story values and works with and through women, and in this instance, *only* with and through a woman.[72]

In the mystery of the incarnation, it seems correct to say that God has treated "male DNA differently from female."[73] In so doing, God has elevated women, *but not to the detriment of men*. Rather than exclusion of one side or the other, there is an unparalleled inclusivity precisely in this process of the incarnation. The virginal conception reveals that the Messiah, whose body

---

nist code' woven into the texture of the biblical 'textile'" ("Toward a Materialist-Feminist Reading," in *A Feminist Introduction*, vol. 1 of *Searching the Scriptures*, ed. Elisabeth Schüssler Fiorenza [New York: Crossroad, 1993], 237–38).

71. Courtney Hall Lee notes: "If the virgin birth is indeed merely mythical, Mary becomes nothing more than the mother of a notable spiritual leader. In other words, she becomes incidental if not wholly irrelevant to the story of Jesus of Nazareth" (*Black Madonna: A Womanist Look at Mary of Nazareth* [Eugene, OR: Cascade, 2017], 60). Lee, utilizing Elisabeth Schüssler Fiorenza's work, also argues that "eliminating the virgin birth is indeed a *kyriarchal* act.... If... Mary were a girl who was seduced or raped, her role would be that of an ordinary female under male domination and without sexual agency, whose baby was lucky enough to be chosen as the Savior" (64).

72. "However, in the case of Christ, who did not have an earthly father, his 'enfleshment,' his body is fully from a woman, thus creating a breathtakingly close link between his body and female flesh." See Julia Baudzej, "Re-telling the Story of Jesus: The Concept of Embodiment and Recent Feminist Reflections on the Maleness of Christ," *Feminist Theology* 17 (2008): 72–91.

73. Lincoln, "Bible, Theology, and the Virgin Birth." See also Kristen Padilla, *Now That I'm Called: A Guide for Women Discerning a Call to Ministry* (Grand Rapids: Zondervan, 2018), 91.

was crucified and resurrected, embraces male and female, and therefore can in a powerfully and beautifully inclusive way save all humans. In short, a male-embodied Savior with female-provided flesh saves all.[74]

The Image of God

With the exegetical and theological assurance of the virginal conception, I turn now to a different set of New Testament texts to attend to another aspect of the incarnate Son. It is the language of Christ as the image of God that provides the avenue to consider the connection between the Savior's revelation of God and of true humanity. Twice the New Testament literature refers to Christ the Son as the "image of God" (εἰκὼν τοῦ θεοῦ [*eikōn tou theou*] 2 Cor 4:4; Col 1:15). The evocative honorific echoes several fields of reference in the writings of Israel. In one stream, the image of God is God's Wisdom or God's Word. Sophia or Logos is that through which God created the world and appears as the manifestation of the divine in the world. For example, Wisdom is "a reflection of eternal light and a spotless mirror of the activity of God and an image of his goodness" (Wis 7:26). Philo states, "for the image of God is his most ancient word" (*On the Confusion of Tongues* 147), and again, "But the divine word which is above these does not come into any visible appearance, inasmuch as it is not like to any of the things that come under the external senses, but is itself an image of God, the most ancient of all the objects of intellect in the whole world, and that which is placed in the closest proximity to the only truly existing God, without any partition or distance being interposed between them" (*On Flight and Finding* 101), and most succinctly, "Now the image of God is the Word, by which all the world was made" (*On the Special Laws* 1.81).[75] In

74. I am suggesting this way of understanding the incarnation would assure a connection to Jesus Christ for biological females, males, and all who find themselves in between. Elisabeth Behr-Sigel captures the sentiment precisely: "The God-Man, who by becoming man, assumed humanity in such a way that no human person is excluded" (*The Ministry of Women in the Church*, trans. Steven Bigham [Crestwood, NY: St. Vladimir's Seminary Press, 1991], 40), and again, "It was from a woman, the Theotokos, that the divine Word took flesh, thus assuming humanity in its totality" (59).

75. Philo also states, "For God gives to the soul a seal, a very beautiful gift, to show that he

this first field of view, then, the Messiah, in line with what was believed about Wisdom or God's Word, is the one who reveals God. From this perspective, theologians have seen references to the eternal Son, the divine person.[76]

Humanity would not be aware of this divine person, however, if the Son had not become a human being. In the two places where the New Testament writings assign this title to Christ, they also offer clues that the "image of God" applies to the incarnate Son. Colossians resonates strongly with a preincarnate Son, who was before creation and the means of divine creation and sustenance, yet this same one made peace through the blood of his cross (Col 1:20). He has brought reconciliation through *the body of his flesh* (1:22). The fullness of deity was pleased to dwell in bodily form (2:9). The image of God both exists previous to creation and entered into creation as a human creature.[77] In 2 Cor 4, Paul states that he preaches the Messiah (Χριστός [*Christos*]) who is the image of God, the man named Jesus, who had a face (2 Cor 4:6). The preaching of a Messiah who died and rose again is a very bodily endeavor complete with scars and the hope for renewal (4:10). The incarnate *imago Dei* reveals God by becoming human.

As further support for the way in which the unique Messiah reveals God, Christian tradition has recognized the pneumatological reality in the revelation of the image of God. John of Damascus states, "We know Christ the Son of God through the Holy Spirit, and in the Son we contemplate the Father."[78] The work of the Spirit reveals the Son to humanity, and when humanity sees the Son, they see the Father. This is the revelatory and gracious work of the Trinity, a work that centers on the Son, the Son who became incarnate. The

has invested with shape the essence of all things which was previously devoid of shape, and has stamped with a particular character that which previously had no character, and has endowed with form that which had previously no distinctive form, and having perfected the entire world, he has impressed upon it an image and appearance, namely, his own word" (*On Dreams* 2.45).

76. See discussion in Marc Cortez, *ReSourcing Theological Anthropology: A Constructive Account of Humanity in Light of Christ* (Grand Rapids: Zondervan, 2017), 99–129.

77. Douglas J. Moo argues for both wisdom and human/Adamic streams in play in this reference (*The Letters to Colossians and Philemon,* The Pillar New Testament Commentary [Grand Rapids: Eerdmans, 2008], 118), as does Marianne Meye Thompson, stating, "Two strands of the Biblical use of 'image of God' are interwoven in this statement" (*Colossians and Philemon,* The Two Horizons New Testament Commentary [Grand Rapids: Eerdmans, 2005], 28; see full discussion on 29–33).

78. John of Damascus, *Third Oration* 18, cited in Sergius Bulgakov, *Icons and the Name of God,* trans. Boris Jakim (Grand Rapids: Eerdmans, 2012), 52–53n72.

language of Sergius Bulgakov evokes the connection as well: "The Holy Spirit *accomplishes* the Image of the Father in the Son, and therefore the Image of the Son is not the Son alone in separation but the Son overshadowed by the Holy Spirit proceeding from the Father."[79] The Holy Spirit reveals Christ as the image of God the Father.

Now I am poised to unite both streams of christological assertions—virginal conception and *imago Dei*. The Spirit-led revelation of the Father was accomplished when the Holy Spirit *overshadowed* the body of a woman (Luke 1:35). When the Holy Spirit cultivated the body of the Son from Mary of Nazareth, the image of God was revealed. If the *incarnate* Son is the image of God who reveals God to humanity, it is his *particular* embodiment that makes this revelation. Consequently, the inclusion of male and female in the body of the incarnate Lord provides the christological justification for rejecting an exclusive maleness in God.

The nature of the inclusion demands clarification. In light of the account of Jesus's unique origination, some have argued that Jesus could have been intersex.[80] Virginia Ramey Mollenkott, in dialogue with Edward L. Kessel's work,[81] makes a connection between the *imago Dei*, Jesus's embodiment, and "the Genesis depiction of a God who is imaged as both male and female and yet is literally neither one nor the other. A chromosomally female, phenotypically male Jesus would come as close as a human body could come to the perfect image of such a God."[82] The connection between creation and Christ, the anthropological *imago Dei*, is striking, but I counter that Jesus does not come *as close as possible* to the perfect image of God. He *is* the perfect image of God. He serves as the template for the affirmation that humans—all hu-

---

79. Bulgakov, *Icons and the Name of God*, 52–53.

80. Megan DeFranza suggests a specific condition for his suggestion of "sex reversal": "a severe case of congenital adrenal hyperplasia in an XX fetus could have produced a substantial enough phallus for sex assignment as male and male secondary sex development" (*Sex Difference in Christian Theology: Male, Female, and Intersex in the Image of God* [Grand Rapids: Eerdmans, 2015], 248).

81. Edward L. Kessel, "A Proposed Biological Interpretation of the Virgin Birth," *Journal of the American Scientific Affiliation* 35 (1983): 129–36.

82. Virginia Ramey Mollenkott, *Omnigender: A Trans-religious Approach* (Cleveland: Pilgrim, 2001), 248. To the contrary, because the triune God is not a creature and therefore beyond sex, God is not imaged "*as* both male and female" but *in* both male and female.

mans—are created in the image of God. In the midst of this intriguing and often fruitful speculation on Jesus as intersex,[83] two things are assured by the text and tradition. First, those around Jesus viewed him as male.[84] Second, his male embodiment was unlike any other naturally conceived *male* because his flesh was taken from a woman alone.[85] All orthodox Christians who affirm the virginal conception would affirm that he—in a way unique to the human race—embraces female and male in his body because his male body came from a female alone. That insight is not new. Augustine says, "He was born of a woman; don't despair men; Christ was happy to be a man. Don't despair, women; Christ was happy to be born of a woman" (Sermon 72a.4).[86] *How* this is true remains a mystery.[87] *That* it is true is not up for debate. In the divine

83. These authors agree "speculation" is the fitting term because there is not widespread agreement that humans can now have empirical access to the body of Christ. At various times throughout the history of the church, some have claimed eucharistic miracles have occurred in which the consecrated communion host has transformed into human flesh and blood, the body of Jesus. See Real Presence Education and Adoration Association, *The Eucharistic Miracles of the World: Catalogue Book of the Vatican International Exhibition* (Bardstown, KY: Eternal Life, 2009), and Joan Carroll Cruz, *Eucharistic Miracles: And Eucharistic Phenomena in the Lives of the Saints* (Charlotte, NC: TAN Books, 2012). For most, the exact nature of his body remains a mystery.

84. Including when he was circumcised, in which no comment is made about anything unusual (Luke 2:21).

85. Elaine Storkey, reviving the explosive insights of Albert Schweitzer, wisely reminds interpreters of the dangers of making Jesus the Messiah in our own image: "God in Christ is not ultimately like us, any of us" ("Who Is the Christ? Issues in Christology and Feminist Theology," in *The Gospel and Gender: A Trinitarian Engagement with Being Male and Female in Christ*, ed. Douglas A. Campbell, Studies in Theology and Sexuality 7 [London: T&T Clark, 2003], 122). This caution applies to feminists who wish to find a female Christa but also to any who would claim that Jesus is male like any other male. Similarly, Angela West cautions, "This faith [Christianity] has the Other at the very centre of its life and recognizes that in all our search to express the divine, we are vulnerable to the desire to domesticate God. . . . God in Christ is not a person like us" (*Deadly Innocence: Feminist Theology and the Mythology of Sin* [London: Cassell, 1995], 185).

86. Augustine, *Sermons 51–94 on the New Testament*, trans. Edmund Hill, OP, Works of Saint Augustine: A Translation for the 21st Century III/3 (Brooklyn, NY: New City Press, 1991), 284.

87. The Eastern assertion of mystery offers a wise course of action: "The most evident idea in theology, namely the sacred incarnation of Jesus for our sakes, is something which cannot be enclosed in words nor grasped by any mind, not even by the leaders among the front ranks of angels. That he undertook to be a man is, for us, entirely mysterious. We have no way of understanding how, in a fashion at variance with nature, he was formed from a virgin's blood"

plan for the incarnation, in which the image of God is revealed, the divine embrace of human embodiment is accomplished by the birth of the Messiah as a virginally conceived male.

Christological discussions have frequently moved into another inquisitive territory as well: Could Christ have been female? The beauty of the incarnation, God becoming human, suggests an answer in the negative. Not because of the sociology of the day, which Jesus and his followers have no trouble pushing against, but because of the most basic biology. To be a human is to be born, born of a woman. The only way it is possible within the system of human procreation for God to involve both sexes in the revelation of divine embodiment is to have the image of God born as a male from the flesh of a female.[88]

God's choice to incarnate as male certainly *could* have excluded women. Kallistos Ware states, "We should keep in view the *particularity* of the incarnation. Christ was born at a specific time and place, from a specific mother. He did not become a human just in an abstract or generalized sense—he became a particular human being. As such he could not be both a male and a female at once, and he was in fact a male."[89]

Ware speaks rightly by emphasizing the maleness of Christ but errs in that he has not kept in view the *particularity* of Christ's maleness by virtue of the mode of the incarnation. The New Testament texts do assert that the Son was born and conceived of this specific mother. Because of that unparalleled conception, he is a male like no other, a male who received his body from God's partnering with a female alone.[90] To forget *this* particularity is to ignore

(Pseudo-Dionysius, *On the Divine Names* 2.9; see Pseudo-Dionysius the Areopagite, *The Complete Works*, trans. Colm Luibheid and Paul Rorem, The Classics of Western Christianity [New York: Paulist, 1987], 65).

88. As Maximus the Confessor states, "by being born of the virgin the separation of human nature into males and females is overcome" (*De ambiguis* [Patrologia Graeca 91:1308–9]; cited in Behr-Sigel, *Women in the Ministry of the Church*, 207). She states, "All men and women are called to grow toward the likeness of God which is communion, through the Spirit, with the God-Man who by becoming man, assumed humanity in such a way that no human person is excluded. He opened to all the possibility of restoring in Himself the unity of all human persons" (*Women in the Ministry of the Church*, 40).

89. Ware, "Man, Woman and the Priesthood of Christ," 26.

90. Although Brittany Wilson doesn't have in view the mode of the incarnation, she reaches a similar conclusion about Jesus's maleness: "Jesus may be a 'man,' but he is a man who differs from other men, not only because he does not adhere to standards of manliness but because he

the mode of the incarnation. To forget *this* particularity leads to a diminished recognition of God's image in women.

Jesus, son of Mary, radically includes females and males in his *imago Dei* body. The body that embraces male and female is the same body that reveals God. God the Father is indeed beyond gender, and this is revealed with striking clarity in the incarnate body of the male Savior Jesus, who was born of a woman. God's choice to incarnate as a male through a woman sets the precedent for the embodied inclusion of both men *and women*, all, in the body of Christ. God cannot be limited to the male, or represented by males alone, because the incarnate body of *the* image of God embraces both male and female.[91]

Revisiting God the Bridegroom

If all humans are so fully and robustly included in Christ, his revelation of God the Father cannot privilege some as more like God than others. Egregious equations between God and maleness are based on a weak understanding of Jesus's particular embodiment. Having presented the male-from-female-alone nature of Jesus Christ, the image of God, I can now return to the way in which Christians should and should not image God, using "bridegroom" as the example.

Barth argues that the image of God as the husband of Israel functioned as a signpost pointing forward to Christ: "The Bridegroom is Jesus the Son of Man, who in His person was to be the Lover, Bridegroom and Husband of His own people sanctified by Himself. It can and must be said that . . . the Old Testament pointed most powerfully beyond itself to the King given to Israel . . .

---

is God in the flesh" (*Unmanly Men: Reconfigurations of Masculinity in Luke-Acts* [Oxford: Oxford University Press, 2015], 201).

91. Feminist philosophers such as Luce Irigaray and Grace Jantzen appreciate the notion of incarnation. It upsets the "binary logic" of spirit versus flesh, affirming the good of all embodied humanity (Jantzen, *Becoming Divine: Toward a Feminist Philosophy of Religion*, Manchester Studies in Religion, Culture and Gender [Manchester: Manchester University Press, 1998], 62; see also 93, 269), but Jantzen counters that Jesus was "only a *partial* incarnation. He could not be the whole, the unique and only one, since he did not encompass all of humanity" (Jantzen, *Becoming Divine*, 17). To the contrary, because Jesus is male from a female alone, the mode of the incarnation allows a male Savior to embrace all humans.

the Son of God and Son of Man, Jesus Christ."[92] In a move practiced with some regularity by various authors of the New Testament,[93] the Son serves as the *ur*-image to a picture of the Old Testament that he then fulfills in his incarnate form. In Israel's Scriptures, the marital relationship that began in the garden, one of delight, fidelity, and mutual service, becomes more focused upon the production of children, and for Israel in its time and place, this focus narrowed to the production of a male heir. The divine proclamation of the good of marriage led to the divine proclamation of the good of childbearing. The bulk of Israel's concern with the family, the "central witness" concerning marriage in its concern for male progeny, points, Barth argues, "to the Son, the expected One."[94] The focus of marriage prepared the way for Christ to come as a child. It was the divine will that the ultimate bridegroom of the church come first as a son of Mary. In other words, for Christian interpreters the incarnate *Son's* relationship with God's people, named as the church, is both the fount and fulfillment of God's marital relationship with Israel.

Ephesians 5 is the "exegetical norm" for all texts portraying the divine-human relationship as marriage, when the *incarnate Son* serves as that picture's author and perfecter, the fount and the telos of the bridegroom imagery.[95] In Eph 5, Paul states with complete clarity that his primary interest is Christ and the church (Eph 5:32). Therefore, all divine-marriage pictures in Scripture are not primarily about the actions of a typical male for a female. Certainly, Paul draws application for actual marriages.[96] Even when good principles for human

---

92. *Church Dogmatics* III/1, §41.3, p. 323.

93. This way of reading the Scriptures appears in the Epistle to the Hebrews, where Jesus is said to be in the order of Melchizedek (5:5; 7:28), but Melchizedek is like the Son of God (7:3). Similarly, Paul gives evidence of this kind of understanding when he asserts that the fulfillment of God's promise to Abraham's descendants is realized in Jesus the Jewish Mesisah and also that he was the original seed to whom the inheritance was promised (Gal 3).

94. *Church Dogmatics* III/1, §41.3, p. 323. So also, "Man and woman become focused on children to lead to the Son" (III/2, §45.3, p. 300).

95. *Church Dogmatics* III/2, §45.3, p. 313.

96. Even on this point, Christ, in his presenting maleness, uses the power afforded to him to serve his bride. Masculinity appears only to subvert its dominance. Husbands learn that God the Son has a curious way of implementing sovereignty over his bride. It is not, as Jesus said, like the "gentiles" do it (Matt 20:25; Phil 2:5–11). Garrett Green calls this masculinity "'kenotic,' an aspect of divine self-emptying." His words best describe the actions of the Son, "God divests himself of all majesty, dominion, and power," not the actions of God the Father ("The Gender

marriages are established, male-female human relationships are not the main point. Marriage between a male and a female is the vehicle of the metaphor but not its tenor. Paul's description first and foremost focuses on the divine actions of God through the unparalleled person of Jesus Christ. Christ as husband is an affirmation of God as sacrificial sovereign. If God is the bridegroom of the people of God, it is not because God is more similar to men than women. It is because God the Father is one with the Son. The bridegroom image is defined by the Son. Christ's bridegroom maleness and therefore Yahweh's role as a husband is determined by the Son's *particular* incarnation as a male.

His sonship, in service to God's people, is incomparable to any male person. He is male but unlike every other male, for his embodied maleness broadens to include the female body from which he came. The particular Savior's body came from a particular Jewish woman. This Jesus as the bridegroom grants no support for God the Father as the exclusively male-imaged husband.

The imagery of the bridegroom and the bride, or God the husband of Israel, or Christ the husband of the church, is a pervasive and treasured image. I wish neither to destroy nor dismiss it, nor to swing the pendulum and demand imaging God as the wife. May God as husband continue to be contemplated and celebrated in Christian circles, but always and only through the lens of the revealed bridegroom, Jesus the incarnate Son.

In Persona Christi

The proof of an appropriate incarnational view of God appears, it seems to me, in the strictures for church leadership. Just as men are encouraged to imagine themselves as members of the bride, women should be freely encouraged to imagine themselves as members of Christ the bridegroom. As men can represent the church, so can women represent Christ. Thomas Hopko argues that for some feminist interpreters "the maleness of Jesus Christ has nothing to

---

of God and the Theology of Metaphor," in *Speaking the Christian God: The Holy Trinity and the Challenge of Feminism*, ed. Alvin F. Kimel Jr. [Grand Rapids: Eerdmans, 1992], 64). See also the argument that Jesus is a "maleness against itself" in Elizabeth Green, "More Musings on Maleness: The Maleness of Jesus Revisited," *Feminist Theology* 20 (1999): 9–27, as well as Tina Beattie, "Sexuality and the Resurrection of the Body: Reflections in the Hall of Mirrors," in *Resurrection Reconsidered*, ed. Gavin D'Costa (Oxford: Oneworld, 1996), 135–49, who suggests that Jesus "liberates women as well as men from the domination of the phallus" (59).

do with the ordained Christian ministry."[97] This may have been true for some who were arguing for the ordination of women in the 1970s.[98] That is not the argument I am seeking to make. It is right to reject previous assertions that dismissed the particularly of Jesus's sex as unimportant or to assert that inclusion is found in the fact that psychologically Jesus carried masculine and feminine qualities (all humans do), or finally that in his resurrected state, Jesus was androgynous.[99] I certainly seek not "to erode the male image of Jesus Christ."[100]

The maleness of Jesus Christ, in my estimation, has *everything* to do not just with Christian ministry but with Christian *life*. If Jesus were not birthed as a male, he would not include male bodies in his recapitulation. If he were not *birthed and conceived from a woman alone*, he would not include female bodies in his recapitulation. I seek not to erode but to emphasize his maleness, the way it came about, to show its unique particularity specifically as it regards male and female. No woman can be excluded from imaging God because his male body came only from a woman.[101]

In my assessment, this eliminates the maleness of Jesus as support for a male-only clergy.[102] The orienting person of the image does not justify any

97. Hopko, "Women and the Priesthood," 181.

98. Rosemary Radford Ruether says this explicitly: "the maleness of Jesus has no ultimate significance" (*Sexism and God-Talk: Toward a Feminist Theology; With a New Introduction* [Boston: Beacon, 1993], 135).

99. Discussed in Belonick, "Spirit of the Female Priesthood," 140.

100. Belonick argues this is the mistake of some feminist interpreters ("Spirit of Female Priesthood," 140). This sentiment might find expression by Susannah Cornwall: "Jesus's historic physical maleness might simply have to be something Christians say *less* about in theological terms; something to which they attach less significance and in which they ground fewer theological and ecclesial suppositions" ("Sex Otherwise: Intersex, Christology, and the Maleness of Jesus," *Journal of Feminist Studies in Religion* 30 [2014]: 23–39). She, however, is arguing more about the negative *implications* of Jesus's maleness than about Jesus's actual existence. One can arrive at the result Cornwall desires, namely, more inclusion for nonmales in Christ, by saying more about Jesus's physical maleness than less.

101. Neil H. Williams concludes his book with this: "We conclude that, in the incarnation, God honors both sexes . . . by being born male, of a woman. 'When the fullness of time had come, God sent his Son, born of a woman' (Galatians 4:4)" (*The Maleness of Jesus: Is It Good News for Women?* [Eugene, OR: Cascade, 2011], 240).

102. Bishop Kallistos Ware argues, "The male character of the Christian priesthood forms an integral element in this pattern of revealed, God-given symbolism, which is not to be tampered with. Christ is the Bridegroom and the Church is his bride. And how can the living icon of the

privileging of one gender of humanity over another in any enactment of the bridegroom with his church, or bride. Males are not more apt to represent the divine husband than the female, because the maleness of the referent in this picture (Jesus Christ) has no peer. Women inadequately image Jesus, but so do men. Nonvirginally conceived males can never perfectly symbolize Jesus's virginally conceived maleness. Males and females can only ever embody a part of Jesus's inclusive body.

The impact, however, is not limited to the women who have aptitude and sense a call to ordained ministry but are barred from Christ's representative role. Representation matters for every woman who claims Christ, whether she stands behind the altar or pulpit or sits in the pew.[103] By seeing women represent God, every woman knows that she, in her distinct embodiment, is included in Christ along with and *no less than* her fellow male confessor.[104] She fully bears the image of God. Kathy Keller offers the encouragement that both men and women "get to play the Jesus role," but with men demonstrating his servant authority and women his submissive servanthood.[105] I agree with the encouragement, but not the bifurcation. The incarnation opens the door to

---

Bridegroom be other than a man?" ("Man, Woman and the Priesthood of Christ," 29). How? Because the bridegroom himself is male like no other.

103. Hopko makes the point that this applies to all women when he states, "No woman is ever called to this vocation [priesthood]—her very womanhood precludes it, since she cannot possibly be a husband and father" ("Women and the Priesthood," 186). Conversely, Behr-Sigel suggests, "every woman carried potentially within her, with the image of Christ, the image of his mother" (*Women in the Ministry of the Church*, 129). She quotes Alexandre Boukharev: "In the presence of a woman . . . may your eyes rise toward the Lord, whose image is imprinted in her according to her human nature and redemptive grace . . . then will be revealed to you in this woman, in this human person, at the same time as in the icon of the Lord, the image . . . of her from whom the Lamb of God condescended to take flesh" (104).

I recognize that I am speaking in binaries, primarily concerning the historic (although it continues in contemporary reality) exclusion of women. I encourage readers to engage with the thoughtful, theologically rigorous, and compassionate works of Mark A. Yarhouse concerning those people who do not fit neatly into either category of male or female. Christ's unique embrace of the sexed reality of human experience offers inclusion not only to both women and men but also to all those who find themselves somewhere in between.

104. The Logia Institute, founded by Christa McKirland, which exists to support women in theological education has this as its tagline: "You can be what you can see" (The Logia Institute, https://logos.wp.st-andrews.ac.uk/logia/).

105. Keller, *Jesus, Justice, and Gender Roles*, 36.

all standing in Christ's authority, which is expressed in Christ's service. Jesus's particular embodiment, and faithful life, denies such fracture of his unified nature along sexed lines.

Church communities may *prefer* to play out the divine drama with men representing the divine, but if this decision is based not upon preference but principle, it is possible that a theological error has crept in. It is leadership that discloses the true meaning of theological language. The claim may be made that God is above gender, but if only men are ever allowed to represent this God, that claim becomes difficult, if not impossible, to believe.[106] If women are not allowed to represent Christ, those Christian communities are utilizing a flattened view of his maleness, one that forgets the mode of the incarnation. This weakened Christology becomes a pathway to the false and damaging male-making of God the Father.[107] The male Savior whose flesh came from the body of a woman provides a radically inclusive embrace of all humanity, a humanity made in the image of God.

Biological Reductionism?

If women are included in the Messiah, in the very image of God, because of the role of Mary the Savior's *mother*, the gain of women's full participation in Christ may have come at the cost of their reduction to maternal bodies.[108] In other words, women are full agents in the Christian life revealing God because and solely because of their biological potential for giving birth, or so it might seem.

This conundrum is a well-trod path dead-ending at a point where the only available options left to women are to be ignored or to be valued only for their

---

106. Jantzen argues that Christendom is the place where masculinity has most clearly "usurped the place of domination" (*Becoming Divine*, 172).

107. Communities may have other reasons for limiting ecclesial leadership to men, including passages in the Pauline Epistles or Jesus's selection of twelve Jewish male apostles. The critique I offer here is focused on reasoning for male-only leadership based on Jesus's maleness.

108. Sensitive to the dangers of lifting up Mary as a symbol, I seek to honor Mary's particularity yet at the same time highlight the inclusion of all, including all women, in her son. See Elizabeth Johnson, *Truly Our Sister: A Theology of Mary in the Communion of Saints* (New York: Continuum, 2003), 95–101.

biology. The work of Luce Irigaray illustrates the difficulty. She aptly named the problem of disdain: "If traditionally, and as mother, woman represents *place* for man, such a limit means that she becomes a *thing*."[109] She also sought to counter this dismissiveness. Writing to correct philosophers who had appropriated but ignored the maternal, she argued for the importance of the womb. In so doing, however, she fell prey to the other side of the problem, limiting the value of women to their reproductive bodies.[110] Tertullian stands guilty, too, says Mayra Rivera, in a way dangerously close to my own project: "Describing Christ as the union of Mary's flesh and God's will was meant as a claim of importance of flesh. But representing carnality as the contribution of women depended on and contributed to hierarchical conceptions of gender that limit the feminine to the realm of a *spiritless materiality*. That legacy haunts contemporary accounts of flesh."[111] I must face the possibility that my account, my passion for affirming the inclusive female-produced body of the male Savior, might very well be haunted.

I desire to honor the shocking fact that God entered the world through the womb of and from the flesh of a woman. I aim to show exegetically and theologically the ways in which that entrance makes a profound difference for the ways humans understand God and themselves, particularly proclaiming a profound valuing of women. The challenge is to do so without reducing women to their spiritless bodies, who matter to God because they are or could become mothers. The legacy Rivera calls attention to seems to demand that an interpreter must choose either one commitment or the other, embrace the mode of the incarnation as well as biological reductionism or reject them both.[112]

109. Luce Irigaray, *An Ethics of Sexual Difference*, trans. Carolyn Burke and Gillian Gill (Ithaca, NY: Cornell University Press, 1993), 10.

110. As stated by Mayra Rivera, "By making the maternal the ultimate site from which to conceive flesh helps reify the feminization of flesh, which establishes a parallel between male/ female and spirit/flesh dualisms" (*Poetics of the Flesh* [Durham, NC: Duke University Press, 2015], 107). Jantzen calls attention to the same problem in Julia Kristeva's *Stabat Mater*, whose work casts "women simply as mothers," or "women who harbour the desire to reproduce" (*Becoming Divine*, 203, 262).

111. Rivera, *Poetics of the Flesh*, 108–9 (emphasis mine).

112. It is important to clarify why I find biological reductionism false and therefore detrimental. First, it is exclusionary; not all women are able to or desire to have children. Second, it is limiting; even women who relish their children have other interests and identities, not all of which are maternal/nurturing.

To the contrary, I believe it is possible to affirm both the mode of the incarnation and the full personhood of women, and to hold both with coherence. Even more, when one does so, each affirmation becomes more robust.

To begin, materiality must be evaluated through the Christian narrative. The Christian imaginary, dependent upon Israel's account of creation, affirms that materiality, even human flesh, is that which God called good (Gen 1:31). That beginning point already calls into question a good (spirit) versus bad (material) dichotomy. From that point on, all humans, according to the good design of God, are born of women.[113] The incarnation in congruence with this affirmation of the goodness of human materiality through human birth unsettles the negative dichotomy further. Mary is not simply the *place* for the God-man, the vessel through which he passes, a *thing*. If the Son of God has flesh, and Christianity has banked its entire system on the affirmation that he does, that flesh is drawn from her. In the Christian imaginary, as centered on the incarnation, that is no small thing. The human body is granted even greater value through this doctrine. God has not only created but *entered into* human flesh. The distinction between divine and human, spirit and flesh, is breached and forever transformed. Consequently, the female contribution of *flesh*, cultivated by the spirit of God, is not the unimportant part but the very contribution where God chose to reveal, and ultimately revealed, the divine identity. Moreover, this is the contribution that, having undergone transformation, will remain forever after being resurrected to eternal life. If, because of the cursed lies of misogyny, many have denigrated "feminized flesh," the Christian God, as Mary said, "hath exalted the humble and meek" (Luke 1:52). In Christianity, flesh is a very good thing, divinely created, blessed, inhabited, and, after resurrection, enduring forever.

Rivera's elegant phrase, "spiritless materiality," illuminates the second way through what is, in my opinion, a false dichotomy between the spirit (sym-

---

113. Jantzen illuminates this point powerfully, calling for "a focus not so much on women as *mothers*, but on all of us, women and men, as *natals*, entering the world of woman born," and "it should be not be necessary to say that not all women are mothers, that women who are not mothers are not thereby inadequate or 'failed' women, and that even for those women who are mothers, motherhood is only one aspect of their lives, even if a very significant one. But although not all women give birth, every person who has ever lived has been born, and born of a woman." Finally, and most poetic, "there can be no other selves than selves of woman born" (*Becoming Divine*, 203, 144, 141). The echoes of Gal 4:4 resound throughout her work.

bolized male) and the flesh (symbolized female), by virtue of which women are reduced to their bodies alone. It is true that Luke clearly portrays Mary willingly offering her *body*. The consensus of the tradition then affirms that it is her flesh that provides the carnality of the Messiah. This act, however, is the precise opposite of *spiritless*. It is possible because and only because the spirit of God hovers over the flesh of Mary and cultivates from her the flesh of God (Luke 1:35). The female contribution is not *spiritless but spirit-filled flesh*. The female body stands not as the opposite of spirituality but as the material from which the ultimate example of the revelation of the Spirit, the incarnate Son of God, exists. Female flesh becomes the epicenter of the Spirit.

Finally, one can affirm the universal impact of the mode of the incarnation without reducing women to their biology because of the breadth of Mary's own story. In the following chapter, I engage in a close reading of all references to her in order to show that the one woman in the Christian narrative who could most easily be reduced to her identity as a biological mother persistently *is not*. Mark's scant reference to her, which holds a particular weight as the earliest gospel tradition, positions motherhood, even her motherhood, in relation to Jesus as an act of faith over and above an act of biology (Mark 3:31–35, where Jesus concludes, "Whoever does the will of God is my brother and sister and mother"). Although Matthew paints a powerful picture of her motherhood, his inclusion of the same conversation precludes any move to limit her importance to biological motherhood alone (Matt 12:46–50). The same is true for Luke (Luke 8:19–21). Hence, this exchange, which some have read as evidence of her limited faith in her son, is instead included so that she might not be limited to the act of bearing her son. Admittedly, John refers to her only by virtue of her biological relationship to Jesus, only as "mother," but even in this position, she does more than mother him. Luke's writings are clearest of all. The author who gives the most confirmation of her biological motherhood also gives her voice as a prophet and narrates her as a gospel proclaimer. If the New Testament limits not even Mary to her motherhood, then her story cannot be used, or used *rightly* at least, to do the same for any other woman. The breadth of her story is the ultimate reason I, as an adherent of Christianity, reject biological reductionism. Feminist theory has with open-eyed honesty named what is already present in Christian Scripture. Women are never limited to their propensity for biological reproduction, and it is Mary who most clearly shows this to be true.

The unique embodiment of the Son of God includes all women by virtue of Mary his mother. Instead of limiting them to their biology, the incarnation affirms female flesh in Christ as divinely valued and Spirit-infused, so that women, with gratefulness for their particular bodies, can, following Mary's example, serve the coming kingdom of God in any and all ways the Spirit might call.

Conclusion

Affirming the birth of the Messiah through a virgin aligns with the coherent witness of the New Testament and Christian tradition. To do so asserts the humanity of Jesus in such a way that all are radically included within the divine image while at the same time making male perceptions of God the Father impossible. The denial of any maleness or masculinity of God appears with no greater force than in the assertion that God the Father is revealed in the incarnate, virginally conceived Son. This God as revealed in the incarnation of Jesus Christ does not favor males and does empower females. The story of the Mother of God serves as proof.

six

Ministry

She was also a co-minister with the disciples of the Lord.

—Pseudo-Maximus the Confessor, *Life of the Virgin*

Mary is known to the world because she was the mother of Jesus, but she did more for God than mother Jesus. She provides a template for all Christians whose primary identity resides in their relationship with Christ,[1] whose Christian identity comes to expression in a rich variety of ways.

God, present with her in the act of child-rearing, grants a holy honor to the call of mothering. She served God not only with her body, as discussed in the second chapter, but also with her character. It was her voice that facilitated Jesus's learning of obedience and creativity, as evidenced in the accounts of the early days of the Messiah by both Luke and John.[2]

1. As Mary becomes more separated from her son, and the unrepeatable role she plays in his arrival, it becomes easier to transform her into an impossible and damaging ideal for women. Andrew Louth notes this shift in "Mary in Patristics," in *The Oxford Handbook of Mary*, ed. Chris Maunder (Oxford: Oxford University Press, 2019), 54–66.

2. "Mary's mothering of Christ is indeed part of the particular and unrepeatable drama of redemption that is the object of our faith." See Angela West, *Deadly Innocence: Feminist Theology and the Mythology of Sin* (London: Cassell, 1995), 212.

Mary performs a divinely enabled and divinely honored service as the mother of Jesus, but divine enablement and support are not exhausted by her maternal role. God also enables and honors her ministry to people other than her son, and in these instances, her ministry is not that of parenting but proclamation. Some have called her a prophet,[3] some a preacher, but both terms can stir up debates that risk distraction from the reality at hand: She has a ministry of the word. The authors of the New Testament portray her speaking truth about God to others. She sings to Elizabeth while she is carrying Jesus. She instructs a group of servants at the beginning of Jesus's ministry, and she testifies to the diverse crowds in Jerusalem at Pentecost. The content of each communiqué discloses a different facet on the prism of God's character, and the form presents an undeniable fact: the God of the New Testament does not silence the verbal ministry of women.[4] In fact, just as was true for her service as mother, it is the spirit of God who enables and amplifies her proclamation.

Even with the infrequent testimony about her, the New Testament shows that Mary ministers inside and outside the home, with acts of service and with speech, as parent and proclaimer. The verisimilitude of the narrative follows the pattern of real life: these roles are not neatly separated. Hence, I consider them roughly in sequence,[5] the proclamation of her Magnificat, her mothering

3. N. Clayton Croy and Alice E. Connor argue that Luke painted Mary as a prophet but did not call her such because of associations with pagan virgin prophetesses. Once this threat of association was not present, several patristic sources, including Eusebius, Theodoret, Basil of Caesarea, Epiphanius, and Cyril of Alexandria, were comfortable with naming her as a prophet ("Mantic Mary? The Virgin Mother as Prophet in Luke 1.26–56 and the Early Church," *Journal for the Study of the New Testament* 34 [2012]: 254–76). Robert W. Jenson calls her the arch prophet in that she speaks the person-word Jesus ("An Attempt to Think about Mary," *Dialog* 31 [1992]: 261).

4. The vast number of interpreters agree, even those who limit women from *certain* forms of proclamation. For example, D. A. Carson rejects the interpretation of 1 Cor 14:34–35 that women should be absolutely silent in the church assembly ("'Silent in the Churches': On the Role of Women in 1 Cor 14:33b–36," in *Recovering Biblical Manhood and Womanhood: A Response to Evangelical Feminism*, rev. ed. [Wheaton, IL: Crossway, 2021], 179–98).

5. Because I am drawing from different evangelists in this chapter, I am intentionally choosing to read the events in the chronological order of my construction, not the individual accounts of the distinct stories of the life of Jesus in isolation. In so doing, I am tracking through the basic events of Mary's experience with Jesus: pregnancy, birth, parenting, then his early ministry, death, and postresurrection.

of twelve-year-old Jesus, her influence over both Jesus and the servants at the wedding of Cana, and finally, her proclamation at Pentecost. Mary is certainly unique as the Mother of God, but her Spirit-inspired multivalent ministry is not. No one else can mother Jesus, but everyone can testify of him.

God's affirmation of Mary's worth does not end with the participation with her flesh but extends to an affirmation of her mind, emotions, will, and voice as well. Mary's continued involvement with God gives evidence of divine valida- tion of the myriads of ministries that women, in line with her central example, can enact. Mary's God enables men *and women* to minister in multiple ways.

Ministry of Proclamation: Magnificat

An analysis of her song discloses her world-changing prophetic gift. Luke places the words of this song of praise upon the lips of Mary.[6] It is profoundly important that the narrator does not say these things; instead, the at-risk girl

---

6. Could Mary, the young first-century Jewish girl, have spoken these words? It would be unlikely for her to have done so in Greek, but some scholars in the past suggested a Hebrew urtext for her song that Luke or a source before him translated into Greek. See R. A. Aytoun, "The Ten Lucan Hymns of the Nativity in Their Original Language," *Journal of Theological Studies* 18 (1917): 247–88; Stephen Farris, *The Hymns of Luke's Infancy Narratives: Their Origin, Meaning and Significance* (London: Bloomsbury, 2015). The songs are, in the words of I. Howard Marshall, "unlikely to have been spontaneous compositions, but serve, like the speeches in ancient his- tories, to express the significance of the moment in appropriate language" (*The Gospel of Luke: A Commentary on the Greek Text*, New International Greek Testament Commentary [Grand Rapids: Eerdmans, 1978], 46). It seems feasible, as several scholars conclude, that Luke used some sources for the birth narrative, maybe from a poor Jewish community (see Raymond E. Brown, *The Birth of the Messiah: A Commentary on the Infancy Narratives in the Gospels of Matthew and Luke*, new updated ed. [New York: Doubleday, 1993], 357–60), or possibly from Mary her- self (33). It is not clear to me why Luke consulting the memories of Mary is "sheer conjecture" (Joseph A. Fitzmyer, *The Gospel according to Luke I–IX*, Anchor Bible 28 [New Haven: Yale Uni- versity Press, 2009], 308), as Richard Bauckham has argued that named eyewitnesses, including the family of Jesus, would have provided their testimony (*Jesus and the Eyewitnesses: The Gospels as Eyewitness Testimony*, 2nd ed. [Grand Rapids: Eerdmans, 2017], 297–98). Having heard from others, then Luke formed the story, including the songs, in his own form, with knowledge of Hannah's song from 1 Sam 2:1–10. Hannah Frankel, a student in my class Mary: Mother of God, captured this text's truth well: "Perhaps the most loving thing God could have done was place that sweet and strong poetry inside of Mary's mouth, even if she never said it herself. Just

does.[7] A close analysis of the song reveals that Mary speaks in a thickly woven tapestry truths about God, herself, and others, in line with Israel's prophets of the past and foretelling the movement of the church in the future. As a trustworthy proclaimer, she sets a deeply influential example.[8]

Her words, like those spoken at the annunciation, are fully self-involved.[9] Mary's first words in the song/poem speak of her comprehensive response to God:[10] "My soul doth magnify the Lord." While "soul" (ψυχῇ [*psychē*]) may connote interiority (Luke 12:19), for this evangelist, more often the term embraces a more comprehensive sense. It is a term he uses to speak of one's whole life.[11] Then she adds the poetic parallel: "My spirit [πνεῦμα (*pneuma*)] rejoices in God my Savior" (1:47). πνεῦμα (*pneuma*), too, when it applies to humans,

---

as Botticelli honors Mary with an indigo cape, could the Holy Spirit, through Luke, not have honored Mary with a song fit for the Mother of God?"

7. I adopt this striking description from Courtney Hall Lee, who notes that Mary is "a woman of a low caste and an oppressed ethnicity. She is a girl who today would be labeled 'at risk'" (*Black Madonna: A Womanist Look at Mary of Nazareth* [Eugene, OR: Cascade, 2017], 112). The words of Elisabeth Schüssler Fiorenza are apt here as well: "it is the young pregnant woman, living in occupied territory and struggling against victimization and for survival and dignity. It is she who holds out the offer of untold possibilities for Christology and theology" (*Jesus: Miriam's Child, Sophia's Prophet; Critical Issues in Feminist Christology* [New York: Continuum, 1994], 187). A few early Latin manuscripts attribute this song to Elisabeth, but the external and internal data support Mary as the speaker. See Bruce M. Metzger, *Textual Commentary on the New Testament*, 2nd ed. (New York: United Bible Societies, 1994), 109.

8. For powerful reflections on the story of Mary as a muse for preaching, see Jerusha Matsen Neal, *Blessed: Monologues for Mary*, Art for Faith's Sake (Eugene, OR: Cascade, 2013), and Neal, *The Overshadowed Preacher: Mary, the Spirit, and the Labor of Proclamation* (Grand Rapids: Eerdmans, 2020).

9. Serene Jones states, "As one who is blessed and lives in recognition of her blessedness, Mary embodies the glory of the God whom she also bears to the world. Imagining the shape of God's kingdom, she steps forward and speaks poetic, prophetic words that are absolutely— also—hers" (*Trauma and Grace: Theology in a Ruptured World*, 2nd ed. [Louisville: Westminster John Knox, 2019], 119). John B. F. Miller also calls attention to the personal nature of the Magnificat; the language keeps "Mary within the scope of the action" in *"Convinced That God Had Called Us": Dreams, Visions, and the Perception of God's Will in Luke-Acts* (Leiden: Brill, 2007), 128.

10. Using the phrase of Claus Westermann, Farris defines the Magnificat as a "declarative psalm of praise," noting that it "exhibits the parallelism which is so characteristic of Hebrew and the burden of [it] is the praise of God" (*Hymns of Luke's Infancy Narratives*), 11.

11. Luke 6:9; 9:24; 12:20; 12:22–23; 14:26; 17:33; 21:19; Acts 2:41, 43; 3:23; 7:14; 15:26; 20:24; 27:10, 22, 37.

denotes the vivifying aspect of the person.[12] Mary with her mind, emotions, body—entire living self—rejoices to magnify God. After the first verse of the Magnificat, God becomes the subject of the actions.

She does magnify God because God is her Savior. As the first instance of the very-important-for-Luke salvation (σῴζω [sōzō]) word group, Mary's term does not replicate something that Gabriel said to her, although it does resonate with the idea that the coming Messiah will reign. Hence the logical implication is that he will therefore *save* Israel from their present unjust rulers (Luke 1:32–33). It is she, however, who is the one to introduce the theme of salvation.

Her soteriological statement about God is richly multivalent. It includes the things from which God has already saved her, namely, the possibility of barrenness and the grief and shame that can accompany it.[13] It also denotes that Mary demonstrates her trust that God *will* save her from the shame this particularly unusual pregnancy would bring. She is the second example in this two-volume narrative, following the barren Elizabeth, of God's saving, in a tangibly familial way, of the disdained. In addition to physical and social components of salvation, Mary's declaration also names a spiritual dimension: God is the Savior of her entire being. The tradition has affirmed God's gracious preparation of her for her task.[14]

Mary's song connects God's salvation of her with God's looking upon her lowliness, specifically the lowliness (ταπείνωσιν [tapeinōsin]) of his slave (δούλης [doulēs]). Because she named *herself* in this role (Luke 1:48), this is a self-reference with the painful paradox of honor discussed in chapter 3. The specificity of her lowliness comes into sharpest relief when compared with her muse in the Scriptures of Israel, Hannah. In her agonizing prayers, Hannah asked God to look upon (ἐπιβλέπω [epiblepō]) the humiliation (ταπείνωσιν [tapeinōsin]) of his slave (δούλη [doulē]) (1 Sam 1:11). Quite the opposite of Mary, however, when she uttered this prayer, Hannah resided in the humilia-

---

12. Luke 1:17 (Elijah), 80 (John); 8:55 (Peter's mother-in-law); 23:46 (Jesus).

13. Yet unlike Hannah (1 Sam 2:5), Mary says nothing explicit about barrenness.

14. Disagreement continues, of course, about the timing and extent of this salvation of Mary, but no tradition denies that God was the Savior of her whole person. See Matthew Levering, who states, "To be mother of the Redeemer ... is a *mission*, rooted entirely in grace and for which Mary is prepared by grace" ("Mary and Grace," *The Oxford Handbook of Mary*, ed. Chris Maunder [Oxford: Oxford University Press, 2019], 289).

tion of barrenness. Mary, by this point in the narrative, does not. Instead, her lowliness has other possible meanings. She might be referring to her economic position, as the hymn itself connects this lowliness with hunger (Luke 1:53), and the temple narrative discloses that she and Joseph have to opt for the less expensive birds rather than the lamb sacrifice (2:24). It could be a reference to a reckoning in a system of honor in which others might (unjustly) deem her shameful for a birth not with her betrothed.[15] It could also be her appropriate recognition of her place before God. Since she has heard and believed that God is the Most High, she knows that she stands, by comparison, in a state of lowliness.[16] Although the familiar translation of "lowliness" could seem self-deprecatory, similar to the paradox of slave language, her marginalized position is a clear-eyed statement of her embodied reality in her society and before God. It is from the platform of such a recognition that the God of Israel works wonders.[17] Unlike Hannah, however, Mary does not beg for God to see her; she states that God already has. God's vision is the reason for her praise. The God who sees has seen her in her lowliness,[18] imposed by her society or embraced as a spiritual discipline or both. For her, being seen by God for who she truly is and how she really exists provides a reason to rejoice.

God will not be the only one to notice her. She will receive blessing from all generations. It begins with her own generation, chiefly in the person of Elizabeth (Luke 1:42, 45). Throughout Luke's Gospel, Jesus has nothing good to say about the current generation, be that people living during his own time or people of the age before his return. Each time he uses the term "generation,"

15. The resonance of unjust humiliation connects with another time Luke uses the word. In the Ethiopian eunuch's recitation of Isaiah's suffering-servant passage, the servant is treated unjustly in a state of humiliation (Acts 8:33).

16. The word group generally denotes that which is low, as compared to the high (Jas 1:10; Luke 3:5; 14:11; 18:14).

17. The God of Israel has a propensity to notice and act on behalf of those who are in a state of humility (Deut 26:7; 1 Sam 9:16; Neh 9:9; Ps 24:18 LXX; 30:8 LXX; 118:153 LXX; 135:23 LXX).

18. El-roi, "the God who sees," as named by Hagar in Gen 16:13. See the treatment of this narrative in Phyllis Trible, *Texts of Terror: Literary-Feminist Readings of Biblical Narratives* (Philadelphia: Fortress, 1984), 9–36, and Delores S. Williams, *Sisters in the Wilderness: The Challenge of Womanist God-Talk* (Maryknoll, NY: Orbis Books, 2013), and Williams, "Hagar in African American Biblical Appropriation," in *Hagar, Sarah, and Their Children: Jewish, Christian, and Muslim Perspectives*, ed. Phyllis Trible and Letty M. Russell (Louisville: Westminster John Knox, 2006), 177–84.

it is to critique or condemn them.[19] Yet even someone from that generation does bless (μακαρία [*makaria*]) Mary (11:27), although Jesus has to correct her reason for doing so since the focus is more on Mary's maternity than her faith.

The generation around her is not the only one to offer blessing. Similar to the promise that her son will have an eternal throne (1:33), she proclaims that each generation—for as long as there are generations—will remember her and call her blessed.[20] The transition from lowliness to perpetual praise will happen because the one who is able to do all things (1:37) has in fact done great things *for her* (1:49). She does not falsely imagine this greatness to be her own possession, but neither does she deny its reality. She shows the strength of humility by naming what *God* has done *for her*.

The Lord is not just good to her alone, she proclaims, but extends mercy to those same perpetual generations who will bless her. God's mercy comes upon those who fear God, Mary says, indicating that the Mighty One is worthy of fear.

With both the expansion of the song's perspective past herself and toward others and also naming the condition of fear, Luke 1:50 transitions to the second half of the poem that speaks of God's corporate actions both toward the appropriately fearful and toward those who are not. Mary says boldly that God possesses a strong arm—an image drawn from the texts of Israel—that scatters those who do not fear.[21] God has completely adequate means to deal with those who are deeply proud. God is, as Mary has already stated, powerful and will depose from their thrones those who imagine themselves powerful. God discloses that their power is temporary.[22] In their place, the Savior will lift

---

19. Luke 1:48, 50; 7:31; 9:41; 11:29–32, 50–51; 16:8; 17:25; 21:32. One neutral example might be Luke 16:8, where the children of this age act shrewdly with the members of their generation. Because interacting with the generation takes shrewdness like that displayed by the unfaithful steward, it is questionable whether this generation is morally exemplary.

20. Interestingly, this language continues in what Stephen J. Shoemaker calls the "earliest clear indication of Marian piety" on a papyrus from Egypt. The prayer calls Mary "the blessed one" ("Marian Liturgies and Devotion in Early Christianity," in *Mary: The Complete Resource*, ed. Sarah Jane Boss [London: Continuum, 2009], 130).

21. For example, Gen 49:24; Wis 11:21.

22. Scot McKnight asserts, "her song belongs . . . on the shelf with socio-spiritual songs of protest against unjust rulers" (*The Real Mary: Why Evangelical Christians Can Embrace the Mother of Jesus* [Brewster, MA: Paraclete, 2007], 20).

up the lowly (ταπεινός [*tapeinos*] 1:52) just as in the lifting up of Mary herself (ταπείνωσιν [*tapeinōsin*] 1:48).

Moving from the level of kingdoms to the level of the kitchen table, she also affirms that God will fill those who are hungry with good things. Her language here resonates most closely with Ps 106:9 LXX, where, in recalling the story of the exodus, the psalmist declares that God filled the hungry soul with good things. Quite possibly she is including herself in this group. If she is poor, as Luke later indicates, she could have experienced hunger, as would many of her neighbors.[23] The rich will not be invited to this feast but will be sent away empty, until the fullness of their bellies no longer clouds their ability to perceive their deeper hunger.

Her words have already been evoking the sacred texts of Israel, so her final stanza only makes explicit that which has been in the background. God is keeping the promise of mercy to Abraham and his seed by supporting (ἀντιλαμβάνω [*antilambanō*]) Israel.[24] Here Mary's words describe Israel as God's παῖς (*pais*), aptly translated as either "child" or "servant." As good poetry does, this line depicts several possible objects of the divine embrace. God takes hold of the people of Israel, the collective child, by aiding the Son upon whom the hopes of Israel rest. Yet God's embrace of this Son must be preceded by God's gathering of another young servant, namely, Mary herself.[25] Mary asserts that God is being faithful to the promises spoken to the ancestors, a group she claims as her own ("our [ἡμῶν] fathers" [Luke 1:55]). She has already declared God's good work with her, so it would be in line with the rest of the chapter to say that God has taken hold of *her* to aid her. She has described herself as a δούλης (*doulēs*), and this bears semantic overlap with a παῖς (*pais*), as a "servant." Both she and this παῖς (*pais*) belong to God (αὐτοῦ [*autou*] 1:48, 54). Hence, the Lord will embrace Israel (read: nation, Jesus, Mary) as a remembrance of the

---

23. Peter Garnsey argued that "famines were rare, but that subsistence crises falling short of famine were common" (*Famine and Food Supply in the Greco-Roman World: Responses to Risk and Crises* [Cambridge: Cambridge University Press, 1985], 6). Stephen J. Friesen postulates that the majority of the population lived near or below subsistence levels ("Injustice or God's Will? Early Christian Explanations of Poverty," in *Wealth and Poverty in Early Church and Society*, ed. Susan R. Holman [Grand Rapids: Baker, 2008], 17–36).

24. ἀντιλαμβάνω (*antilambanō*) is employed to denote literally "grabbing" (Gen 48:17) but comes to take on the meaning of "aid" or "help."

25. It is possible that Luke also evokes echoes to another servant (δοῦλος [*doulos*]) who has heard God's word (ῥῆμα [*rhēma*]) of promise, namely, David (2 Sam 7:25).

divine mercy spoken at the beginning of covenant history to Abraham and to his seed (read: nation, Jesus, Mary).[26] Of this embrace, there will be no end. God spoke promises to Abraham about his lineage being the source of blessing to all peoples, and just recently God, through Gabriel, has remembered those merciful promises by inviting Mary to fulfill them.

The truth of Mary's proclamation is borne out by its multiple witnesses. From the past, the law and the prophets affirm her statements. In the future, the actions of Jesus and the Spirit-infused church carry out the magnification of God about which she has hymned. When the Savior is born (Luke 2:11), he confirms her proclamation with word and deed as he enacts the great reversal in his ministry. In his first public teaching, he says that he has come to bring good news to the poor and release to the oppressed (4:18–19). After that, his words frequently echo hers: "Blessed are you who are hungry now, for you will be filled." "Woe to you who are full now, for you will be hungry" (6:21, 25). And again, "For all who exalt themselves will be humbled, and those who humble themselves will be exalted" (14:11; 18:14). He often teaches on the judgment that comes to those who idolize their riches (8:14; 12:21; 16:19–31; 18:23–25), the parable of the rich man and Lazarus being a poignant example of the reversal of the hungry and the full (16:19–31). After instructing his simple band of followers on the necessity of humility, he promises them thrones (22:30). So too, the summary of what the church does in its early days resonates with her words. There was no lack, as her song had foretold (1:53; Acts 12:45). They received their food in gladness as she had rejoiced (ἠγαλλίασεν [ēgalliasen] Luke 1:47; Acts 2:46). People were being saved, just as it had been foretold to her (Luke 1:69, 71, 77; Acts 2:47). The connections between Luke's two-volume work show Mary to be an exemplary and trustworthy proclaimer, even if the proclamations need to be interpreted along the way in light of the surprising ministry of Jesus.[27]

As fulcrum between past and future, she is also a prime example of one who speaks truly about God. She proclaims that God the Most High has saved

26. The association between Mary and Israel finds affirmation in the similarities between Gabriel's address to Mary (χαῖρε [chaire]) in Luke 1:28 and the same address to Daughter Zion in Zeph 3:14 and Zech 9:9. See Hans Urs von Balthasar and Joseph Cardinal Ratzinger, *Mary: The Church at the Source* (San Francisco: Ignatius, 2005), 64–67.

27. See Miller, *Convinced That God Had Called Us*, esp. 133–43. He notes, "Without these hymns (Mag and Benedictus) there would be nothing in Luke's narrative describing the messianic expectations that had to be reshaped in order to understand Jesus's actual earthly ministry" (143).

her, noticed her, done great things for her, exalted her, filled her, aided her, remembered her, all because she believed that God has spoken to her. This may be Mary meek, but this is not Mary mild. She hymns boldly with true humility that God has done unparalleled great things *for her*. Because God is so great and so compassionate and so merciful and so good, God has indeed magnified *her*.

At the same time, the Magnificat magnifies God. Mary proclaims that God is God as Israel's story affirms: holy and powerful. The God of the Magnificat, a theological sketch reiterated in Zechariah's Benedictus,[28] presents the Lord: mighty, holy, worthy of fear. God remains the sovereign: the magnified, praised, holy, and powerful Master. No chance for reversal of this dynamic; no equality between God's power and that of humanity.

This power, however, is not a zero-sum equation between the divine and the human, even between the divine κύριος (*kyrios*) and the human female. It is not the case that, as God is lifted up, others are brought low. In fact, it is quite the opposite. Without diminishment of any of this strength, God sees this young woman, saves her, gives her deep joy, makes her great, and makes her greatness known among others in perpetuity. The sovereign God, whom Mary magnifies, has already and will continue to honor and lift up Mary. Consequently, even as it affirms what God has done for her, the Magnificat also proclaims what is true about God's actions for others, particularly other women and the poor and oppressed, who have been debased.[29] God's actions

28. What she has hymned comes true in the birth of John the Baptist. Zechariah, his father, does not displace Mary's speech. I adopt the reading of Brittany E. Wilson, who in disagreement with some feminist scholarship does not see Zechariah as an example of men speaking more than women but as confirmation of his subsidiary position: "Because he agreed on the divinely given name, Zechariah can now (belatedly!) join his voice with Mary and Elizabeth, for he has joined them by becoming dependent on God" (*Unmanly Men: Reconfigurations of Masculinity in Luke-Acts* [Oxford: Oxford University Press, 2015], 110). He acts as her supporting witness. Based on her song, there is absolutely no doubt who has more honor, Mary or Zechariah, in God's system. As the Benedictus shows, God's attention to Mary becomes a template for God's attention to the rest of God's people. God looks upon them (Luke 1:68), doing great things for them, namely, redemption (1:68), rescue, and granting fearlessness (1:74). God grants them extended time to serve (1:75), saves them (1:69–70, 77), speaks to them (1:70), does mercy (1:72, 78), and remembers the holy covenant (1:72).

29. Elisabeth Behr-Sigel shows the connection: "Among those of low degree, we must count women with whom Mary, the 'lowly handmaiden' is in solidarity. In her and with her, believing

with her provide a window into God's actions with all like her. God notices and exalts the lowly, meets their needs richly, takes hold of them as one would embrace a child, mercifully remembering the mercy promised to the seed of Abraham. It is she who tells the reader that this powerful God is in the business of exalting the lowly.[30] As Mary tells the story, if anyone wishes to find security, a place to hold one's head high, it is in relationship with this God.[31]

The tender embrace of her and them includes the concomitant rejection of those who are not humble before this mighty Lord. God powerfully deals with their pride and power and greed.[32] The great, powerful, holy Lord God mercifully saves the lowly and the God-fearing in faithfulness to divine promises. Holding the vulnerable and strong-arming the threat away; this is the holy power of God that Mary proclaims.[33]

The Spirit has come over Mary, and now Mary has spoken truth about God, herself, and others. She has affirmed promises in the past and predicted the

---

women know that they are saved, honored, and glorified" (*Ministry of Women in the Church* [New York: St. Vladimir's Seminary Press, 2004], 210).

30. Courtney Hall Lee proclaims, "Few symbols of the New Testament's concern for 'the least' are as powerful as the one shaped by Mary" (*Black Madonna*, 118).

31. Citing examples of poor and oppressed women who find a *compañera* in Mary, Elizabeth Johnson concludes, "Honoring her puts one in solidarity with God's own option for the poor, and with the poorest of the poor, colonialized women in violent situations, most of all" (*Truly Our Sister: A Theology of Mary in the Communion of Saints* [New York: Continuum, 2003], 13).

32. Focusing through the lens of ancient masculinity on Zechariah, Wilson concludes, "In the downfall, silence, and restoration of Zechariah in Luke 1, we shall see how Luke subtly refigures elite masculine mores and expectations of where power dwells. Power does not reside, Luke maintains, with men, but with God. God is the one who wields supreme authority, but it is a destabilizing authority, for God dismantles traditional power structures, bringing down the powerful, silencing those who typically speak, and turning fathers to their wives and children" (*Unmanly Men*, 81). Luke has portrayed Zechariah's problem as lacking faith, not as being prideful, powerful, and greedy, but the revocation of his status allows readers to contemplate the dismantling of those in his same position who are not so righteous.

33. As confirmation of this image arising from the Scriptures of Israel, Jon D. Levenson comments about the texts of Israel, "It would be a mistake to see in these words a call to justice *tempered* by compassion, or to a compassion that *goes beyond* justice . . . Rather, justice here is *constituted* by compassion, by special solicitude for the powerless and disadvantaged, a determination that they not be victimized" (*Creation and the Persistence of Evil: The Jewish Drama of Divine Omnipotence* [Princeton: Princeton University Press, 1994], 104).

kingdom shape of the future. She is a Spirit-inspired trustworthy proclaimer who speaks prophetically.[34]

Elizabeth

As stated, Mary's unparalleled role in the drama of salvation is chiefly in the bearing of the Messiah. At the same time, she is not a class unto herself as regards Spirit-inspired proclamation. As immediate proof, in this same account, Luke asserts that the Holy Spirit has also blessed Elizabeth and led her into the proclamation of truth. Her words confirm two things: Mary's unique standing in God's plan can never be replicated, but also her inspired speech proclaiming that plan can be voiced by others.

Luke suggests, by the words he uses and the structure of the passage, that Mary goes to see Elizabeth with little lost time. Her trip to the house of Zechariah to see Elizabeth is "in those days" and she goes "with haste" (Luke 1:39; cf. 2:16). Luke's point is that she is not sluggish. She is quick in her actions, but Luke does not provide her motivation for being so.[35] Readers know only that Gabriel had spoken of Elizabeth's God-empowered conception, but whether Mary goes to confirm, celebrate, or receive comfort is not clear.[36]

What Luke does reveal in this encounter between these kin is the fulfill-

---

34. Beverly Roberts Gaventa concludes, "Mary's role in this scene warrants identifying her as a prophet" (*Mary: Glimpses of the Mother of Jesus*, Personalities of the New Testament [Minneapolis: Fortress, 1999], 58). The aorist tense of her verbs proclaims not only what will happen, but what has already begun, hence they should be interpreted as prophetic. See Joel B. Green, *The Gospel of Luke*, New International Commentary on the New Testament (Grand Rapids: Eerdmans, 1997), 100. Or in the terminology Daniel B. Wallace uses, the proleptic (futuristic) aorist, God's actions she proclaims are "as good as done" (*The Basics of New Testament Syntax: An Intermediate Greek Grammar* [Grand Rapids: Zondervan, 2000], 242).

35. Miller makes a convincing case that her actions stem from her visionary experience with Gabriel (*Convinced That God Had Called Us*, 125).

36. Green states, "Mary's journey is apparently unmotivated. She does not go in obedience to the angel, who gave her no such instructions. . . . this lack of detail and reflection highlights the orientation of this narrative segment on her action, accented further by her 'haste.' And this prepares for the sharp contrast with the following material wherein Luke introduces two pauses in the narrative to allow for concentrated reflection on the meaning of these events. Moreover,

ment of the angelic messages. First, the infant John receives the Holy Spirit *in utero*. Gabriel had promised to Zechariah that the child would be filled with the Holy Spirit while still in the location of his mother's womb (κοιλίας μητρὸς [*koilias mētros*] Luke 1:15). When Elizabeth hears Mary's greeting, this happens. Strikingly, though, Luke does not state the baby's filling explicitly. Instead, Luke leads the reader to surmise his filling in this space because twice Luke mentions Elizabeth's womb, both in his narrated words and the spoken words of Elizabeth (1:41, 44), and twice he notes that the baby made an unusual movement. John leapt (σκιρτάω [*skirtaō*] 1:41, 44), which Elizabeth interprets as a sign of rejoicing (ἀγαλλίασις [*agalliasis*] 1:44), precisely the reaction that would ensue at John's coming (1:14). This attention to John's unusual movement in his mother's womb *suggests* his filling, but Luke says explicitly that *Elizabeth herself* is filled with the Holy Spirit (1:41). Mary's arrival then fulfills what Gabriel had said about John but in a *maternally focused* way. Elizabeth is the one who is filled, and John benefits. Maybe this is what Gabriel had intended by the fact that John was to be filled in his mother's womb—that he would be filled as his mother was filled—but it should not escape notice that Luke does not assume Elizabeth in John's filling. Instead, it is the opposite. Luke makes explicit the Holy Spirit's pouring out upon her and suggests that the blessing also comes to John. God blesses Elizabeth directly, and she knows it in her body.[37]

The second fulfilled promise concerns Jesus. The pregnancy foretold by Gabriel and accepted by Mary has now occurred. The text does not reveal the moment this happens. Instead, Luke allows Elizabeth's words to provide the reader with the knowledge of the pregnancy. Elizabeth's speech, which begins right after she has been filled with the Spirit, thereby highlighting its credibility, states that there is fruit of Mary's womb. Again, there is a very personal particularity in this divinely inspired speech. Mary herself matters in the eyes of God; God has blessed *her*. The child is the fruit of *her* womb. She is not just a nameless and expendable vessel. It is her body that has allowed the formation of the body; she is now a mother (Luke 1:43). "Blessed are you among women,

---

it allows for a closer parallel with the previous scene related to John's conception, juxtaposing as tightly as possible the promise of a sign and the sign itself" (*Gospel of Luke*, 95).

37. For an analysis of the body in early Christian thought, see Jennifer Glancy, *Corporal Knowledge: Early Christian Bodies* (New York: Oxford University Press, 2010). About this encounter, she vividly imagines, "the round-bellied old woman Elizabeth embraces the round-bellied young woman Mary" (83).

and blessed is the fruit of your womb," Elizabeth proclaims (1:42). She states that Mary has entered a blessedness in comparison with other women and that her child has procured a blessing from God.

Such blessings on Mary and her babe, however, are not common ones. Elizabeth then expresses disbelief at her great fortune. Mary's coming, simply a visit from her younger relative, has now become a visitation from the mother of her Lord. Elizabeth's words—as was true in Gabriel's proclamation to Zechariah (Luke 1:17)—name Mary's baby as the Lord. κύριος (*kyrios*) could indicate his superiority to her, especially as the Messiah, but thus far in his account, Luke has utilized κύριος (*kyrios*) as the title for the God of Israel (1:16, 32), thus establishing an intriguing association between her son and God.[38]

Because the reader knows that this child is blessed in a different and superior way, the parallel statement about Mary carries the same weight. She is blessed among women, but she is also blessed above those women, for she, unlike any before or after, is bearing the Lord (Luke 1:43). This is apparent in what Mary's arrival accomplishes. Mary's presence, even only through the vehicle of her voice, brings the promise of the Spirit and its outpouring onto Elizabeth. Gabriel had not disclosed how this filling of John would happen, but now the reader knows that God has done it *through Mary*. As a microcosm of the Christian story as a whole, she is the means of divine fulfillment. Hence, with her embodied obedience, she stands as both uniquely blessed and as a blessing.

Elizabeth's statement about Mary resonates with that one spoken by a woman in the crowd when Jesus is teaching (Luke 11:27). The unnamed woman cries out, "Blessed is the womb that bore you and the breasts that nursed you!" Both include a reference to Mary's womb (κοιλία [*koilia*]) and both to a state of blessedness (εὐλογέω [*eulogeō*] 1:42; μακαρία [*makaria*] 1:45; 11:27). In chapter 11, Jesus's response to the woman directs attention to a person's response to God ("Blessed rather are those who hear the word of God and obey it!" [11:28]), and so too does Elizabeth's final statement: "Blessed [μακαρία (*makaria*)] is the woman who believes that completion will come for the things

---

38. See the expert analysis of *kyrios* in Luke 1:43 in C. Kavin Rowe, *Early Narrative Christology: The Lord in the Gospel of Luke* (Berlin: de Gruyter, 2006), 34–49, where he concludes, "the lack of direct identification of Jesus with the Father does not preclude a continuity in their identity" (49). Wilson draws the same conclusion: "Luke applies the title 'Lord' to both Jesus and the God of Israel throughout his two volumes, and Elizabeth's identification of Jesus as 'Lord' is simultaneously an identification of Jesus as God" (*Unmanly Men*, 88).

spoken to her from the Lord" (1:45). Elizabeth's point is that Mary has heard from God through Gabriel and has believed that the amazing pronouncement about a virginal conception could happen and assented to it happening to her (1:38), and, as her song has shown, also believed that all the angel said about her son will come to its perfect end. In both Luke 1 and 11, Mary stands as blessed because of what she hears and believes and does. Jesus's statement is not a denigration of her motherhood over and against her faith, for she has shown her belief in God, not exclusively but primarily *through* her motherhood. This interpretation fits Jesus's statement about his mother and brothers as those who hear the word of God and do it (8:21). She is *uniquely* blessed by God as mother of the Lord, yet she is happily blessed by God like *all others can be* who hear and believe and obey. Paralleled is how Jesus describes the good soil, those who hear the word, hold fast to it, and produce good fruit (8:15). After being filled by the Holy Spirit, it is Elizabeth who proclaims this truth about Mary, lifting her up as an example for all other followers of her son.

That expansion to others begins with Elizabeth herself. Elizabeth's last statement, "Blessed is she who believed," applies not only to Mary but also to her. The narrative has not made it clear how she knows that Mary is pregnant, much less bearing the Messiah, only when she hears Mary's greeting (Luke 1:41, 44). Had Zechariah told her about the angelic visitation, he would have had to write it down, as he did John's name (see 1:63), but nothing in the angel's words said anything clear and explicit about a particular Messiah, much less that the Messiah would be born from Elizabeth's relative Mary. Hence the logic of the narrative assumes that both Mary and Elizabeth are believing women (ἡ πιστεύσασα [hē pisteusasa]), particularly women who have believed what the Lord has spoken to them. Readers are simply not privy to the moment when God reveals to Elizabeth directly. It must, however, have happened, for there is no other way for her to know about Mary's pregnancy.

Only Mary is the mother of the Lord, but both she and Elizabeth have heard God speak, have trusted that revelation, have been gifted the Spirit, and have spoken truth about God's salvific plan. Therefore, the title "prophet" is a fitting one for both. Just one chapter over, Luke presents another female prophet, Anna, whose life is filled with prayer and fasting (Luke 2:36–37). When she sees Jesus, she breaks forth in praise (2:38). Mary, the God-inspired proclaimer, is not alone.[39]

---

39. About this passage, Richard Bauckham concludes, "the actions of Elizabeth and Mary

Ministry of Mothering

Luke asserts that Jesus "grew in wisdom and in stature, in favor with God and humanity" (Luke 2:52). It should not escape notice that the one Luke proclaims as the Son of God *grew*. This maturation of the Son appears in Hebrews as well, where it offers up one of this letter's many conundrums. It seems nonsensical that the one through whom the ages were created, who is granted a name superior to the angels (Heb 1:1–5), who bears the identity of God,[40] stands in need of perfecting (2:10; 5:9; 7:28). The problem has several plausible and complementary solutions, including his maturation as a human.[41] Hebrews 5 explicitly locates this process of perfecting "in the days of his flesh." The situation described here is a painful one: he cries out to God with tears and passion, reverently trusting that he would be saved from death (5:7). Through this kind of suffering, he learns obedience and becomes perfect. Scholars debate which event might be in the mind of the author: Gethsemane, the cross, the temptation,[42] but his education in obedience would not have been limited to the climactic moments of his adult life. He would have learned obedience through difficulty from the time that he was cognizant. For even if one is sinless (Heb 4:15), life presents hardship, so within this reality, he had to learn to obey.

In his early years, it would have fallen to his parents to facilitate this process. The one event the canonical gospels record of his childhood displays this type of learning. Here, while Joseph is present, Mary his mother is the parent who does the explicit teaching. Similarly, when the evangelist John portrays the

---

are the focus of attention and supply the dominant perspectives that readers are invited to share" (*Gospel Women*, 54).

40. The Son is "the radiance of God's glory and the imprint of God's being." Richard Bauckham employs the phrase "Christology of Divine Identity," in *Jesus and the God of Israel: God Crucified and Other Studies on the New Testament's Christology of Divine Identity* (Grand Rapids: Eerdmans, 2008). See his argument in the chapter on Hebrews, "The Divinity of Jesus in the Letter to the Hebrews," 233–53.

41. See David Peterson, *Hebrews and Perfection: An Examination of the Concept of Perfection in the "Epistle to the Hebrews,"* Society for New Testament Studies Monograph Series 47 (Cambridge: Cambridge University Press, 1982). Madison N. Pierce offers an analysis of the suggestions in *Divine Discourse in the Epistle to the Hebrews: The Recontextualization of Spoken Quotations of Scripture*, Society for New Testament Studies Monograph Series 178 (Cambridge: Cambridge University Press, 2020), 128–33.

42. Luke Timothy Johnson, *Hebrews: A Commentary* (Louisville: Westminster John Knox, 2006), 145–46.

inaugural sign of Jesus's ministry, it is his mother's influence that prods him to meet needs even as he carries out the divine will. In both instances, she facilitates his learning of what it is to obey God. She mothers God. God not only allows it but also benefits from it.

Second Temple Visit

For the second time in Luke's second chapter, the evangelist recounts the holy family's travels to Jerusalem. It is not the second time they have attended, because Luke says it was the practice of Jesus's parents to attend Passover in Jerusalem each year. Such a multiple-day journey on an annual basis for the celebration of Passover is testament to their piety[43] because while the law asked men to attend the festivals (Exod 23:17; 34:23; Deut 16:16), families were not required. Many families did probably attend, so Mary and Jesus are not unique, but such attendance does demonstrate this family to be serious in their participation of covenant.[44] They fulfill the days of Passover (Luke 2:43) and begin to return home.[45]

This instance proves memorable because Jesus stays in Jerusalem without their knowledge. They assume he is with the group on the road back to Nazareth, possibly because this had been Jesus's practice in the past. At the end of that first day of travel, they look for him among family and friends, and, when they do not find him, they turn back to Jerusalem. Without any further specification of timing, the gravity of the situation suggests that Joseph and Mary make this journey in the evening, so that puts them walking through the night. It takes three days before they find him in the temple. How Luke might be counting the days here is not completely clear,[46] but such an extended absence,

---

43. James R. Edwards, *The Gospel according to Luke*, Pillar New Testament Commentary (Grand Rapids: Eerdmans, 2015), 97.

44. Drawing from Josephus (*Jewish Antiquities* 11.109), E. P. Sanders concludes, "They were times for feasting and rejoicing, and men brought their families" (*Judaism: Practice and Belief, 63 BCE–66 CE* [London: SCM, 1992], 131).

45. Passover lasts for a week (Exod 12:14–20), but there is also evidence that pilgrims needed attend Jerusalem for only the first two days. See François Bovon, *Luke 1: A Commentary on the Gospel of Luke 1:1–9:50* (Minneapolis: Fortress, 2002), 111.

46. "The search for Jesus probably does not require an additional three days, for a search of the temple, and even Jerusalem, would not require so much time. 'After three days' (v. 46) is

in this story, shows the care and persistence one would assume in parents. Narratively, Luke is surely foreshadowing another three-day period when Jesus will be absent. Retelling this event allows the evangelist an echo with Jesus's resurrection, the only other instance where three days appears in the gospel (Luke 9:22; 18:33; 24:7, 21, 46).

When they finally find him, they are amazed (ἐκπλήσσω [*ekplēssō*])— a word different from when they marveled at Simeon's words (θαυμάζω [*thaumazō*] Luke 2:33) but with a similar use in Luke's writings. This is how people react to Jesus or the story about him (4:32; 9:43; Acts 13:12). They react with this sentiment because they find Jesus at the center of the action in the midst of the teachers. He is listening to them and asking them questions, and he is also providing answers. He plays the role of both a learner and a teacher, inquisitive and confident, and he plays both roles well. He dazzles the teachers.

Mary and Joseph are not equally impressed. More than simple amazement, any pride in their son is also mixed with equal parts frustration. In what has become Luke's method in the birth narrative (in both the annunciation [Luke 1:26-27] and the Simeon account [2:33-34]), he starts with a description of both parents and then focuses on Mary. It is she who speaks to the child Jesus. "Child [τέκνον (*teknon*)], why did you do to us in this way?" (2:48). Very similar to Jesus's response to his mother at Cana, it is hard not to hear this titular direct address and question as accusatory. τέκνον (*teknon*) as a direct address, as evidenced by Luke's use of it, can convey tenderness (as the father to the prodigal son [15:31]) or blame (Abraham to the rich man [16:25]). The latter seems likely in light of the rest of her statement. She sees Jesus's way of acting toward her and Joseph as that which has caused pain (ὀδυνώμενοι [*odynōmenoi*]).[47]

He responds to both his parents: "Why were you seeking me? Did you not know that it was necessary for me to be in my Father's house?" (Luke 2:49). Jesus had not intended to cause them pain. Jesus's words suggest that he thought they should have known that he would stay behind in the temple. It was necessary that he be about his Father's business in his Father's house.[48]

---

more likely inclusive, i.e., a day for the outbound trip, a day to return, and finding Jesus on the third day in the temple" (Edwards, *Gospel according to Luke*, 93).

47. Gaventa asks interpreters to pause and consider the anguish (as informed by this word's appearance in Tobit and the Maccabean literature) Mary expresses here (*Mary*, 68).

48. "The things of my Father" (ἐν τοῖς τοῦ πατρός μου [*en tois tou patros mou*]) could support either the location of the temple, or the work of God more generally, or both (Bovon, *Luke 1*, 114).

They had after all, when he was only an infant, dedicated him to the Lord (2:22). He thought it would be obvious what he was doing and where he was, so they need not have been unsure in their search. His questions suggest that twelve-year-old Jesus imagined he was to start his independent vocation at this point.

His parents, Luke says, did not understand the word spoken to them (Luke 2:50). They serve as examples of a lack of understanding featured throughout the gospel. In Luke 8:10, Jesus cites Isa 6 to his followers. They, the insiders, have been given knowledge, but the outsiders do not understand. Similar to the evangelist Mark, Luke portrays Jesus's definition of insider and outsider with playful reversibility.[49] Even with this knowledge, later in Luke 18, it is the twelve disciples who do not understand about his death (18:34), and they come to understand it only after the resurrection when he grants them understanding (24:27, 31–32). In this instance in the temple, Mary and Joseph are among those to whom Jesus speaks with clarity, but for them, as is true for the other disciples and readers, it does not make sense at the time.[50] Jesus asks, "Did you not know that it is necessary for me to be among the things of my Father?" "What do you mean?" they might reply. "We've had you among the things of your Father by bringing you annually to celebrate the festival." They would have no reason yet to fully understand the implications of his identity, precisely what *those things* of his Father are, namely, a ministry of both fame and rejection that will culminate in death and resurrection.[51] Simeon had left Mary on an ominous note (Luke 2:34–35), but nothing said to them up to this point would reveal that kind of detailed information. It is not a sign of doubt or obstinacy that they do not understand; it is only a sign of their humanness in the particular time in which they exist.[52]

49. See Laura C. Sweat, *The Theological Role of Paradox in the Gospel of Mark*, The Library of New Testament Studies 492 (London: Bloomsbury T&T Clark, 2013).

50. Michal Beth Dinkler describes Jesus's question to his parents as "a purposeful riddle," which "stirs readerly curiosity" (*Silent Statements: Narrative Representations of Speech and Silence in the Gospel of Luke* [Berlin: de Gruyter, 2013], 59).

51. Mark Coleridge concurs: "The effect of the ambiguity is to leave the readers sharing the parents' perplexity and asking what it might mean to be 'in the things of my father'" (*The Birth of the Lukan Narrative: Narrative as Christology in Luke 1–2* [Sheffield: JSOT Press, 1993], 203), which will be answered in the course of the entire Lukan narrative.

52. Green articulates a similar conclusion: "Where will this radical identification with God's

The conversation might very well affirm a similar, and nonsinful, misunderstanding in Jesus. In order to do so, it is important to clarify precisely which aspect of his word they do not understand. If the rest of the narrative coheres with this vignette, Mary and Joseph are well aware who his Father is.[53] His divinely caused existence is not the issue. Instead, what they do not understand could include why he is questioning their seeking of him.[54] "Why were you seeking me?" Jesus asks. "Why?" they might reply with exasperation. "Because we love you and are responsible for you!"

They might also not understand why he thought it was necessary to remain at the temple *at that point*, and their lack of understanding would be justified. It is plausible that he in his humanity does not fully understand how being among his Father's things is not meant to begin *at that moment*. Luke's description of him paints a zealous young man who thinks himself capable of independence— at twelve he is ready to start his ministry—even though Mary and Joseph, as well as the authoritative narrator, recognize that he is a child. Mary addresses him as child (τέκνον [*teknon*]) in Luke 2:48, which agrees with the narrator's description of him as a child (παῖς [*pais*]) in 2:43.[55] It is possible that he, too, does not fully understand, not in a sinful way, but in a naive way because he is fully human. In this encounter, Luke shows that this includes being fully a human at that headstrong sunset of childhood.[56] Theirs is a rather classic moment of mutual misunderstanding. His parents cannot understand why he remained in the temple. He cannot understand why they did not know that he would.

---

salvific program lead? This is not yet clear, and it is not surprising that Luke records the inability of Mary and Joseph to understand. . . . here the reader is invited to respond in kind, to put aside hasty conclusions and to maintain an openness to the course the narrative will take as it develops these themes further" (*Gospel of Luke*, 157).

53. Coleridge captures the shift clearly: "Joseph's paternity is emphasized in v. 48 in order to prepare for its transcendence in v. 49" (*Birth of the Lukan Narrative*, 198).

54. Coleridge notes, "If Mary's question seems reasonable and natural, Jesus's reply by contrast seems unreasonable and unnatural, even priggish or impertinent . . . it is a surprising first word from the character who will dominate the Gospel narrative and who will often speak in surprising ways" (*Birth of the Lukan Narrative*, 199).

55. Henk J. de Jonge catalogs ancient thinkers who believed that "a boy of twelve had not yet put his childhood behind him, and had not yet reached the first stage of maturity" ("Sonship, Wisdom, and Infancy: Luke 2:41–51a," *New Testament Studies* 24 [1978]: 321).

56. Although he is speaking about Jesus's teaching, Bovon includes a commensurate comment: "he remains quite human throughout the course of the account" (*Luke 1*, 115).

Seeing and hearing that he has wounded them, Jesus descends from the temple with them, leaves the center of the activity of God for the smallness of Nazareth, and is obedient to them. His bold naivete is chided in the incident, and he responds accordingly. He grows up, Luke literally says, gaining wisdom and stature and grace with God, and also with humans (Luke 2:52). Note that it is *after this* conversation with Mary that he grows in wisdom, which means he still had some to gain when he was twelve. Maybe this indicates that he does not hurt his parents in this way again. He is patient to wait until he is fully ready for his independent departure into the ministry God has for him.

The final word on Mary in Luke's infancy narrative says that Mary holds all these words in her heart (Luke 2:51). At this point, that includes Gabriel's words, the shepherd's words, Simeon's, Anna's, and now Jesus's. As would be true for any mother, she would never forget the three-day period in which her child was missing. She may not fully understand all these words and events, but she does not give up thinking about them, and as she does, she parents this boy who is growing into a young man.

Luke gives clear evidence, in this well-known yet rather provocative story, that Joseph and prominently Mary positively shape Jesus through their parenting of him. They ensure he experiences the reenactment of God's redemption of the people of Israel by taking him yearly to the temple, and then they bring him home from the temple. She is honest with him about the impacts of his actions: she and Joseph had to seek for him, and it caused them pain. Despite their lack of understanding in the exchange of words, something occurs by which Jesus decides to leave the temple and accompany them home. Mary and Joseph have influenced him, parented him, for his betterment. It was under their care that he was able to grow in wisdom and stature and favor. God allowed Joseph his father and Mary his mother to mold the actions and character of the Son of God. God blessed their ministry of parenting.[57]

---

57. Luke's corpus does not idolize the nuclear family. Parents deserve respect and children deserve care, but the family is put under the priority of following Jesus's gospel call. See the discussion of ascetic features in Luke in Turid Karlsen Seim, "The Virgin Mother: Mary and Ascetic Discipleship in Luke," in *Feminist Companion to Luke*, Feminist Companion to the New Testament and Early Christian Writings 3, ed. Amy-Jill Levine and Marianne Blickenstaff (London: Sheffield Academic, 2002), and Christopher M. Hays, "Hating Wealth and Wives: An Examination of Discipleship Ethics in the Third Gospel," *Tyndale Bulletin* 60 (2009): 47–68.

Ministry of Parenting and Proclamation: Wedding at Cana

By the time Jesus is grown and entering into his public ministry, Mary is not parenting him the same way any longer—he is no longer a child—but she does still exercise influence over him. She does so in this event because of her relationship with him. She is still, even though he is grown, his mother. At the same time, Mary influences more than just Jesus in this account. Whereas Luke has Mary and Elizabeth proclaiming truth, but only to the limited audience of one another in the privacy of Elizabeth's own home, the evangelist John preserves another more expansive example of Mary's proclamation. Here she verbally points the servants of the home toward active trust in her son. At Cana, she is both parenting and proclaiming. God allows and blesses both.

A story abundantly rich as the wine at its center, the wedding at Cana affirms the mundane realities of Mary and Jesus's familial relationship. She is at a wedding, and so it makes sense that her son is invited (John 2:1–2). As John unfolds the narrative, it seems that people were already aware of the type of person Jesus was, a teacher who had gathered followers or disciples (1:38–51), and in addition to him, his whole band was invited along (2:2). His mother, he, and his followers were invited to a wedding, a celebration of life and love.[58] Such an invitation eliminates any view of him as too holy to participate in the joys of normal life. The shared tradition between Matthew and Luke corroborates this, as it records Jesus as one who had a reputation among the religious elite as a glutton and a drunkard (Matt 11:19; Luke 7:34). Such gossip probably arose from some reality that Jesus and his followers knew how to enjoy life. He came to support and participate in the celebration of this couple and these families and, in the end, only increased the conviviality of the event.

The way in which John tells the event indicates that Mary has a close connection with the family hosting the wedding.[59] John names her presence in the list of notable (to the reader) attendees and then adds that when the wine

---

58. Craig S. Keener cites Jer 33:11; John 3:29; Rev 19:7; Mark 2:19; Babylonian Talmud Berakhot 6b; Jerusalem Talmud Pe'ah 1:1, §15; 1 Macc 1:27; 9:39–41; 3 Macc 4:6; Jer 7:34; 16:9; 25:10; Joel 2:16; Rev 18:23; Josephus, *Jewish War* 6.301; Leviticus Rabbah 20:3; Ecclesiastes Rabbah 2:2, §4, as evidence that "Jewish people emphasized joyous celebration at wedding feasts" (*The Gospel of John: A Commentary* [Peabody, MA: Hendrickson, 2003], 1:498n54).

59. Ritva H. Williams, "The Mother of Jesus at Cana: A Social-Science Interpretation of John 2:1–12," *Catholic Biblical Quarterly* 59 (1997): 684–85.

runs out, she knows about it. It would have been socially embarrassing, even shameful, to have run out of wine.[60] Presumably, if everyone knew this unfortunate turn of events, she would not have needed to tell Jesus, so she must be connected with the family in such a way that allows her access to the behind-the-scenes workings of the festivities. When she learns of the problem, she goes to him. At base, this is an indication that, with no mention of Joseph, Jesus served as a resource for his mother.

It could indicate more, of course. John has nothing to say about the birth of Jesus through Mary, but he has declared with bold clarity that Jesus is God come in the flesh (John 1:14). His prebirth divine state seems a fact with which his mother, the one who gave birth to him, would have been acquainted. In this reading, she goes to him because she knew already that he of all people would have answers to difficult problems. His mother would know he has that potential to help even if he had not acted on it previously (as this is described as his first sign). If this problem is going to be solved, she knows he is the one to do something about it.

Jesus speaks to her with uncomfortably direct words. First, "What is it to me and to you, woman?" The direct address of γύναι (gynai), "woman," to his mother strikes many readers as harsh. Tone is imported in reading a text, and because Jesus addresses the Samaritan woman (John 4:21), the woman caught in adultery (8:10), and his mother again from the cross (19:26), it does not have to be a sign of disrespect but the Johannine way that Jesus speaks.[61] Second, he says, "My hour has not yet come" (2:4). In so doing, he shares

60. "To ensure that an appropriate quantity and quality of food and drink are available, the groom must have drawn on the resources of some of his colleagues. In such circumstances, running out of wine represents a loss of honor, since it makes it evident to all that the groom lacks both material and social resources" (Williams, "Mother of Jesus at Cana," 684).

61. This is a way of speaking recorded in other Second Temple Jewish writings; just this word appears in Josephus (Jewish Antiquities 17.74) when "the wife of Pheroras tells Herod (the Great) how her husband summoned her in his illness. . . . The example is important, since Pheroras had great affection for his wife." See George R. Beasley-Murray, John, 2nd ed. Word Biblical Commentary 36 (Nashville: Thomas Nelson, 1999), 34. Gail O'Day concludes, "'Woman' is an unusual way to address one's own mother, but it is not a hostile or rude address (see Matt 15:28; Luke 22:57; John 4:21). Jesus's words communicate that he is under no obligation to respond simply because the woman who speaks is his mother (see his similar response to his brothers in 7:1–10). Instead, Jesus's hour will dictate how and when he acts (v. 4)." See Gail R. O'Day and Susan E. Hylen, John (Louisville: Westminster John Knox, 2006), 35.

his reservations about getting involved in the stated problem. He responds with a dual hesitancy: neither the type of connection it would establish with the family nor the timing of a public event are right. He does not want to be bound to this family in an exchange of reciprocity.[62] Viewed within a world of reciprocal relationships, were he to perform this miracle openly at this time, this family would be bound to him in some sense to return the favor, and then he to them to do the same, but he is about to begin his itinerant ministry and therefore needed to be free of boundedness to this particular family.[63] Second, he does not want to reveal himself fully. In his response, he mentions a sensitive theological topic, the necessary delay of his hour.[64] This oblique reference to the cross could imply a shared knowledge of his identity and call, just the kind of thing a leader would share only with those close to him. It shows the expected dynamics of her maternal relationship to him.

Even in light of his hesitancies, he does not, however, deny her request. Mary, through continued action on the problem, is not displaying any kind of flagrant disobedience, because he has not said no to her. He has only presented implications he must avoid. John commands respect for the character of Mary as she threads the needle. She neither disagrees with Jesus nor challenges him but goes to the servants. Moreover, she does not instruct them *to do* much of anything but only to go to the *right person*.

"See that person over there. Walk over and see what he tells you to do. Whatever it is, do it." She remains hopeful that Jesus will grant her request, and she acts on that hope. She is persistent. At the same time, she gives Jesus the

---

62. Williams develops this argument: "Jesus's words are a recognition that he is being drawn into the local system of reciprocal relationships" ("Mother of Jesus at Cana," 689).

63. In his analysis of patron-client relationships, David A. deSilva comments, "imprecision in accountability . . . led these relationships to be ongoing, almost interminable. Mutual bonds of favor and the accompanying bonds of indebtedness provided the glue that maintained social cohesion" ("Exchanging Favor for Wrath: Apostasy in Hebrews and Patron-Client Relationships," *Journal of Biblical Literature* 115 [1996]: 92). Admittedly, being bound to others does not keep Jesus from performing future signs, hence, the timing of this one is the greatest hesitancy.

64. The word for hour in John (ὥρα [*hōra*]) often takes on powerful symbolism as the time of salvation (John 4:21, 23; 5:25, 28), related to his death and resurrection (7:30; 8:20; 12:23, 27; 13:1; 17:1).

freedom to say anything. He might tell the servants, "Be at peace!" and nothing about the lack of wine would change. Her actions indicate her belief that *if* anything is going to happen, Jesus will be the one to do it. She communicates that hope with respectful ambiguity to the servants. She directs her hope and the activity of the servants to the right person. He might act, he might not, but either way, she points them toward *him*.

Her persistent trust propels the servants to act in ways that show their trust in this man Jesus. The servants, following her lead, treat him with the respect of obedience. The reader has no knowledge that the servants know who Jesus is—other than they might have heard that he is a teacher collecting a following—yet when he tells them to do something, they do it. He says to fill up the water jugs, and they fill them up to the top, obeying him to the highest degree (John 2:7). Then he tells them to draw some water out and take it to the headwaiter. They obey.

This would not be a simple errand in light of the time in which Jesus asks them to do it. The headwaiter is busy with a wedding feast and, in addition to that, is stressed by the depleting wine supplies. It would take gumption for an underling to ask him to pause to take a drink of water in that moment.[65] It is especially interesting to imagine when the water actually became wine. As he is tasting, he tastes water that had become wine (John 2:9). The grammar (γεγενημένον [*gegenēmenon*], perfect of γίνομαι [*ginomai*]) allows the possibility that the change does not occur until he takes the cup to drink.[66] If that is the case, then the obedience demonstrated by the servants is even more amazing. Because Jesus told them to do so, they take a cup of water, used for the washing of utensils and hands,[67] to their supervisor at a horrible time. It is

65. So also, Marcus Dods comments, "They knew very well they had only put in water, and they knew that to offer water to the governor of a marriage feast would be to insure their own punishment; but they did not hesitate" (*The Gospel of St. John* [New York: Armstrong and Son, 1903], 1:74).

66. About John 2:9, J. Ramsey Michaels comments, "At this point, the miracle is already accomplished, but no one except Jesus knows it. The reader will find out first, from the expression, 'the water-turned-to-wine.' The servants who drew the water will find out next, presumably from the banquet master's comment (v. 10)" (*The Gospel of John*, New International Commentary on the New Testament [Grand Rapids: Eerdmans, 2010], 151).

67. Karen H. Jobes, *John through Old Testament Eyes: A Background and Application Com-*

a costly obedience, but they do it nonetheless. They follow Mary's lead to be persistent in their respectful obedience to Jesus.

They are left in the dust of the headwaiter's flabbergasted confusion as he goes to confront the bridegroom with his uncanny sommelier planning. The evangelist had one more thing to say about them. Even though the headwaiter did not know from where the wine had come, John is explicit. The servants, the very ones who drew the water, knew from where it had come, namely, the word of Jesus. John concludes the story by saying that in this event in which Jesus revealed his glory, his disciples came to believe in him. Surely this includes the disciples who had joined him for the wedding (John 2:2), but since the servants were a part of that very small group who knew of the glorious sign, the chances are high that they had joined the group designated as followers of Jesus.[68] Second in the narrative only to Nathaniel's declaration of trust in Jesus (1:49), this event fulfills the promise of the prologue that those who trust in him would become part of God's family (1:7, 12). Even if they did not physically join the band of followers when they left for Capernaum, they had come to know what Jesus could do; they had experienced his glory. They did so because Mary spoke to them and pointed them toward Jesus. She was, for them, a pointer toward the miraculous and glorious news about her son.

As the evangelist tells the story, Jesus performs this sign because Mary has brought it to his attention and because the servants have followed his command. The trust and activity of the humans move his hand, yet without changing his will.[69]

Jesus's will, as stated to Mary, is that he not bind himself to this family

---

mentary (Grand Rapids: Kregel Academic, 2021), 59; Andreas J. Köstenberger, *John*, Baker Exegetical Commentary on the New Testament (Grand Rapids: Baker, 2004), 96.

68. Köstenberger also includes the servants in the list of people receiving an "early glimpse of his messianic identity" (*John*, 99).

69. Marian misunderstanding or error, or both, also appears as an interpretive trope. When she asks Jesus to turn the water into wine, some think she is grasping for his honor and grossly misunderstanding the path of shame he must walk before his glorification. See discussion in Raymond E. Brown et al., eds., *Mary in the New Testament* (New York: Paulist, 1978), 189, as well as Beth Kreitzer, "The Wedding at Cana," in *Reforming Mary: Changing Images of the Virgin Mary in Lutheran Sermons of the Sixteenth Century*, Oxford Studies in Historical Theology (Oxford: Oxford University Press, 2004), 93–108. For the reasons articulated in my own exegesis, I do not think this is the most compelling reading.

and that he not yet begin his hour. By the end of the story, he has avoided his concerns and thus accomplished his will. The family does not know where the wine came from. The headwaiter thinks the bridegroom has done it, and the reader does not know what the bridegroom thinks but is given no clear indication that he comes to believe in Jesus at this point. Consequently, the family remains unaware and so are not duty-bound to Jesus and he to them in a reciprocity of good deeds. The family keeps—and increases!—the honor of their self-sufficiency, and Jesus is free to proceed with his ministry.

It is also true that even at the end of this event, his hour has not been ushered in. While this event stands at the beginning of his self-revelation, it shows a part of that identity to only a small band of followers.

Even as his will remains unchanged and is in fact accomplished, the believing and active faith of Mary—and through her influence, the active faith of the servants—prompts him to fulfill her request. He retains his ultimate goals while also meeting her needs. She is trusting and respectful; he is sovereign and responsive. Human faith propels divine action even as it does not change divine will.

The divine action meets the human need in a striking way. The rest of the signs—and John records seven of them—are miracles of necessity, interventions that meet dire situations (John 4:46–54; 5:1–15; 6:5–14; 6:16–24; 9:1–7; 11:1–45), such as healing children close to death, restoring limbs and blind eyes, calming dangerous storms, and providing food for the hungry. They culminate in the raising of Lazarus from the dead—the direst situation of all. This first sign, starkly, is not. It is a miracle that prevents shame, but that is not the same as healing a person without the ability to walk or raising a lifeless man. This miracle, therefore, sits oddly among the rest.

Its arresting quality only increases when the reader does the math to consider its rich abundance. It is rich in the sense that he transforms the water into something extraordinarily good, something lavish, something of unexpected quality.[70] This is not the lesser wine; this is the good (ὁ καλός [ho kalos]) wine

---

70. Laura Sweat Holmes points out that the presence of the wine in the purificatory jars shows that "Jesus's presence and words could purify his disciples . . . [he] provided the joyful, abundant presence of God." See Laura Sweat Holmes and George Lyons, *John 1–12: A Commentary in the Wesleyan Tradition* (Kansas City: Beacon Hill, 2020), 90.

that is normally put out first.[71] It is abundant because Jesus makes a great deal of this top-quality drink. He fills up what is lacking in the jars and tells the servants to bring the water to the brim, all the way to the top (John 2:7). At two to three measures each,[72] this creates over one hundred gallons.[73] This is top-shelf wine in wholesale quantities. He overwhelms them with this lavishness.

When Jesus began to reveal his identity through the performance of miraculous signs, he did so by blessing and continuing a celebration. He performed a miracle not to meet a need but to meet a desire for honor and joy in community. Because he does so, a manager avoids reproach, a family avoids shame, but for almost everyone else there, he does so simply so that their joyful celebration can continue and even improve. Jesus does not have to do this— people will not die if he refuses. Its oddity, therefore, and its prominence as the first sign prohibit its dismissal or relegation. Instead, the evangelist affirms that this, too, counts as the kind of miracle the Son of God is in the business of doing. In fact, it stands as the first, the lens through which all other signs are viewed. Therefore, such a sign attests that God works miraculously not just to save lives but also to make life worth living. At times, God simply grants the delights of the community, and not just their needs. In Johannine terms, his performance of this miracle allows those gathered to experience life and experience it more abundantly (John 10:10), now and as a pointer toward the eternal life to come. Mary has respectfully yet tenaciously shaped the actions of God, and she has done so as his mother and as his witness. Her ministry of parenting and proclamation intertwine and propel the first of his signs, which acts as a signpost to the abundance of his salvation.

71. John uses καλός (*kalos*) in the rest of the gospel to describe Jesus (10:11, 14) and his work (10:32–33).

72. The word μετρητής (*metrētēs*) is used for liquid measurement and in the papyri frequently for wine. It equals roughly forty liters, or close to nine gallons, see "μετρητής," in Frederick W. Danker et al., *Greek-English Lexicon of the New Testament and Other Early Christian Literature*, 3rd ed. (Chicago: University of Chicago Press, 2000), 643.

73. Raymond E. Brown calls attention to the echoes of God's eschatological abundance in Amos 9:13–14; Hos 14:7; Jer 31:12; 1 Enoch 10.19; 2 Bar. 29.5 (*The Gospel according to John I–XII*, Anchor Bible 29 [Garden City, NY: Doubleday, 1966], 105).

Ministry of Proclamation: Pentecost

Luke explicitly mentions Mary only once in Acts (1:14). This singular reference continues her story into the Christian movement and shows God empowering her public ministry of proclamation.

From that one reference, where she is present with the other disciples in the upper room gathered for prayer, it is plausible to imagine her as being present for certain periods of time described in the beginning of Acts. Luke notes that Jesus gives instructions through the Holy Spirit to the apostles he has chosen (Acts 1:2). Clearly that includes the Twelve (Luke 6:13), but as Luke has recounted in the birth narrative, God also chose Mary. Moreover, these statements in Acts 1:1–5 apply to the long period of time after the resurrection, and it seems incredulous that Mary would not ever have encountered her risen son.[74] If she is referenced in Peter's speech, as I will argue, then he affirms that those speaking with him were witnesses of his resurrection (2:32).

Luke moves from Jesus's general teaching during this forty-day period to a more specific conversation (Acts 1:6–8). A nondescript "they" come together (1:6) to ask him about the restoration of the kingdom of Israel, and Jesus points them to the coming of the Holy Spirit upon them (1:8).

At this point, Jesus ascends, and the two men robed in white correct the angle of the group's vision. These two figures address the group as the "Men of Galilee" (ἄνδρες Γαλιλαῖοι [*andres Galilaioi*]), the strongest point against an argument for Mary's presence at the ascension. It is also possible that others are gathered there, and only the men from Galilee keep their eyes to the heavens, or that when addressing a mixed gender crowd, the two white-robed beings use a masculine form of address.[75] It becomes clear that more than the

---

74. See also Acts 13:31: "and for many days he appeared to those who came up with him from Galilee to Jerusalem, and they are now his witnesses to the people." Chris Maunder argues that it is plausible to see Mary, the mother of Jesus, as present at the tomb, and many in the Christian tradition assumed this ("Mary and the Gospel Narratives," in *The Oxford Handbook of Mary*, ed. Chris Maunder [Oxford: Oxford University Press, 2019], 33–35). See the in-depth analysis of the presence of the women at the tomb in Kara J. Lyons-Pardue, *Gospel Women and the Long Ending of Mark*, The Library of New Testament Studies 614 (London: Bloomsbury T&T Clark, 2020).

75. Noting the frequency with which ancients addressed crowds as "men" (ἄνδρες [*andres*]), as in Acts 1:11; 2:14, 22; 3:12; 5:35; 13:16; 21:28; 17:22; 19:35, Craig S. Keener suggests that in 2:14, Peter "retains the convention of addressing only adult males even though others might

Eleven are present, because when they select another member of the Twelve, they choose from two men who have been with them "beginning from the baptism of John until when he was taken up from us" (Acts 1:22). Whoever the members of the group might be, which certainly includes the eleven disciples whose names Luke presents again (1:13), the "they" return to Jerusalem and to the upper room. If Mary was there at the ascension, God has allowed her to see the fulfillment of the promise that her son the Lord would reign with God eternally, a fulfillment of Gabriel's announcement (1:33) beyond what she could have imagined at the time. Even if she was not there, she would have heard a report about it from the men of Galilee gathered there when they returned to the upper room. Nevertheless, Luke puts his focus upon the actions she took *after* hearing of his ascension.

Luke places her in the upper room where the apostles are staying in Jerusalem, the room where they all return after the ascension. They are all gathered close (προσκαρτερέω [*proskartereō*]), with unified zeal (ὁμοθυμαδόν [*homothymadon*]) in prayer. Other women are present, as well as the brothers of Jesus,[76] but in addition to the eleven apostles, Mary is the only other person whom Luke names (Acts 1:14).

In these days after the ascension, marked by communal prayer (Acts 1:14–15), Peter rises to instigate the choice for another disciple to complete the symbolic number of twelve in order to demonstrate the connection between Jesus's followers and the people of Israel.[77] They choose from two men who have been with them "beginning from the baptism of John until when he was taken up from us" (1:22). Mary would have joined in the prayer before the selection of Matthias and seen another fulfillment of her son's kingdom as it now would include a symbolically full twelve representatives. This symbolism

---

be welcome to listen and profit" (*Acts: An Exegetical Commentary* [Grand Rapids: Baker, 2012], 1:868). In 1:11, however, he concludes, "those so designated are, presumably, literally male. 'They,' in 1:12–13 are specified as apostles (i.e., the eleven; 1:2, 26), to which the 'women' of 1:14 are added" (*Acts*, 1:730).

76. If it is the case that his brothers had not been followers of him until his resurrection (Mark 3:20–21, 30–31; John 7:5), she would know the intense joy of her kinship relations now united with her Messiah relations.

77. So also Keener: "The primary emphasis of Acts 1:15–26 is the selection of a twelfth apostle to prepare for Israel's renewal and restoration" (*Acts*, 1:774).

of fullness prepares the way for the promise for which Jesus instructed his followers to wait.

Luke keeps the focus on the full group at the beginning of chapter 2. As the scene transitions, Luke records, "When the day of Pentecost had come they were all together" (Acts 2:1), as the best manuscripts record.[78] This is a comprehensive description, much like that of 1:14, where Mary is explicitly present. A very similarly sounding "all" were together at the same place (2:1) when the wind and fire of the Spirit fall upon them.

This suggests that she remained with the community of disciples fervent in the unity of prayer and obedient to Jesus to stay where he told them to wait (Acts 1:12–14). In this faithful community, she is putting herself in the place to receive the Holy Spirit. Luke portrays the coming of the Holy Spirit at Pentecost similarly to the pneumatological arrival with Mary in two ways. First, he emphasizes the directional movement from heaven to earth (from heaven [2:2] and rested upon [2:3]; Most High *over*shadow [Luke 1:35]). Second, he notes that both are oracular events (the words of Gabriel [1:28, 30, 35]; the sound of the Holy Spirit [Acts 2:2]). There, however, the similarities cease. The sound of Pentecost is a forceful (βίαιος [*biaios*]) wind accompanied by tongues like fire (πυρός [*pyros*]). Such intensity illuminates the contrast of the lack of such intensity in Luke's portrayal of the annunciation. With such an intense arrival, the Holy Spirit fills everyone gathered and gives the gift of foreign speech, or the ability to hear foreign speech, to all. Despite the fact that Luke portrays Mary conceiving by the Holy Spirit, he never says in the birth narrative that Mary herself is *filled* with the Holy Spirit—an odd omission given that John (Luke 1:15), Elizabeth (1:41), and Zechariah (1:67) are all filled. Moreover, Elizabeth and Zechariah, when filled, burst forth in praise. When Mary sings her song of praise, Luke gives no explicit indication that the Holy Spirit fills her, leading to her speech. The absence of "filling" language does not indicate that God is absent from Mary—neither are Simeon and Anna filled with the Holy Spirit explicitly. The Spirit interacts with them (2:35–37), and they insightfully see God's work and respond. This omission early in the gospel does, however, suggest that when she is filled with the Holy Spirit at Pentecost, it is a distinct work God is doing in her.[79] Her bearing of the Son of God does not

---

78. A few miniscule manuscripts (614, 326, 1505 p* t) have "all the apostles."

79. Sergius Bulgakov interprets similarly, distinct from the annunciation when the Holy

exempt her from the need to be filled with the promised Holy Spirit along with all the other disciples of Jesus. She is filled with the Holy Spirit at the same time and in the same way that the other disciples receive the Holy Spirit.[80] She is not elevated above them, but neither is she excluded from them.

The comprehensive language continues. They *all* speak in different tongues, uttering just what the Spirit allowed them to utter (Acts 2:4), testifying vocally and publicly to "God's deeds of power" (2:11) to those gathered in Jerusalem (designated as "men" [2:5, 14, 22, 29]).

It is possible that Luke intends to depict only the twelve disciples (the full symbolic number just having been restored with the selection of Matthias) as those who preach publicly. The twelve apostles do take a prominent place as those who stand with Peter (Acts 2:14) and those who receive a question from the crowd (2:37).

Luke leaves several markers, however, to indicate that though the apostles are easily seen, they are not the only ones being heard. Instead, the testifying group includes them *as well as* all those who gathered waiting for the coming of the Spirit. Luke leaves clues that the testifying group specifically includes Mary.

First, those who testify are called "Galileans," which Luke established in his gospel that Mary is (Luke 1:26). Second, Luke specifies that the listening crowd is made of men; he uses the more gender-specific term ἀνήρ (*anēr*) and not the more general human term ἄνθρωπος (*anthrōpos*). Because he uses the terms with some fluidity, this could simply be his way of referring to a mixed-gender crowd with a masculine term. It is striking, however, that in the same

---

Spirit overshadows Mary, "as a human being, for the sake of her own nature begotten in original sin, *as indeed every human being*, she needed baptism and the reception of the Holy Spirit and she received the fiery tongue of the Holy Spirit *along with and equally with* all the apostles, with the whole Church" (*The Burning Bush: On the Orthodox Veneration of the Mother of God*, trans., ed., and intro. Thomas Allan Smith [Grand Rapids: Eerdmans, 2009], 67).

80. Augustine's statements on Mary and the church are fitting here: "Because Mary is part of the Church, a holy member, a quite exceptional member, the supremely wonderful member, but still a member of the whole body" (Sermon 72a, in *Sermons 51–94 on the New Testament*, trans. Edmund Hill, OP, Works of Saint Augustine: A Translation for the 21st Century III/3 [Brooklyn, NY: New City Press, 1991], 288; quoted in Tina Beattie, "Mary in Patristic Thought," in *Mary: The Complete Resource*, ed. Sarah Jane Boss [London: Continuum, 2009], 94).

passage where he describes the crowd as men *four times*,[81] he never uses the same term for "men" to describe those who are testifying.

Most important for Mary's inclusion in this group is Peter's extensive citation of the prophecy of Joel.[82] After the gospel cacophony, Peter rises to speak: What you have seen and heard, he says, is not drunkenness but a demonstration of the spirit of God being poured upon sons *and daughters*. The balanced phrase is not an example of inclusive translation. "Daughters" appears in the Greek of Peter's speech, and "daughters" appears in the Hebrew of Joel's prophecy (Joel 2:28–29). His cited text from Joel also calls the anointed ones male and female slaves (δούλη [*doulē*]). This is a designation that Luke uses only two other times in his two-volume work, and in both instances, this word describes Mary, in her climactic yes to the invitation to the incarnation (Luke 1:38) and in her Magnificat (1:48). It is little surprise that many in the Christian tradition have believed that Mary was present at Pentecost.[83] Mary, therefore (along with the other unnamed women), testified vocally and publicly to the fulfillment of God's promises in her son Jesus. There is no other way to account for the specifics of Peter's speech. He could not have said that "this is what was spoken through the prophet Joel" (Acts 2:16), the fulfillment that the crowd is seeing and hearing, if Mary and the other slave-daughters of the Lord had remained silent.

Luke shows the divine choice to include her in this group who obeys, is filled, and then testifies. As the only named female representative, she shows that the language of daughters and female slaves is not just the decor of inclusion but is the way God's Spirit acts. God gives her the Spirit issuing forth in the gift of speech to proclaim the gospel. She like all the others is given voice to speak in tongues that will propel the good news of her son to many. She had remained faithful and therefore was used by God not only to bring the Son but also, empowered by the Spirit, to join with others to continue his work (Acts 1:2).

81. In line with the rhetorical convention. See footnote 76, above.

82. "The gender inclusiveness of the gift of the Spirit comes to the fore when Peter speaks out to explain Pentecost to the gathering crowd. He quotes the prophet Joel" (Johnson, *Truly Our Sister*, 255, 300–301).

83. See Timothy Verden, *Mary in Western Art* (New York: Hudson Mills, 2005), 168–76. Vladimir Lossky notes that she often appears in Orthodox icons of Pentecost (*In the Image and Likeness of God* [London: Mowbrays, 1975], 206).

Conclusion

When Peter rises and defends those speaking from the slander of drunkenness,[84] he retells, for the first of many times in Acts, the grand story of God's salvation. Picturing Mary present, listening to Peter's Spirit-inspired words after having just spoken of her own, provides a perspective on Peter's speech that confirms and expands the miraculous nature of God's faithful work in and through her life. When Peter speaks of God's power, wonder, and signs that God did through Jesus (Acts 2:19), Mary recalls the wonders and signs at the very beginning: the miracle of her bodily knowledge of a child conceived by the Spirit, the angelic signs and wonders the shepherds shared with her, and the wonder of a young son who could teach the teachers. If readers of Luke's text know Matthew's story as well, they recall her knowledge of a moving star in the heavens, the worship of the magi, and the protection through dreams. Along with the wonder, she would also call to mind the pain. The plan and foreknowledge of God that he would be opposed by many (Acts 2:23) had been spoken to her by Simeon when he was just an infant (Luke 2:34), and she had lived to see it. She was present at the end of his earthly life as well. Finally, she, too, is witness of his resurrection, as Peter says to the crowd (2:32). She has seen that God would truly give her son the throne of his father David *forever* (Luke 1:32–33), with not even death a barrier to that reign.

She has seen it all, and she has participated in it all. She bore and mothered God, and she became his witness. From the privacy of a home to one female family member (Elizabeth), to a group of servants behind the scenes at a wedding, to the crowds in Jerusalem on the day of Pentecost, to the countless millions who through the canonical Scriptures have read, memorized, and sung her words, she proclaimed his story.[85]

The charge that the Christian tradition portrays Mary as only a passive

---

84. Interestingly, Hannah, Luke's muse for Mary's Magnificat, was thought drunk, too, before she uttered her song of praise (1 Sam 1:12).

85. For a treatment of the Magnificat in liturgy, see Jennifer Knust and Tommy Wasserman, "The Biblical Odes and the Text of the Christian Bible: A Reconsideration of the Impact of Liturgical Singing on the Transmission of the Gospel of Luke," *Journal of Biblical Literature* 133 (2014): 341–65. See also Ruth Ann Foster, "Mary's Hymn of Praise in Luke 1:46–55: Reflections on Liturgy and Spiritual Formation," *Review and Expositor* 100 (2003): 451–63.

vessel strikes me as implausible in light of all this.[86] She is not just vessel. She is virtuous mother. She is gospel proclaimer. She is not the only one—the First and Second Testament include stories of other influential women in various roles—but, for Christians, she is the central example.

In 1611, the same year the King James Bible was produced, Aemilia Lanyer, trailblazing female poet, wrote of Jesus: "without the assistance of man [he was] begotten of a woman, borne of a woman, nourished of a woman, obedient to a woman."[87] If God entrusted himself to her body and instruction and his story to her voice, then no other proof is necessary. Woefully insufficient would be the tepid claim that the Christian God is *not opposed* to the ministering of women. Instead, Mary shows this unassailable good news: through invitation, empowerment, and amplification, God has deemed the bodies and voices of women worthy of gospel participation, from raising the next generation to the act of testifying to countless generations. God values women.

86. Mary's yes to God has functioned as the quintessential template for "female subjection"; so argues Marina Warner, *Alone of All Her Sex: The Myth and the Cult of the Virgin Mary*, new edition (Oxford: Oxford University Press, 2016), 50. She goes on to describe the common image of Mary as sweet, submissive, and passive (191). Mary Daly sees her as the image of the "weak normal woman" in *Gyn/Ecology: The Metaethics of Radical Feminism* (Boston: Beacon, 1978), 231. Here, "normal" is used in the sense of "domesticated," as Mary encouraged women to be hemmed within male power. Lisa Isherwood and Dorothea McEwan view her as one who "does not seek power; she accepts her fate as dictated by others" (*Introducing Feminist Theology*, ed. Lisa Isherwood and Dorothea McEwan, 2nd ed. [Sheffield: Sheffield Academic, 2001], 69). She is "self-effacing" in the reading of Margaret Daphne Hampson (*After Christianity* [London: SCM, 1996], 194). These scholars argue that her story proves problematic for women across the spectrum of strength. She makes weak women weaker. Her story tells them that "suffering is natural and that their meek and mild acceptance of all the world throws at them is holy and reflects the example of the Virgin" (Isherwood and McEwan, *Introducing Feminist Theology*, 58). And, as previously mentioned, they argue she provides no example for strong women to run their own lives. These scholars are correct that her story has been misused, but the reading I've suggested here discloses that as she is in line with the ways of a good God, Mary provides an incredible example of strength.

87. *The Poems of Aemilia Lanyer: Salve Deus Rex Judaeorum*, ed. Susanne Woods (Oxford: Oxford University Press, 1993), 49–50. Thanks to Jim Wilhoit for bringing this to my attention.

Conclusion

At my son's recent eight-year-old birthday party, a conversation organically unfolded about gender. "I like boys better," one of the male attendees shared. "Why is that?" I queried. "Because God is a boy." From the mouths of babes. I could not have articulated the problem this book seeks to address with any greater clarity.

Readers dulled by familiarity with the Christmas story may be numb to both the potential and dangers that lurk in Gabriel's words to Mary: "The Holy Spirit will come upon you." For the Christian faith, distinct even from its fellow Abrahamic religions, countless questions and struggles, debates and divisions, and potentials for heresy and oppression inhere in this moment.[1] A divine messenger proclaims that God is going to cause a pregnancy. Readers who allow themselves to entertain the unmentionable questions are excused for wondering about the character and nature of this Father God, who seems in this moment to play the role of the decisive and overpowering male. Moreover, it is also no secret that the woman addressed in the statement is a cause of deep division. Beliefs about her mark out the territory between the different branches of the Christian faith, and she often becomes the lightning rod

---

1. In a conversation on the annunciation and consent that took place during the Society for Equitable Philosophy of Religion Round Table Discussion in December 2020, one of the panelists noted, "If God could save the world another way, the fact that God goes the way of impregnating a teenage girl seems profoundly problematic." I appreciated the clear-eyed recognition of the scandal at the heart of the Christian confession voiced in this comment, and this book is, in some ways, an extended response to that concern. See Blake Hereth, "Mary, Did You Consent?," *Religious Studies* (2021): 1–24.

for post-Christian disdain of them all. Wrestling with this event is well worth the intellectual controversy and theological risk, for the blessing obtained is nothing short of, in my assessment, the undeniable value of women that arises out of a fresh vision of God.

One may imagine that these fields of study, theology proper and gender studies, may be kept neatly apart. Theology proper need not become entangled in the complications of gender studies. This assumption is false. The basic Christian confession, that Jesus of Nazareth is God in the flesh, necessitates that the two be considered together. For if God does not care to be bothered about or even disdains women, that God stands at odds with the one revealed in the incarnation. The pervasive and deep hunger for good news on gender is met in the proper theology of this story, which is the story of God, yes, but by God's election, it is at the same time the story of Mary of Nazareth.

While many examples of the divine valuing of women exist in Israel's Scriptures, the New Testament, and church history, it is the epicenter—Mary's story—that is most important, for this is how God chose to enter the world. This book has considered anew the story of Mary, calling attention to riches previously unearthed. The evangelists portray her as one who welcomes the holy presence of God, exercises agency in strength, and then serves the coming kingdom of that God in word and deed.

That inspiring account of God's honoring of her and her active faith might have stood on its own as a nice and largely unthreatening look at Mary—and how daringly brave for a Protestant to do so!—but, for such a time as this, heralding the positive alone would have been incomplete as well as ineffective. God may do nice things for women, but if that God really ultimately prefers males, the nice things for women are sad second-class substitutes for true respect due anyone who is graced with the *imago Dei*. Hence, it was necessary as well to consider the ways Christians speak of and therefore think of God. Preference for divine masculinity cannot stand in the face of the event in which God caused a pregnancy. God the Father is not male. God the Father is not masculine. The son Jesus is embodied male but, because of the mode of his incarnation, is male like no other, denying the necessity that only males represent him. God the Father is rightly "Father" because God is Father of the eternal Son Jesus the Messiah, whose mother was Mary of Nazareth.

The Theotokos, the Mother of God, is not only for women, although they have been my focus here. Cyril proclaims the impact on all humanity because of God's choice to manifest in this way: "He had no need of temporal birth, in the last days of the world, for his own nature. No, he meant to bless the very origin of our existence, though a woman's giving birth to him united with flesh, meant too that the curse on the whole race which dispatches our earthly bodies to death should cease . . . he intended to prove true the prophet's utterance '. . . God took away every tear from every countenance.'"[2] The incarnation affirms, for all humans, their creation by God as well as the coming resurrection out of death. The curse upon Eve affects women in particular ways, but it is not limited to them, for everyone is born of a woman, everyone is born in this fallen world to death, but God choosing to have a mother broke that curse for all.

Because I make these dual claims rooted in the incarnation—God does not prefer men, and God values women—readers both more conservative and more critical than I will find aspects for disagreement. May the conversation continue! At this juncture, allow me to be as clear as possible. On one hand, I am not asking all readers to embrace the choice I have made to submit to the Christian tradition only to grant that affirming the goodness of the Son of God's conception and birth of a woman is neither exegetically naive nor necessarily oppressive. Many women can attest that even with the painful and misogynistic failures of our faith, in relationship with this God, we have found deep and lasting value for our lives.[3] On the other, neither am I asking all readers to affirm that women should serve in the home and the church based on their giftedness rather than their sex. These practices enacted on the basis of gender arise out of various (and often even opposite) but nonetheless plausible exegetical decisions.[4] I ask only that any who hold that persuasion

2. Cyril of Alexandria, "Third Letter to Nestorius," *Select Letters*, ed. and trans. Lionel R. Wickham (Oxford: Clarendon, 1983), 29.

3. See Beth Allison Barr's personal narrative in *The Making of Biblical Womanhood: How the Subjugation of Women Became Gospel Truth* (Grand Rapids: Brazos, 2021), esp. 201–5.

4. To this point, much more needs to be said. Readers will notice the glaring absence of Pauline texts in a book wrestling with Christian ideas of gender. My personal and pedagogical experience confirms that previous generations' stark divisions over the meaning of Mary's story continue to haunt many Protestants, leaving us hamstrung in our interminable conversations on gender roles. To approach the conversation through Mary's story, especially as a Protestant, offered new insights and fresh perspectives. Moreover, God, Jesus, Holy Spirit, and Mary offered enough material for one book. Now that it is done, an incarnational reading of Pauline texts might be the next logical step.

resist maintaining those role distinctions on the basis of any inappropriate projection of either maleness or masculinity upon the persons of the triune God. The mode of the incarnation—the reality of Mary—where God elected to achieve salvation and reveal Godself most definitively, will not allow it.

We need Mary not only for that debate about gender roles, however. She speaks to our spiritual hunger for the presence of God in the ordinary and our keen desire for justice. Catholic and Orthodox siblings serve as insightful guides to Protestants who do not quite know what to do with the gnawing ache alerting us to the truth that we are missing something vital. The field of Mariology greatly rewards those willing to traverse it. I only hope to whet the appetite with the simple affirmation that Mary stands in the Christian story as an undeniable reminder that God achieved the salvation of the world by choosing to manifest through the will, body, mind, emotions, soul, spirit, and voice of a woman.

I present this book as an apologia of the unwavering conviction that drives my life, that the Christian God loves women, a conviction most keenly felt, I should say, not in the library, where I feel God's pleasure in discovery, not even in the classroom, which I love more than I can articulate, but chiefly when I stand at the altar each week, where I cross the cross emblazoned over my chest as one who has been granted the supremely undeserved grace to come in the name of the Lord. Throughout the years in which I have struggled through texts and conversations that whispered that God's love was less for me because I am female, the Lord I met at the table each week would never allow me to believe the lie. Constructing this work has helped me live into the meaning of my name, *Beloved*, and I pray all readers will experience the same.

Appendix: God the Good Father

We should be more startled than we are by the kinship titles in the Bible.

—Janet Soskice, *Kindness of God*

One of the ways to correctly understand the masculine paternal language for God is to attend to what the text does and does not say. This prevents charging the text with oppressiveness that may be, in fact, absent. One does not know for sure until the texts are investigated closely.

This educative option is insufficient on its own. Close exegetical and theological attention to the text cannot provide the final answer to the problem of a male God explored in this book. The God and Father of the Jewish Messiah Jesus of Nazareth might very well be a good Father, but if that Father is still viewed as a "He," deep problems remain. Close attention to the goodness of God does not in any way remove the specter of a male God. Benevolence is no sure safeguard against heresy and its offshoot, oppression, to the detriment of both men and women, as parts of Christian history woefully demonstrate.

Nevertheless, knowledge of the New Testament picture of God's Fatherhood is an important aspect of this conversation. I offer this treatment in the hopes that tracing the character of God the Father throughout the New Testament might be a beneficial resource to readers.

God the Good Father

As a Christian academic who views theological concepts as fascinating intellectual puzzles and who finds myself comfortable within the Christian fold, I have needed tangible reminders that paternal language for God, for many, elicits strong reactions. Be it damaging personal experience or visceral righteous anger against patriarchy, many reject this language outright.

The texts of the canonical Scriptures challenge the idea that divine paternity appears in order to solidify selfish power and demand oppressive subjection. Instead, the authors consistently employ those schemas where God is Father to show God's care, love, and even self-sacrifice for the members of the family. The Scripture shows that God the Father is good.

In order to validate that claim, I showcase insightful critiques against paternal language for God but also demonstrate how biblical texts stand up to those critiques.[1]

A General God

Without question, divine "Father" language can bring damaging associations with certain negative conceptions of fatherhood. Such associations become possible because "father" is such a Rorschach-like term, a malleable canvas capable of absorbing any or all cultural or personal narratives. The meanings of the general statement "God is Father" find their limit only in the number of the experiences of the individuals who hear it.

The texts of the New Testament—dependent upon Israel's Scriptures as interpreted through the Christ event—do not present a statement about God's fatherhood in a general way, however. They make extremely particular claims about divine fatherhood. God is not generally father, whatever that could mean, but is the Father of Jesus of Nazareth, the Jewish Messiah. The fatherhood of God finds its breadth and depth as it is based on a very specific story with very particular meanings.[2]

---

1. Similar to the way in which Kierkegaard referred to Feuerbach as a "godly traitor" (*Kierkegaard's Journals and Notebooks* 6:340; quoted in Adam Neder, *Theology as a Way of Life* [Grand Rapids: Baker, 2019], 57), I read the critiques of some feminists, even and maybe especially those who have left Christianity, as an act of blessing as they expose false views of God that need to be abandoned.

2. Writing about Paul (which seems applicable to the entire New Testament), J. Ross Wager arrives at a similar position: "the apostle's discourse about God as Father remains consistently

Paul

As a chief example, in his Epistle to the Romans,[3] Paul lays out his gospel to address some of their needs as well as his own.[4] Paul defines the "good news" in his first sentence. God promised this good news through the prophets in the Scriptures of Israel, and the good news concerns God's Son who would come from the seed of David according to the flesh (Rom 1:3). God appointed the same Son of God in power according to the spirit of holiness from the resurrection of the dead.[5] This Son of God is Jesus the Messiah whom both Paul and the Romans confess as Lord (1:4). Grace and peace come from him as well as from his Father and theirs, a Father who is God (1:5). Paul's initial statements in Romans capture what he means by divine fatherhood with both brevity and clarity. Their Lord Jesus, the Messiah of Israel, is the Son of God, and so, because of that unique relationship, God is also Father to Paul and his congregants.[6]

---

and unabashedly particularistic. . . . For Paul, God's identity as Father is inseparable from the narrative of God's saving deeds in Jesus Christ" ("Is God the Father of Jews Only, or Also of Gentiles? The Peculiar Shape of Paul's 'Universalism,'" in *The Divine Father: Religious and Philosophical Concepts of Divine Parenthood in Antiquity*, ed. Felix Albrecht and Reinhard Feldmeier [Boston: Brill, 2014], 238, 245). See also N. T. Wright, *Paul and the Faithfulness of God* (Minneapolis: Fortress, 2013), 661–66.

3. A communiqué Paul writes to a congregation he has not founded but among whom he has many friends (cf. Rom 1:10–15; 16).

4. For the various motivations for Romans, see Karl P. Donfried, *The Romans Debate*, rev. and exp. ed. (Peabody, MA: Hendrickson, 1991). See also the thorough description of the possibilities in Robert Jewett's commentary where he argues for a missional motivation that comprises several of the previously discussed internal and external reasons for writing (*Romans: A Commentary*, Hermeneia [Minneapolis: Fortress, 2007], 41–91).

5. Many interpreters agree that Paul is drawing from a shared confession as a way of connecting with what he and the Romans already share. Nontypical Pauline terms and themes (Jesus as Son of David, the verb ὁρίζω [*horizō*], the phrase "spirit of holiness") have led to this near consensus. See Joseph A. Fitzmyer, *Romans: A New Translation with Introduction and Commentary*, Anchor Bible 33 (New Haven: Yale University Press, 2007), 230; James G. D. Dunn, *Romans 1–8*, Word Biblical Commentary 38A (Grand Rapids: Zondervan, 2015), 5; Douglas Moo, *The Letter to the Romans*, New International Commentary on the New Testament, 2nd ed. (Grand Rapids: Eerdmans, 2018), 45.

6. Dunn makes the distinction in the comparison between the sonship of Jesus and other humans: "it is obvious that a sonship is envisaged different from that affirmed of believers in the regular opening greeting (v 7)" (*Romans 1–8*, 11). This distinction constructs the identity upon which Paul builds his letters: "while he describes his identity and his audiences' identity

Throughout his writings, Paul continues to set divine paternity in relationship to the Lord Jesus Christ. Most prominent for Paul is the affirmation that
God is the Father of "our Lord Jesus Christ" (Rom 15:6; 2 Cor 1:3; 11:31), or
stated as its complement, Jesus is God's "Son" (Rom 1:3, 4, 9; 5:10; 8:3, 29, 32;
1 Cor 1:9; 2 Cor 1:19; Gal 1:16; 2:20; 1 Thess 1:10).[7]

Since Paul portrays himself and his congregations in relationship with this
Messiah and this God, it is not surprising that he depicts them relating to God
as their Father (1 Cor 1:3; 2 Cor 1:2; 6:18; Gal 1:3, 4; Eph 1:2, 5; 2:18; Phil 1:2; 4:20;
Col 1:2, 12; 1 Thess 1:2, 3; 3:11, 13; 2 Thess 1:1, 2; 2:16; Phlm 3).[8] Consequently,
the Pauline norm is to refer to fellow confessors of Jesus Christ as siblings, no-
menclature that occurs 130 times throughout the letters that bear his name.[9]

The funneling of God's fatherhood through God's relationship with Jesus
Christ suggests that Paul's use of paternal language for God is most influenced
by the Christian confession that precedes him. Many have seen a pre-Pauline
formula in his gospel definition at the beginning of Romans,[10] and even more
clearly, as the citations of Rom 8:15 and Gal 4:6 demonstrate, Paul's use of

in relation to God and Jesus, he constructs joint identity in terms of kinship relationship with
God." See Abera M. Mengestu, *God as Father in Paul: Kinship Language and Identity Formation
in Early Christianity* (Eugene, OR: Pickwick, 2013), 165.

7. The same pattern continues in letters where Pauline authorship is questioned. Multiple
statements affirm that God is Father (Eph 1:17; 3:14; 4:6; 5:20; Col 1:12; 3:17; 1 Tim 1:2; 2 Tim
1:2; Titus 1:4), which align with the more precise definition that God is the Father of our Lord
Jesus Christ (Eph 1:3; Col 1:3) and Jesus is God's Son (Eph 4:13; Col 1:13).

8. In Wagner's words, "God's paternal relationship to believers is thus firmly linked both to
Jesus's self-giving in death, by the will of God, 'for us' and to God's mighty act of raising him
from the dead" ("Is God the Father of Jews Only," 240).

9. God is named as "Father" (41 times total) at least once in each letter that bears Paul's
name: Romans (4), 1 Corinthians (3), 2 Corinthians (4), Galatians (4), Ephesians (8), Colossians (4), Philippians (3), 1 Thessalonians (4), 2 Thessalonians (3), the Pastoral Epistles
(1 each), Philemon (1). Jesus as Son is less frequent (17) but still present in most of the corpus:
Romans (7), 1 Corinthians (2), 2 Corinthians (1), Galatians (4), Ephesians (1), Colossians (1),
1 Thessalonians (1). See also Mengestu's analysis of the data (*God as Father in Paul*, 16–17).

10. Matthew Bates argues that this formulation seems to precede Paul because, for example,
it resonates with the received tradition in 1 Cor 15:3–5 as well as its inclusion of non-Pauline
words ("A Christology of Incarnation and Enthronement," *Catholic Biblical Quarterly* 77 [2015]:
107–27, esp. 109–10). Matthew Novenson, after weighing the arguments, concludes similarly
(*Christ among the Messiahs: Christ Language in Paul and Messiah Language in Ancient Judaism*
[New York: Oxford University Press, 2012], 169–70).

the Aramaic term strongly suggests that this is one of the Jesus traditions of which he was aware.[11] If scholars no longer tout Jesus as utterly unique in his affirmation that one could address God as "Abba," they are no less confident to assert that Jesus taught this concept.[12] Hence, Paul can use this paternal and filial language for God without argumentation because it was part of the accepted tradition that came before him. In other words, such language was not controversial for those to whom he is writing. He views the God of Israel, the God of the patriarchs, the God of his Scriptures as a Father; and he views the one revealed as Lord, Jesus the Messiah, as that God's Son. He neither makes nor tells of any arguments on this point, in great contrast to other contested issues in the communities to whom he writes. To them, he need not prove Jesus is Son of God the Father; he need only state it as part of their shared understanding. Paul's letters demonstrate that Christian communities thought of God as Father, even their Father, because Jesus their Lord was God's Son.

John

Another theological giant in the New Testament, the author of the Gospel of John, particularizes divine paternity in the same way. Kinship language first appears in the Gospel of John as it pertains to the many children rather than the one Son. Having talked about Jesus as the Word (John 1:1–3) and as the light (1:4–9), the evangelist then asserts that as many as receive the one who is the light receive authority to become children of God (1:12). These are born not in any of the normal ways—blood, flesh, or the will of men—but from God (1:13). When people believe in the name of the sent one, they are born as God's children.

The topic being broached, the author now reflects on the one who comes into the world as a child of God. When the Word took on flesh, he demonstrated

11. Moo, *Letter to the Romans*, 502–3; Richard N. Longenecker, *The Epistle to the Romans*, New International Greek Testament Commentary (Grand Rapids: Eerdmans, 2016), 702–3; Jewett, *Romans*, 499; James D. G. Dunn, *The Epistle to the Galatians*, Black's New Testament Commentaries (Grand Rapids: Baker, 1993), 221; Martinus C. de Boer, *Galatians: A Commentary*, New Testament Library (Louisville: Westminster John Knox, 2011), 266.

12. See the history of the debate in Marianne Meye Thompson, *The Promise of the Father: Jesus and God in the New Testament* (Louisville: Westminster John Knox, 2000), 21–34, and Erin M. Heim, *Adoption in Galatians and Romans: Contemporary Metaphor Theories and the Pauline* Huiothesia *Metaphors* (Leiden: Brill, 2017), 161–64.

a particular glory, full of grace and truth, the glory of a unique one from the Father. Because μονογενής (*monogenēs*) tends to be used as a reference to an only child (Judg 11:34; Luke 7:12; 8:42; 9:38; Heb 11:17; Tob 3:15; 6:11; 8:17; Wis. 18:4), and because John says the μονογενής (*monogenēs*) is unique from the *Father*, "only child" is an apt translation.[13] The singular language appears dissonant. John has just stated that God is in the business of bearing children—many of them—but now the Word has a glory fitting of an only child of God. This raises a question of precision. Does God have many children or only one? John has introduced a paradox he will tease out throughout his gospel.

John the Evangelist puts forth John the Baptist to elucidate the conundrum.[14] The baptist's testimony (John 1:7) asserts the Word's primacy. Even though John is the herald, the one testifying about the one to come (1:15), the person about whom he testifies has actually come before him, giving him primacy over John (1:15).

John's forerunning for the one who has come before him clarifies that the evangelist has followed a similar model with his kinship language. His affirmation that God births many children appears in John 1:12, but the only child mentioned in 1:14, in reality, comes first. It is from his fullness, John says, that the many receive grace upon grace (1:16). Through Jesus Christ—his name and honorific title appearing for the first time in 1:17—comes grace and truth. The way someone becomes a child of God is to receive him (1:11) and to believe in his name (1:12). Hence, the only begotten child of God is so abundant in grace and truth that his status as the singular child of God is not compromised when its glory overflows to birth other children of God. He is, in some sense, one Son among many, but he remains unique because only through him, Jesus Christ, can others stand in relationship to God as Father.[15]

---

13. Contra Craig S. Keener, *The Gospel of John: A Commentary* (Grand Rapids: Baker, 2010), 1:412–13. My argument is not based on etymology but on use.

14. Notice that the evangelist does not call him the one who baptizes until 1:25.

15. Similarly, Carlos Raúl Sosa Siliezar concludes, "the Word who became flesh possesses a unique relationship with the Father that is distinguishable from that of those who believe in ὁ λόγος" (*Creation Imagery in the Gospel of John*, The Library of New Testament Studies 546 [London: T&T Clark, 2015], 52). Thompson notes that "even more than the other Gospels or than the Pauline epistles, John emphasizes the unique relationship of the Son and the Father" (*Promise of the Father*, 133).

Marianne Meye Thompson calls attention to the important distinction in the terminology of John's writings: "Jesus is always called Son (υἱός [*huios*]), whereas believers are always designated children (τέκνα [*tekna*]). While there are many 'children' of God, there is only *one* Son."[16] In fact, the evangelist says that the unique only begotten God who was close to the heart of his Father is the only one who can explain God because no one else has seen God.[17] The Son of God's level of connection with God the Father *as God and yet as distinguishable from God* affords him unparalleled ability to reveal and relate God the Father to those who will be children.

As is evident, the evangelist works with many schemas in his opening section: Logos, light, John's testimony, and, as a preview of things to come, kinship language, which does significant work for him. First, it contributes to the exaltation of Jesus the Messiah. He is in a unique filial relationship with God. His status as only begotten is the particular manifestation of his glory (John 1:14). This glory puts him in immediate proximity with God and allows him to be the only one with such an intimate connection so that he can explain God to others. Second, it demonstrates the character of the God who spreads this intimate relationship to others. The only begotten God who possesses both grace and truth (1:14) gives to others, who then have authority to become children of God (1:12). Instead of hording his relationship with God—his intimacy and superiority—he shares its fullness with others. They are children of God because the only child of God has allowed them to be. This inclusion was the will of God. John makes it clear here in chapter 1 as well as throughout

16. Thompson, *Promise of the Father*, 136. She goes on to say, "the Father has given life to the Son and through the Son mediated life to others, who become 'children of God' (1:12; 11:52; see 1 John 3:1–2)" (137).

17. The high christological reading "only begotten God" is the best attested in the manuscripts. Writing against Francis Maloney, who argues that the reading "the only God" would be "somewhat clumsy in this context and within the overall Christology and theology of the Fourth Gospel (cf. 3:16, 18; 1 John 4:9)," Raymond E. Brown reads *theos* but translates *monogenēs* in apposition to *theos*, hence, "God the only Son." He states, "It is the unique relation of the Son to the Father, so unique that John can speak of 'God the only Son,' that makes his revelation the supreme revelation" (*The Gospel according to John I–XII*, Anchor Bible 29 [Garden City, NY: Doubleday, 1966], 17, 36). Sosa sums up well the reading I adopt: "Since the phrase (μονογενὴς θεὸς) can lead the reader to think that John has collapsed God into Jesus Christ, the following phrase clarifies that this μονογενὴς θεὸς exists in the bosom of the Father" (*Creation Imagery in the Gospel of John*, 52).

the gospel that the Father and the only Son, both God, are united, so therefore both the Father and the Son willed for the fullness of grace and truth to
envelop the many children.[18] Stated differently, John has shown that the God
of all, Father and only begotten, desires many children. The only way to be in
relationship with this divine Father is through this divine Son.

Jesus frequently aims to get this message to his followers. In one of the
final conversations of the gospel narrative, Jesus tells them of the household
of his Father. He asserts that they know the way to this location (John 14).

Thomas disagrees. He does not know the more basic information, namely,
where Jesus is going, so how can he know the way? Based on this conversation and previous ones (John 10:15–18; 12:23–33), it seems that Thomas should
know that Jesus is returning to his Father and that the way is through his death
and being lifted up. This obtuse question allows the evangelist to present Jesus's
clear and compelling answer in the penultimate "I am" of the gospel; Jesus
states that he is the way and the truth and the life (14:6). He does make it clear
that his destination is to be with the Father, and the way to the Father is only
through him. In addition to being the means of approach, he is also revelation
of the Father. If his followers know him, they will know the Father; they, in fact,
do know the Father and have seen God, a privilege not ever before allowed
(14:7), a fact that serves as a realization of John 1:18 ("No one has ever seen
God. It is God the only Son, who is close to the Father's heart, who has made
him known" [NRSV]).

Philip does not believe, so he asks to see the Father, because it seems
that seeing Jesus does not line up with his expectations of seeing God. Jesus
answers in a frustrated tone. "Have I been with you all this time, Philip, and you
still do not know me? Whoever has seen me has seen the Father" (John 14:9
NRSV). The evangelist is trading in an epistemically weighty kind of seeing.
It is not just to observe Jesus but to see him for who he is. Philip does not yet
have this type of vision. Jesus asks Philip whether he believes the assertion
Jesus has made so many times, namely, that he is in the Father and the Father

---

18. "Christ's equality with the Father is, therefore, as eternal as his generation from the Fa-
ther. The term 'equal' (*isos*) in 5:18 expresses the notion of equal nature and will." See Adesola
Akala, "Sonship, Sending, and Subordination in the Gospel of John," in *Trinity without Hierarchy:
Reclaiming Nicene Orthodoxy in Evangelical Theology*, ed. Michael F. Bird and Scott Harrower
(Grand Rapids: Kregel Academic, 2019), 31.

is in him and that his words and works are not his own. Jesus commandingly asks Philip and the others to believe his claim about his relationship with the Father, but if they are not yet ready to believe the claim, they can believe his works. Works point toward his identity in relationship with God. One could hardly ask for a closer association between Jesus and God. To see Jesus is to have seen God, to follow Jesus is to go to the Father.

Jesus's prayer from John 17 displays the same invitation. Loved and glorified before the world began, Jesus looks forward to sharing eternally the same glory and love with those who believe in his relation to the Father. The unity of the Father and the Son embraces the followers of Jesus, those who hear and receive the word about him. He also hopes that this unity will ultimately embrace the world who currently does not know and even hates God. Anyone can claim God as Father, as long as they come through Jesus.[19]

These two influential theological voices provide the example affirmed in the rest of the New Testament: God is Father of Jesus Christ. Rescued from a bland generality that could be twisted to indicate any kind of father, good or ill, the New Testament assertion of divine paternity is extremely particular, even exclusive. In that exclusivity, the fatherhood of God is defined and accessed through the sonship of the Jewish Messiah. The hope is that all the world, people and creation, will be included in that relationship.[20] That kind of particular-

---

19. With more punch, the Johannine epistles affirm the same idea. A confession of the Son means a retention of the Father (1 John 2:22–24), or in 2 John, a "having" of the Father and the Son (2 John 9). Jesus's identity as Son has been testified to them by none less than God (stated twice 1 John 5:9, 10). The one who believes has internally received this testimony (5:10), but if it is not believed and received, rejection is the same as calling God a liar (5:10). If any do not retain this confession of Jesus as the Messiah come in the flesh from God, they will be in opposition to the Son but also against his Father and cannot retain a relationship with either.

20. This precision is apparent even in Eph 3:14–15, a statement that highlights God's role as Father over all the families in the heavens and on the earth. This is an affirmation of God's standing as Creator (for a lucid discussion, see Frank Thielman, *Ephesians*, Baker Exegetical Commentary on the New Testament [Grand Rapids: Baker, 2010], 227–28), and yet, this cannot be separated from God's identity as the Father of Jesus Christ. Andrew T. Lincoln states, "God is not only Father as Redeemer but also as Creator. Yet the two notions cannot be held apart for the writer of Ephesians. The God who is the Father of all families is the same God who is the Father of Jesus Christ" (*Ephesians*, Word Biblical Commentary 42 [Grand Rapids: Zondervan, 2014], 203).

ity, grounded in the story told in these texts, provides responses to the possibly damaging connotations that could arise with a general fatherhood.[21]

A Distant God

If the fatherhood of God is not general and therefore open to any connotations, the specificity of the Father of Jesus Christ has created other critiques worthy of consideration. Distance is one aspect that colors a common picture of the Father God. Personal experiences, more common in times and cultures where labor necessities or mores about emotion kept fathers removed from their children, resulted in this image of God. Riet Bons-Storm gives voice to this assumption when she argues that God conceived as only Father and not as Father/Mother portrays God as "the Lonely Powerful Male."[22] In these pictures, God the Father appears inaccessible, needing the kind of mediation of "eating with the outcast" Jesus or, if Jesus becomes too staunch, his all-compassionate mother.[23] With such an image, God the Father simply cannot convey intimacy and care. Bons-Storm draws sharp lines between the two

21. Early Christian interpreters arrived at the same conclusion about the particularity of God's fatherhood. Peter Widdicombe summarizes Origen's thought: "Origen thinks that although God is Father we can only come to know him as Father through our participation in the Son. We come to know God as Father through a step-by-step progression to the status of adopted sons and thus to a share in the eternal relationship of the Father and the Son" (*The Fatherhood of God from Origen to Athanasius* [Oxford: Clarendon, 2000], 93).

22. Riet Bons-Storm, "Back to Basics: 'The Almighty Father' Revisited," *HTS Telogiese Studies/Theological Studies* 67 (2011): 2. She offers further details: "'God the Mother' calls into existence a world of meanings totally different from the meanings attached to 'God the Father'. God the Father sits on top of the power ladder. He can be called 'Lord'. . . . As such He is almighty, Lord of everything." She asserts, "The average woman has an idea of love different from that of men. Many men suppose that it is possible to love from a distance. Many earthly fathers will maintain that they love their wife and children whilst they only see them a small part of their time, being otherwise engaged with important business. Women, on the whole, associate love with nearness. They are trained to accept as their role to be there for children, husbands, (elderly) parents, friends and whoever needs care. Hence they long for a God who loves them in the sense of being near them" (5).

23. As Louis-Marie Grignon de Montfort says, "through Mary we take Christ by his weak side" (*A Treatise on the True Devotion to the Blessed Virgin*, trans. Frederick William Faber [London: Burns and Lambert, 1863], 101). Also Alphonsus Ligouri states, "If God is angry with a

pictures of God, opposing "God the Almighty Father" with "a God who walks with Her or His friends through life and death, always near them in gracious and inspiring, empowering love, not almighty but honoring the responsibility She or He gave them."[24]

Such a reading undergirds the gendered stereotypes that many no longer accept. Not all fathers are distant, and not all mothers are intimate; ideas of parental love do not fall so sharply into two genders. Nevertheless, this kind of critique of the masculine language for God connects with a pervasive understanding of a distant and fearful sovereign.

When the canonical texts use Father language for God, however, their descriptions could hardly paint a more intimate, and hence less distant, relationship between God and God's people. This Father is indeed worthy of glory and reverence (Eph 1:17; 3:14; 4:6; Phil 2:11; 4:20), but chiefly so because of what God has done with compassion *for others*.

Paul

The Pauline literature affirms this positive tone to God's fatherhood. God the Father loves us, Paul tells his communities (Rom 1:7; 2 Thess 2:16), as does the Son (Gal 2:20), and in that self-giving love, God gave the Son (Rom 8:32), and the Son gave himself (Gal 2:20; Phil 2:8). The result is that sin is condemned (Rom 8:3), so a rescue can happen (Col 1:13; 1 Thess 1:10; Gal 1:4) resulting in new life (Rom 6:4), holiness and blamelessness (1 Thess 3:13), blessing (Eph 1:3), and reconciliation and salvation (Rom 5:10). People are now in the fellowship of God (1 Cor 1:9), in the very family of God.[25] In the present, God the Father gives grace and peace,[26] guidance (1 Thess 3:11), mercy, and consolation (2 Cor 1:3). In the future, God the Father gives hope (2 Thess 2:16) and an inheritance (Col 1:12). In all these ways, Paul can call the divine Father faithful (1 Cor 1:9), blessed (Eph 1:3), and worthy of thanks (Eph 5:20; Col 1:3, 12; 3:17). God the Father has said "Yes" to humanity in the Son (2 Cor 1:19).

---

sinner and Mary takes him under her protection, she withholds the avenging arm of her Son" (*The Glories of Mary* [New York: Edward Duncan and Brother, 1852], 133).

24. Bons-Storm, "Back to Basics," 5.

25. Rom 8:14, 15, 29, 32; 9:26; 2 Cor 6:18; Gal 1:16; Eph 2:18; 4:13; Phil 4:20; 1 Thess 5:5; 2 Thess 1:1.

26. Rom 1:3, 7; 1 Cor 1:3; 2 Cor 1:2; Gal 1:3; Eph 1:2; Phil 1:2; Col 1:2; 1 Thess 1:1; 2 Thess 1:2; 2:16; 1 Tim 1:2; 2 Tim 1:2; Titus 1:4; Phlm 3.

God's fatherhood, through Jesus Christ, is deeply good news for Paul and his communities (Rom 1:3, 9). Such a catalog reiterates that paternal language is not only extremely prevalent but also that its prevalence focuses upon God's good care. When Paul speaks of the magnanimity of God toward humanity, he frequently does so by referring to God as Father.

An exegete could ask for no better articulation of this theme than Paul's theologically and rhetorically exultant Rom 8, which offers a victorious crescendo after the angst-filled discord of chapter 7, and key parts of that crescendo come in the tones of familial language. In this section, by appealing to the work of the spirit of God, Paul affirms his and his readers' identity as children of God. He grounds that identity experientially in the current reality of their suffering, thereby putting them into the pattern of the life of Jesus the Son of God. He then concludes with his stirring proclamation of God's love for them. Consequently, his presentation of God's Fatherhood is extremely positive, yet with full recognition of the less than positive reality they are currently experiencing.

To illuminate this relationship in more detail, I focus on the second section of the chapter, where Paul makes their present identity explicit. In Rom 8:12, for the first time in the chapter, Paul addresses his readers directly as ἀδελφοί (adelphoi). Putting kinship on their mental schema, he evokes the previous section by referring to the many who are being led by the spirit of God. As he urges them toward a certain way of living—here, putting to death the deeds of the body—he then draws the implication that those being so led by the Spirit are sons of God (8:14).[27] He is careful to distinguish this relationship from one of fearful slavery, from which one has nothing to say. In contrast, they have received a spirit of adoption (υἱοθεσία [huiothesia]),[28] in which they are able to cry out and address God as "Abba, Father" (8:15). This is a relationship of intimacy, indicated by the fact that they can have conversation with God and even more so by the familiar paternal term used in that conversation. Most importantly and valuably, this adoptive spirit allows people to talk to God

---

27. The exhortation resonates with that of 2 Cor 6.

28. See Heim's discussion that indicates the best interpretation here is "adoption" and not the more general sonship (*Adoption*, 118–21), including referring to the same conclusions by James M. Scott, *Adoption as Son of God: An Exegetical Investigation into the Background of ΥΙΟΘΕΣΙΑ in the Pauline Corpus*, Wissenschaftliche Untersuchungen zum Neuen Testament 2/48 (Tübingen: Mohr Siebeck, 1992), xiv.

like Jesus did. This spirit of adoption, which seems to be a synonymous way of describing the spirit of God since both are internal (8:9, 15),[29] testifies with their spirit that they are children of God. Their actions—being led by the Spirit—and their prayer—as made possible by the Spirit—assures them of their familial standing before God.

As this identity allows a particularly intimate type of prayer in the present, so it also allows a hope for the future. Children generally inherit from their father, so the Romans to whom Paul is writing also have an inheritance to which they look forward, just as Jesus looks forward to his inheritance (Rom 8:17). They are heirs of God and also fellow heirs with the Messiah. That inheritance includes future glorification but also includes the path of present suffering that leads toward glorification—hence the need for intimate and bold prayer now as they suffer. Sonship, forged and confirmed spiritually, allows them to participate in the life of Christ to join him in his suffering and in his glorification.

Having mentioned suffering, Paul then reflects on that current reality. He does not deny its existence but counters that it will pale in comparison to future glory (Rom 8:18). Part of the greatness of that glory is that it will include more than just the children of God themselves. All creation holds its breath for the revelation of the sons of God. Paul's synonymous language is repetitive, and hence rhetorically emphatic, on this point: the eager expectation (ἀποκαραδοκία [*apokaradokia*]) of creation eagerly awaits (ἀπεκδέχεται [*apekdechetai*]) the revelation of the sons of God, likely the revelation of their glorified state (8:19), with its ethical implications,[30] since creation is still awaiting the revelation.[31] Although presently, creation is subjected, the one who

29. Dunn, *Romans 1–8*, 452; Jewett, *Romans*, 498; Michael F. Bird, *Romans*, The Story of God Bible Commentary (Grand Rapids: Zondervan, 2016), 267; Moo, *Letter to the Romans*, 501–2. Contra Longenecker, *Epistle to the Romans*, 703.

30. Jewett calls attention to the implications of this hope that should not have to wait completely for the eschaton: "When Paul speaks of their 'revelation/unveiling' there is a clear reference to God's glory advancing in the world, in this instance, through the triumph of the gospel. As the children of God are redeemed by the gospel, they begin to regain a rightful dominion over the created world (Gen 1:28–30; Ps 8:5–8); in more modern terms, their altered lifestyle and revised ethics begin to restore the ecological system that had been thrown out of balance by wrongdoing (1:18–32) and sin (Rom 5–7)" (*Romans*, 512).

31. Moo, *Letter to the Romans*, 515; Longenecker, *Epistle to the Romans*, 723. See also Douglas J. Moo and Jonathan A. Moo, *Creation Care: A Biblical Theology of the Natural World*, Biblical Theology for Life (Grand Rapids: Zondervan, 2018).

subjected it did so for hope (8:20). Just as the sons of God have been set free, creation looks forward to freedom as well (8:21). Paul's audience did not receive a spirit of slavery *again* (8:15); instead, they are in freedom (8:21). Creation looks forward to a similar release from the slavery of decay, but now it groans and experiences labor pains. Humans join creation in this hopefulness, because they have the firstfruits of the Spirit, by which they know they have been adopted and can cry out to God. They, too, like creation, are groaning for the adoption that will redeem their bodies. They, too, like creation, hope (8:24) and eagerly await their hope (8:25). They both have already received adoption and also look forward to adoption. Heim captures the paradox beautifully: "Thus, the emotional content evoked by the two υἱοθεσία metaphors in Romans 8 expresses the existential tension of the present ambiguity, and gives the believers a space to groan under an intense emotional burden for God's final action, while they simultaneously rest in the assurance of their identity as sons of God."[32]

Having proclaimed their identity as God's children, and the future glory and present suffering that entails, Paul returns to the work of the Spirit in the midst of their prayer. It is the Spirit who takes hold of their weakness; it is the Spirit who intercedes for them with inarticulate groaning (Rom 8:23, 26). God can see to that inward part where the Spirit is praying. Although there is not family language in this section of Romans (8:26–27), it reiterates some of the same themes of the heavenly kinship section of 8:12–17. In both places, the Spirit forges an intimacy of conversation and understanding between God and the believer.

Then again, as he did in Rom 8:17, 23, Paul returns to the idea of the believer being patterned off of Jesus. All things—even the hardships of the present— will work together toward good, because this was God's plan to make others like his Son, to make him the first among his brothers (8:29), those who share in his suffering and glorification.

Hence, their standing as children/sons of God is extremely christological. They suffer as he suffered and will be glorified as he is now glorified. That future glorification will include the redemption of their bodies just as it did for his, and their glorified bodies will open the doors to the redemption of all creation. Consequently, when they act like Jesus, being led by the Spirit, pray like Jesus— addressing God as "Abba" as the Spirit allows—they and all creation know that

32. Heim, *Adoption*, 243.

they have begun to walk the path he has already completed, a path that leads to incomparable glory for all things. Paul constructs their identity in a christological mode but with one important difference; only they have received adoption. The Spirit facilitates this transfer, as well as its subsequent life of prayer and ultimate reality of hope. Hence, their standing as sons of God is also extremely pneumatological.

In the final section of the chapter, Paul assures them of the present, extremely good implications of their relationship with God. God is for them (Rom 8:31). If God did not spare even the Son but gave him over to deal with sin and death, will God who gave him not also give all things (8:32)? Will God accuse or will Jesus Christ condemn God's elect? These are incredulous questions since God is righteous and Jesus Christ has died, been raised, sits at God's right hand, and intercedes *for them*. Anything they are presently suffering, from the internal war waged against the sin in their flesh to external persecution, is not a sign of God's absence but a sign of being with Christ the Son, their brother, on the way to his inheritance of victory. They will persevere and overcome because of the one who loved them (8:37), and Paul clarifies that this love is God's love in Christ. No created thing can stand between this love and God's people.

Through the Spirit, God's love incorporates the elect into God's Son Christ and, as it does so, demands a participation in the Son's suffering, and promises an inheritance in the Son's glorification. An apt example of my previous overview of Paul's kinship language for the divine, in Rom 8, God is a *loving* Father, and Jesus is a loving firstborn Son. Paul highlights God's paternity of this congregation as he emphasizes God's presence in the midst of their suffering and redemptive plan for their suffering.[33] Yet again loving fatherhood motifs become especially prominent when the current suffering is also in view. According to Paul, through the Spirit and the Son, his communities are in relationship with a present and good Father God.

Paul's presentation is impervious to the charge of a patriarchal, distant Father God. In the densest treatment of the family of God in Paul's writ-

---

33. C. E. B. Cranfield notes that this type of prayer, one that cries out to God as Father, illumined by the use of κράζω (*krazō*) in the Psalms, denotes "an urgent and sincere crying to God" (*A Critical and Exegetical Commentary on Romans*, vol. 1, International Critical Commentary [New York: T&T Clark, 1975], 399).

ing—Rom 8, with its dual mention of adoption and the inclusion of the Abba prayer—Paul focuses on the fatherhood of God *as he discusses* God's sustaining presence with them in the midst of suffering. Bons-Storm's description of the opposite of the Almighty Father God actually seems a fitting description of Rom 8: "God who walks with Her or His friends through life and death, always near them in gracious and inspiring, empowering love." Paul says that God the Father is present now with them in his Spirit and guarantees the redemption of their souls, bodies, and all creation from their current causes of suffering. This is all accomplished by the one whom they are to call "Abba." It is certainly the case that some traditions developed in theology and art that depict God as harsh and inaccessible, but that does not seem fitting to the text, particularly this high-water mark of the Pauline corpus.

General Epistles

The General Epistles provide a salient example of this theme of God's father-hood as well. These texts are uncompromising letters. Written by authors un-afraid to call for obedience and call out sin, one might expect their portrayal of God as Father to be similarly rigid. Their portrayal does include an element of judgment, but the picture that dominates is one of mercy, love, and even maternal tenderness.[34] Birth and sustenance, therefore, provide the grid to analyze the references to the divine paternal theme in these letters.

The letters of James, Peter, and Jude describe features of God's fatherhood through God's birthing of the communities to whom they are writing. James writes to confirm in their minds the consistent character of God. God is not tempted and does not tempt (Jas 1:13); only good comes from God. James says that there is not even one variation or turning to the dark side in God. James's example of this goodness is God's desire to give birth to (ἀποκυέω [*apokyeō*]) this community.[35] The birth takes place in association with the

34. Let me be clear that I am not affirming the stereotype that mothers are gentle and fathers are firm. Yet, because, for example, 1 Pet 2:2 speaks of the *milk* of the Lord, this is a *maternal* image of tenderness. Since only mothers can breastfeed and breastfeeding has to be done with gentleness (if it is not, the mother will be bitten!), the text portrays the Lord with a particularly maternal (due to the biology of breastfeeding) tenderness.

35. An unusual word in the Christian Scriptures, it appears in the New Testament only in James 1:15, 18 and in the Septuagint texts only in 4 Maccabees 15:17. This is the word Philo uses for

word of truth. Depending upon the meaning of the case, truth functions as a sort of midwife of the Lord or as a seed implanted in the infant (the word is an implanted thing just a few statements later in 1:21), which is meant to grow into the maturity of hearing and action (1:22–23). Either way, as is fitting to an unchangeable God, the Father's birthing process is characterized by truth. Finally, James asserts that their birth contains within it a promise for the future. Their truthful generation is only the first act of a continuing drama. They are the firstfruits of God's intention for the creation. Everything will be born by the word of truth. If they are tempted to doubt God's future goodness, they need only look to their origin and see within it the guarantee for how things will be in the future.[36]

The First Letter of Peter also explicitly uses the language of birth associated with God as Father. God is Father of "our Lord Jesus Christ," who bore us again (ἀναγεννάω [*anagennaō*]).[37] God's great mercy was the motivating factor for this birth (1 Pet 1:2). God's work with them was an act of mercy. Peter appeals to their birth again when he reminds them that they have been reborn (ἀναγεννάω [*anagennaō*]) through the word of the living God. He clarifies that this is the word that was gospeled to them. It was the good news that brought about their birth from God. Hence, God's birthing them is associated with truth, love, mercy, and good news. God sounds not like a distant father but an intimate and good one.

God's good parenting extends past the moment of birth to the life of the child as well. God the Father sustains the children whom God has generated. James's first encouragement to those who may be wondering whether God is responsible for the bad in their lives is that God, the Father of lights (rather than shadows, a description that emphasizes God's clear consistency), is responsible for every good and perfect gift that comes down (Jas 1:17). The continual gift-giving of God the Father shows God's paternal presence and care

---

the birthing process (*On the Creation of the World* 161) and also metaphorically for generation, as when one number generates another (*Allegorical Interpretation* 1.15).

36. "The idea appears to be that believers are that section of creation harvested by God as part of the new creation." See Chris Vlachos, *James*, Exegetical Guide to the Greek New Testament (Nashville: Broadman & Holman, 2013), 50.

37. This specific form of the verb appears only in Peter's first letter, but its use in Josephus and Philo attests to an idea of reappearance of a thing in a new form. See Josephus, *Jewish War* 4.484 (ashes in fruit) and Philo, *On the Eternity of the World* 8 (the Stoic belief of regeneration).

throughout life. Peter pairs the continuing work of God with each mention of God's birthing. In 1 Pet 1:3–4, the birth motivated by mercy has hope as its result. This is a hope that lives, which denotes a present experience of hope, as well as a hope that looks forward to an inheritance, a fitting thing for which to hope when one is a child. This inheritance, much like the character of God in James, is made unassailable by the agents of corruption, impurity, or dullness, because it is being preserved safe in heaven.[38] They are currently being guarded by the power of God. This powerful guard is present even though they are currently experiencing trials, trials that God's power allows in the knowledge that it will refine them and make them more fit to give glory and honor to their Messiah when he is revealed (1:7). So too in 1:23, they have been reborn through the living *and abiding* word of God. God's word, as Isaiah says (Isa 40:8), will remain forever; that which was present at their birth will sustain them into eternity when they possess their unfading inheritance.

The most striking presentation of God's parental sustenance follows immediately on the heels of Peter's presentation of God's abiding word. If this gospel word bore them and continues to sustain them, their lives should reflect this rebirth. His vivid picture of such a life is that of an infant, newly born, who greatly desires the milk of her mother. They, too, should so desire the pure milk that would allow them, just as is true for any infant, to grow. They, however, are growing not into adulthood but into salvation. Since God is the agent behind their rebirth—and based on 1:2, the Father, the Spirit, and Jesus the Messiah are all involved—the most plausible reading is that God is also the one who is feeding them. The next verse supports this picture. If they long for this milk, they will taste the truth that the Lord is kind. God's sustaining milk is gentleness, care, and protection for those who rest on him. In the revised edition of the *Women's Bible Commentary*, Gail O'Day reaches a conclusion about the paternal language for God in John, which seems fitting to literature previously discussed as well: "God as Father does not evoke conventional gender cate-

---

38. The passive of τηρέω (*tēreō*) seems likely to be a divine passive, in that the inheritance is kept safe by God. Karen H. Jobes's comments point in this direction when she says, "now their new inheritance is secure, for it is even now being kept 'in heaven' for them, far beyond the reach of the events of the world" (*1 Peter*, Baker Exegetical Commentary on the New Testament [Grand Rapids: Baker, 2005], 87).

gories. John speaks of God as Father neither to reinforce patriarchy . . . nor to reinforce the primacy of the male gender. . . . Jesus calls God Father in John in order to evoke a new world in which intimate, loving relations with God and one another are possible."[39]

An Infantilizing God

A Father who births and cares for children may solve the problem of distance but introduces another concern. For some, calling God "Father" is not just a gendered problem but a more basic issue of human flourishing and freedom. If God is Father, then the humans in relationship with God are children, and children do not act on their own. "Fatherhood" language serves to infantilize, discouraging adherents from autonomous decision-making and therefore stunting their ability to mature.[40] Calling God "our Father," or even "our Mother," according to this critique, creates problems for any adult, man or woman.

Such inert cowardice could arise from paternal language, but that reaction would be at odds with the grain of the text. Those in relationship with the divine Father of the New Testament are not infantilized but, instead, empowered. God gives much to them, and in turn God demands much of them. They must grow in maturity to rise to these demands and to experience these benefits.

It is true that the Pauline writings describe God's paternal actions as ones of rescue (Col 1:13; 1 Thess 1:10; Gal 1:4), which implies that humans are in a situation that demands it. Paul is rather adamant that humans cannot manage

---

39. Gail O'Day, "Gospel of John," in *Women's Bible Commentary*, eds. Carol A. Newsom, Sharon H. Ringe, and Jacqueline E. Lapsley, rev. and upd. 20th anniversary ed. (Louisville: Westminster John Knox, 2012), 530.

40. Rosemary Radford Ruether articulates it this way: "Patriarchal theology uses the parent image for God to prolong spiritual infantilism as virtue and to make autonomy and assertion of free will a sin" (*Sexism and God-Talk: Toward a Feminist Theology; With a New Introduction* [Boston: Beacon, 1993], 69). Rita Nakashima Brock concurs when she states that Christianity "leads the focus of feeling and action away from self-awareness, away from our inner selves, our contexts, and our history" because "this parent-child fusion serves to maintain the independence of the parent and the dependence of the child" (*Journeys by Heart: A Christology of Erotic Power* [Eugene, OR: Wipf & Stock, 2008], 54).

to save themselves.[41] After this rescue, however, God the Father demands that the children of the divine family not remain inactive and immature. When the glory of the Father raises the Son, in whose death and new life believers participate through resurrection, the participants are not to remain in their sin, nor are they to wait for God to act, but they are instructed to walk in the new life given to them (Rom 6:4). This is an active and demanding response. It does not seem that Paul's exhortations of the faith "lead the focus of feeling and action away from self-awareness, away from our inner selves, our contexts, and our history."[42] Instead, Paul places weighty ethical demands on the members of God's family, asking them to consider seriously their own responses in their own particular contexts in light of their history, that is, a history caught into God's story. Paul rejects any idea that his congregations would remain immature and inactive infants; instead, he desires that they actively grow into mature adult children of God. It is true that Paul urges for neither autonomy nor independence, yet his ethics are not a flat binary where the opposite of these is infantile inactivity. Instead, dependence upon God as Father encourages willful actions and growth in maturity.

The Johannine gospel also argues that belief in God as Father should have a transformative effect on the lives of those who so believe. They, too, will do the works that Jesus has done and even greater (John 14). Whatever they ask, the Son will do so that the Father will be glorified through the Son by the works of those who believe in the Son. All they need to do is ask in the Son's name. This is another picture of the overflowing abundance of the Father and the Son. There is no hoarding of amazing works but a profligate giving to their followers.

This is an immense blessing, but this relationship also comes with responsibility. He also asks them to remain in that love (John 15:9). The way to do so is to keep the commandments, following the example of Jesus, who has kept his Father's commandments and so remained in the Father's love. He reminds them that he chose them and appointed them for what he is calling them to

---

41. This may be a point at which those who do not see the human situation as corrupted by sin simply raise a fundamental disagreement with the text and, therefore, see any language of God's rescue as infantilizing. I find Paul's assessment that humans are in need of rescue apropos of lived reality.

42. Brock, *Journeys by Heart*, xiv.

do: bear fruit that remains. To this end, he will request that his Father will give them a comforter, the Spirit of truth. God the Father makes provisions so that those who have become children activate their faith.

The First Epistle of John is similarly replete with kinship language for God and God's people that invites mature response. God's commandment is that they believe in the name of his Son Jesus Christ and love one another, which is exactly what Jesus told them to do (1 John 3:23). This is a tangible love (3:13–22). To remain in what they have heard is to remain in the Son and the Father (2:24). The one who loves the begetter also loves the one begotten (5:1), a statement that could apply both to the Father and the Son, as well as the Father and the many children. In 2 John, the familial titles appear in the greeting. He wishes them grace, mercy, and peace from God the Father and from Jesus Christ the Son of the Father (2 John 3), and he is delighted to hear that the children of the lady to whom he writes are walking in truth just as their Father had commanded them (2 John 4).

This corpus shares the family identity of God's giving love to the Son, extending through the Spirit to those who believe in the Son. Love is promised, and confession and obedient love demanded, for the continuation of God's blessings. The fatherhood of God as John portrays it avoids shoals both of power-hungry domination, for nothing is not shared, and also of apathetic spoiling, for much—continual love, obedience, and even one's life—is demanded.

The First Letter of Peter displays a similar dynamic. The readers should lay aside all evil and deceit, hypocrisy, jealousy, and slander, a list likely influenced by Peter's citation of Ps 33 (LXX), which follows. If Ps 33 does exert influence on this epistle, then God's gentleness is not incommensurate with God's judgment (see 33:11, 16, 21 LXX). Peter's readers should live in particular ways because they address as Father the one who judges (1 Pet 1:17). This is an impartial judgment administered according to the work of each. Hence, there is an extremely tender care to God's nature as Father, and judgment of wrong actions is an aspect of that care. If judgment is a part of the relationship, immaturity will not be condoned.

In the view of the author of Hebrews, the community is experiencing difficulties because God is offering those realities for them in their identity as sons. This is the only explicitly nonsacrificial use of "offer" (προσφέρω [*prospherō*]) in Hebrews. Possibly, he is capturing the idea that as Jesus (Heb 5:1, 7; 9:14,

21, 28; 10:12) and they (13:16, 21) offer pleasing things to God, so too is God
offering something ultimately pleasing to them. He begins from the argument
simply that this is what fathers do: Train the children who belong to them.[43]
For what son is there whom a father does not discipline (12:7)? All of them
are experiencing this discipline, because if they were not, that would indicate
that they are not in a filial relationship with God. As children of God, then,
they should expect no less. In fact, they should expect more. God does not
discipline just by what *seems* good like their fathers of the flesh (12:9), but God
knows the benefit that will come through discipline. Moreover, that benefit is
not just human maturity but a maturity of divine likeness, stepping into the
very qualities of God: life (3:12; 9:14; 10:31; 12:22), holiness, peace (13:20),
and righteousness (6:10). The author employs a *synkrisis* argument yet again:[44]
If they respected their earthly fathers, how much more should they submit to
God, the Father of their spirits (12:9).[45] Such knowledge should give them
strength: the circumstances they are enduring are not outside of God's plan

43. Harold W. Attridge (*The Epistle to the Hebrews*, Hermeneia 58 [Minneapolis: Fortress,
1989], 361) and Mary Ann Beavis and HyeRan Kim-Cragg (*Hebrews*, Wisdom Commentary
[Collegeville, MN: Liturgical, 2015], 160–63) present a helpful discussion of the common
paideic assumptions upon which this passage is built.

44. Alan C. Mitchell draws attention to the fact that while this is a comparative statement, it
could be a transitional one as well: "Even though he appeals to the readers' former relationship
to their parents, he does so in the past tense. They 'had' parents and they 'respected' them. It is
as if they have left the natural parental relationship behind in order to enter into fictive kinship
in the Christian community, where God now functions as the spiritual parent" (*Hebrews*, Sacra
Pagina 13 [Collegeville, MN: Liturgical, 2007], 275). If this is true, separation from their families
could sharpen the struggles they experience as confessors of Jesus as Messiah and Lord.

45. "Father of spirits" language works in two ways here. First, it distinguishes biological fathers from the nonbiological relationship they have with God. Second, if Hebrews looks forward
to resurrected bodies, as some have argued, then we see "the litany of faithful ones in 11:1–12:2
who are witnesses for the audience of what it looks like to live as those who look forward to the
'better resurrection.' These faithful ones will *live*, and Jesus is the chief example." See David M.
Moffitt, *Atonement and the Logic of Resurrection in the Epistle to the Hebrews*, Supplements to
Novum Testamentum 141 (Leiden: Brill, 2011), 255. See also Michael Kibbe, *Godly Fear or Ungodly Failure? Hebrews 12 and the Sinai Theophanies*, Beihefte zur Zeitschrift für die neutestamentliche Wissenschaft 216 (Berlin: de Gruyter, 2016), 180–81. Scott D. Mackie argues the author
could be saying that presently God is Father of their spirits but not yet their renewed bodies
(*Eschatology and Exhortation in the Epistle to the Hebrews*, Wissenschaftliche Untersuchungen
zum Neuen Testament 2/223 [Tübingen: Mohr Siebeck, 2007], 95–98, 169–70).

but in it; they will not last forever but for a season (12:11), and they will bring inequitably abundant rewards in comparison with the present grief.[46]

The author's aim is for them to reinterpret what they are already going through. God is right there with them in the midst of suffering. In fact, God is allowing it for them so that they can reap the joy of a divine-likeness maturity that follows. Rather than despise God or give up, they should surrender to God's good plan.

If they hold onto this encouragement (Heb 12:5), the community members can strengthen one another so that they can all stay on a smooth path together. The author instructs them to attend to their bodies, to set right failing hands and disabled knees. He exhorts them to make straight paths for their feet so that healing can come to those who are lame. He asks them to pursue peace and sanctification (12:14), the very qualities God's discipline is said to produce (12:10–11). God's discipline does not weaken them but gives them strength— agency even—for themselves and others to pursue the end God is working in them. To accept God's discipline is to find great power as they accept their role as children of the all-knowing and good God.

The Johannine apocalypse also affirms the Father-Son relationship between God and Jesus, and subsequently includes the faithful followers of Jesus in that family, as a way of shoring up the mature endurance they will need as they face persecution.

The family relationship appears at the beginning in John's letter to the churches. Jesus the Messiah is, among other things, the firstborn from the dead and the ruler over the nations. Both πρωτότοκος (*prōtotokos*) and a possible allusion to Ps 2 in the reference to him ruling over the kings of the earth suggest a Son of God trope. This royal theme then becomes explicit when Jesus makes the churches a kingdom and priests to God his Father (Rev 1:6). Several more times, the author refers to God in this way: the Father gave authority to Jesus (2:28), the Father receives Jesus's confession of the names of the faithful ones (3:5), Jesus sits with his Father on his throne (3:21), and God is the Father of Jesus, whose name is written on the martyrs' foreheads (14:1).

Jesus then includes his followers in his royal inheritance. Jesus gives them authority over the nations to rule them with an iron rod (Rev 2:26–27). The conquerors get to sit on his throne (3:21). In the closing sections, God explic-

---

46. This assertion resonates with Paul's comparison of present struggles with the weight of glory (Rom 8:18).

itly names them as heirs and children (21:7). All of these moves, God's paternal relationship with the royal Son and his inclusion of his followers in this royal family appear at the beginning of Revelation and recur throughout until the clear pronouncement by God of filial identity at the end. This is one more means by which the author encourages them to endure: knowledge of their present identity and its future promise in the Son Jesus the Messiah. Their Father has an inheritance waiting for them if they endure. Such strength could not be expected of young children.

I will allow the Jesus tradition to have the final word on this point: Matthew's presentation of God as Father is summed up nicely in Jesus's line from the Sermon on the Mount. God, the heavenly Father, is perfect (Matt 5:48). This is the closing statement in Jesus's series of "You have heard it said" statements (5:21, 27, 33, 38, 43), a bookend to the previously stated high standard that his listeners' righteousness should exceed that of the scribes and Pharisees (5:20). As God their heavenly Father is perfect, so too should they be.

In the surrounding context, God's perfection is manifest in God's fairness to all of God's creation. The sun and the rain come upon the evil and unrighteous just as they do the good and righteous. They, too, should not just do right by their friends and beloved but should show love and friendship even to their enemies. This is a way to excel above the status quo (Matt 5:47); this is how to reach perfection.[47] God the Father's perfection is that God shows care to all without discrimination; if the listeners want to follow Jesus, God expects the same high standard of them.

The Father of Jesus Christ is present with the many sons and daughters in the divine family as they suffer but deems them worthy agents of participating in the demanding task of maturation. Children of God are not infantilized, because so much is demanded of them. Only with strength and maturity can they give their lives to God and for others.[48]

47. The other instance of perfection (τέλειος [teleios]) in Matthew also involves a high moral standard, namely, Jesus's command that the man seeking eternal life (Matt 19:16) sell his goods and give them to the poor (19:21).

48. This does not negate the reality that Jesus lifts up children as examples for being a part of the kingdom of God (Matt 18:1–7; Mark 10:13–16). Dependence and trust in God are not incommensurate with a thoughtful and difficult pledge of one's life.

A Cruel God

God the Father, then, may not be distant, or infantilizing, but the heavy demands that come in the intimate relationship with this God might be cruel. As Revelation shows, the children of God reign as martyrs with the lamb who was slain because God demands the sacrifice of one's entire life.

Some critics see the Father of Christian theology as brutal because this God was willing to sacrifice the Son by means of a shameful and painful death. Rather than demonstrating a character of love, this is seen as evidence of an unfeeling or even abusive God.[49] The praxis this theology legitimates is especially damning. For if God honors the righteous and silent suffering of his Son, will God not also honor the silent suffering of those who are abused?[50] A Father who is willing to kill his own child will do little to intervene in the suffering of people who call on his name, and will even encourage them to suffer—to sacrifice their life—for the sake of some greater cause.

The text does not support this interpretation. First, the authors of the New Testament portray Jesus going to his death not easily but willingly. Second, God the Father does not cause the suffering experienced by Jesus's followers but remains present with them during the suffering they experience and uses it for their benefit. God the Father, in relationship with Jesus and with Jesus's followers, is not cruel.

Jesus

The nighttime scene in the garden of Gethsemane captures Jesus's decision to die with the most pathos (Matt 26:36–46; Mark 14:32–42; Luke 22:39–46).

49. Brock argues that these ideas arise out of cultures that accepted the abuse of children: "Our oppressive patriarchal doctrines are a result of the abusive treatment of children in a patriarchal culture" (*Journeys by Heart*, 50). She concludes, "Such doctrines of salvation reflect by analogy I believe images of the neglect of children or even worse child abuse, making it acceptable as divine behavior—cosmic child abuse, as it were" (56).

50. So argue Joanne Carlson Brown and Rebecca Walker: "Christianity has been a primary— in many women's lives the primary—force in shaping our acceptance of abuse. The central image of Christ on the cross as the Savior of the world communicates the message that suffering is redemptive. If the best person who ever lived gave his life for others, then to be of value we should likewise sacrifice ourselves" ("For God So Loved the World?," in *Christianity, Patriarchy, and Abuse: A Feminist Critique*, ed. Joanne Carlson Brown and Carole R. Bohn [Cleveland: Pilgrim, 1989], 2).

When the moment is upon him, that which he had spoken in factual terms now seems unbearable. He prays to his Father that he might avoid the death that is fast approaching. The text leaves no indication that the Father either rejects or chides the Son for this display of emotional angst; to the contrary, the Father will vindicate the one who engaged in such despair.[51] After this struggle, ultimately, the Son agrees to go through with the plan.[52] Once he has committed to the task, the gospels never again display him faltering. God the Father does not have to force him; he willingly stays committed to the plan until its completion.

The Good Shepherd Discourse verbally captures this assuredness as it is lived out in the passion. In this extended simile, Jesus asserts three times that he will give his soul for the sheep (John 10:11). No one takes his life; Jesus himself gives it. He has authority both to give it and to take it up again (10:18). The interweaving of the action of the Father and the action of the Son is very tight here. The Father commands the Son to have authority, and the Son uses that authority to give his life for the sheep and take it up again.

Paul's presentation of the story concurs. God the Father, Paul says, did give the Son (Rom 8:32), and this includes the Son's experience of death (5:8). Paul also says that God raised the Son (8:11) and gave all things to the Son (1 Cor 15:28), but even as great an undoing as the resurrection, ascension, and session at God's right hand would not remove the charge against God if the handing over to death was an abusive act. The charge does not stick, because Paul also says that the Son gave himself (Gal 2:20; Phil 2). His death was a willing act. Moreover, as Paul describes the situation, the pervasive reality of sin was so damaging that all of reality needed a reboot, a rebirth as it were, and the divinely willed and divinely willing death dealt with the real and pervasive problem of sin. Hence, Paul's presentation of the death of the Messiah on the

---

51. For the problematic nature of Jesus's emotive display in the ancient world, see Brittany E. Wilson, *Unmanly Men: Reconfigurations of Masculinity in Luke-Acts* (Oxford: Oxford University Press, 2015), 217–22, and in the interpretive tradition, see Kevin Madigan, "Ancient and High-Medieval Interpretations of Jesus in Gethsemane: Some Reflections on Tradition and Continuity in Christian Thought," *Harvard Theological Review* 88 (1995): 157–73.

52. Robert H. Stein argues, "Herein lies faith: the ability to request openly another destiny than the one God has chosen, but ultimately submitting to God's will whatever this may involve" (*Mark*, Baker Exegetical Commentary on the New Testament [Grand Rapids: Baker, 2010], 662).

cross is not abusive, because it was willingly embraced by the Son, and it was not caused by God but demanded by the problem of sin.

Finally, in Heb 10, the author puts the words of Ps 39 LXX upon the lips of Jesus. When he is coming into the world, he pledged to God—willingly—to do God's will. This will involved the body God had prepared for the Son (Heb 10:7), an offering of that body for sanctification (10:10). In conclusion, the text of the New Testament never displays Jesus as a weak child cowering underneath the wrath of his divine Father, but rather as a man with great authority who yields that authority to the Roman leadership to allow his death to occur.

Equally important, God the Father does not leave the Son to languish in the death he chose to endure. According to Paul, it was the glory of the Father that raised Christ from the dead (Rom 6:4). This act defines the identity of God the Father (Gal 1:1). As such in the resurrection, God displays great continuity with the story of Israel. The God who raised the Son is the same God who freed Israel, or as Robert Jenson states, "God is whoever raised Jesus from the dead, having before raised Israel from Egypt."[53] Again and particularly through death, God the Father reveals the divine identity as particularly the redemptive God, Father of Jesus the Jewish Messiah.

Other Children

If the definitive relationship of God's fatherhood is not abusive, it is much less likely that God's derivative relationships would be abusive. The way in which many authors of the New Testament portray the fatherhood of God confirms this argument.

The letters of John provide an initial example. When one attends to the character of God sketched with this language in the First Epistle of John, yet again, the prominence of love rises to the fore. Because of the Father's sending of the Son, they have fellowship with him and with the Father (1 John 1:3). When Jesus advocates for their sin, he does so before their Father. This is no placation of an angry and distant deity but the intercession before the Father who loves them and has already established a relationship with them. The Father accepts Jesus's intercession for their sin (1:9–2:2).

---

53. Robert W. Jenson, *The Triune God*, vol. 1 of *Systematic Theology* (Oxford: Oxford University Press, 1997), 63.

This is also true in the Synoptics. The good care of the divine Father appears as a theme in the Sermon on the Mount. In Matt 7, Jesus speaks of God as a parent in comparison with human parents. His followers should ask and seek from God, being confident that just as they give good rather than ill when their children request it, God the Father in heaven will do the same and even more. Although they give good gifts, Jesus says they are evil, but God, who is perfect, can be trusted even more to give good gifts when asked.

At the very least, one could say that Luke's divine Father is just as gracious as any other parent. If evil humans give good gifts, God the heavenly Father can certainly be expected to give good gifts as well (Luke 11:13). God is aware as any other parent of the basic needs of the child, and God will provide these things (11:30).

Yet even in this similarity of providing basics, Luke asserts more for God. While all parents try to maintain the life of their children, only God the Father can accept the spirit of his dying Son and henceforth vindicate it (Luke 23:39). For the other children of God, God provides not only sustenance and clothing but also the kingdom (22:29). Moreover, Jesus says that the Father will give the Holy Spirit (11:13). The Holy Spirit is the great promise of the Father (24:49; Acts 1:4; 2:33). The good of the Holy Spirit is no small gift in Luke's narrative.

The most intense instantiation of God's paternal compassion might be the theme's first appearance in Luke's version of Jesus's sermon to his disciples (Luke 6:17–49). In the same context as Matthew, in which the First Evangelist urges love, even of enemies, Luke includes the admonition to lend to those who cannot repay. For this version then, in order to be "sons" of God (your Father in heaven [Matt 5:45]; the Most High [Luke 6:35]), one must love enemies but also do good and graciously lend. These rewarding actions reflect the character of these children's God, who is kind (χρηστός [chrēstos]) not just to the good but even to those who are ungrateful and those who are evil. God, as Father, responds kindly even when it is not deserved. The conclusion should be obvious by this point in the address: Jesus's listeners should be compassionate just as their Father is compassionate (6:36).

Luke dramatizes the Father's graciousness twice more in the gospel. First, in the passion narrative, Jesus prays to his Father to forgive those who are crucifying him (Luke 23:34). The manuscript history suggests that Luke did not write this, but at least it can be said that an early commentator saw that this prayer fit with the character of the compassionate God previously revealed in the gospel.[54]

Second, and most developed, is the parable of the prodigal son. In one of the most well-known of all Jesus's parables, the two sons could hardly be more undeserving, and the father hardly more compassionate. He gives all that is his to the wayward son and to the sulky son. This is a father of even humiliating compassion. Any charge that God as Father is a cruel authoritarian finds no warrant in the writings of Luke.

Possibly the hardest text to deal with in an argument that the New Testament portrays God as a *good* Father is Heb 12. Having evaluated it as a text that demands maturity, I return to it as a text that presents a disciplining God. Those listening to this sermon have circumstances in their lives that are making it hard to hold fast to God because those circumstances seem to indicate that God might not any longer be holding fast to them. With the confiscation of their property, imprisonment, and shame (10:32–34; 12:4; 13:3), they might imagine that this God and the reigning Son are not to be trusted to take care of those who confess him, the members of his own household (3:6). Hence, the author responds with a rousing exhortation to keep running the race of the faithful. Then, he offers another word of encouragement, this time from Prov 3. It takes the form of a proclamation of their identity, blessings, and responsibilities *as children of God*.

While the author puts forward several powerful *suggestions* that the audience members are children of God, he does not name this identity with clear assurance until he names this identity in association with their challenging situation. This is a text spoken (as all the texts in Hebrews are) but spoken specifically to them *as sons*. He makes the quotation even more intimate by adding a μου (*mou*), "my," after the vocative υἱέ (*huie*), "son." This emendation is not attested in versions of the Septuagint, and this not only increases the

<hr />

54. "The logion, though probably not a part of the original Gospel of Luke, bears self-evident tokens of its dominical origin, and was retained . . . in its traditional place where it had been incorporated by unknown copyists relatively early in the transmission of the Third Gospel." See Bruce M. Metzger, *Textual Commentary on the New Testament*, 2nd ed. (New York: United Bible Societies, 1994), 154.

rhetorical power of the direct address speech but also aligns this text with the one first spoken by God in Hebrews. To both the Son and the many sons, God says, "my son" (Heb 1:5; 12:5).[55]

The content of the spoken proverb, however, may seem like something less than an encouragement, in that it calls for the embrace of discipline, reproof, and even whipping (μαστιγόω [mastigoō]).[56] These are hard words not to be taken lightly, and much of the literature shows how often interpreters wrestle with them. In the history of interpretation, texts like these have been used in abusive and diabolical ways.[57] In recognition of this reality, a hermeneutics of suspicion could be a healthy place to begin,[58] as long as it is paired with a hermeneutics of grace. Understanding the original setting of the comments, as well as their power for healing as well as damage, allows the possibility of the texts to expand beyond oppression.[59] In the original context, the author offers these comments to those who are already suffering, which radically shifts the meaning of the passage. The author is not asking them to seek out

55. For a fuller discussion of this point, see Amy L. B. Peeler, *You Are My Son: The Family of God in the Epistle to the Hebrews*, The Library of New Testament Studies 486 (London: T&T Clark, 2014), 149–51. For the gendered nature and implications of the language of sonship in Hebrews, see Peeler, "'Leading Many Sons to Glory': Historical Implications of Exclusive Language in the Epistle to the Hebrews," *Religions* 12 (2021), https://doi.org/10.3390/rel12100844.

56. This reading comes from the Greek translation. The Masoretic Text, on the other hand, reads, "for the Lord reproves the one he loves, as a father the son in whom he delights" (Prov 3:12 NRSV).

57. Annie Imbens and Ineke Jonker, *Christianity and Incest* (London: Burns & Oates, 1992), present horrible examples of this reality.

58. Beavis and Kim-Cragg, *Hebrews*, 163.

59. Ulrike Wagener notes, "In church history, these kinds of statements have poisoned the image of God by portraying God in the image of a father whose love is inseparably intertwined with violence. Such theological imagery has to be rejected today and thoroughly scrutinized in view of its effects throughout history of support of domestic violence of fathers and husbands" ("Hebrews: Strangers in the World," in *Feminist Biblical Interpretation: A Compendium of Critical Commentary on the Books of the Bible and Related Literature*, ed. Luise Schottroff and Marie-Theres Wacker, trans. Lisa E. Dahill et al. [Grand Rapids: Eerdmans, 2012], 867). She continues, "On the other hand, the theological attempt to bring the experience of injustice and suffering into a connection with God can, when done by those who suffer under them, be an important step against resignation and thus function as an act of survival. . . . such theological assertions highly risk being easily perverted; they reflect unmistakably the contextuality and confessional nature of every form of God language" (868).

suffering for God's sake but to process the suffering they are already enduring.[60] One can vigorously reject abuse without rejecting this passage and, with it, this author's portrayal of God as Father. The author is not extolling arbitrary paternal discipline for the sake of violence. Quite the contrary, his aim is to show that their difficulties are not signs of God's absence but of God's intimate presence, not causing but being present in the midst of challenge for the sake of their maturity.

After the citation, the author asserts that they are in need of endurance (which he already stated in Heb 10:36). The author relates their endurance to discipline in that they are to endure their situation *interpreted* as God's discipline.[61] If the author has in mind some direct supernatural chastisement for sins, he does not describe it.[62] Much more likely is that he views their present sufferings as allowed by God and utilized by God for their good. This does not get God off the hook because, as an interpretive lens for understanding the persecution they are facing, he does state that God himself is offering (προσφέρεται [*prospheretai*], a middle form) this discipline to them (12:7). It may not be direct, but even the allowance of difficulty raises the issue of potential maltreatment. Why would God allow the persecution? Why would God want them, his children, to endure it? The author's answer is that God is acting in relationship with them as a wise and good Father.

---

60. In his study of suffering throughout the letter, this is precisely what Bryan R. Dyer argues for Hebrews as a whole and this passage in particular: "In this way, the author of Hebrews presents the challenging notion that suffering and being a member of the Christian community are linked. . . . Outside of a context of situation that includes present suffering, this is a difficult, almost cruel, belief. . . . Here is where our thesis regarding the epistle's context of situation becomes so important. It must be remembered that the author was writing to a community that was already experiencing suffering and affliction. This author is not challenging them to seek suffering but to interpret their current suffering through a theological lens" (*Suffering in the Face of Death: The Epistle to the Hebrews and Its Context of Situation*, The Library of New Testament Studies 568 [London: T&T Clark, 2017], 177).

61. So also Dyer: "Given the context of hardships described in the audience's background (10:23–34) and in the immediate context of 12:1–4, what the audience is to 'endure' is certainly some type of hardship, trial, or difficulty" (*Suffering*, 103n101).

62. N. Clayton Croy has, in my opinion, made a convincing case for a nonpunitive view of discipline in Hebrews (*Endurance in Suffering: Hebrews 12:1–13 in Its Rhetorical, Religious, and Philosophical Context*, Society for New Testament Studies Monograph Series 98 [Cambridge: Cambridge University Press, 2005], 192–213).

Discipline need not be the same as abuse. In fact, at times, lack of discipline is evidence of abuse via neglect. For the author of Hebrews, God is a good Father who does what is necessary, even if it is not pleasant, for the children in the divine family. God allows suffering so that they will mature. They approach the God who is judge (Heb 12:23), who can see the innermost parts of themselves and purify them. God is a consuming fire (12:29), burning off that which will entangle.

As discussed, this particular wisdom of endurance, the process of getting from where they are to where they should be, begins by knowing God's character and trusting it. By drawing from a section of Proverbs that reflects upon the beauty, desirability, and blessings of Sophia, God's Wisdom, the author of Hebrews urges the audience to wisely accept the particular type of relationship God has established with them, namely, kinship.[63] To be God's son does mean to look forward to an inheritance of glorious salvation (Heb 1:14; 2:3), but this standing receives greatest attention when the author reminds them of God's presence with them in suffering. God's fatherhood of them is most tangible for this author in God's wise support of them in the midst of their darkest moments and God's transformation of their darkest moments for their eternal good. The most prominent evocation of God's paternal relationship with the readers emphasizes not God's majesty or blessings but God's presence in and sovereignty over hardship. Therefore, instead of "reject[ing] the interpretation of suffering as divine discipline," an acceptance that God's divine discipline is to be a transformative Father with the community in the midst of their suffering issues forth precisely in the call to mend the lame and restore them, a "call to open for all the oppressed a new and living way."[64] God the Father did not abuse the Son or the many children in relationship with him but grants divine presence and empowerment with them in the midst of difficulty so that they might mature.

---

63. It must be acknowledged that the author makes no appeals to the personification of Sophia, a trope that many feminist writers find encouraging. Nevertheless, the commentators of the recent Hebrews commentary in the Wisdom Commentary series seek to call attention to the "audible, if muted, voice of Sophia in Hebrews" (Beavis and Kim-Cragg, *Hebrews*, xliii).

64. Mary Rose D'Angelo, "Hebrews," in *Feminist Bible Commentary*, ed. Carol A. Newsom, Sharon H. Ringe, and Jacqueline E. Lapsley, rev. and upd. 20th anniversary ed. (Louisville: Westminster John Knox, 2012), 612.

Conclusion: God the Good Father

Fathers can be anything—distant, harsh autocrats who stunt the growth of their children or intimate and wise disciplinarians who empower the growth of their children. A first step to deal with the problems of divine Father language in the text is to assess what the authors of the New Testament actually say. To use the paternal language of Scripture without close attention to the texts is a major contributor to the oppressive application of the language. Part of the way to work against negative connotations is to pay careful attention to the text and what it says—and what it does not—about the God named as Father. Without disagreement, the texts say that this God is a good Father.[65]

65. "In speaking the Christian God, anyone who claims that masculine metaphors such as these are 'oppressive to women' is interpreting them out of context . . . the theological cure for such abstract thinking is re-immersion in the concrete text of Scripture." See Garrett Green, "The Gender of God and the Theology of Metaphor," in *Speaking the Christian God: The Holy Trinity and the Challenge of Feminism*, ed. Alvin F. Kimel Jr. (Grand Rapids: Eerdmans, 1992), 60.

Bibliography

Achtemeier, Elizabeth. "Exchanging God for 'No Gods': A Discussion of Female Language for God." Pages 1–16 in *Speaking the Christian God: The Holy Trinity and the Challenge of Feminism*. Edited by Alvin F. Kimel Jr. Grand Rapids: Eerdmans, 1992.

Aghiorgoussis, Maximos. *Women Priests?* Brookline, MA: Holy Cross Orthodox, 1976.

Akala, Adesola. "Sonship, Sending, and Subordination in the Gospel of John." Pages 23–38 in *Trinity without Hierarchy: Reclaiming Nicene Orthodoxy in Evangelical Theology*. Edited by Michael F. Bird and Scott Harrower. Grand Rapids: Kregel Academic, 2019.

Anderson, Ray. "The Incarnation of God in Feminist Christology: A Theological Critique." Pages 288–312 in *Speaking the Christian God: The Holy Trinity and the Challenge of Feminism*. Edited by Alvin F. Kimel Jr. Grand Rapids: Eerdmans, 1992.

Annan, Kent. "Reading Luke's Christmas Story with Those in Haiti." Pages 8–10 in *Global Perspectives in the New Testament*. Edited by Mark Roncace and Joseph Weaver. Boston: Pearson, 2014.

The Ante-Nicene Fathers. Edited by Alexander Roberts and James Donaldson. 1885–1887. 10 vols. Repr., Peabody, MA: Hendrickson, 1994.

Arcadi, James. *An Incarnational Model of the Eucharist*. Cambridge: Cambridge University Press, 2018.

Argyle, A. W. *The Gospel according to Matthew*. Cambridge: Cambridge University Press, 1963.

Aristotle. Translated by H. P. Cooke et al. 23 volumes. Loeb Classical Library. Cambridge: Harvard University Press, 1938–1995.

Attridge, Harold W. *The Epistle to the Hebrews*. Hermeneia 58. Minneapolis: Fortress, 1989.

Augustine. *Sermons 51–94 on the New Testament*. The Works of Saint Augustine: A Translation for the 21st Century III/3. Translation and notes by Edmund Hill, OP. Brooklyn, NY: New City Press, 1991.

Aytoun, R. A. "The Ten Lucan Hymns of the Nativity in Their Original Language." *Journal of Theological Studies* 18 (1917): 247–88.

Balthasar, Hans Urs von. *Dramatis Personae: Persons in Christ*. Vol. 3 of *Theo-Drama: Theological Dramatic Theory*. Translated by Graham Harrison. San Francisco: Ignatius, 1992.

Balthasar, Hans Urs von, and Joseph Cardinal Ratzinger. *Mary: The Church at the Source*. Translated by Adrian Walker. San Francisco: Ignatius, 1997.

Barr, Beth Allison. *The Making of Biblical Womanhood: How the Subjugation of Women Became Gospel Truth*. Grand Rapids: Brazos, 2021.

Barresi, Michael J. F., and Scott F. Gilbert. *Developmental Biology*. 12th ed. Oxford: Oxford University Press, 2019.

Bartchy, S. Scott. "Slaves and Slavery in the Roman World." Pages 169–78 in *The World of the New Testament*. Edited by Joel B. Green and Lee Martin McDonald. Grand Rapids: Baker, 2013.

Barth, Karl. *Church Dogmatics*, III/1. Edited by G. W. Bromiley and T. F. Torrance. Translated by J. W. Edwards, O. Bussey, and H. Knight. London: T&T Clark, 2004.

———. *Church Dogmatics*, III/2. Edited by G. W. Bromiley and T. F. Torrance. Translated by H. Knight, G. W. Bromiley, J. K. S. Reid, and R. H. Fuller. London: T&T Clark, 2001.

Bates, Matthew W. *The Birth of the Trinity: Jesus, God, and Spirit in New Testament and Early Christian Interpretations of the Old Testament*. Oxford: Oxford University Press, 2015.

———. "A Christology of Incarnation and Enthronement." *Catholic Biblical Quarterly* 77 (2015): 107–27.

Bauckham, Richard. *Gospel Women: Studies of the Named Women in the Gospels*. Grand Rapids: Eerdmans, 2002.

———. *Jesus and the Eyewitnesses: The Gospels as Eyewitness Testimony*. 2nd ed. Grand Rapids: Eerdmans, 2017.

———. *Jesus and the God of Israel: God Crucified and Other Studies on the New Testament's Christology of Divine Identity*. Grand Rapids: Eerdmans, 2008.

Baudzej, Julia. "Re-telling the Story of Jesus: The Concept of Embodiment and Recent Feminist Reflections on the Maleness of Christ." *Feminist Theology* 17 (2008): 72–91.

Beasley-Murray, George R. *John*. 2nd ed. Word Biblical Commentary 36. Nashville: Thomas Nelson, 1999.

Beattie, Tina. *God's Mother, Eve's Advocate: A Marian Narrative of Women's Salvation.* London: Continuum, 2002.

———. "Mary in Patristic Thought." Pages 75–106 in *Mary: The Complete Resource.* Edited by Sarah Jane Boss. London: Continuum, 2009.

———. *New Catholic Feminism: Theology and Theory.* London: Routledge, 2006.

———. "Sexuality and the Resurrection of the Body: Reflections in the Hall of Mirrors." Pages 135–49 in *Resurrection Reconsidered.* Edited by Gavin D'Costa. Oxford: Oneworld, 1996.

Beavis, Mary Ann, and HyeRan Kim-Cragg. *Hebrews.* Wisdom Commentary. Collegeville, MN: Liturgical Press, 2015.

Behr-Sigel, Elisabeth. *The Ministry of Women in the Church.* Translated by Steven Bigham. Crestwood, NY: St. Vladimir's Seminary Press, 1991.

Belonick, Deborah. "The Spirit of the Female Priesthood: Women and the Priesthood." Pages 135–68 in *Women and the Priesthood.* Edited by Thomas Hopko. Crestwood, NY: St. Vladimir's Seminary Press, 1983.

Bernard of Clairvaux. *Homilies in Praise of the Virgin Mary.* Translated by Mary-Bernard Saïd. Cistercian Fathers Series 18a. Kalamazoo, MI: Cistercian, 1993.

Bettini, Maurizio. *Women and Weasels: Mythologies of Birth in Ancient Greece and Rome.* Translated by Emlyn Eisenach. Chicago: University of Chicago Press, 2013.

Bird, Michael F. *Romans.* The Story of God Bible Commentary. Grand Rapids: Zondervan, 2016.

"Blessed Be the Name of the Lord: Why 'Creator, Redeemer, Sanctifier' is Somewhere between Heresy and Idolatry." *Christianity Today* 52 (2008): 21.

Block, Darrell L. *Luke.* IVP New Testament Commentary Series 3. Downers Grove, IL: InterVarsity Press, 1994.

Bloesch, Donald G. *The Battle for the Trinity: The Debate over Inclusive God-Language.* Ann Arbor: Servant, 1985.

Boer, Martinus C. de. *Galatians: A Commentary.* New Testament Library. Louisville: Westminster John Knox, 2011.

Bons-Storm, Riet. "Back to Basics: 'The Almighty Father' Revisited." *HTS Telogiese Studies/Theological Studies* 67 (2011): Art. #902. DOI: 10.4102/hts.v67i1.902.

Boss, Sarah Jane. *Empress and Handmaid: Nature and Gender in the Cult of the Virgin Mary.* London: Cassell, 2000.

———, ed. *Mary: The Complete Resource.* Oxford: Oxford University Press, 2007.

———. "The Title Theotokos." Pages 50–55 in *Mary: The Complete Resource.* Edited by Sarah Jane Boss. London: Continuum, 2009.

Bourgeault, Cynthia. *The Holy Trinity and the Law of Three: Recovering the Radical Truth at the Heart of Christianity.* Boston: Shambhala, 2013.

Bovon, François. *Luke 1: A Commentary on the Gospel of Luke 1:1–9:50.* Minneapolis: Fortress, 2002.

Bowles, Nellie. "Jordan Peterson, Custodian of the Patriarchy." *New York Times,* May 18, 2018. https://www.nytimes.com/2018/05/18/style/jordan-peterson -12-rules-for-life.html.

Brock, Rita Nakashima. *Journeys by Heart: A Christology of Erotic Power.* Eugene, OR: Wipf & Stock, 2008.

Brown, Joanne Carlson, and Rebecca Walker. "For God So Loved the World?" Pages 1–30 in *Christianity, Patriarchy, and Abuse: A Feminist Critique.* Edited by Joanne Carlson Brown and Carol R. Bohn. Cleveland: Pilgrim, 1989.

Brown, Raymond E. *The Birth of the Messiah: A Commentary on the Infancy Narratives in the Gospels of Matthew and Luke.* New updated ed. New York: Doubleday, 1993.

———. *The Gospel according to John I–XII.* Anchor Bible 29. Garden City, NY: Doubleday, 1966.

———. *The Gospel according to John XIII–XXI.* Anchor Bible 29A. Garden City, NY: Doubleday, 1970.

Brown, Raymond E., Karl P. Donfried, Joseph A. Fitzmyer, and John Reumann, eds. *Mary in the New Testament.* New York: Paulist, 1978.

Bruce, Michael, and G. E. Duffield, eds. *Why Not? Priesthood and the Ministry of Women.* Abingdon: Marcham Manor, 1972.

Brugarolas, Miguel, ed. *Gregory of Nyssa: Contra Eunomium I; An English Translation with Supporting Studies.* Leiden: Brill, 2018.

Bruner, Frederick Dale. *The Christbook: Matthew 1–12.* Vol. 1 of *Matthew: A Commentary.* Rev. and exp. ed. Grand Rapids: Eerdmans, 2007.

Budapest, Zsuzsanna E. "Self-Blessing Ritual." Pages 269–72 in *Womanspirit Rising: A Feminist Reader in Religion.* Edited by Carol P. Christ and Judith Plaskow. San Francisco: Harper & Row, 1979.

Bulgakov, Sergius. *The Burning Bush: On the Orthodox Veneration of the Mother of God.* Translated, edited, and with an introduction by Thomas Allan Smith. Grand Rapids: Eerdmans, 2009.

———. *Icons and the Name of God*. Translated by Boris Jakim. Grand Rapids: Eerdmans, 2012.

Calvin, John. *A Harmony of the Gospels: Matthew, Mark, and Luke*. Edited by David W. Torrance and Thomas F. Torrance. Translated by T. H. L. Parker. 3 vols. Grand Rapids: Eerdmans, 1972.

Carson, D. A. "'Silent in the Churches': On the Role of Women in 1 Cor 14:33b–36." Pages 179–98 in *Recovering Biblical Manhood and Womanhood: A Response to Evangelical Feminism*. Rev. ed. Wheaton, IL: Crossway, 2021.

Catchpole, D. J. *Jesus People: The Historical Jesus and the Beginnings of Community*. London: Darton, Longman & Todd, 2006.

Central Board of Finance of the Church of England. *The Ordination of Women to the Priesthood: A Second Report by the House of Bishops of the General Synod of the Church of England*. London: General Synod of the Church of England, 1988.

Charlesworth, James H., ed. *Old Testament Pseudepigrapha*. 2 vols. New York: Doubleday, 1983–1985.

Chen, Diane. *God as Father in Luke-Acts*. Studies in Biblical Literature 92. New York: Lang, 2005.

Choi, Hoon. "Encouraging Male Participation in the Life of the Church." *New Theology Review* 31 (2018): 1–10.

Claassens, Juliana M. *Mourner, Mother, Midwife: Reclaiming God's Delivering Presence in the Old Testament*. Louisville: Westminster John Knox, 2012.

Clark, Elizabeth A. *Women in the Early Church*. Message of the Fathers of the Church 13. Collegeville, MN: Liturgical, 1983.

Clark, John C., and Marcus Peter Johnson. *The Incarnation of God: The Mystery of the Gospel as the Foundation of Evangelical Theology*. Wheaton, IL: Crossway, 2015.

Clines, David J. A. "Alleged Female Language about the Deity in the Hebrew Bible." *Journal of Biblical Literature* 140 (2021): 229–49.

———. "The Most High Male: Divine Masculinity in the Bible." Pages 61–82 in *Hebrew Masculinities Anew*. Edited by Ovidiu Creanga. Hebrew Bible Monographs 79. Sheffield: Sheffield Phoenix, 2019.

Coakley, Sarah. *God, Sexuality, and the Self: An Essay 'On the Trinity.'* Cambridge: Cambridge University Press, 2013.

———. *Powers and Submissions: Spirituality, Philosophy and Gender*. Malden, MA: Wiley-Blackwell, 2002.

Cobb, L. Stephanie. *Dying to Be Men: Gender and Language in Early Christian Martyr Texts*. New York: Columbia University Press, 2008.

Cohen, Shaye J. D. "Menstruants and the Sacred in Judaism and Christianity." Pages

273–300 in *Women's History and Ancient History*. Edited by Sarah B. Pomeroy. Chapel Hill: University of North Carolina Press, 1991.

———. *Why Aren't Jewish Women Circumcised? Gender and Covenant in Judaism.* Berkeley: University of California Press, 2005.

Cohick, Lynn. *Women in the World of the Earliest Christians: Illuminating Ancient Ways of Life.* Grand Rapids: Baker, 2009.

Coleridge, Mark. *The Birth of the Lukan Narrative: Narrative as Christology in Luke 1–2.* Sheffield: JSOT Press, 1993.

Connolly, R. Hugh, ed. and trans. *Didascalia Apostolorum: The Syriac Version; Translated and Accompanied by the Verona Latin Fragments.* Ancient Texts and Translations. Eugene, OR: Wipf & Stock, 2010.

Conway, Colleen M. "'Behold the Man!' Masculine Christology and the Fourth Gospel." Pages 163–80 in *New Testament Masculinities.* Edited by Stephen D. Moore and Janice Capel Anderson. Semeia Studies 45. Leiden: Brill, 2004.

———. "Masculinity Studies." Pages 77–94 in *The Oxford Handbook of New Testament, Gender, and Sexuality.* Edited by Benjamin H. Dunning. Oxford: Oxford University Press, 2019.

Cornwall, Susannah. "Sex Otherwise: Intersex, Christology, and the Maleness of Jesus." *Journal of Feminist Studies in Religion* 30 (2014): 23–39.

Cortez, Marc. *ReSourcing Theological Anthropology: A Constructive Account of Humanity in Light of Christ.* Grand Rapids: Zondervan, 2017.

Cranfield, C. E. B. *A Critical and Exegetical Commentary on Romans.* Vol. 1. International Critical Commentary. New York: T&T Clark, 1975.

Crisp, Oliver. *Analyzing Doctrine: Toward a Systematic Theology.* Waco, TX: Baylor University Press, 2019.

———. *God Incarnate: Explorations in Christology.* London: T&T Clark, 2009.

Crossan, John Dominic. "Virgin Mother or Bastard Child?" Pages 37–55 in *A Feminist Companion to Mariology.* Edited by Amy-Jill Levine and Maria Mayo Robbins. New York: T&T Clark, 2005.

Croy, N. Clayton. *Endurance in Suffering: Hebrews 12:1–13 in Its Rhetorical, Religious, and Philosophical Context.* Society for New Testament Studies Monograph Series 98. Cambridge: Cambridge University Press, 2005.

Croy, N. Clayton, and Alice E. Connor. "Mantic Mary? The Virgin Mother as Prophet in Luke 1.26–56 and the Early Church." *Journal for the Study of the New Testament* 34 (2012): 254–76.

Cruz, Joan Carroll. *Eucharistic Miracles: And Eucharistic Phenomena in the Lives of the Saints*. Charlotte, NC: TAN Books, 2012.

Cunneen, Sally. *In Search of Mary: The Woman and the Symbol*. New York: Ballantine Books, 1996.

Cunningham, Mary B. *Gateway of Life: Orthodox Thinking on the Mother of God*. Foundations Series 7. Yonkers, NY: St. Vladimir's Seminary Press, 2015.

Cyril of Alexandria. *Selected Letters*. Edited and translated by Lionel R. Wickham. Oxford: Clarendon, 1983.

Dalarun, Jacques. *Francis of Assisi and the Feminine*. Saint Bonaventure, NY: Franciscan Institute, 2006.

Daly, Mary. *Gyn/Ecology: The Metaethics of Radical Feminism*. Boston: Beacon, 1990.

———. *Pure Lust: Elemental Feminist Philosophy*. Minneapolis: Women's Press, 1998.

D'Angelo, Mary Rose. "Hebrews." Pages 608–12 in *Feminist Bible Commentary*. Edited by Carol A. Newsom, Sharon H. Ringe, and Jacqueline E. Lapsley. Rev. and upd. 20th anniversary ed. Louisville: Westminster John Knox, 2012.

Danker, Frederick W., Walter Bauer, William F. Arndt, and F. Wilbur Gingrich. *Greek-English Lexicon of the New Testament and Other Early Christian Literature*. 3rd ed. Chicago: University of Chicago Press, 2000.

Dean-Jones, Lesley. *Women's Bodies in Classical Greek Science*. Oxford: Clarendon, 1994.

DeFranza, Megan. *Sex Difference in Christian Theology: Male, Female, and Intersex in the Image of God*. Grand Rapids: Eerdmans, 2015.

DeSilva, David A. "Exchanging Favor for Wrath: Apostasy in Hebrews and Patron-Client Relationships." *Journal of Biblical Literature* 115 (1996): 91–116.

Dinkler, Michal Beth. *Silent Statements: Narrative Representations of Speech and Silence in the Gospel of Luke*. Berlin: de Gruyter, 2013.

DiNoia, J. A. "Knowing and Naming the Triune God: The Grammar of Trinitarian Confession." Pages 162–87 in *Speaking the Christian God*. Edited by Alvin F. Kimel Jr. Grand Rapids: Eerdmans, 1992.

Diogenes Laertius, *Lives of Eminent Philosophers*. Translated by R. D. Hicks. 2 vols. Loeb Classical Library. Cambridge: Harvard University Press, 1972.

Dionysius of Halicarnassus. *Roman Antiquities*. Translated by Earnest Cary. 7 vols. Loeb Classical Library. Cambridge: Harvard University Press, 1937.

Dods, Marcus. *The Gospel of St. John*. 2 vols. New York: Armstrong and Son, 1903.

Donfried, Karl P. *The Romans Debate*. Rev. and exp. ed. Peabody, MA: Hendrickson, 1991.

Douglas, Mary. *Purity and Danger: An Analysis of Concepts of Pollution and Taboo.* London: Routledge, 2005.

Duff, Nancy J. "Mary, the Servant of the Lord: Christian Vocation at the Manger and the Cross." Pages 59–70 in *Blessed One: Protestant Perspectives on Mary.* Edited by Beverly Roberts Gaventa and Cynthia L. Rigby. Louisville: Westminster John Knox, 2002.

Dunn, James D. G. *Christology in the Making: A New Testament Inquiry into the Origins of the Doctrine of the Incarnation.* 2nd ed. Grand Rapids: Eerdmans, 1996.

———. *The Epistle to the Galatians.* Black's New Testament Commentaries. Grand Rapids: Baker, 1993.

———. *Romans 1–8.* Word Biblical Commentary 38A. Grand Rapids: Zondervan, 2015.

Dunning, Benjamin H. "The New Testament and Early Christian Literature." Pages 1–15 in *The Oxford Handbook of New Testament, Gender, and Sexuality.* Edited by Benjamin H. Dunning. Oxford: Oxford University Press, 2019.

Dyer, Bryan R. *Suffering in the Face of Death: The Epistle to the Hebrews and Its Context of Situation.* The Library of New Testament Studies 568. London: T&T Clark, 2017.

Edwards, James R. *The Gospel according to Luke.* The Pillar New Testament Commentary. Grand Rapids: Eerdmans, 2015.

Ehrman, Bart D., ed. *After the New Testament: A Reader in Early Christianity.* New York: Oxford University Press, 1998.

Eilberg-Schwartz, Howard. "The Father, the Phallus, and the Seminal World: Dilemmas of Patrilineality in Ancient Judaism." Pages 27–42 in *Gender, Kinship, Power: A Comparative and Interdisciplinary History.* Edited by Mary Jo Maynes, Ann Waltner, Birgitte Soland, and Ulrike Strasser. New York: Routledge, 1996.

———. *God's Phallus: And Other Problems for Men and Monotheism.* Boston: Beacon, 1994.

Eisenbaum, Pamela M. "A Remedy for Having Been Born of Woman: Jesus, Gentiles, and Genealogy in Romans." *Journal of Biblical Literature* 123 (2004): 671–702.

Ephrem the Syrian. *Hymns.* Translated by Kathleen E. McVey. The Classics of Western Spirituality. New York: Paulist, 1989.

Erbele-Küster, Dorothea. *Body, Gender and Purity in Leviticus 12 and 15.* London: Bloomsbury T&T Clark, 2017.

Evans, C. F. *Saint Luke.* London: SCM, 1990.

Evans, Craig A., and Stanley E. Porter, eds. *Dictionary of New Testament Background.* Downer's Grove, IL: InterVarsity Press, 2005.

Fantham, Elaine. "Purification in Ancient Rome." Pages 59–66 in *Rome, Pollution and Propriety: Dirt, Disease and Hygiene in the Eternal City from Antiquity.* Edited by Mark Bradley. Cambridge: Cambridge University Press, 2012.

Farris, Stephen. *The Hymns of Luke's Infancy Narratives: Their Origin, Meaning and Significance.* London: Bloomsbury, 2015.

Filson, F. V. *The Gospel according to St. Matthew.* London: Harper & Row, 1960.

Fitzmyer, Joseph A. *The Gospel according to Luke I–IX.* Anchor Bible 28. New Haven: Yale University Press, 2009.

———. *Romans: A New Translation with Introduction and Commentary.* Anchor Bible 33. New Haven: Yale University Press, 2007.

———. *To Advance the Gospel: New Testament Studies.* Grand Rapids: Eerdmans, 1998.

Fonrobert, Charlotte Elisheve. *Menstrual Purity: Rabbinic and Christian Reconstructions of Biblical Gender.* Stanford: Stanford University Press, 2009.

Forde, Gerhard O. "Naming the One Who Is Above Us." Pages 110–19 *Speaking the Christian God: The Holy Trinity and the Challenge of Feminism.* Edited by Alvin F. Kimel Jr. Grand Rapids: Eerdmans, 1992.

Foster, Ruth Ann. "Mary's Hymn of Praise in Luke 1:46–55: Reflections on Liturgy and Spiritual Formation." *Review and Expositor* 100 (2003): 451–63.

Frame, John M. "Male and Female in the Image of God." Pages 225–32 in *Recovering Biblical Manhood and Womanhood: A Response to Evangelical Feminism.* Edited by Wayne Grudem and John Piper. Wheaton, IL: Crossway, 2006.

Fredriksen, Paula. "Did Jesus Oppose the Purity Laws?" *Bible Review* 11 (1995): 18–25.

Freed, Edwin. D. *The Stories of Jesus' Birth: A Critical Introduction.* London: T&T Clark, 2004.

Friesen, Stephen J. "Injustice or God's Will? Early Christian Explanations of Poverty." Pages 17–36 in *Wealth and Poverty in Early Church and Society.* Edited by Susan R. Holman. Grand Rapids: Baker, 2008.

Galen. Translated by A. J. Brock et al. 8 vols. Loeb Classical Library. Cambridge: Harvard University Press, 1916–2020.

Garnsey, Peter. *Famine and Food Supply in the Greco-Roman World: Responses to Risk and Crises.* Cambridge: Cambridge University Press, 1985.

Gaventa, Beverly Roberts. *Mary: Glimpses of the Mother of Jesus.* Personalities of the New Testament. Minneapolis: Fortress, 1999.

———. *Our Mother Saint Paul.* Louisville: Westminster John Knox, 2007.

Genig, Joshua D. *Viva Vox: Rediscovering the Sacramentality of the Word through the Annunciation.* Emerging Scholars. Minneapolis: Fortress, 2015.

Glancy, Jennifer. *Corporeal Knowledge: Early Christian Bodies*. New York: Oxford University Press, 2010.

———. *Slavery in Early Christianity*. Minneapolis: Fortress, 2006.

Gleason, Maud W. *Making Men: Sophists and Self-Presentation in Ancient Rome*. Princeton: Princeton University Press, 1995.

Goldstein, Elizabeth W. *Impurity and Gender in the Hebrew Bible*. Lanham, MD: Lexington Books, 2017.

Goldstein, Elyse. *The Women's Torah Commentary: New Insights from Women Rabbis on the 54 Weekly Torah Portions*. Woodstock, VT: Jewish Lights, 2000.

Green, Elizabeth. "More Musings on Maleness: The Maleness of Jesus Revisited." *Feminist Theology* 20 (1999): 9–27.

Green, Garrett. "The Gender of God and the Theology of Metaphor." Pages 44–64 in *Speaking the Christian God: The Holy Trinity and the Challenge of Feminism*. Edited by Alvin F. Kimel Jr. Grand Rapids: Eerdmans, 1992.

Green, Joel B. *The Gospel of Luke*. New International Commentary on the New Testament. Grand Rapids: Eerdmans, 1997.

———. "The Social Status of Mary in Luke 1:5–2:52: A Plea for Methodological Integration." *Biblica* 73 (1992): 457–72.

Green-McCreight, Kathryn. *Feminist Reconstructions of Christian Doctrine: Narrative Analysis and Appraisal*. New York: Oxford University Press, 2000.

Gregory the Great. *The Letters of Gregory the Great*. Translated by John R. C. Martyn. 2 vols. Toronto: Pontifical Institute of Medieval Studies, 2004.

Gregory of Nyssa. *Homilies on the Song of Songs*. Translated with introduction and notes by Richard A. Norris Jr. Atlanta: Society of Biblical Literature, 2012.

Grenz, Stanley J. "Is God Sexual?" Pages 190–212 in *This Is My Name Forever: The Trinity and Gender Language for God*. Edited by Alvin F. Kimel Jr. Downers Grove, IL: InterVarsity Press, 2001.

———. *Theology for the Community of God*. Grand Rapids: Eerdmans, 2000.

Grossman, Susan. "Women and the Jerusalem Temple." Pages 15–38 in *Daughters of the King: Women and the Synagogue; A Survey of History, Halakhah, and Contemporary Realities*. Edited by Susan Grossman and Rivka Haut. Philadelphia: Jewish Publication Society, 1993.

Gunderson, Erik. *Staging Masculinity: The Rhetoric of Performance in the Roman World*. Ann Arbor: University of Michigan Press, 2000.

Hagner, Donald A. *Matthew 1–13*. Word Biblical Commentary 33a. Dallas: Word, 1993.

Hamori, Esther J. "Divine Embodiment in the Hebrew Bible and Some Implications for Jewish and Christian Incarnational Theologies." Pages 161–83 in *Bodies, Embodiment, and Theology of the Hebrew Bible*. Edited by S. Tamar Kamionkowski and Wonil Kim. New York: T&T Clark, 2010.

———. *"When Gods Were Men": The Embodied God in Biblical and Near Eastern Literature*. Berlin: de Gruyter, 2008.

Hampson, Daphne. *After Christianity*. London: SCM, 1996.

Harrill, James Albert. *Slaves in the New Testament: Literary, Social, and Moral Dimensions*. Minneapolis: Fortress, 2006.

Harrison, Nonna Verna. "The Breast of the Father." Pages 327–32 in *Feminism and Theology*. Edited by J. M. Soskice and D. Lipton. Oxford: Oxford University Press, 2003.

———. "Gender, Generation, and Virginity." *Journal of Theological Studies* 47 (1996): 38–68.

———. "The Trinity and Feminism." Pages 519–30 in *The Oxford Handbook of the Trinity*. Edited by Gilles Emery and Matthew Levering. Oxford: Oxford University Press, 2011.

Hays, Christopher M. "Hating Wealth and Wives: An Examination of Discipleship Ethics in the Third Gospel." *Tyndale Bulletin* 60 (2009): 47–68.

Hays, Richard B. *Reading Backwards: Figural Christology and the Fourfold Gospel Witness*. Waco, TX: Baylor University Press, 2014.

Heim, Erin M. *Adoption in Galatians and Romans: Contemporary Metaphor Theories and Pauline* Huiothesia *Metaphors*. Leiden: Brill, 2017.

Hensell, Eugene. "The Annunciation to St. Joseph: Reflections on Matthew 1:18–25." *Priest* 74 (2018): 41.

Hereth, Blake. "Mary, Did You Consent?" *Religious Studies* (2021): 1–24.

Hippocrates. *Generation. Nature of the Child. Diseases 4. Nature of Women. Barrenness*. Edited and translated by Paul Potter. Loeb Classical Library 520. Cambridge: Harvard University Press, 2012.

Holmes, Laura Sweat, and George Lyons. *John 1–12: A Commentary in the Wesleyan Tradition*. Kansas City: Beacon Hill, 2020.

Homer. *The Iliad*. Translated by A. T. Murray. Revised by William F. Wyatt. 2 vols. Loeb Classical Library 171. Cambridge: Harvard University Press, 1999.

———. *The Odyssey*. Translated by A. T. Murray. Revised by George E. Dimock. 2 vols. Loeb Classical Library 104. Cambridge: Harvard University Press, 1995.

Hopkins, M. K. "The Age of Roman Girls at Marriage." *Population Studies* 18 (1965): 309–27.

Hopko, Thomas. "On the Male Character of Christian Priesthood." Pages 97–134 in *Women and the Priesthood*. Edited by Thomas Hopko. Crestwood, NY: St. Vladimir's Seminary Press, 1983.

———, ed. *Women and the Priesthood*. Crestwood, NY: St. Vladimir's Seminary Press, 1983.

———. "Women and the Priesthood: Reflections on the Debate." Pages 169–90 in *Women and the Priesthood*. Edited by Thomas Hopko. Crestwood, NY: St. Vladimir's Seminary Press, 1983.

Hornblower, Simon, and Antony Spawforth, eds. *The Oxford Classical Dictionary*. 4th ed. Oxford: Oxford University Press, 2012.

Humphrey, Edith M. *Further Up and Further In: Orthodox Conversations with C. S. Lewis on Scripture and Theology*. Crestwood, NY: St. Vladimir's Seminary Press, 2017.

Ilan, Tal. *Jewish Women in Greco-Roman Palestine*. Peabody, MA: Hendrickson, 1996.

Imbens, A., and I. Jonker. *Christianity and Incest*. London: Burns & Oates, 1992.

Irigaray, Luce. *An Ethics of Sexual Difference*. Translated by Carolyn Burke and Gillian C. Gill. Ithaca, NY: Cornell University Press, 1993.

———. *Marine Lover of Friedrich Nietzsche*. Translated by Gillian C. Gill. New York: Columbia University Press, 1991.

———. *Sex and Genealogies*. Translated by Gillian Gill. New York: Columbia University Press, 1993.

Isherwood, Lisa, and Dorothea McEwan, eds. *Introducing Feminist Theology*. 2nd ed. Sheffield: Sheffield Academic, 2001.

Jantzen, Grace. *Becoming Divine: Toward a Feminist Philosophy of Religion*. Manchester Studies in Religion, Culture and Gender. Manchester: Manchester University Press, 1998.

Jenson, Blanche A. "The Movement and the Story: Whatever Happened to 'Her'?" Pages 276–87 in *Speaking the Christian God: The Holy Trinity and the Challenge of Feminism*. Edited by Alvin F. Kimel Jr. Grand Rapids: Eerdmans, 1992.

Jenson, Robert W. "An Attempt to Think about Mary." *Dialog* 31 (1992): 261.

———. *The Triune God*. Vol. 1 of *Systematic Theology*. Oxford: Oxford University Press, 1997.

Jeremias, Joachim. *Jerusalem in the Time of Jesus: An Investigation into Economic and Social Conditions during the New Testament Period*. Translated by F. H. and C. H. Cave. Philadelphia: Fortress, 1969.

Jewett, Robert. *Romans: A Commentary*. Hermeneia. Minneapolis: Fortress, 2007.

———. "Second Temple Judaism, Jesus, and Women Yeast of Eden." *Biblical Interpretation* 2 (1994): 8–33.

Jobes, Karen H. *1 Peter.* Baker Exegetical Commentary on the New Testament. Grand Rapids: Baker, 2005.

———. *John through Old Testament Eyes: A Background and Application Commentary.* Grand Rapids: Kregel Academic, 2021.

John Paul II. "Mulieris Dignitatem: Apostolic Letter of the Supreme Pontiff John Paul II on the Dignity and Vocation of Women on the Occasion of the Marian Year." The Holy See. https://www.vatican.va/content/john-paul-ii/en/apost_let ters/1988/documents/hf_jp-ii_apl_19880815_mulieris-dignitatem.html.

———. "Redemptoris Mater: Ioannes Paulus PP. II on the Blessed Virgin Mary in the Life of the Pilgrim Church." The Holy See. https://www.vatican.va/content /john-paul-ii/en/encyclicals/documents/hf_jp-ii_enc_25031987_redemptoris -mater.html.

Johnson, Elizabeth A. *Truly Our Sister: A Theology of Mary in the Communion of Saints.* New York: Continuum, 2003.

Johnson, Luke Timothy. *Hebrews: A Commentary.* Louisville: Westminster John Knox, 2006.

Jones, Serene. *Trauma and Grace: Theology in a Ruptured World.* 2nd ed. Louisville: Westminster John Knox, 2019.

Jonge, H. J. de. "Sonship, Wisdom, and Infancy: Luke 2:41–51a." *New Testament Studies* 24 (1978): 317–54.

Julian of Norwich. *Showings: Authoritative Text, Contexts, Criticism.* Edited by Denise Nowakowski Baker. New York: Norton, 2005.

Just, Arthur A., Jr., ed. *Luke.* Ancient Christian Commentary on Scripture. Downers Grove, IL: InterVarsity Press, 2003.

Kahl, Brigitte. "Toward a Materialist-Feminist Reading." Pages 225–40 in *A Feminist Introduction.* Vol. 1 of *Searching the Scriptures.* Edited by Elisabeth Schüssler Fiorenza. New York: Crossroad, 1993.

Kalkun, Andreas. "How to Ask Embarrassing Questions about Women's Religion: Menstruating Mother of God." Pages 97–114 in *Orthodox Christianity and Gender: Dynamics of Tradition, Culture and Lived Practice.* Edited by Helena Kupari and Elina Vuola. New York: Routledge, 2020.

Kartzow, Marianne Bjelland. *The Slave Metaphor and Gendered Enslavement in Early Christian Discourse: Double Trouble Embodied.* New York: Routledge, 2018.

Kasher, Aryeh, and Eliezer Witsum. *King Herod: A Persecuted Persecutor; A Case Study in Psychohistory and Psychobiography.* Berlin: de Gruyter, 2007.

Kateusz, Ally. *Mary and Early Christian Women: Hidden Leadership.* Cham: Palgrave MacMillan, 2019.

Keener, Craig S. *Acts: An Exegetical Commentary*. Vol. 1. Grand Rapids: Baker, 2012.
————. "Adultery, Divorce." Pages 6–16 in *Dictionary of New Testament Background*. Edited by Craig A. Evans and Stanley E. Porter. Downers Grove, IL: InterVarsity Press, 2005.
————. *The Gospel of John: A Commentary*. 2 vols. Peabody, MA: Hendrickson, 2003.
Kellenbach, Katharina von. *Anti-Judaism in Feminist Religious Writings*. Atlanta: Scholars Press, 1994.
Keller, Kathy. *Jesus, Justice, and Gender Roles: A Case for Gender Roles in Ministry*. Grand Rapids: Zondervan, 2012.
Kessel, Edward L. "A Proposed Biological Interpretation of the Virgin Birth." *Journal of the American Scientific Affiliation* 35 (1983): 129–36.
Kessler, Gwynn. *Conceiving Israel: The Fetus in Rabbinic Narratives*. Philadelphia: University of Pennsylvania Press, 2009.
Kibbe, Michael. *Godly Fear or Ungodly Failure? Hebrews 12 and the Sinae Theophanies*. Beihefte zur Zeitschrift für die neutestamentliche Wissenschaft 216. Berlin: de Gruyter, 2016.
Kimel, Alvin F., Jr. "The God Who Likes His Name: Holy Trinity, Feminism, and the Language of Faith." Pages 188–208 in *Speaking the Christian God: The Holy Trinity and the Challenge of Feminism*. Edited by Alvin F. Kimel Jr. Grand Rapids: Eerdmans, 1992.
————, ed. *Speaking the Christian God: The Holy Trinity and the Challenge of Feminism*. Grand Rapids: Eerdmans, 1992.
————, ed. *This Is My Name Forever: The Trinity and Gender Language for God*. Downers Grove, IL: InterVarsity Press, 2001.
King, Helen. *The One Sex Body on Trial: The Classical and Early Modern Evidence*. New York: Routledge, 2013.
King, Nicholas. "The Significance of the Inn for Luke's Infancy Narrative." Pages 67–76 in *New Perspectives on the Nativity*. Edited by Jeremy Corley. London: T&T Clark, 2009.
Kirk, Daniel J. R. *A Man Attested by God: The Human Jesus of the Synoptic Gospels*. Grand Rapids: Eerdmans, 2016.
Klawans, Jonathan. *Impurity and Sin in Ancient Judaism*. Oxford: Oxford University Press, 2000.
————. *Purity, Sacrifice, and the Temple: Symbolism and Supersessionism in the Study of Ancient Judaism*. New York: Oxford University Press, 2009.

Knafl, Anne K. *Forming God: Divine Anthropomorphism in the Pentateuch.* Winona Lake, IN: Eisenbrauns, 2014.

Knust, Jennifer, and Tommy Wasserman. "The Biblical Odes and the Text of the Christian Bible: A Reconsideration of the Impact of Liturgical Singing on the Transmission of the Gospel of Luke." *Journal of Biblical Literature* 133 (2014): 341–65.

Kochenash, Michael. "'Adam, Son of God' (Luke 3.38): Another Jesus-Augustus Parallel in Luke's Gospel." *New Testament Studies* 64 (2018): 307–25.

Köstenberger, Andreas J. *John.* Baker Exegetical Commentary on the New Testament. Grand Rapids: Baker, 2004.

Kraemer, Ross Shepherd. "Jewish Religion in the Diaspora World of Late Antiquity." Pages 46–72 in *Jewish Women in Historical Perspective.* Edited by Judith Reesa Baskin. 2nd ed. Detroit: Wayne State University Press, 1998.

Kreitzer, Beth. "The Wedding at Cana." Pages 93–108 in *Reforming Mary: Changing Images of the Virgin Mary in Lutheran Sermons of the Sixteenth Century.* Oxford Studies in Historical Theology. Oxford: Oxford University Press, 2004.

Laes, Christian. *Children in the Roman Empire: Outsiders Within.* Cambridge: Cambridge University Press, 2011.

Lampe, G. W. H., ed. *A Patristic Greek Lexicon.* Oxford: Clarendon, 1961.

Laqueur, Thomas. *Making Sex: Body and Gender from the Greeks to Freud.* Cambridge: Harvard University Press, 1990.

Lee, Courtney Hall. *Black Madonna: A Womanist Look at Mary of Nazareth.* Eugene, OR: Cascade, 2017.

Lefkowitz, Mary R. *Women in Greek Myth.* 2nd ed. Baltimore: Johns Hopkins University Press, 2007.

Lettsome, Raquel S. "Mary's Slave Songs: The Tensions and Turnarounds of Faithfully Reading *Doulē* in the Magnificat." *Interpretation* 75 (2021): 6–18.

Levenson, Jon D. *Creation and the Persistence of Evil: The Jewish Drama of Divine Omnipotence.* Princeton: Princeton University Press, 1994.

Levering, Matthew. "Mary and Grace." Pages 289–302 in *The Oxford Handbook of Mary.* Edited by Chris Maunder. Oxford: Oxford University Press, 2019.

Levine, Amy-Jill. "Jewish Women in the New Testament." *Shalvi/Hyman Encyclopedia of Jewish Women.* https://jwa.org/encyclopedia/article/jewish-women-in-the-new-testament.

Lewis, C. S. "Priestesses in the Church." Pages 255–62 in *God in the Dock.* Edited by Walter Hooper. Grand Rapids: Eerdmans, 2014.

———. *That Hideous Strength.* New York: Scribner, 2003.

Lewis, Jody Vaccaro. "The Inn, the Manger, the Swaddling Cloths, the Shepherds, and the Animals." Pages 224–38 in *The Oxford Handbook of Christmas.* Edited by Timothy Larsen. Oxford: Oxford University Press, 2020.

Liddell, Henry George, Robert Scott, and Henry Stuart Jones. *A Greek-English Lexicon.* 9th ed. with revised supplement. Oxford: Clarendon, 1996.

Ligouri, Alphonsus. *The Glories of Mary.* New York: Edward Duncan and Brother, 1852.

Lillie, Celene. *The Rape of Eve: The Transformation of Roman Ideology in Three Early Christian Retellings of Genesis.* Philadelphia: Fortress, 2017.

Lincoln, Andrew T. "The Bible, Theology, and the Virgin Birth: Continuing a Conversation?" *Journal of Theological Interpretation* 14 (2020): 267–85.

———. *Born of a Virgin? Reconceiving Jesus in the Bible, Tradition, and Theology.* Grand Rapids: Eerdmans, 2013.

———. *Ephesians.* Word Biblical Commentary 42. Grand Rapids: Zondervan, 2014.

Litwa, David. *Iesus Deus: The Early Christian Depiction of Jesus as a Mediterranean God.* Philadelphia: Fortress, 2014.

Livy. Translated by B. O. Foster et al. 14 vols. Loeb Classical Library. Cambridge: Harvard University Press, 1919–1959.

Loader, William R. G. *The New Testament on Sexuality.* Grand Rapids: Eerdmans, 2012.

"Logia." The Logia Institute. https://logos.wp.st-andrews.ac.uk/logia.

Longenecker, Richard N. *The Epistle to the Romans.* New International Greek Testament Commentary. Grand Rapids: Eerdmans, 2016.

Lossky, Vladimir. *In the Image and Likeness of God.* London: Mowbrays, 1975.

Louth, Andrew. "Mary in Patristics." Pages 54–66 in *The Oxford Handbook of Mary.* Edited by Chris Maunder. Oxford: Oxford University Press, 2019.

Lüdemann, Gerd. *Virgin Birth? The Real Story of Mary and Her Son Jesus.* Translated by John Bowden. Harrisburg, PA: Trinity Press International, 1998.

Luther, Martin. *Luther's Works.* Edited by Jaroslav Pelikan et al. 55 vols. Saint Louis: Concordia, 1955.

Lyons-Pardue, Kara J. *Gospel Women and the Long Ending of Mark.* The Library of New Testament Studies 614. London: Bloomsbury T&T Clark, 2020.

Mackie, Scott D. *Eschatology and Exhortation in the Epistle to the Hebrews.* Wissenschaftliche Untersuchungen zum Neuen Testament 2/223. Tübingen: Mohr Siebeck, 2007.

Macquarrie, John. *Mary for All Christians*. 2nd ed. Edinburgh: T&T Clark, 2001.

Madigan, Kevin. "Ancient and High-Medieval Interpretations of Jesus in Gethsemane: Some Reflections on Tradition and Continuity in Christian Thought." *Harvard Theological Review* 88 (1995): 157–73.

Mankowski, Paul. "The Gender of Israel's God." Pages 35–61 in *This Is My Name Forever: The Trinity and Gender Language for God*. Edited by Alvin F. Kimel Jr. Downers Grove, IL: InterVarsity Press, 2001.

Markschies, Christoph. *God's Body: Jewish, Christian, and Pagan Images of God*. Waco, TX: Baylor University Press, 2019.

Marshall, I. Howard. *The Gospel of Luke: A Commentary on the Greek Text*. New International Greek Testament Commentary. Grand Rapids: Eerdmans, 1978.

Mathis, David. "More on the Masculine Feel of Christianity." Desiring God. https://www.desiringgod.org/articles/more-on-the-masculine-feel-of-christianity.

McKnight, Scot. *The Real Mary: Why Evangelical Christians Can Embrace the Mother of Jesus*. Brewster, MA: Paraclete, 2007.

Mengestu, Abera M. *God as Father in Paul: Kinship Language and Identity Formation in Early Christianity*. Eugene, OR: Pickwick, 2013.

Metzger, Bruce M. *Textual Commentary on the New Testament*. 2nd ed. New York: United Bible Societies, 1994.

Michaels, J. Ramsey. *The Gospel of John*. New International Commentary on the New Testament. Grand Rapids: Eerdmans, 2010.

Middelton, Deborah F. "The Story of Mary: Luke's Version." *New Blackfriars* 70 (1989): 555–64.

Migliore, Daniel L. "Woman of Faith: Toward a Reformed Understanding of Mary." Pages 117–30 in *Blessed One: Protestant Perspectives on Mary*. Edited by Beverly Roberts Gaventa and Cynthia L. Rigby. Louisville: Westminster John Knox, 2002.

Milgrom, Jacob. *Leviticus: A Book of Ritual and Ethics*. Philadelphia: Fortress, 2004.

———. *Leviticus 1–16: A New Translation with Introduction and Commentary*. Anchor Bible 3. New York: Doubleday, 1998.

———. *Leviticus 17–22: A New Translation with Introduction and Commentary*. Anchor Bible 3A. New York: Doubleday, 2000.

———. *Leviticus 23–27: A New Translation with Introduction and Commentary*. Anchor Bible 3B. New York: Doubleday, 2001.

Miller, John B. F. *"Convinced That God Had Called Us": Dreams, Visions, and the Perception of God's Will in Luke-Acts*. Leiden: Brill, 2007.

Mitchell, Alan C. *Hebrews*. Sacra Pagina 13. Collegeville, MN: Liturgical, 2007.

Moffitt, David M. *Atonement and the Logic of Resurrection in the Epistle to the Hebrews*. Supplements to Novum Testamentum 141. Leiden: Brill, 2011.

Mollenkott, Virginia Ramey. *The Divine Feminine: The Biblical Imagery of God as Female*. Eugene, OR: Wipf & Stock, 1984.

―――. *Omnigender: A Trans-religious Approach*. Cleveland: Pilgrim, 2001.

Moltmann, Jürgen. "The Motherly Father: Is Trinitarian Patripassianism Replacing Theological Patriarchalism?" Pages 51–56 in *God as Father?* Edited by Johann Baptist Metz, Edward Schillebeeckx, and Marcus Lefébure. Translated by G. W. S. Knowles. Edinburgh: T&T Clark; New York: Seabury, 1981.

Montfort, Louis-Marie Grignon de. *A Treatise on the True Devotion to the Blessed Virgin*. Translated by Frederick William Faber. London: Burns and Lambert, 1863.

Moo, Douglas J. *The Letters to Colossians and Philemon*. The Pillar New Testament Commentary. Grand Rapids: Eerdmans, 2008.

―――. *The Letter to the Romans*. 2nd ed. New International Commentary on the New Testament. Grand Rapids: Eerdmans, 2018.

Moo, Douglas, and Jonathan A. Moo. *Creation Care: A Biblical Theology of the Natural World*. Biblical Theology for Life. Grand Rapids: Zondervan, 2018.

Moore, Stephen D. *God's Gym: Divine Male Bodies of the Bible*. New York: Routledge, 1996.

Morris, Joan. *The Lady Was a Bishop: The Hidden History of Women with Clerical Ordination and the Jurisdiction of Bishops*. New York: Macmillan, 1973.

Moss, Candida R., and Joel S. Baden. *Reconceiving Infertility: Biblical Perspectives on Procreation and Childlessness*. Princeton: Princeton University Press, 2015.

Moyise, Steve. *Was the Birth of Jesus according to Scripture?* Eugene, OR: Cascade Books, 2013.

Myers, Alicia. *Blessed among Women? Mothers and Motherhood in the New Testament*. Oxford: Oxford University Press, 2017.

National Council of Churches. *An Inclusive Language Lectionary*. Atlanta: John Knox, 1982.

Neal, Jerusha Matsen. *Blessed: Monologues for Mary*. Art for Faith's Sake. Eugene, OR: Cascade, 2013.

―――. *The Overshadowed Preacher: Mary, the Spirit, and the Labor of Proclamation*. Grand Rapids: Eerdmans, 2020.

Neder, Adam. *Theology as a Way of Life*. Grand Rapids: Baker, 2019.

Newman, Barbara. *From Virile Woman to Woman Christ: Studies in Medieval Religion and Literature*. Middle Ages Series. Philadelphia: University of Pennsylvania Press, 1995.

Newsom, Carol A., Sharon H. Ringe, and Jacqueline E. Lapsley, eds. *Women's Bible Commentary*. Rev. and upd. 20th anniversary ed. Louisville: Westminster John Knox, 2012.

The Nicene and Post-Nicene Fathers, Series 1. Edited by Philip Schaff. 1886–1889. 14 vols. Repr., Peabody, MA: Hendrickson, 1994.

The Nicene and Post-Nicene Fathers, Series 2. Edited by Philip Schaff and Henry Wace. 1890–1900. 14 vols. Repr., Peabody, MA: Hendrickson, 1994.

Nicholson, Ernest W. *God and His People: Covenant and Theology in the Old Testament*. Oxford: Clarendon, 1986.

Nolland, John. *The Gospel of Matthew: A Commentary on the Greek Text*. New International Greek Testament Commentary. Grand Rapids: Eerdmans, 2005.

———. *Luke 1:1–9:20*. Word Biblical Commentary 35A. Dallas: Word, 1989.

Novenson, Matthew V. *Christ among the Messiahs: Christ Language in Paul and Messiah Language in Ancient Judaism*. New York: Oxford University Press, 2012.

O'Day, Gail. "Gospel of John." Pages 517–35 in *Women's Bible Commentary*. Edited by Carol A. Newsom, Sharon H. Ringe, and Jacqueline E. Lapsley. Rev. and upd. 20th anniversary ed. Louisville: Westminster John Knox, 2012.

O'Day, Gail R., and Susan E. Hylen. *John*. Louisville: Westminster John Knox, 2006.

Origen. *Commentary on the Epistle to the Romans Books 1–5*. Translated by Thomas P. Scheck. Fathers of the Church 103. Washington, DC: Catholic University of America Press, 2001.

Padilla, Kristen. *Now That I'm Called: A Guide for Women Discerning a Call to Ministry*. Grand Rapids: Zondervan, 2018.

Parrinder, Geoffrey. *The Son of Joseph: The Parentage of Jesus*. London: T&T Clark, 1992.

Patrologia Graeca. Edited by Jacques-Paul Migne. 162 vols. Paris, 1857–1886.

Paul VI. "Inter Insigniores: Declaration on the Question of Admission of Women to the Ministerial Priesthood." The Holy See. https://www.vatican.va/roman_cu ria/congregations/cfaith/documents/rc_con_cfaith_doc_19761015_inter-insi gniores_en.html.

Peeler, Amy. "Joseph, Husband of Mary." *Bible Odyssey*. http://www.bibleodyssey .org/en/people/related-articles/joseph-husband-of-mary.

———. "'Leading Many Sons to Glory': Historical Implications of Exclusive Language in the Epistle to the Hebrews." *Religions* 12 (2021). https://doi.org/10 .3390/rel12100844.

———. *You Are My Son: The Family of God in the Epistle to the Hebrews*. The Library of New Testament Studies 486. London: T&T Clark, 2014.

Pelikan, Jaroslav. *Mary through the Centuries: Her Place in the History of Culture*. New Haven: Yale University Press, 1996.

Pelikan, Jaroslav, and Valerie R. Hotchkiss, eds. *Creeds and Confessions of Faith in the Christian Tradition*. Vol. 1. New Haven: Yale University Press, 2003.

Peppard, Michael. *The Son of God in the Roman World: Divine Sonship in Its Social and Political Context*. Oxford: Oxford University Press, 2011.

———. *The World's Oldest Church: Bible, Art, and Ritual at Dura-Europos, Syria*. Illustrated edition. New Haven: Yale University Press, 2016.

Peterson, David. *Hebrews and Perfection: An Examination of the Concept of Perfection in the "Epistle to the Hebrews."* Society for New Testament Studies Monograph Series 47. Cambridge: Cambridge University Press, 1982.

Philo. Translated by F. H. Colson et al. 10 vols. Loeb Classical Library. Cambridge: Harvard University Press, 1929–1962.

Pierce, Madison N. *Divine Discourse in the Epistle to the Hebrews: The Recontextualization of Spoken Quotations of Scripture*. Society for New Testament Studies Monograph Series 178. Cambridge: Cambridge University Press, 2020.

Pietersma, Albert, and Benjamin G. Wright, eds. *A New English Translation of the Septuagint*. New York: Oxford University Press, 2007.

Piper, John. "'The Frank and Manly Mr. Ryle': The Value of a Masculine Ministry." Desiring God. https://www.desiringgod.org/messages/the-frank-and-manly-mr-ryle-the-value-of-a-masculine-ministry.

Plaskow, Judith. *Standing Again at Sinai: Judaism from a Feminist Perspective*. San Francisco: HarperSanFrancisco, 1991.

Plutarch. *Lives*. Translated by Bernadotte Perrin. 11 vols. Loeb Classical Library. Cambridge: Harvard University Press, 1999.

———. *Moralia*. Translated by Edwin L. Minar Jr., F. H. Sandbach, and W. C. Helmbold. 15 vols. Loeb Classical Library. Cambridge: Harvard University Press, 1969.

Pomata, Gianna. "Blood Ties and Semen Ties: Consanguinity and Agnation in Roman Law." Pages 43–66 in *Gender, Kinship, and Power: A Comparative and Interdisciplinary History*. Edited by Mary Jo Maynes, Ann Waltner, Brigitte Soland, and Ulrike Strasser. New York: Routledge, 1995.

Pope, Michael. "Gabriel's Entrance and Biblical Violence in Luke's Annunciation Narrative." *Journal of Biblical Literature* 137 (2018): 701–10.

———. "Luke's Seminal Annunciation: An Embryological Reading of Mary's Conception." *Journal of Biblical Literature* 138 (2019): 791–807.

Pseudo-Dionysius the Areopagite. *The Complete Works.* Translated by Colm Luibheid and Paul Rorem. The Classics of Western Spirituality. New York: Paulist, 1987.
————. *The Divine Names and Mystical Theology.* Milwaukee: Marquette University Press, 1980.

Putthoff, Tyson L. *Gods and Humans in the Ancient Near East.* Cambridge: Cambridge University Press, 2020.

Rahner, Karl. "The Fundamental Principle of Marian Theology." Translated by Philip Endean. Pages 292–99 in *Mary: The Complete Resource.* Edited by Sarah Jane Boss. Oxford: Oxford University Press, 2007.

Räisänen, Heikki. "Begotten by the Holy Spirit." Pages 321–42 in *Sacred Marriages: The Divine-Human Sexual Metaphor from Sumer to Early Christianity.* Edited by Martti Nissinen and Risto Uro. Winona Lake, IN: Eisenbrauns, 2008.

Real Presence Education and Adoration Association. *The Eucharistic Miracles of the World: Catalogue Book of the Vatican International Exhibition.* Bardstown, KY: Eternal Life, 2009.

Rigby, Cynthia L. "Mary and the Artistry of God." Pages 145–58 in *Blessed One: Protestant Perspectives on Mary.* Edited by Beverly Roberts Gaventa and Cynthia L. Rigby. Louisville: Westminster John Knox, 2002.

Rivera, Mayra. *Poetics of the Flesh.* Durham, NC: Duke University Press, 2015.

Roberts, Kyle. *A Complicated Pregnancy: Whether Mary Was a Virgin and Why It Matters.* Minneapolis: Fortress, 2017.

Rowe, C. Kavin. *Early Narrative Christology: The Lord in the Gospel of Luke.* Berlin: de Gruyter, 2006.

Ruether, Rosemary Radford. *Sexism and God-Talk: Toward a Feminist Theology; With a New Introduction.* Boston: Beacon, 1993.

Sanders, E. P. *Judaism: Practice and Belief, 63 BCE–66 CE.* London: SCM, 1992.

Saward, John. *The Mysteries of March: Hans Urs von Balthasar on the Incarnation and Easter.* Washington, DC: Catholic University of America Press, 1990.
————. *Redeemer in the Womb: Jesus Living in Mary.* San Francisco: Ignatius, 1993.

Schaberg, Jane. *The Illegitimacy of Jesus: A Feminist Theological Interpretation of the Infancy Narratives.* Sheffield: Sheffield Academic, 1995.

Schearing, Linda S. "Double Time . . . Double Trouble? Gender, Sin, and Leviticus 12." Pages 429–50 in *Leviticus: Composition and Reception.* Edited by Rolf Rendtorff, Robert A. Kugler, and Sarah Smith Bartel. Leiden: Brill, 2003.

Schmemann, Alexander. *Celebration of Faith.* Vol. 3 of *The Virgin Mary.* Yonkers, NY: St. Vladimir's Seminary Press, 2001.

————. *For the Life of the World: Sacraments and Orthodoxy.* Crestwood, NY: St. Vladimir's Seminary Press, 2004.

Schmidt, Thomas. "The Christological Phallicy in the Gospels." Pages 88–107 in *This Is My Name Forever: The Trinity and Gender Language for God.* Edited by Alvin F. Kimel Jr. Downers Grove, IL: InterVarsity Press, 2001.

Schüssler Fiorenza, Elisabeth. *Jesus: Miriam's Child, Sophia's Prophet; Critical Issues in Feminist Christology.* New York: Continuum, 1994.

Scott, David A. "Creation as Christ: A Problematic Theme in Some Feminist Theology." Pages 236–57 in *Speaking the Christian God: The Holy Trinity and the Challenge of Feminism.* Edited by Alvin F. Kimel Jr. Grand Rapids: Eerdmans, 1992.

Scott, James M. *Adoption as Son of God: An Exegetical Investigation into the Background of ΥΙΟΘΕΣΙΑ in the Pauline Corpus.* Wissenschaftliche Untersuchungen zum Neuen Testament 2/48. Tübingen: Mohr Siebeck, 1992.

Seim, Turid Karlsen. "The Virgin Mother: Mary and Ascetic Discipleship in Luke." Pages 89–105 in *Feminist Companion to Luke.* Feminist Companion to the New Testament and Early Christian Writings 3. Edited by Amy-Jill Levine and Marianne Blickenstaff. London: Sheffield Academic, 2002.

Sharp, Carolyn J. "Character, Conflict, and Covenant in Israel's Origin Tradition." Pages 41–73 in *The Hebrew Bible: Feminist and Intersectional Perspectives.* Edited by Gale A. Yee. Minneapolis: Fortress, 2018.

Shaw, B. "The Age of Roman Girls at Marriage: Some Reconsiderations. *Journal of Roman Studies* 77 (1987): 28–46.

Shoemaker, Stephen J., trans. *The Life of the Virgin: Maximus the Confessor.* New Haven: Yale University Press, 2012.

————. "Marian Liturgies and Devotion in Early Christianity." Pages 130–45 in *Mary: The Complete Resource.* Edited by Sarah Jane Boss. London: Continuum, 2009.

————. *Mary in Early Christian Faith and Devotion.* New Haven: Yale University Press, 2016.

Siliezar, Carlos Raúl Sosa. *Creation Imagery in the Gospel of John.* The Library of New Testament Studies 546. London: T&T Clark, 2015.

Smith, Mark S. *The Early History of God: Yahweh and the Other Deities in Ancient Israel.* 2nd ed. The Biblical Resource Series. Grand Rapids: Eerdmans, 2002.

————. *Where the Gods Are: Spatial Dimensions of Anthropomorphism in the Biblical World.* New Haven: Yale University Press, 2016.

Smith, Paul R. *Is It Okay to Call God "Mother"? Considering the Feminine Face of God.* Peabody, MA: Hendrickson, 1993.

Smyth, Herbert Weir. *Greek Grammar*. Rev. ed. Revised by Gordon M. Messing. Cambridge: Harvard University Press, 1984.

Sommer, Benjamin D. *The Bodies of God and the World of Ancient Israel*. New York: Cambridge University Press, 2009.

Soskice, Janet Martin. "Can a Feminist Call God Father?" Pages 81–94 in *Speaking the Christian God: The Holy Trinity and the Challenge of Feminism*. Edited by Alvin F. Kimel Jr. Grand Rapids: Eerdmans, 1992.

———. *The Kindness of God: Metaphor, Gender, and Religious Language*. Oxford: Oxford University Press, 2008.

Soulen, R. Kendall. *The Divine Name(s) and the Holy Trinity*. Vol. 1 of *Distinguishing the Voices*. Louisville: Westminster John Knox, 2011.

Spencer, F. Scott. *Salty Wives, Spirited Mothers, and Savvy Widows: Capable Women of Purpose and Persistence in Luke's Gospel*. Grand Rapids: Eerdmans, 2012.

Stein, Robert H. *Mark*. Baker Exegetical Commentary on the New Testament. Grand Rapids: Baker, 2010.

Storkey, Elaine. "Who Is the Christ? Issues in Christology and Feminist Theology." Pages 105–23 in *The Gospel and Gender: A Trinitarian Engagement with Being Male and Female in Christ*. Edited by Douglas A. Campbell. Studies in Theology and Sexuality 7. London: T&T Clark, 2003.

Sweat, Laura C. *The Theological Role of Paradox in the Gospel of Mark*. The Library of New Testament Studies 492. London: Bloomsbury T&T Clark, 2013.

Talbert, Charles H. "Miraculous Conceptions and Births in Mediterranean Antiquity." Pages 79–86 in *The Historical Jesus in Context*. Edited by Amy-Jill Levine, Dale C. Allison Jr., and John Dominic Crossan. Princeton Readings in Religion 31. Princeton: Princeton University Press, 2006.

Tannehill, Robert C. *The Gospel according to Luke*. Vol. 1 of *The Narrative Unity of Luke-Acts: A Literary Interpretation*. Philadelphia: Fortress, 1986.

———. *Luke*. Abingdon New Testament Commentaries. Nashville: Abingdon, 1996.

Tanner, Kathryn. *Christ the Key*. Current Issues in Theology. Cambridge: Cambridge University Press, 2010.

Thielman, Frank. *Ephesians*. Baker Exegetical Commentary on the New Testament. Grand Rapids: Baker, 2010.

Thiessen, Matthew. "Luke 2:22, Leviticus 12, and Parturient Impurity." *Novum Testamentum* 54 (2012): 16–29.

Thomas Aquinas. *Summa Theologica*. Translated by Fathers of the English Dominican Province. 5 vols. New York: Benziger Brothers, 1947.

Thompson, Marianne Meye. *Colossians and Philemon.* The Two Horizons New Testament Commentary. Grand Rapids: Eerdmans, 2005.

———. *The Promise of the Father: Jesus and God in the New Testament.* Louisville: Westminster John Knox, 2000.

Tonstad, Linn Marie. *God and Difference: The Trinity, Sexuality, and the Transformation of Finitude.* New York: Routledge, 2016.

———. "The Logic of Origin and the Paradoxes of Language: A Theological Experiment." *Modern Theology* 30 (2014): 50–73.

Torrance, Alan. "Call No Man Father! The Trinity, Patriarchy and Godtalk." Pages 179–97 in *The Gospel and Gender: A Trinitarian Engagement with Being Male and Female in Christ.* Edited by Douglas A. Campbell. Studies in Theology and Sexuality 7. New York: T&T Clark, 2003.

Torrance, Thomas F. "The Christian Apprehension of God the Father." Pages 120–43 in *Speaking the Christian God: The Holy Trinity and the Challenge of Feminism.* Edited by Alvin F. Kimel Jr. Grand Rapids: Eerdmans, 1992.

———. *The Doctrine of Jesus Christ.* Eugene, OR: Wipf & Stock, 2002.

———. *The Incarnation: Ecumenical Studies in the Nicene-Constantinopolitan Creed A.D. 381.* Eugene, OR: Wipf & Stock, 1998.

Treier, Daniel J. "Virgin Territory?" *Pro Ecclesia* 23 (2014): 372–79.

Trenchard, Warren C. *The Complete Vocabulary Guide to the Greek New Testament.* Rev. ed. Grand Rapids: Zondervan, 1998.

Trible, Phyllis. *Texts of Terror: Literary-Feminist Readings of Biblical Narratives.* Philadelphia: Fortress, 1984.

"The Trinity: God's Love Overflowing." Presbyterian Mission. https://www.presby terianmission.org/resource/trinity-gods-love-overflowing/.

Tuana, Nancy. "The Weaker Seed: The Sexist Bias of Reproductive Theory." *Hypatia* 3 (1988): 35–59.

Verden, Timothy. *Mary in Western Art.* New York: Hudson Mills, 2005.

Vlachos, Chris. *James.* Exegetical Guide to the Greek New Testament. Nashville: Broadman & Holman, 2013.

Wagener, Ulrike. "Hebrews: Strangers in the World." Pages 857–69 in *Feminist Biblical Interpretation: A Compendium of Critical Commentary on the Books of the Bible and Related Literature.* Edited by Luise Schottroff and Marie-Theres Wacker. Translated by Lisa E. Dahill et al. Grand Rapids: Eerdmans, 2012.

Wagner, Andreas. *God's Body: The Anthropomorphic God in the Old Testament.* New York: T&T Clark, 2019.

———. *Göttliche Körper—Göttliche Gefühle: Was leisten anthropomorphe und anthropopathische Götterkonzepte im Alten Orient und Alten Testament?* Göttingen: Vandenhoeck & Ruprecht, 2014.

Wagner, J. Ross. "Is God the Father of Jews Only, or Also of Gentiles? The Peculiar Shape of Paul's 'Universalism.'" Pages 233–54 in *The Divine Father: Religious and Philosophical Concepts of Divine Parenthood in Antiquity*. Edited by Felix Albrecht and Reinhard Feldmeier. Themes in Biblical Narrative 18. Boston: Brill, 2014.

Wainwright, Geoffrey. "Trinitarian Worship." Pages 209–21 in *Speaking the Christian God: The Holy Trinity and the Challenge of Feminism*. Edited by Alvin F. Kimel Jr. Grand Rapids: Eerdmans, 1992.

Wallace, Daniel B. *The Basics of New Testament Syntax: An Intermediate Greek Grammar*. Grand Rapids: Zondervan, 2000.

Ware, Kallistos. "Man, Woman and the Priesthood of Christ." Pages 9–37 in *Women and the Priesthood*. Edited by Thomas Hopko. Crestwood, NY: St. Vladimir's Seminary Press, 1983.

Warner, Maria. *Alone of All Her Sex: The Myth and Cult of the Virgin Mary*. Oxford: Oxford University Press, 2013.

Webb, Stephen H. *Jesus Christ, Eternal God: Heavenly Flesh and the Metaphysics of Matter*. New York: Oxford University Press, 2012.

West, Angela. *Deadly Innocence: Feminist Theology and the Mythology of Sin*. London: Cassell, 1995.

West, Christopher. *Theology of the Body Explained: A Commentary on John Paul II's Man and Woman He Created Them*. Rev. ed. Boston: Pauline, 2007.

———. *Theology of the Body for Beginners*. West Chester, PA: Ascension, 2004.

Wevers, John William, ed. *Deuteronomium*. Volume 3/2 of *Septuaginta Vetus Testamentum Graecum: Auctoritate Academiae Scientiarum Gottingensis editum*. Göttingen: Vandenhoeck & Ruprecht, 1977.

Whitear, Sarah. "Solving the Gender Problem in Leviticus 12: From Philo to Feminism." *Annali di Storia dell'Esegesi* 37 (2020): 299–319.

Widdicomb, Peter. *The Fatherhood of God from Origen to Athanasius*. Oxford: Clarendon, 2000.

Wijk-Bos, Johanna W. H. van. *Reimagining God: The Case for Scriptural Diversity*. Louisville: Westminster John Knox, 1995.

Williams, Delores S. "Hagar in African American Biblical Appropriation." Pages 177–84 in *Hagar, Sarah, and Their Children: Jewish, Christian, and Muslim Per-*

spectives. Edited by Phyllis Trible and Letty M. Russell. Louisville: Westminster John Knox, 2006.

―――. *Sisters in the Wilderness: The Challenge of Womanist God-Talk*. Maryknoll, NY: Orbis Books, 2013.

Williams, Neil H. *The Maleness of Jesus: Is It Good News for Women?* Eugene, OR: Cascade, 2011.

Williams, Ritva H. "The Mother of Jesus at Cana: A Social-Science Interpretation of John 2:1–12." *Catholic Biblical Quarterly* 59 (1997): 679–92.

Wilson, Brittany E. *The Embodied God: Seeing the Divine in Luke-Acts and the Early Church*. Oxford: Oxford University Press, 2021.

―――. *Unmanly Men: Reconfigurations of Masculinity in Luke-Acts*. Oxford: Oxford University Press, 2015.

Wilson, Sarah Hinlicky. *Woman, Women and the Priesthood in the Trinitarian Theology of Elisabeth Behr-Sigel*. London: Bloomsbury T&T Clark, 2013.

Woods, Susanne, ed. *The Poems of Aemilia Lanyer: Salve Deus Rex Judaeorum*. Oxford: Oxford University Press, 1993.

Wright, Christopher J. H. *Knowing God the Father through the Old Testament*. Downers Grove, IL: InterVarsity Press, 2007.

Wright, N. T. *Paul and the Faithfulness of God*. Minneapolis: Fortress, 2013.

Yannaras, Christos. *Elements of Faith: An Introduction to Orthodox Theology*. Edinburgh: T&T Clark, 1991.

Yarbro Collins, Adela, and John J. Collins. *King and Messiah as Son of God: Divine, Human, and Angelic Messianic Figures in Biblical and Related Literature*. Grand Rapids: Eerdmans, 2008.

Yarhouse, Mark A. *Understanding Gender Dysphoria: Navigating Transgender Issues in a Changing Culture*. Christian Association for Psychological Studies Books. Downers Grove, IL: IVP Academic, 2015.

Zizioulas, John D. *Being as Communion: Studies in Personhood and the Church*. London: Darton, Longman & Todd, 1985.

―――. *Communion and Otherness: Further Studies in Personhood and the Church*. Edited by Paul McPartlan. London: T&T Clark, 2006.

―――. *Lectures in Christian Dogmatics*. Edited by Douglas H. Knight. London: T&T Clark, 2008.

Index of Authors

Frankel, Hannah, 154n6
Fredriksen, Paula, 34, 36n9
Freed, Edwin D., 125n29, 128n41
Freud, Sigmund, 107n55
Friesen, Stephen J., 159n23

Garnsey, Peter, 159n23
Gaventa, Beverly Roberts, 48nn52–53,
49n55, 50n57, 51n60, 55–56n76, 62n96,
85, 102n37, 124n21, 131n53, 163n34,
169n47
Genig, Joshua D., 69n15
Gilbert, Scott F., 94n13
Glancy, Jennifer A., 23n42, 51n61, 58n83,
62n96, 78n37, 164n37
Gleason, Maud W., 109n61
Goldstein, Elizabeth W., 37n14, 38, 40
Goldstein, Elyse, 40
Green, Elizabeth, 144n96
Green, Garrett, 112n71, 143n96, 223n65
Green, Joel B., 52n64, 53n69, 54n72,
73n23, 74n28, 78n39, 163n34, 163n36,
170n52
Green-McCreight, Kathryn, 17n20
Grenz, Stanley J., 3n5, 102n40, 134n63
Grossman, Susan, 35, 38
Gunderson, Erik, 109n61

Hagner, Donald A., 43, 50n59
Hamori, Esther J., 16n17
Hampson, Margaret Daphne, 185–86n86
Harrill, James Albert, 80n45
Harrison, Nonna Verna, 98–99n26,
99n27, 99–100n28, 100n29
Hays, Christopher M., 172n57
Hays, Richard B., 128n40
Heim, Erin M., 195n12, 202n28, 204

Hensell, Eugene, 48n53
Hereth, Blake, 187
Holmes, Laura Sweat, 178n70. *See also*
Sweat, Laura C.
Hopkins, M. K., 83n51
Hopko, Thomas, 118n2, 119, 144,
146n103
Hotchkiss, Valerie R., 100n29, 100n30
Humphrey, Edith M., 106n54, 112n70
Hylen, Susan E., 174n61

Ilan, Tal, 49n56, 55n74
Imbens, Annie, 220n57
Irigaray, Luce, 9n1, 25–26, 59n86, 95n14,
142n91, 148
Isherwood, Lisa, 77n36, 87n67,
185–86n86

Jantzen, Grace, 7n13, 91n5, 95n14, 95n16,
107n55, 108n58, 116, 142n91, 147n106,
148n110, 149
Jenson, Blanche, 89
Jenson, Robert W., 153n3, 217
Jeremias, Joachim, 67n5
Jewett, Robert, 193n4, 203n29, 203n30
Jobes, Karen H., 176n67, 208n38
John Paul II, 6n12, 68–69n11, 101, 122
Johnson, Elizabeth, 48n53, 85, 147n108,
162n31, 184n82
Johnson, Keith, 115n84
Johnson, Luke Timothy, 167n42
Johnson, Marcus Peter, 121n13
Jones, Henry Stuart, 90n3
Jones, Serene, 23–24, 50n58, 155n9
Jonge, Henk J. de, 171n55
Jonker, Ineke, 220n57
Just, Arthur A., Jr., 60n92

Index of Subjects

Index of Scripture and Other Ancient Sources